P9-BIW-430

THE SOCIAL REALITY OF CRIME

THE SOCIAL REALITY OF CRIME

RICHARD QUINNEY
New York University

LITTLE, BROWN AND COMPANY Boston

LIBRARY OF CONGRESS CATALOG CARD NO. 70-100791

FIRST PRINTING

Published simultaneously in Canada
by Little, Brown & Company (Canada) Limited

PRINTED IN THE UNITED STATES OF AMERICA

Preface

My purpose in this book is to provide a reorientation to the study of crime. I have attempted to accomplish this task by developing a theoretical perspective by means of which research and writing in criminology can be reinterpreted.

The nominalistic position is my starting point: a thing exists only when it is given a name; any phenomenon is real to us only when we can imagine it. Without imagination there would be nothing to experience. So it is with crime. In our relationships with others we construct a *social reality of crime*. This reality is both conceptual and phenomenal, a world of meanings and events constructed in reference to crime.

This theoretical approach to crime consists of several related processes: (1) how criminal definitions are formulated; (2) how criminal definitions are applied; (3) how behavior patterns develop in relation to criminal definitions; and (4) how criminal conceptions are constructed. The social reality of crime is constantly being created.

I have felt it necessary to reinterpret criminology for more than academic reasons. Much of our criminology lacks a sense of the contemporary. I seek a sociology of crime that fits into our own times. I am, also, explicitly interested in the ideals of justice and individual freedom. When we find ourselves able to examine crime as a human construct, then we can raise questions about the justice of criminal law. It is my hope that the theory of the social reality of crime has the power of forcing us to consider libertarian ideals. I contend that a relevant criminology can be attained o when we allow our personal values to provide a vision for the s y of crime.

chard Quinney

Contents

1 A THEORY OF CRIME

ONE
The Social Reality of Crime 3

Assumptions: Explanation in the Study of Crime
Assumptions: Man and Society in a Theory of Crime
Theory: The Social Reality of Crime
A Theoretical Perspective for Studying Crime

2 FORMULATION OF CRIMINAL DEFINITIONS

TWO
Criminal Law in Politically Organized Society 29

The Study of Criminal Law
From Sociological Jurisprudence to Sociology of Criminal Law
Law in Politically Organized Society
The Interest Structure
Formulation and Administration of Criminal Law
Interests in Contemporary Society

THREE
Interests in the Formulation of Criminal Laws 43

Emergence of Criminal Law
Criminal Law in Colonies and Territories

Protection of the Political Order
Religious Foundations of Criminal Law
Sunday Law
The Law of Theft
Antitrust Laws
Pure Food and Drug Laws
Sexual Psychopath Laws
Protection of Morality and Public Order

3 APPLICATION OF CRIMINAL DEFINITIONS

FOUR
Enforcement of Criminal Law 101

Police Discretion
Legal Regulation of Law Enforcement
Law Enforcement Systems
Community Context of Law Enforcement
Police Organization and Law Enforcement
Police Ideology and Law Enforcement
The Encounter Between Police and Citizens
The Offense Situation and Selective Law Enforcement

FIVE
Administration of Criminal Justice 137

Politicality of Justice
Discretion and Decision-Making in the Judicial Process
Prosecution and Nontrial Adjudication
The Criminal Lawyer in the Adversary System
The Criminal Trial and the Jury
Judicial Sentencing

SIX
Penal and Correctional Administration 169

Organization and Supervision of Probation
Social Organization of Penal Custody

Administration of Institutional Treatment
Administration of Capital Punishment
Parole Decisions and Supervision
Prevention Programs in the Community
Removal of Criminal Definitions

4 DEVELOPMENT OF BEHAVIOR PATTERNS IN RELATION TO CRIMINAL DEFINITIONS

SEVEN
Societal Organization and the Structuring of Behavior Patterns 207

Segmental Organization of Society
Behavior Patterns and Probability of Criminal Definitions
Structuring of Behavior Patterns
Ecology of Behavior Patterns and Criminal Definitions
General Cultural Themes in Segmental Society

EIGHT
Action Patterns of the Criminally Defined 234

Achievement of Self
Association, Identification, and Commitment
Personal Action Patterns as Responses to Criminal Definition
Behavior Systems of the Criminally Defined
Personal Meaning of Action

5 CONSTRUCTION OF CRIMINAL CONCEPTIONS

NINE
Public Conceptions of Crime 277

Social Reaction to Crime
Diffusion of Criminal Conceptions

Social Types in the World of Crime
Public Attitudes Toward Crime
Public Attitudes Toward the Control of Crime
Consequences of Criminal Conceptions

TEN
The Politics of Reality 303

Periodic Investigations of Crime
The President's Crime Commission
The Law and Order Challenge
Crime and Legitimacy of Authority in a Free Society
Conclusion

Index to Names 319

Index to Subjects 325

THE SOCIAL REALITY OF CRIME

CHAPTER ONE

The Social Reality of Crime

The history of contemporary sociology is characterized by a progressive loss in faith — faith that anything exists beyond man's imagination. We are consequently being led to new assumptions about our craft and the substance of our labors. New ways of attacking old problems are making this a dynamic period for sociology.

Perhaps in no other sociological realm is intellectual revisionism more apparent than in the study of crime. In these pages I will indicate how current thoughts and trends in the sociological study of crime can culminate in a theory of crime. The theory that I will present — *the theory of the social reality of crime* — rests upon theoretical and methodological assumptions that reflect the happenings of our time; it is meant to provide an understanding of crime that is relevant to our contemporary experiences.[1]

ASSUMPTIONS: EXPLANATION IN THE STUDY OF CRIME

Until fairly recent times studies and writings in criminology were shaped almost entirely by the criminologist's interest in "the crim-

[1] An earlier version of the theory of the social reality of crime was contained in a paper I presented at the 63rd annual meeting of the American Sociological Association, August 28, 1968. This chapter is a revision of my later paper, "The Social Reality of Crime," in Jack D. Douglas (ed.), *Crime and Justice in American Society* (Indianapolis: Bobbs-Merrill, 1970).

inal." In the last few years, however, those who study crime have realized that crime is relative to different legal systems, that an absolute conception of crime — outside of legal definitions — had to be replaced by a relativistic (that is, legalistic) conception. Many criminologists have therefore turned to studying how criminal definitions are constructed and applied in a society.

Two schools of thought have developed. Some argue that crime is properly studied by examining the offender and his behavior. Others are convinced that the criminal law is the correct object: how it is formulated, enforced, and administered. The two need not become deadlocked in polemics. The long overdue interest in criminal definitions happily corrects the absurdities brought about by studying the offender alone; the two approaches actually complement one another. A synthesis of the criminal behavior and criminal definition approaches can provide a new theoretical framework for the study of crime.

The theory I am proposing rests upon certain assumptions about theoretical explanation: these assumptions are in regard to (1) ontology, (2) epistemology, (3) causation, and (4) theory construction.

Ontology. What is the world really like? I mean, what is it we pretend to separate ourselves from when we go about our observations? I adopt a nominalistic position contrary to that of the positivists. Accordingly, I can accept no universal essences. The mind is unable to frame a concept that corresponds to an objective reality. We cannot be certain of an objective reality beyond man's conception of it. Thus, we have no reason to believe in the objective existence of anything. We must, instead, formulate theories that give meaning to our experiences.[2]

Epistemology. Implied in the ontological assumption is the epistemological assumption that we as observers cannot "copy" anything that may be regarded as an objective reality, since we are skeptical of the existence of such a reality. Our observations, instead, are based on our own mental *constructions,* not on essences beyond our

[2] I have developed this position in *The Problem of Crime* (New York: Dodd, Mead, 1970), chap. 3.

experiences. Expressed in a more romantic way: "Beauty is in the eye of the beholder." Thus, our concern is not with any correspondence between "objective reality" and observation, but between observation and the utility of such observations in understanding our own subjective, multiple social worlds.

Causation. Much of criminological theory, based on positivistic assumptions, has sought to explain the "causes" of crime. That search continues, but the modern concept of causation employed in the philosophy of science is considerably different from that used by criminologists.[3] The strategy toward causation that I propose for a theory of crime is consistent with the above assumptions about the world and the way in which we understand it, as well as with current usage in the philosophy of science. This strategy has three parts.

First, causal explanation need not be the sole interest of criminologists.[4] The objective of any science is not to formulate and verify theories of causation, but to construct an order among observables. Explanations as generalized answers to the question "why?" may be presented in other than causal form. For example, explanations in terms of probability statements, functional relationships, and developmental stages can be formulated into propositions that do not depend upon causal explanation. A science of human social behavior is obviously possible without the notion of causation.

Second, a statement of causation does not necessarily state the

[3] For a discussion of the usage of causation in modern philosophy of science and in the physical sciences, see Percy W. Bridgman, "Determinism in Modern Science," in Sidney Hook (ed.), *Determinism and Freedom in the Age of Modern Science* (New York: Collier, 1961), pp. 57–75; Mario Bunge, *Causality: The Place of the Causal Principle in Modern Science* (New York: The World Publishing Co., 1963); Werner Heisenberg, *Physics and Philosophy: The Revolution in Modern Science* (New York: Harper & Row, 1958).

[4] Alternatives in causal explanation in criminology have been suggested in Hermanus Bianchi, *Position and Subject Matter of Criminology: Inquiry Concerning Theoretical Criminology* (Amsterdam: North Holland, 1956); Nathaniel Cantor, "The Search for Causes of Crime," *Journal of Criminal Law, Criminology and Police Science, 22* (March–April, 1932), pp. 854–863; Peter Lejins, "Pragmatic Etiology of Delinquent Behavior," *Social Forces,* 29 (March, 1951), pp. 317–321; David Matza, *Delinquency and Drift* (New York: John Wiley, 1964); Walter C. Reckless, *Criminal Behavior* (New York: McGraw-Hill, 1940). Acceptance of causal analysis in contemporary criminology is found in Travis Hirshi and Hanan C. Selvin, *Delinquency Research: An Appraisal of Analytic Methods* (New York: The Free Press, 1967).

nature of reality, but is a *methodological construction* of the observer: "Causes certainly are connected by effects; but this is because our theories connect them, not because the world is held together by cosmic glue."[5] The scientist who defines a causal relationship has to see that it is a construct imposed by himself in order to give meaning to a significant theoretical problem. Confused, we often inadvertently turn the causational construct into a description of reality.[6] Initially a heuristic device, a methodological tool, causation does not necessarily describe the substance of our observations.

Third, we must not use the causational construct as it has often been applied in physical science. Causative explanations of crime have tended in particular to be based on the mechanistic conception of causation. What is required in the explanation of crime, *if* a causative explanation is formulated, is a conception of causation that is attuned to the nature of social phenomena.

The world of social phenomena studied by the social scientist has meaning for the human beings living within it. The world of nature, on the other hand, which the physical scientist studies, means nothing to the physical objects. Therefore, the social scientist's constructs have to be founded upon the *social reality* created by man: "The constructs of the social sciences are, so to speak, constructs of the second degree, that is, constructs of the constructs made by the actors on the social scene, whose behavior the social scientist has to observe and to explain in accordance with the procedural rules of his science."[7] As social scientists we may well conceive of a *substantive causal process*, as part of a social reality that is constructed by man, and distinct from the causal constructs formulated as methodological devices by the physical scientist. Thus, causation could be used substantively to explain crime in the special sense of *social causation*. To the extent that man defines situations, that is, con-

[5] Norwood Russell Hanson, *Patterns of Discovery* (Cambridge: Cambridge University Press, 1965), p. 64.

[6] On the confusion between nominal and real constructs in general, see Robert Bierstedt, "Nominal and Real Definitions in Sociological Theory," in Llewellyn Gross (ed.), *Symposium in Sociological Theory* (Evanston, Ill.: Row, Peterson, 1959), pp. 121–144.

[7] Alfred Schutz, "Concept and Theory Formation in the Social Sciences," in Maurice Nathanson (ed.), *Philosophy of the Social Sciences* (New York: Random House, 1963), p. 242.

structs his own world in relation to others, the student of social life may conceive of a social causation as part of a social reality.

Theory Construction. The appropriate structure of a theory is far from certain in sociology. Many have worked toward establishing a research methodology, but little has been done about developing theoretical methods. Since we lack criteria for building theories, Homans has suggested that a theory must consist of propositions that state relationships and form a deductive system.[8] But we cannot ignore explanations that may be formulated in forms other than the deductive. These may contain propositions which are not deductive, but which are probabilistic, functional, or genetic.[9] Such propositions need not necessarily be deductive, in the sense that another set of propositions must be deduced from them in order for the original set of propositions to be regarded as a theory.

More important, propositions must be consistent with one another and must be integrated into a system.[10] The conclusions drawn from one proposition must not contradict those derived from another, and any conclusions obtained from the theory must be derivable within the system. Other standards to be adhered to in constructing theories are: the propositions must be testable; their validity must be determined by subsequent research; and they must be useful, enabling us to understand the problem that inspired us to formulate the theory.

Within the theory that I am constructing are several propositions that are consistent and integrated into a theoretical system. One or more specific statements express in probability form the relationships within the proposition. Further, the propositions are arranged according to a *system of proposition units*. The propositions express relationships that are both coexistent and sequential. The theory

[8] George Casper Homans, "Contemporary Theory in Sociology," in Robert E. L. Faris (ed.), *Handbook of Modern Sociology* (Chicago: Rand McNally, 1964), pp. 951–977.

[9] See Robert Brown, *Explanation in Social Science* (Chicago: Aldine, 1963); Morris R. Cohen and Ernest Nagel, *An Introduction to Logic and Scientific Method* (New York: Harcourt, Brace, 1934), pp. 197–222; Abraham Kaplan, *The Conduct of Inquiry: Methodology for the Behavioral Sciences* (San Francisco: Chandler Publishing Co., 1964), pp. 327–369.

[10] David Miller, *Scientific Sociology: Theory and Method* (Englewood Cliffs, N.J.: Prentice-Hall, 1967), pp. 9–10.

thus assumes that patterns of phenomena develop over a period of time.[11] Each proposition unit within the theoretical model requires explanation, and each unit relates to the others. Ultimately, the theoretical system provides the basis for an integrated theory of crime.

ASSUMPTIONS: MAN AND SOCIETY IN A THEORY OF CRIME

In studying any social phenomenon we must hold to some general perspective. Two of those used by sociologists, and by most social analysts for that matter, are the *static* and the *dynamic* interpretations of society. Either is equally plausible, though most sociologists take the static viewpoint.[12] This emphasis has relegated forces and events, such as deviance and crime, which do not appear to be conducive to stability and consensus, to the pathologies of society.

My theory of crime, however, is based on the dynamic perspective. The theory is based on these assumptions about man and society: (1) process, (2) conflict, (3) power, and (4) social action.

Process. The dynamic aspect of social relations may be referred to as "social process." Though in analyzing society we use static descriptions, that is, we define the structure and function of social relations, we must be aware that social phenomena fluctuate continually.[13]

We apply this assumption to all social phenomena that have duration and undergo change, that is, all those which interest the sociologist. A social process is a continuous series of actions, taking place in time, and leading to a special kind of result: "a system of social

[11] For discussions of sequential theories, see Howard S. Becker, *Outsiders: Studies in the Sociology of Deviance* (New York: The Free Press of Glencoe, 1963), pp. 22–25; Clarence Schrag, "Elements of Theoretical Analysis in Sociology," in Llewellyn Gross (ed.), *Sociological Theory: Inquiries and Paradigms* (New York: Harper & Row, 1967), pp. 242–244.

[12] See Robert A. Nisbet, *The Sociological Tradition* (New York: Basic Books, 1966); Reinhard Bendix and Bennett Berger, "Images of Society and Problems of Concept Formation in Sociology," in Gross, *Symposium on Sociological Theory,* pp. 92–118.

[13] Howard Becker, *Systematic Sociology on the Basis of the Beziehungslehre and Gebildelehre of Leopold von Wiess* (New York: John Wiley & Sons, 1932).

change taking place within a defined situation and exhibiting a particular order of change through the operation of forces present from the first within the situation."[14] Any particular phenomenon, in turn, is viewed as contributing to the dynamics of the total process. As in the "modern systems approach," social phenomena are seen as generating out of an interrelated whole.[15] The methodological implication of the process assumption is that any social phenomenon may be viewed as part of a complex network of events, structures, and underlying processes.

Conflict. In any society conflicts between persons, social units, or cultural elements are inevitable, the normal consequences of social life. Conflict is especially prevalent in societies with diverse value systems and normative groups. Experience teaches that we cannot expect to find consensus on all or most values and norms in such societies.

Two models of society contrast sharply: one is regarded as "conflict" and the other, "consensus." With the consensus model we describe social structure as a functionally integrated system held together in equilibrium. In the conflict model, on the other hand, we find that societies and social organizations are shaped by diversity, coercion, and change. The differences between these contending but complementary conceptions of society have been best characterized by Dahrendorf.[16] According to his study, we assume in postulating the consensus (or integrative) model of society that: (1) society is a relatively persistent, stable structure, (2) it is well integrated, (3) every element has a function — it helps maintain the system, and (4) a functioning social structure is based on a consensus on values. For the conflict (or coercion) model of society, on the other hand, we assume that: (1) at every point society is subject to change, (2) it displays at every point dissensus and conflict, (3) every element contributes to change, and (4) it is based on the coercion of some of its members by others. In other words, so-

[14] Robert MacIver, *Social Causation* (New York: Ginn, 1942), p. 130.

[15] Walter Buckley, "A Methodological Note," in Thomas J. Scheff, *Being Mentally Ill* (Chicago: Aldine, 1966), pp. 201–205.

[16] Ralf Dahrendorf, *Class and Class Conflict in Industrial Society* (Stanford: Stanford University Press, 1959), pp. 161–162.

ciety is held together by force and constraint and is characterized by ubiquitous conflicts that result in continuous change: "values are ruling rather than common, enforced rather than accepted, at any given point of time."[17]

Although in society as a whole conflict may be general, according to the conflict model, it is still likely that we will find stability and consensus on values among subunits in the society. Groups with their own cultural elements are found in most societies, leading to social differentiation with conflict between the social units; nonetheless integration and stability may appear within specific social groups: "Although the total larger society may be diverse internally and may form only a loosely integrated system, within each subculture there may be high integration of institutions and close conformity of individuals to the patterns sanctioned by their own group."[18]

Conflict need not necessarily disrupt society. Some sociologists have been interested in the *functions* of social conflict, "that is to say, with those consequences of social conflict which make for an increase rather than a decrease in the adaptation or adjustment of particular social relationships or groups."[19] It seems that conflict can promote cooperation, establish group boundaries, and unite social factions. Furthermore, it may lead to new patterns that may in the long run be beneficial to the whole society or to parts of it.[20] Any doubts about its functional possibilities have been dispelled by Dahrendorf: "I would suggest . . . that all that is creativity, innovation, and development in the life of the individual, his group, and his society is due, to no small extent, to the operation of conflicts between group and group, individual and individual, emotion and emotion within one individual. This fundamental fact alone seems to me to justify the value judgment that conflict is essentially 'good' and 'desirable.' "[21] Conflict is not always the disruptive agent in a

[17] Ralf Dahrendorf, "Out of Utopia: Toward a Reorientation in Sociological Analysis," *American Journal of Sociology*, 67 (September, 1958), p. 127.

[18] Robin M. Williams, Jr., *American Society*, 2nd ed. (New York: Alfred A. Knopf, 1960), p. 375.

[19] Lewis A. Coser, *The Functions of Social Conflict* (New York: The Free Press, 1956), p. 8.

[20] Lewis A. Coser, "Social Conflict and the Theory of Social Change," *British Journal of Sociology*, 8 (September, 1957), pp. 197–207.

[21] Dahrendorf, *Class and Class Conflict in Industrial Society*, p. 208. The importance of conflict in society is also discussed in, among other works, George

society; at certain times it may be meaningful to see it as a cohesive force.

Power. The conflict conception of society leads us to assume that coherence is assured in any social unit by coercion and constraint. In other words, *power* is the basic characteristic of social organization. "This means that in every social organization some positions are entrusted with a right to exercise control over other positions in order to ensure effective coercion; it means, in other words, that there is a differential distribution of power and authority."[22] Thus, conflict and power are inextricably linked in the conception of society presented here. The differential distribution of power produces conflict between competing groups, and conflict, in turn, is rooted in the competition for power. Wherever men live together conflict and a struggle for power will be found.

Power, then, is the ability of persons and groups to determine the conduct of other persons and groups.[23] It is utilized not for its own sake, but is the vehicle for the enforcement of scarce values in society, whether the values are material, moral, or otherwise. The use of power affects the distribution of values and values affect the distribution of power. The "authoritative allocation of values" is essential to any society.[24] In any society, institutional means are used to officially establish and enforce sets of values for the entire population.

Simmel, *Conflict,* trans. Kurt H. Wolff (New York: The Free Press, 1955); Irving Louis Horowitz, "Consensus, Conflict and Cooperation: A Sociological Inventory," *Social Forces,* 41 (December, 1962), pp. 177–188; Raymond W. Mack, "The Components of Social Conflict," *Social Problems,* 12 (Spring, 1965), pp. 388–397.

[22] Dahrendorf, *Class and Class Conflict in Industrial Society,* p. 165.

[23] Max Weber, *From Max Weber: Essays in Sociology,* trans. H. H. Gerth and C. Wright Mills (New York: Oxford University Press, 1946); Hans Gerth and C. Wright Mills, *Character and Social Structure* (New York: Harcourt, Brace, 1953), especially pp. 192–273; C. Wright Mills, *The Power Elite* (New York: Oxford University Press, 1956); George Simmel, *The Sociology of George Simmel,* trans. Kurt H. Wolff (New York: The Free Press, 1950), pp. 181–186; Robert Bierstedt, "An Analysis of Social Power," *American Sociological Review,* 15 (December, 1950), pp. 730–738.

[24] David Easton, *The Political System* (New York: Alfred A. Knopf, 1953), p. 137. Similar ideas are found in Harold D. Lasswell, *Politics: Who Gets What, When, How* (New York: McGraw-Hill, 1936); Harold D. Lasswell and Abraham Kaplan, *Power and Society* (New Haven: Yale University Press, 1950).

Power and the allocation of values are basic in forming *public policy*. Groups with special *interests* become so well organized that they are able to influence the policies that are to affect all persons. These interest groups exert their influence at every level and branch of government in order to have their own values and interests represented in the policy decisions.[25] Any interest group's ability to influence public policy depends on the group's position in the political power structure. Furthermore, access to the formation of public policy is unequally distributed because of the structural arrangements of the political state. "Access is one of the advantages unequally distributed by such arrangements; that is, in consequence of the structural peculiarities of our government some groups have better and more varied opportunities to influence key points of decision than do others."[26] Groups that have the power to gain access to the decision-making process also inevitably control the lives of others.

A major assumption in my conception of society, therefore, is the importance of interest groups in shaping public policy. Public policy is formed so as to represent the interests and values of groups that are in positions of power. Rather than accept the pluralistic

[25] Among the vast amount of literature on interest groups, see Donald C. Blaisdell, *American Democracy Under Pressure* (New York: Ronald Press, 1957); V. O. Key, Jr., *Politics, Parties, and Pressure Groups* (New York: Thomas Y. Crowell, 1959); Earl Latham, *Group Basis of Politics* (Ithaca, N.Y.: Cornell University Press, 1952); David Truman, *The Governmental Process* (New York: Alfred A. Knopf, 1951); Henry W. Ehrmann (ed.), *Interest Groups on Four Continents* (Pittsburgh: University of Pittsburgh Press, 1958); Henry A. Turner, "How Pressure Groups Operate," *Annals of the American Academy of Political and Social Science,* 319 (September, 1958), pp. 63–72; Richard W. Gable, "Interest Groups as Policy Shapers," *Annals of the American Academy of Political and Social Science,* 319 (September, 1958), pp. 84–93; Murray S. Stedman, "Pressure Group and the American Tradition," *Annals of the American Academy of Political and Social Science,* 319 (September, 1958), pp. 123–219. For documentation on the influence of specific interest groups, see Robert Engler, *The Politics of Oil* (New York: Macmillan, 1961); Oliver Garceau, *The Political Life of the American Medical Association* (Cambridge: Harvard University Press, 1941); Charles M. Hardin, *The Politics of Agriculture: Soil Conservation and the Struggle for Power in Rural America* (New York: The Free Press of Glencoe, 1962); Grant McConnell, *Private Power and American Democracy* (New York: Alfred A. Knopf, 1966); Harry A. Millis and Royal E. Montgomery, *Organized Labor* (New York: McGraw-Hill, 1945); Warner Schilling, Paul Y. Hammond, and Glenn H. Snyder, *Strategy, Politics and Defense* (New York: Columbia University Press, 1962); William R. Willoughby, *The St. Lawrence Waterway: A Study in Politics and Diplomacy* (Madison: University of Wisconsin Press, 1961).

[26] Truman, *The Governmental Process,* p. 322.

conception of the political process, which assumes that all groups make themselves heard in policy decision-making, I am relying upon a conception that assumes an unequal distribution of power in formulating and administering public policy.[27]

Social Action. An assumption of man that is consistent with the conflict-power conception of society asserts that man's actions are purposive and meaningful, that man engages in voluntary behavior. This *humanistic* conception of man contrasts with the oversocialized conception of man. Man is, after all, capable of considering alternative actions, of breaking from the established social order.[28] Once he gains an awareness of self, by being a member of society, he is able to choose his actions. The extent to which he does conform depends in large measure upon his own self-control.[29] Nonconformity may also be part of the process of finding self-identity. It is thus *against* something that the self can emerge.[30]

By conceiving of man as able to reason and choose courses of action, we may see him as changing and becoming, rather than merely being.[31] The kind of culture that man develops shapes his

[27] Evaluations of the pluralistic and power approaches are found in Peter Bachrach and Morton S. Baratz, "Two Faces of Power," *American Political Science Review,* 61 (December, 1962), pp. 947–952; Thomas I. Cook, "The Political System: The Stubborn Search for a Science of Politics," *Journal of Philosophy,* 51 (February, 1954), pp. 128–137; Charles S. Hyneman, *The Study of Politics* (Urbana: University of Illinois Press, 1959); William C. Mitchell, "Politics as the Allocation of Values: A Critique," *Ethics,* 71 (January, 1961), pp. 79–89; Talcott Parsons, "The Distribution of Power in American Society," *World Politics,* 10 (October, 1957), pp. 123–143; Charles Perrow, "The Sociological Perspective and Political Pluralism," *Social Research,* 31 (Winter, 1964), pp. 411–422.

[28] For essentially this aspect of man see Peter Berger, *Invitation to Sociology: A Humanistic Perspective* (New York: Doubleday, 1963), chap. 6; Max Mark, "What Image of Man for Political Science?" *Western Political Quarterly,* 15 (December, 1962), pp. 593–604; Dennis Wrong, "The Oversocialized Conception of Man in Modern Sociology," *American Sociological Review,* 26 (April, 1961), pp. 183–193.

[29] Tamotsu Shibutani, *Society and Personality: An Interactionist Approach to Social Psychology* (Englewood Cliffs, N.J.: Prentice-Hall, 1961), especially pp. 60, 91–94, 276–278. Also see S. F. Nadel, "Social Control and Self-Regulation," *Social Forces,* 31 (March, 1953), pp. 265–273.

[30] Erving Goffman, *Asylums* (New York: Doubleday, 1961), pp. 318–320.

[31] Richard A. Schermerhorn, "Man the Unfinished," *Sociological Quarterly,* 4 (Winter, 1963), pp. 5–17; Gordon W. Allport, *Becoming: Basic Considerations for a Psychology of Personality* (New Haven: Yale University Press, 1955).

ability to be creative. Through his culture he may develop the capacity to have greater freedom of action.[32] Not only is he shaped by his physical, social, and cultural experiences, he is able to select what he is to experience and develop. The belief in realizing unutilized human potential is growing and should be incorporated in a contemporary conception of human behavior.[33]

The *social action* frame of reference that serves as the basis of the humanistic conception of man is drawn from the work of such writers as Weber, Znaniecki, MacIver, Nadel, Parsons, and Becker.[34] It was originally suggested by Max Weber: "Action is social in so far as, by virtue of the subjective meaning attached to it by the acting individual (or individuals), it takes account of the behavior of others and is thereby oriented in its own course."[35] Hence, human behavior is *intentional,* has *meaning* for the actors, is *goal-oriented,* and takes place with an *awareness* of the consequences of behavior.

Because man engages in social action, a *social reality* is created. That is, man in interaction with others constructs a meaningful world of everyday life.

> It is the world of cultural objects and social institutions into which we are all born, within which we have to find our bearings, and with which we have to come to terms. From the outset, we, the actors on the social scene, experience the world we live in as a world both of nature and of culture, not as a private but as an intersubjective one, that is, as a world common to all of us, either actually given or potentially accessible to everyone; and this involves intercommunication and language.[36]

Social reality consists of both the social meanings and the products of the subjective world of persons. Man, accordingly, con-

[32] Herbert J. Muller, *The Uses of the Past* (New York: Oxford University Press, 1952), especially pp. 40–42.

[33] Julian Huxley, *New Bottles for New Wines* (New York: Harper, 1957).

[34] Florian Znaniecki, *Social Actions* (New York: Farrar and Rinehart, 1936); MacIver, *Social Causation;* S. F. Nadel, *Foundations of Social Anthropology* (New York: The Free Press, 1951); Talcott Parsons, *The Structure of Social Action* (New York: The Free Press, 1949); Howard Becker, *Through Values to Social Interpretation* (Durham: Duke University Press, 1950).

[35] Max Weber, *The Theory of Social and Economic Organization,* trans. A. M. Henderson and Talcott Parsons (New York: The Free Press), p. 88.

[36] Alfred Schutz, *The Problem of Social Reality: Collected Papers I* (The Hague: Martinus Nijhoff, 1962), p. 53.

structs activities and patterns of actions as he attaches meaning to his everyday existence.[37] Social reality is thus both a *conceptual reality* and a *phenomenal reality*. Having constructed social reality, man finds a world of meanings and events that is real to him as a conscious social being.

THEORY: THE SOCIAL REALITY OF CRIME

The theory contains six propositions and a number of statements within the propositions. With the first proposition I define crime. The next four are the explanatory units. In the final proposition the other five are collected to form a composite describing the social reality of crime. The propositions and their integration into a theory of crime reflect the assumptions about explanation and about man and society outlined above.[38]

PROPOSITION 1 (DEFINITION OF CRIME): *Crime is a definition of human conduct that is created by authorized agents in a politically organized society.*

This is the essential starting point in the theory — a definition of crime — which itself is based on the concept of definition. Crime is a *definition* of behavior that is conferred on some persons by others. Agents of the law (legislators, police, prosecutors, and judges), representing segments of a politically organized society, are responsible for formulating and administering criminal law. Persons and behaviors, therefore, become criminal because of the *formulation* and *application* of criminal definitions. Thus, *crime is created.*

By viewing crime as a definition, we are able to avoid the commonly used "clinical perspective," which leads one to concentrate on the quality of the act and to assume that criminal behavior is an

[37] See Peter L. Berger and Thomas Luckmann, *The Social Construction of Reality* (Garden City, N.Y.: Doubleday, 1966).

[38] For earlier background material, see Richard Quinney, "A Conception of Man and Society for Criminology," *Sociological Quarterly,* 6 (Spring, 1965), pp. 119–127; Quinney, "Crime in Political Perspective," *American Behavioral Scientist,* 8 (December, 1964), pp. 19–22; Quinney, "Is Criminal Behavior Deviant Behavior?" *British Journal of Criminology,* 5 (April, 1965), pp. 132–142.

individual pathology.[39] Crime is not inherent in behavior, but is a judgment made by some about the actions and characteristics of others.[40] This proposition allows us to focus on the formulation and administration of the criminal law as it touches upon the behaviors that become defined as criminal. Crime is seen as a result of a process which culminates in the defining of persons and behaviors as criminal. It follows, then, that *the greater the number of criminal definitions formulated and applied, the greater the amount of crime.*

PROPOSITION 2 (FORMULATION OF CRIMINAL DEFINITIONS): *Criminal definitions describe behaviors that conflict with the interests of the segments of society that have the power to shape public policy.*

Criminal definitions are formulated according to the interests of those *segments* (types of social groupings) of society which have the *power* to translate their interests into *public policy.* The interests — based on desires, values, and norms — which are ultimately incorporated into the criminal law are those which are treasured by the dominant interest groups in the society.[41] In other words, those who

[39] See Jane R. Mercer, "Social System Perspective and Clinical Perspective: Frames of Reference for Understanding Career Patterns of Persons Labelled as Mentally Retarded," *Social Problems,* 13 (Summer, 1966), pp. 18–34.

[40] This perspective in the study of social deviance has been developed in Becker, *Outsiders*; Kai T. Erikson, "Notes on the Sociology of Deviance," *Social Problems,* 9 (Spring, 1962), pp. 307–314; John I. Kitsuse, "Societal Reactions to Deviant Behavior: Problems of Theory and Method," *Social Problems,* 9 (Winter, 1962), pp. 247–256. Also see Ronald L. Akers, "Problems in the Sociology of Deviance: Social Definitions and Behavior," *Social Forces,* 46 (June, 1968), pp. 455–465; David J. Bordua, "Recent Trends: Deviant Behavior and Social Control," *Annals of the American Academy of Political and Social Science,* 369 (January, 1967), pp. 149–163; Jack P. Gibbs, "Conceptions of Deviant Behavior: The Old and the New," *Pacific Sociological Review,* 9 (Spring, 1966), pp. 9–14; Clarence R. Jeffery, "The Structure of American Criminological Thinking," *Journal of Criminal Law, Criminology and Police Science,* 46 (January–February, 1956), pp. 658–672; Austin T. Turk, "Prospects for Theories of Criminal Behavior," *Journal of Criminal Law, Criminology and Police Science,* 55 (December, 1964), pp. 454–461.

[41] See Richard C. Fuller, "Morals and the Criminal Law," *Journal of Criminal Law, Criminology and Police Science,* 32 (March–April, 1942), pp. 624–630; Thorsten Sellin, *Culture Conflict and Crime* (New York: Social Science Research Council, 1938), pp. 21–25; Clarence R. Jeffery, "Crime, Law and Social Structure," *Journal of Criminal Law, Criminology and Police Science,* 47 (November-December, 1956), pp. 423–435; John J. Honigmann, "Value Conflict and Legislation," *Social Problems,* 7 (Summer, 1959), pp. 34–40; George Rusche and Otto Kirchheimer, *Punishment and Social Structure* (New York: Columbia

have the ability to have their interests represented in public policy regulate the formulation of criminal definitions.

That criminal definitions are formulated is one of the most obvious manifestations of *conflict* in society. By formulating criminal law (including legislative statutes, administrative rulings, and judicial decisions), some segments of society protect and perpetuate their own interests. Criminal definitions exist, therefore, because some segments of society are in conflict with others.[42] By formulating criminal definitions these segments are able to control the behavior of persons in other segments. It follows that *the greater the conflict in interests between the segments of a society, the greater the probability that the power segments will formulate criminal definitions.*

The interests of the power segments of society are reflected not only in the content of criminal definitions and the kinds of penal sanctions attached to them, but also in the *legal policies* stipulating how those who come to be defined as "criminal" are to be handled. Hence, procedural rules are created for enforcing and administering the criminal law. Policies are also established on programs for treating and punishing the criminally defined and for controlling and preventing crime. In the initial criminal definitions or the subsequent procedures, and in correctional and penal programs or policies of crime control and prevention, the segments of society that have power and interests to protect are instrumental in regulating the behavior of those who have conflicting interests and less power.[43]

University Press, 1939); Roscoe Pound, *An Introduction to the Philosophy of Law* (New Haven: Yale University Press, 1922).

[42] I am obviously indebted to the conflict formulation of George B. Vold, *Theoretical Criminology* (New York: Oxford University Press, 1958), especially pp. 203–242. A recent conflict approach to crime is found in Austin T. Turk, "Conflict and Criminality," *American Sociological Review,* 31 (June, 1966), pp. 338–352.

[43] Considerable support for this proposition is found in the following studies: William J. Chambliss, "A Sociological Analysis of the Law of Vagrancy," *Social Problems,* 12 (Summer, 1964), pp. 66–77; Kai T. Erikson, *Wayward Puritans* (New York: John Wiley, 1966); Jerome Hall, *Theft, Law and Society,* 2nd ed. (Indianapolis: Bobbs-Merrill, 1952); Clarence R. Jeffery, "The Development of Crime in Early England," *Journal of Criminal Law, Criminology and Police Science,* 47 (March–April, 1957), pp. 647–666; Alfred R. Lindesmith, *The Addict and the Law* (Bloomington: Indiana University Press, 1965); Rusche and Kirchheimer, *Punishment and Social Structure;* Andrew Sinclair, *Era of Excess: A Social History of the Prohibition Movement* (New York: Harper & Row, 1964); Edwin H. Sutherland, "The Sexual Psychopath

Finally, law changes with modifications in the interest structure. When the interests that underlie a criminal law are no longer relevant to groups in power, the law will be reinterpreted or altered to incorporate the dominant interests. Hence, *the probability that criminal definitions will be formulated is increased by such factors as (1) changing social conditions, (2) emerging interests, (3) increasing demands that political, economic, and religious interests be protected, and (4) changing conceptions of the public interest.* The social history of law reflects changes in the interest structure of society.

PROPOSITION 3 (APPLICATION OF CRIMINAL DEFINITIONS): *Criminal definitions are applied by the segments of society that have the power to shape the enforcement and administration of criminal law.*

The powerful interests intervene in all stages in which criminal definitions are created. Since interests cannot be effectively protected by merely formulating criminal law, enforcement and administration of the law are required. The interests of the powerful, therefore, operate in *applying* criminal definitions. Consequently, crime is "political behavior and the criminal becomes in fact a member of a 'minority group' without sufficient public support to dominate the control of the police power of the state."[44] Those whose interests conflict with the interests represented in the law must either change their behavior or possibly find it defined as "criminal."

The probability that criminal definitions will be applied varies according to the extent to which the behaviors of the powerless conflict with the interests of the power segments. Law enforcement efforts and judicial activity are likely to be increased when the interests of the powerful are threatened by the opposition's behavior. Fluctuations and variations in the application of criminal definitions reflect shifts in the relations of the various segments in the power structure of society.

Law," *Journal of Criminal Law, Criminology and Police Science,* 40 (January–February, 1950), pp. 543–554.

[44] Vold, *Theoretical Criminology,* p. 202. Also see Irving Louis Horowitz and Martin Liebowitz, "Social Deviance and Political Marginality: Toward a Redefinition of the Relation Between Sociology and Politics," *Social Problems,* 15 (Winter, 1968), pp. 280–296.

Obviously, the criminal law is not applied directly by the powerful segments. They delegate enforcement and administration of the law to authorized *legal agents,* who, nevertheless, represent their interests. In fact, the security in office of legal agents depends on their ability to represent the society's dominant interests.

Because the interest groups responsible for creating criminal definitions are physically separated from the groups to which the authority to enforce and administer law is delegated, local conditions affect the manner in which criminal definitions are applied.[45] In particular, communities vary in the law enforcement and administration of justice they expect. Application is also affected by the visibility of acts in a community and by its norms about reporting possible offenses. Especially important are the occupational organization and ideology of the legal agents.[46] Thus, *the probability that criminal definitions will be applied is influenced by such community and organizational factors as (1) community expectations of law enforcement and administration, (2) the visibility and public reporting of offenses, and (3) the occupational organization, ideology, and actions of the legal agents to whom the authority to enforce and*

[45] See Michael Banton, *The Policeman and the Community* (London: Tavistock, 1964); Egon Bittner, "The Police on Skid-Row: A Study of Peace Keeping," *American Sociological Review,* 32 (October, 1967), pp. 699–715; John P. Clark, "Isolation of the Police: A Comparison of the British and American Situations," *Journal of Criminal Law, Criminology and Police Science,* 56 (September, 1965), pp. 307–319; Nathan Goldman, *The Differential Selection of Juvenile Offenders for Court Appearance* (New York National Council on Crime and Delinquency, 1963); James Q. Wilson, *Varieties of Police Behavior* (Cambridge: Harvard University Press, 1968).

[46] Abraham S. Blumberg, *Criminal Justice* (Chicago: Quadrangle Books, 1967); David J. Bordua and Albert J. Reiss, Jr., "Command, Control and Charisma: Reflections on Police Bureaucracy," *American Journal of Sociology,* 72 (July, 1966), pp. 68–76; Aaron V. Cicourel, *The Social Organization of Juvenile Justice* (New York: John Wiley, 1968); Arthur Niederhoffer, *Behind the Shield: The Police in Urban Society* (Garden City, N.Y.: Doubleday, 1967); Jerome H. Skolnick, *Justice Without Trial: Law Enforcement in Democratic Society* (New York: John Wiley, 1966); Arthur L. Stinchcombe, "Institutions of Privacy in the Determination of Police Administrative Practice," *American Journal of Sociology,* 69 (September, 1963), pp. 150–160; David Sudnow, "Normal Crimes: Sociological Features of the Penal Code in a Public Defender Office," *Social Problems,* 12 (Winter, 1965), pp. 255–276; William A. Westley, "Violence and the Police," *American Journal of Sociology,* 59 (July, 1953), pp. 34–41; Arthur Lewis Wood, *Criminal Lawyer* (New Haven: College & University Press, 1967).

administer criminal law is delegated. Such factors determine how the dominant interests of society are implemented in the application of criminal definitions.

The probability that criminal definitions will be applied in *specific situations* depends on the actions of the legal agents. In the final analysis, a criminal definition is applied according to an *evaluation* by someone charged with the authority to enforce and administer the law. In the course of "criminalization," a criminal label may be affixed to a person because of real or fancied attributes: "Indeed, a person is evaluated, either favorably or unfavorably, not because he *does* something, or even because he *is* something, but because others react to their perceptions of him as offensive or inoffensive."[47] Evaluation by the definers is affected by the way in which the suspect handles the situation, but ultimately their evaluations and subsequent decisions determine the criminality of human acts. Hence, *the more legal agents evaluate behaviors and persons as worthy of criminal definition, the greater the probability that criminal definitions will be applied.*

PROPOSITION 4 (DEVELOPMENT OF BEHAVIOR PATTERNS IN RELATION TO CRIMINAL DEFINITIONS): *Behavior patterns are structured in segmentally organized society in relation to criminal definitions, and within this context persons engage in actions that have relative probabilities of being defined as criminal.*

Although behavior varies, all behaviors are similar in that they represent the *behavior patterns* of segments of society. Therefore, all persons — whether they create criminal definitions or are the objects of criminal definitions — act according to *normative systems* learned in relative social and cultural settings.[48] Since it is not the

[47] Turk, "Conflict and Criminality," p. 340. For research on the evaluation of suspects by policemen, see Irving Piliavin and Scott Briar, "Police Encounters with Juveniles," *American Journal of Sociology,* 70 (September, 1964), pp. 206–214.

[48] Assumed within the theory of the social reality of crime is Sutherland's theory of differential association. See Edwin H. Sutherland, *Principles of Criminology,* 4th ed. (Philadelphia: J. B. Lippincott, 1947). An analysis of the differential association theory is found in Melvin L. De Fleur and Richard Quinney, "A Reformulation of Sutherland's Differential Association Theory and a Strategy for Empirical Verification," *Journal of Research in Crime and Delinquency,* 3 (January, 1966), pp. 1–22.

quality of the behavior but the action taken against the behavior that makes it criminal, that which is defined as criminal in any society is relative to the behavior patterns of the segments of society that formulate and apply criminal definitions. Consequently, *persons in the segments of society whose behavior patterns are not represented in formulating and applying criminal definitions are more likely to act in ways that will be defined as criminal than those in the segments that formulate and apply criminal definitions.*

Once behavior patterns are established with some regularity within the respective segments of society, individuals are provided with a framework for developing *personal action patterns*. These patterns continually develop for each person as he moves from one experience to another. It is the development of these patterns that gives his behavior its own substance in relation to criminal definitions.

Man constructs his own patterns of action in participating with others. It follows, then, that *the probability that a person will develop action patterns that have a high potential of being defined as criminal depends on the relative substance of (1) structured opportunities, (2) learning experiences, (3) interpersonal associations and identifications, and (4) self-conceptions.* Throughout his experiences, each person creates a conception of himself as a social being. Thus prepared, he behaves according to the anticipated consequences of his actions.[49]

During experiences shared by the criminal definers and the criminally defined, personal action patterns develop among the criminally defined because they are so defined. After such persons have had continued experience in being criminally defined, they learn to manipulate the application of criminal definitions.[50]

Furthermore, those who have been defined as criminal begin to conceive of themselves as criminal; as they adjust to the definitions

[49] On the operant nature of criminally defined behavior, see Robert L. Burgess and Ronald L. Akers, "A Differential Association-Reinforcement Theory of Criminal Behavior," *Social Problems,* 14 (Fall, 1966), pp. 128–147; C. R. Jeffery, "Criminal Behavior and Learning Theory," *Journal of Criminal Law, Criminology and Police Science,* 56 (September, 1965), pp. 294–300.

[50] A discussion of the part the person plays in manipulating the deviant defining situation is found in Judith Lorber, "Deviance as Performance: The Case of Illness," *Social Problems,* 14 (Winter, 1967), pp. 302–310.

imposed upon them, they learn to play the role of the criminal.[51] Because of others' reactions, therefore, persons may develop personal action patterns that increase the likelihood of their being defined as criminal in the future. That is, *increased experience with criminal definitions increases the probability of developing actions that may be subsequently defined as criminal.*

Thus, both the criminal definers and the criminally defined are involved in reciprocal action patterns. The patterns of both the definers and the defined are shaped by their common, continued, and related experiences. The fate of each is bound to that of the other.

PROPOSITION 5 (CONSTRUCTION OF CRIMINAL CONCEPTIONS): *Conceptions of crime are constructed and diffused in the segments of society by various means of communication.*

The "real world" is a social construction: man with the help of others creates the world in which he lives. Social reality is thus the world a group of people create and believe in as their own. This reality is constructed according to the kind of "knowledge" they develop, the ideas they are exposed to, the manner in which they select information to fit the world they are shaping, and the manner in which they interpret these conceptions.[52] Man behaves in reference to the *social meanings* he attaches to his experiences.

Among the constructions that develop in a society are those which determine what man regards as crime. Wherever we find the concept of crime, there we will find conceptions about the relevance of crime, the offender's characteristics, and the relation of crime to the social order.[53] These conceptions are constructed by communication. In fact, *the construction of criminal conceptions depends on the por-*

[51] Edwin M. Lemert, *Human Deviance, Social Problems, and Social Control* (Englewood Cliffs, N.J.: Prentice-Hall, 1964), pp. 40–64; Edwin M. Lemert, *Social Pathology* (New York: McGraw-Hill, 1951), pp. 3–98. A related and earlier discussion is in Frank Tannenbaum, *Crime and the Community* (New York: Columbia University Press, 1938), pp. 3–81.

[52] See Berger and Luckmann, *The Social Construction of Reality*. Relevant research on the diffusion of information is discussed in Everett M. Rogers, *Diffusion of Innovations* (New York: The Free Press of Glencoe, 1962).

[53] Research on public conceptions of crime is only beginning. See Alexander L. Clark and Jack P. Gibbs, "Social Control: A Reformulation," *Social Problems,* 12 (Spring, 1965), pp. 398–415; Thomas E. Dow, Jr., "The Role of Identification in Conditioning Public Attitude Toward the Offender," *Journal of Criminal Law, Criminology and Police Science*, 58 (March, 1967), pp. 75–79; William P. Lentz, "Social Status and Attitudes Toward Delinquency Control,"

trayal of crime in all personal and mass communications. By such means, criminal conceptions are constructed and diffused in the segments of a society. The most critical conceptions are those held by the power segments of society. These are the conceptions that are certain of becoming incorporated into the social reality of crime. In general, then, *the more the power segments are concerned about crime, the greater the probability that criminal definitions will be created and that behavior patterns will develop in opposition to criminal definitions.* The formulation and application of criminal definitions and the development of behavior patterns related to criminal definitions are thus joined in full circle by the construction of criminal conceptions.

PROPOSITION 6 (THE SOCIAL REALITY OF CRIME): *The social reality of crime is constructed by the formulation and application of criminal definitions, the development of behavior patterns related to criminal definitions, and the construction of criminal conceptions.*

These five propositions can be collected into a composite. The theory, accordingly, describes and explains phenomena that increase the probability of crime in society, resulting in the social reality of crime.

Since the first proposition is a definition and the sixth is a composite, the body of the theory consists of the four middle propositions. These form a model, as diagrammed in Figure 1.1, which relates the propositions into a theoretical system. Each proposition is related to the others forming a theoretical system of developmental propositions interacting with one another. The phenomena denoted in the propositions and their relationships culminate in what is regarded as the amount and character of crime in a society at any given time, that is, in the social reality of crime.

Journal of Research in Crime and Delinquency, 3 (July, 1966), pp. 147–154; Jennie McIntyre, "Public Attitudes Toward Crime and Law Enforcement," *Annals of the American Academy of Political and Social Science*, 374 (November, 1967), pp. 34–46; Anastassios D. Mylonas and Walter C. Reckless, "Prisoners' Attitudes Toward Law and Legal Institutions," *Journal of Criminal Law, Criminology and Police Science*, 54 (December, 1963), pp. 479–484; Elizabeth A. Rooney and Don C. Gibbons, "Social Reactions to 'Crimes Without Victims,'" *Social Problems*, 13 (Spring, 1966), pp. 400–410.

FIGURE 1.1
Model of the
Social Reality of Crime

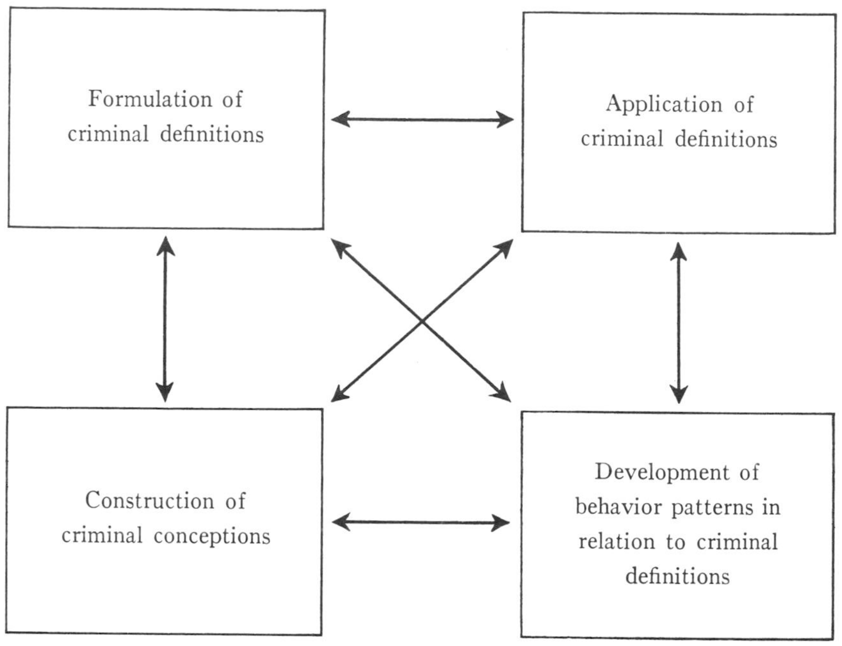

A THEORETICAL PERSPECTIVE FOR STUDYING CRIME

The theory as I have formulated it is inspired by a change currently altering our view of the world. This change, found at all levels of society, has to do with the world that we all construct and, at the same time, pretend to separate ourselves from in assessing our experiences. Sociologists, sensing the problematic nature of existence, have begun to revise their theoretical orientation, as well as their methods and subjects of investigation.

For the study of crime, a revision in thought is directing attention to the process by which criminal definitions are formulated and applied. In the theory of the social reality of crime I have attempted to show how a theory of crime can be consistent with some revisionist assumptions about theoretical explanation and about man and society. The theory is cumulative in that the framework incorporates the diverse findings from criminology.

The synthesis has been brought about by conceiving of crime as a constructive process and by formulating a theory according to a system of propositions. The theory is integrative in that all relevant phenomena contribute to the process of creating criminal definitions, the development of the behaviors of those who are involved in criminal defining situations, and the construction of criminal conceptions. The result is the social reality of crime that is constantly being constructed in society.

The theory of the social reality of crime is used as a *theoretical perspective* throughout this book. It has allowed me to organize a considerable amount of material into a coherent framework, giving a perspective for a sociological study of crime. The theory can be useful to the extent that it helps us to understand crime as we experience it today.

2

Formulation of Criminal Definitions

CHAPTER TWO

Criminal Law in Politically Organized Society

In roughly a decade social scientists have amassed an impressive amount of research on criminal law. Yet, in spite of the research, a theory of criminal law has not developed. We are not at the moment theoretically equipped to generalize beyond the empirical studies or to formulate theoretically relevant research questions. In this chapter, I will develop a theoretical perspective to assist in these tasks. For this perspective I have elaborated on my general proposition describing how criminal definitions are formulated in the social reality of crime.[1]

THE STUDY OF CRIMINAL LAW

Paradoxically, with law and social science gradually converging, we have no greater theoretical understanding of legal matters than we did all of half a century ago. The rapprochement that we are currently witnessing is not novel; a similar trend appeared in the United States shortly after the turn of the century. At that time social scientists, the early American sociologists in particular, were incorporating law into their scheme of things. E. A. Ross

[1] Portions of this chapter are adapted, with the publisher's permission, from the introduction to my *Crime and Justice in Society* (Boston: Little, Brown and Company, 1969), pp. 20–30.

referred to law as "the most specialized and highly furnished engine of control employed by society."[2] Lester F. Ward, an advocate of government control and social planning, foresaw a day when legislation would undertake to solve "questions of social improvement, the amelioration of the condition of all the people, the removal of whatever privations may still remain, and the adoption of means to the positive increase of the social welfare, in short the organization of human happiness."[3] The possibility of social reform, through legal means available to the state, was also emphasized by Albion W. Small.[4]

The ideas of the early sociologists directly influenced the school of legal philosophy that became a major force in American legal thought — sociological jurisprudence — in which Roscoe Pound was the principal figure. He drew from the early sociologists in asserting that law should be studied as a social institution.[5] Pound saw law as a specialized form of social control that brings pressure to bear upon each man "in order to constrain him to do his part in upholding civilized society and to deter him from anti-social conduct, that is, conduct at variance with the postulates of social order."[6] Moreover, in his theory of interests, Pound provided one of the few starting points for the study of law as a social phenomenon.

Recent writing and research have documented the role of interest groups in the political process. The techniques and tactics of interest groups, relations between the groups, their internal organization and politics, and overlapping group membership have been ex-

[2] E. A. Ross, *Social Control* (New York: Macmillan, 1922), p. 106 (originally published in 1901).

[3] Lester F. Ward, *Applied Sociology* (Boston: Ginn, 1906), p. 339.

[4] Albion W. Small, *General Sociology* (Chicago: University of Chicago Press, 1925).

[5] The relationship between early American sociologists and the development of Pound's sociological jurisprudence is discussed in Gilbert Geis, "Sociology and Jurisprudence: Admixture of Lore and Law," *Kentucky Law Journal,* 52 (Winter, 1964), pp. 267–293. Also see Edwin M. Schur, *Law and Society* (New York: Random House, 1968), pp. 17–50.

[6] Roscoe Pound, *Social Control Through Law* (New Haven: Yale University Press, 1942), p. 18. Earlier statements by Pound are found in Roscoe Pound, *An Introduction to the Philosophy of Law* (New Haven: Yale University Press, 1922); Roscoe Pound, *Outline of Lectures on Jurisprudence* (Cambridge: Harvard University Press, 1928).

amined.[7] In addition, studies have been conducted on how specific groups operate.[8] But almost no research has been directed at finding how much influence the interests have in formulating and administering law.[9] Moreover, few have attempted to revise Pound's theory of interests to reflect recent sociological developments. As it has been observed, "Sociologists to date have paid virtually no attention to Pound's doctrine, either in terms of rejecting it, refining it for their purposes, or supplementing it with sociological material of more recent vintage."[10]

[7] Donald C. Blaisdell, *American Democracy Under Pressure* (New York: Ronald Press, 1957); V. O. Key, Jr., *Politics, Parties and Pressure Groups* (New York: Thomas Y. Crowell, 1959); Earl Latham, *Group Basis of Politics* (Ithaca, N.Y.: Cornell University Press, 1952); David B. Truman, *The Governmental Process* (New York: Alfred A. Knopf, 1951); Henry W. Ehrmann (ed.), *Interest Groups on Four Continents* (Pittsburgh: University of Pittsburgh Press, 1958); Henry A. Turner, "How Pressure Groups Operate," *Annals of the American Academy of Political and Social Science,* 319 (September, 1958), pp. 63–72; Richard W. Gable, "Interest Groups as Policy Shapers," *Annals of the American Academy of Political and Social Science,* 319 (September, 1958), pp. 84–93; Murray S. Stedman, "Pressure Groups and the American Tradition," *Annals of the American Academy of Political and Social Science,* 319 (September, 1958), pp. 123–129.

[8] Robert Engler, *The Politics of Oil* (New York: Macmillan, 1961); Oliver Garceau, *The Political Life of the American Medical Association* (Cambridge: Harvard University Press, 1941); Charles M. Hardin, *The Politics of Agriculture: Soil Conservation and the Struggle for Power in Rural America* (New York: The Free Press of Glencoe, 1962); Grant McConnell, *Private Power and American Democracy* (New York: Alfred A. Knopf, 1966); Harry A. Millis and Royal E. Montgomery, *Organized Labor* (New York: McGraw-Hill, 1945); Warner Schilling, Paul Y. Hammond, and Glenn H. Snyder, *Strategy, Politics and Defense* (New York: Columbia University Press, 1962); William R. Willoughby, *The St. Lawrence Waterway: A Study in Politics and Diplomacy* (Madison: University of Wisconsin Press, 1961).

[9] Other social orientations to the law may be found among sociological jurists, among the so-called legal realists, and among current legal historians. See, in particular, Oliver Wendell Holmes, "The Path of the Law," *Harvard Law Review,* 10 (March, 1897), pp. 457–478; Thurman W. Arnold, *Symbols of Government* (New Haven: Yale University Press, 1935); Jerome Frank, *Courts on Trial* (Princeton: Princeton University Press, 1949); K. N. Llewellyn and E. Adamson Hoebel, *The Cheyenne Way: Conflict and Case Law in Primitive Jurisprudence* (Norman: University of Oklahoma Press, 1941); J. Willard Hurst, *Law and Economic Growth: The Legal History of the Lumber Industry in Wisconsin, 1836–1915* (Cambridge, Mass.: The Belknap Press, 1964).

[10] Geis, "Sociology and Sociological Jurisprudence: Admixture of Lore and Law," p. 292.

In the current movement by social scientists toward research into law and the use by lawyers of social science research, an interest approach might well help us to construct a theory of criminal law that would integrate research findings and provide direction for future research. For sociological purposes, however, Pound's approach necessarily requires reformulation and extension into a sociological theory of criminal law.

FROM SOCIOLOGICAL JURISPRUDENCE TO SOCIOLOGY OF CRIMINAL LAW

Law is not merely a complex of rules and procedures; Pound taught us that in calling for the study of "law in action." For some purposes it may be useful to think of law as autonomous within society, developing according to its own logic and proceeding along its own lines. But law also simultaneously reflects society and influences it, so that, in a social sense, it is both social product and social force. In Pound's juristic approach, however, law represents the consciousness of the total society. This *consensus* model of (criminal) law has been described in the following way: "The state of criminal law continues to be — as it should — a decisive reflection of the social consciousness of a society. What kind of conduct an organized community considers, at a given time, sufficiently condemnable to impose official sanctions, impairing the life, liberty, or property of the offender, is a barometer of the moral and social thinking of a community."[11] Similarly, Pound, formulating his theory of interests, felt that law reflects the needs of the well-ordered society. In fact, the law is a form of "social engineering" in a civilized society:

> For the purpose of understanding the law of today, I am content to think of law as a social institution to satisfy social wants — the claims and demands involved in the existence of civilized society — by giving effect to as much as we may with the least sacrifice, so far as such wants may be satisfied or

[11] Wolfgang Friedmann, *Law in a Changing Society* (Harmondsworth, England: Penguin Books, 1964), p. 143. A similar statement is found in Jerome Michael and Mortimer J. Adler, *Crime, Law and Social Science* (New York: Harcourt, Brace, 1933), pp. 2–3.

> such claims given effect by an ordering of human conduct through politically organized society. For present purposes I am content to see in legal history the record of a continually wider recognizing and satisfying of human wants or claims or desires through social control; a more embracing and more effective securing of social interests; a continually more complete and effective elimination of waste and precluding of friction in human enjoyment of the goods of existence—in short, a continually more efficacious social engineering.[12]

Thus, the interests Pound had in mind would maintain and, ultimately, improve the social order. His was a *teleological* as well as consensus theory of interests: men must fulfill some interests for the good of the whole society; these interests are to be achieved through law. In Pound's theory, only the right law can emerge in a civilized society.

Jurisprudence has generally utilized a *pluralistic* model with respect to law as a social force in society. Accordingly, law regulates social behavior and establishes social organization; it orders human relationships by restraining individual actions and by settling disputes in social relations. In recent juristic language, law functions "first, to establish the general framework, the rules of the game so to speak, within and by which individual and group life shall be carried on, and secondly, to adjust the conflicting claims which different individuals and groups of individuals seek to satisfy in society."[13] For Pound, the law adjusts and reconciles conflicting interests:

> Looked at functionally, the law is an attempt to satisfy, to reconcile, to harmonize, to adjust these overlapping and often conflicting claims and demands, either through securing them directly and immediately, or through securing certain individual interests, or through delimitations or compromises of individual interests, so as to give effect to the greatest total

[12] Pound, *An Introduction to the Philosophy of Law,* pp. 98–99.

[13] Carl A. Auerbach, "Law and Social Change in the United States," *U.C.L.A. Law Review,* 6 (July, 1959), pp. 516–532. Similarly, see Julius Stone, *The Province and Function of Law* (Cambridge: Harvard University Press, 1950), Part III; Julius Stone, *Social Dimensions of Law and Justice* (Stanford: Stanford University Press, 1966), chaps. 4–8.

> of interests or to the interests that weigh most in our civilization, with the least sacrifice of the scheme of interests as a whole.[14]

In Pound's theory of interests, law provides the general framework within which individual and group life is carried on, according to the postulates of social order. Moreover, as a legal historian has written, "The law defines the extent to which it will give effect to the interests which it recognizes, in the light of other interests and of the possibilities of effectively securing them through law; it also devises means for securing those that are recognized and prescribes the limits within which those means may be employed."[15] In the interest theory of sociological jurisprudence, then, law is an instrument that controls interests according to the requirements of social order.

Pound's theory of interests included a threefold classification of interests, including the individual, the public, and the social:

> Individual interests are claims or demands or desires involved immediately in the individual life and asserted in the title of that life. Public interests are claims or demands or desires involved in life in a politically organized society and asserted in the title of that organization. They are commonly treated as the claims of a politically organized society thought of as a legal entity. Social interests are claims or demands or desires involved in social life in a civilized society and asserted in the title of that life. It is not uncommon to treat them as the claims of the whole social group as such.[16]

Pound warned that the types are overlapping and interdependent and that most can be placed in all the categories, depending upon one's purpose. He argued, however, that it is often expedient to put claims, demands, and desires in their most general form; that is, into the category of social interests.

[14] Roscoe Pound, "A Survey of Social Interests," *Harvard Law Review,* 57 (October, 1943), p. 39.

[15] George Lee Haskins, *Law and Authority in Early Massachusetts* (New York: Macmillan, 1960), p. 226.

[16] Pound, "A Survey of Social Interests," pp. 1–2.

Surveying the claims, demands, and desires found in legal proceedings and in legislative proposals, Pound suggested that the most important social interest appears to involve security against actions that threaten the social group.[17] Others are interest in the security of domestic, religious, economic, and political institutions; morals; conservation of social resources; general progress, including the development of human powers and control over nature to satisfy human wants; and individual life, especially the freedom of self-assertion. According to Pound, any legal system depends upon the way in which these interests are incorporated into law.

My theoretical perspective on criminal law departs from the general tradition of the interest theory of sociological jurisprudence in a number of ways. First, my perspective is based on a special conception of society. Society is characterized by diversity, conflict, coercion, and change, rather than by consensus and stability. Second, law is a *result* of the operation of interests, rather than an instrument that functions outside of particular interests. Though law may control interests, it is in the first place *created* by interests. Third, law incorporates the interests of specific persons and groups; it is seldom the product of the whole society. Law is made by men, representing special interests, who have the power to translate their interests into public policy. Unlike the pluralistic conception of politics, law does not represent a compromise of the diverse interests in society, but supports some interests at the expense of others. Fourth, the theoretical perspective of criminal law is devoid of teleological connotations. The social order may require certain functions for its maintenance and survival, but such functions will not be considered as inherent in the interests involved in formulating substantive laws. Fifth, the perspective proposed here includes a conceptual scheme for analyzing interests in the law. Finally, construction of the perspective is based on findings from current social science research.

[17] Pound, "A Survey of Social Interests," pp. 1–39. Other aspects of the theory of interest's are discussed by Pound in the following publications: *The Spirit of the Common Law* (Boston: Marshall Jones, 1921), pp. 91–93, 197–203; *An Introduction to the Philosophy of Law,* pp. 90–96; *Interpretations of Legal History* (New York: Macmillan, 1923), pp. 158–164; *Social Control through Law,* pp. 63–80.

LAW IN POLITICALLY ORGANIZED SOCIETY

Authority relations are present in all social collectivities: some persons are always at the command of others. As order is established in a society, several systems of control develop to regulate the conduct of various groups of persons. Human behavior is thus subject to restraint by varied agencies, institutions, and social groupings — families, churches, social clubs, political organizations, labor unions, corporations, educational systems, and so forth.

The control systems vary considerably in the forms of conduct they regulate, and most provide means for assuring compliance to their rules. Informal means, spontaneously employed by some persons, such as ridicule, gossip, and censure, may ensure conformity to some rules. Control systems may, in addition, rely upon formal and regularized means of sanction.

The *legal system* is the most explicit form of social control. The law consists of (1) specific rules of conduct, (2) planned use of sanctions to support the rules, and (3) designated officials to interpret and enforce the rules.[18] Furthermore, law becomes more important as a system of control as societies increase in complexity. Pound wrote that "in the modern world law has become the paramount agent of social control. Our main reliance is upon force of a politically organized state."[19]

Law is more than a system of formal social control; it is also a body of specialized rules created and interpreted in a *politically organized society,* or the state, which is a territorial organization with the authorized power to govern the lives and activities of all the inhabitants. Though other types of organized bodies may possess formal rules, only the specialized rule systems of politically organized societies are regarded here as systems of law.[20]

[18] F. James Davis, "Law as a Type of Social Control," in F. James Davis, Henry H. Foster, Jr., C. Ray Jeffery, and E. Eugene Davis, *Society and the Law* (New York: The Free Press of Glencoe, 1962), p. 43.

[19] Pound, *Social Control through Law,* p. 20.

[20] The rule systems of societies other than those which are politically organized may be adequately referred to, for comparative purposes, in any number of quasilegal ways, such as nonstate law, primitive law, or "lawways." Perhaps, even better, such systems of rules could be described simply as "tradition," "normative system," or "custom." The concept of law is expanded to

Law, as a special kind of institution, again is more than an abstract body of rules. Instead of being autonomous within society and developing according to its own logic, law is an integral part of society, operating as a force in society and as a social product. The law is not only that which is written as statutes and recorded as court opinions and administrative rulings, but is also a method or *process* of doing something.[21] As a process, law is a dynamic force that is continually being *created* and *interpreted.* Thus, law in action involves the making of specialized (legal) decisions by various *authorized agents.* In politically organized society, human actions are regulated by those invested with the authority to make specified decisions in the name of the society.

Furthermore, law in operation is an aspect of politics — it is one of the methods by which public policy is formulated and administered for governing the lives and activities of the state's inhabitants. As an act of politics, law and legal decisions do not represent the interests of all persons in the society. Whenever a law is created or interpreted, the values of some are necessarily assured and the values of others are either ignored or negated.

THE INTEREST STRUCTURE

Modern societies are characterized by an organization of differences. The social differentiation of society, in turn, provides the basis for the state's political life. Government in a politically organized society operates according to the interests that characterize the socially differentiated positions. Because varied interests are distributed among the positions, and because the positions are differently equipped with the ability to command, public policy represents

---

include the control systems of other than politically organized society among such writers as Bronislaw Malinowski, *Crime and Custom in Savage Society* (London: Routledge and Kegan Paul, 1926); E. Adamson Hoebel, *The Law of Primitive Man* (Cambridge: Harvard University Press, 1954); William M. Evan, "Public and Private Legal Systems," in William M. Evan (ed.), *Law and Sociology* (New York: The Free Press of Glencoe, 1962), pp. 165–184; Philip Selznick, "Legal Institutions and Social Controls," *Vanderbilt Law Review*, 17 (December, 1963), pp. 79–90.

[21] For this conception of law, as applied to criminal law, see Henry M. Hart, Jr., "The Aims of the Criminal Law," *Law and Contemporary Problems,* 23 (Summer, 1958), pp. 401–441.

specific interests in the society. Politically organized society, therefore, may be viewed as a differentiated *interest structure.*

Each *segment* of society has its own values, its own norms, and its own ideological orientations. When these are considered to be important for the existence and welfare of the respective segments, they may be defined as *interests.*[22] Further, interests can be categorized according to the ways in which activities are generally pursued in society; that is, according to the *institutional orders* of society. The following may then serve as a definition of interests: *the institutional concerns of the segments of society.* Thus, interests are grounded in the segments of society and represent the institutional concerns of the segments.

The institutional orders within which interests operate may be classified into fairly broad categories.[23] For our use, these may be called: (1) *the political,* which regulates the distribution of power and authority in society; (2) *the economic,* which regulates the production and distribution of goods and services; (3) *the religious,* which regulates the relationship of man to a conception of the supernatural; (4) *the kinship,* which regulates sexual relations, family patterns, and the procreation and rearing of children; (5) *the educational,* which regulates the formal training of the society's members; and (6) *the public,* which regulates the protection and maintenance of the community and its citizens. Each segment of society has its own orientation to these orders. Some, because of their authority position in the interest structure, are able to have their interests represented in public policy.

The segments of society differ in the extent to which their interests are organized. The segments themselves are broad statistical aggregates containing persons of similar age, sex, class, status, occupation, race, ethnicity, religion, or the like. All these have *formal interests;* those which are advantageous to the segment but which are not consciously held by the incumbents and are not organized

[22] The view here that interests are not distributed randomly in society but are related to one's position in society follows Marx's theory of economic production and class conflict. See Ralf Dahrendorf, *Class and Class Conflict in Industrial Society* (Stanford: Stanford University Press, 1959), especially pp. 3–35.

[23] The conception of institutional orders closely follows that of Hans Gerth and C. Wright Mills, *Character and Social Structure* (New York: Harcourt, Brace, 1953), especially pp. 25–26.

for action. *Active interests,* on the other hand, are manifest to persons in the segments and are sufficiently organized to serve as the basis for representation in policy decisions.[24]

Within the segments, groups of persons may become aware of and organize to promote their common interests; these may be called *interest groups.* Public policy, in turn, is the result of the success gained by these groups.

The interest structure is characterized by the unequal distribution of *power* and *conflict* among the segments of society. It is differentiated by diverse interests and by the ability of the segments to translate their interests into public policy. Furthermore, the segments are in continual conflict over their interests. Interests thus are structured according to differences in power and are in conflict.

Power and conflict are linked in this conception of interest structure. Power, as the ability to shape public policy, produces conflict among the competing segments, and conflict produces differences in the distribution of power. Coherence in the interest structure is thus ensured by the exercise of force and constraint by the conflicting segments. In the conflict-power model, therefore, politically organized society is held together by conflicting elements and functions according to the coercion of some segments by others.

The conflict-power conception of interest structure implies that public policy results from differential distribution of power and conflict among the segments of society. Diverse segments with specialized interests become so highly organized that they are able to influence the policies that affect all persons in the state. Groups that have the power to gain access to the decision-making process are able to translate their interests into public policy. Thus, the interests represented in the formulation and administration of public policy are those treasured by the dominant segments of the society. Hence, public policy is created because segments with power differentials are in conflict with one another. Public policy itself is a manifestation of an interest structure in politically organized society.

24 The distinction between formal interests and active interests is similar to the distinction Dahrendorf makes between latent and manifest interests. See Dahrendorf, *Class and Class Conflict in Industrial Society,* pp. 173–179.

FORMULATION AND ADMINISTRATION OF CRIMINAL LAW

Law is a form of public policy that regulates the behavior and activities of all members of a society. It is *formulated* and *administered* by those segments of society which are able to incorporate their interests into the creation and interpretation of public policy. Rather than representing the institutional concerns of all segments of society, law secures the interests of particular segments, supporting one point of view at the expense of others.

Thus, the content of the law, including the substantive regulations and the procedural rules, represents the interests of the segments of society that have the power to shape public policy. Formulation of law allows some segments of society to protect and perpetuate their own interests. By formulating law, some segments are able to control others to their own advantage.

The interests that the power segments of society attempt to maintain enter into all stages of legal administration. Since legal formulations do not provide specific instructions for interpreting law, administration of law is largely a matter of discretion on the part of *legal agents* (police, prosecutors, judges, juries, prison authorities, parole officers, and others). Though implementation of law is necessarily influenced by such matters as localized conditions and the occupational organization of legal agents, the interest structure of politically organized society is responsible for the general design of the administration of criminal justice.

Finally, the formulation and administration of law in politically organized society are affected by changing social conditions. Emerging interests and increasing concern with the protection of various aspects of social life require new laws or reinterpretations of old laws. Consequently, legal changes take place within the context of the changing interest structure of society.

INTERESTS IN CONTEMPORARY SOCIETY

Interests not only are the principal forces behind the creation and interpretation of law, but they are changing the very nature of government. For centuries the state was the Leviathan, protector, repository of power, main source of the community's economic and social life. The state unified and controlled most of the activities of the society. In recent times, however, it is apparent that some groups and segments of society have taken over many of the state's functions:

> The question must be raised in all seriousness whether the "overmighty subjects" of our time — the giant corporations, both of a commercial and non-commercial character, the labor unions, the trade associations, farmers' organizations, veterans' legions, and some other highly organized groups — have taken over the substance of sovereignty. Has the balance of pressures and counter-pressures between these groups left the legal power of the State as a mere shell? If this is a correct interpretation of the social change of our time, we are witnessing another dialectic process in history: the national sovereign State — having taken over effective legal political power from the social groups of the previous age — surrenders its power to the new massive social groups of the industrial age.[25]

Some analysts of the contemporary scene have optimistically forecasted that checks of "countervailing power" will adequately balance the interests of the well organized groups.[26] This pluralistic conception disregards the fact that interest groups are grossly unequal in power. Groups that are similar in power may well check each others' interests, but groups that have little or no power will not have the opportunity to have their interest represented in public policy. The consequence is government by a few powerful private interest groups.

Furthermore, the politics of private interests tends to take place outside of the arena of the public governmental process. In private politics, interest groups receive their individual claims in return for allowing other groups to press for their interests.[27] Behind public politics a private government operates in a way that not only guarantees rewards to well organized groups but affects the lives of us all.

If there be any check in this contemporary condition, it is in the

[25] Friedmann, *Law in a Changing Society*, pp. 239–240.

[26] John Kenneth Galbraith, *Modern Capitalism* (Boston: Houghton Mifflin, 1952).

[27] See Theodore Lowi, "The Public Philosophy: Interest-Group Liberalism," *American Political Science Review*, 61 (March, 1967), pp. 5–24.

prospect that the "public interest" will take precedence over private interests. Interest groups, if for no other reason than their concern for public relations, may bow to the commonweal. Optimistically, the public interest may become an ideal fulfilled, no matter what the source of private power.

But the fallacy in any expectation of the achievement of the public good through the "public interest" is that the government which could foster such a condition will become again in a new age an oppressive interest in itself. That age, in fact, seems to be upon us. Increasingly, as Reich has argued, "Americans live on government largess — allocated by government on its own terms, and held by recipients subject to conditions which express 'the public interest.' "[28] While the highly organized, scientifically planned society, governed for the social good of its inhabitants, promises the best life that man has ever known, not all of our human values will receive attention, and some may be temporarily or permanently negated.

In raw form we cannot hold optimistically to either government by private interests or public interest by government largess. The future for individual man appears to lie in some form of protection from both forms of government. Decentralized government offers some possibility for the survival of the individual in a collective society. But more immediately, that protection must be sought in procedural law, a law that must necessarily be removed from the control of either the interests of private groups or public government. The challenge for law of the future is that it create an order providing fulfillment for individual values that are now within our reach, values that paradoxically are imminent because of the existence of interests from which we must now seek protection. A new society is indeed coming: Can a law be created apart from private interests which assures individual fulfillment within a good society?

[28] Charles A. Reich, "The New Property," *Yale Law Journal*, 73 (April, 1964), p. 733.

CHAPTER THREE

Interests in the Formulation of Criminal Laws

The perspective on criminal law in politically organized society provides the basis for understanding how particular criminal laws are formulated. Following this perspective, criminal laws — including the enactments of legislatures, court decisions, and administrative rulings — are formulated by those segments of society which have the power to shape public policy. The formulation of criminal law is thus an act of politics: Public policy is established by some for governing the lives and affairs of all inhabitants of a society. Crime, then, is a definition of human conduct that is created in the course of the political life of the community.

Lawmaking, according to this perspective, represents the translation of specific group interests into public policy. For the most part, criminal laws support particular interests to the neglect or negation of other interests, thus representing the concerns of only some members of society. Though some criminal laws may involve a compromise of conflicting interests, more likely than not, criminal laws mark the victory of some groups over others. The notion of a compromise of conflicting interests is a myth perpetuated by a pluralistic model of politics. Some interests never find access to the lawmaking process. Other interests are overwhelmed in it, not compromised. But ultimately some interests succeed in becoming criminal law, and are able to control the conduct of others.

EMERGENCE OF CRIMINAL LAW

The very emergence of criminal law is historically a political phenomenon. Because of the interests of particular social segments, criminal law was created: it has continued to operate in various social contexts for the benefit of diverse and shifting interests, including the interests of the state itself.

Early law was a private matter in that injured individuals and their families had the responsibility of securing retribution from the parties that had wronged them. The concept of criminal law developed only when the notion of private vengeance was replaced by the principle that in some instances the community was also injured when harm came to its members. Thus, the right of action arising from a wrong ceased to be restricted to the immediate victim and was granted in the case of certain offenses to all citizens, or to the politically organized society. "True criminal law," as distinguished from elementary tort and primitive law, contains several new legal concepts:

> (1) It will recognize the principle that attacks upon the persons or property of individuals, or rights thereto annexed, as well as offenses that affect the state directly, may be violations of the public peace and good order. (2) It will provide, as part of the ordinary machinery of government, means by which such violations may be punished by and for the state, and not merely by the individual who may be directly affected. (3) The protection it offers will be readily available to the entire body politic, and not restricted to particular groups or classes of citizens.[1]

Criminal law as we know it today in the Western world emerged in several different social contexts, notably, those of Greece, Rome, and England, and has shaped our conception of "criminal" in several ways. Contemporary criminal law embodies notions on (1) the public character of criminal law, (2) the state nature of criminal law, and (3) the role of political unity in criminal law. Each of these concepts in the emergence of criminal law was shaped by social interests.

[1] George M. Calhoun, *The Growth of Criminal Law in Ancient Greece* (Berkeley: University of California Press, 1927), p. 5.

Criminal Law and Democracy in Greece. The decisive step in the emergence of criminal law was taken in Athens at the beginning of the sixth century B.C. At that time, Solon, after being appointed *nomothete,* with dictatorial powers, instituted several formal enactments which gave every citizen the right of action in the prosecution of certain offenses. Greek society was in the throes of a political crisis. The enactments of Solon, which formed the basis for the development of criminal law in Greece, were part of an attempt toward solving the crisis and rehabilitating Greek government.

A number of facts surrounding the Athenian political struggle have been established.[2] At the time all functions of government were exclusively in the hands of the *eupatrids,* an hereditary class of Athenian aristocrats. The inferior orders of citizens, the peasant proprietors (the *georgi*) and the artisans (the *demurgi*), had no part in government except by attaching themselves to a member of the aristocracy. Below this level was the lowest class of freemen, the propertyless population (variously named *thetes, hectemori,* and *pelatae*), whose members had few rights and were in many cases virtually serfs. Still lower were the slaves, without rights of any kind.

The class and political structure of Athens thus consisted of an oligarchy of the wealthy and privileged that ruled over a large proletariat. The lower classes were politically subjugated and were made the object of merciless economic exploitation. The oppressiveness of the situation, accompanied by the increasing economic strength of the proletariat, eventually produced discontent among those excluded from the process of government. The ruling aristocrats reacted to the situation through compromise:

> In such a situation the alternative to revolution and perhaps tyranny was compromise, and this the ruling class, or some of them, were wise enough to see. And we must believe that these wiser men were keenly alive to the menace which confronted them in the presence of a prosperous alien population, chafing under the denial of the political rights to which their economic strength entitled them, ready at the first opportunity to fan

[2] See Calhoun, *The Growth of Criminal Law in Ancient Greece,* especially p. 44.

> into the flame of revolution the smouldering discontent of the native proletariat.[3]

The political compromise that resulted from the class conflict of ancient Greece provided the beginnings for the criminal law of the Western world. The step taken toward criminal law consequently protected citizens from one another and from government itself, in this case protecting the lower classes of Athens from the aggression of the rich and powerful. Through legal reform, as an alternative to possible revolution, Solon and his council established popular courts, provided for appeal from the decisions of magistrates, and assured the right of all citizens to initiate prosecutions. It may be suggested that Greece became the "cradle of democracy" through the creation of criminal law. At least, whatever the connection may be, the foundations of democratic government and the emergence of criminal law occurred together in a relationship that was mutually supportive of both.

Criminal Law in the Roman State. The concept of criminal law developed slowly among the Romans. Although eventually a distinction was made between *civilis* and *criminalis,* law in Rome was devoted primarily to private legal matters and civil procedure. When a criminal law did develop, its principal concern was with offenses against the state and with the punishment of such offenders. The Romans were more the efficient administrators of their empire than students and practitioners of justice.

The law of the Twelve Tables — of the middle of the fifth century B.C. — was based on the idea of the right of the injured party to private vengeance. Punishment was inflicted by the state, however, for crimes which were committed directly against the commonwealth. While most of the provisions of the Twelve Tables, as codifications of Roman customary law, rested on the concept of private law, the Twelve Tables were originally created as a safeguard for a portion of the population. In effect the Twelve Tables protected the plebeians against the unfair treatment of the patricians.[4]

[3] Calhoun, *The Growth of Criminal Law in Ancient Greece,* p. 52.

[4] Hans Julius Wolff, *Roman Law: An Historical Introduction* (Norman: University of Oklahoma Press, 1951), pp. 54–61. Also Barry Nicholas, *An Introduction to Roman Law* (Oxford: Oxford University Press, 1962), pp. 208–209.

As Rome grew from a rural community to a powerful city-state, the "private criminal law" of the Twelve Tables proved increasingly inadequate.

> The "private criminal law" of the Twelve Tables reflected the conditions of a primitive commonwealth of modest dimensions and rustic character. It was bound to prove increasingly inadequate as Rome developed into a metropolis dominated by powerful social tensions; and the growth of the urban proletariat and of the slave population was certainly accompanied by a rise in criminality which demanded vigorous measures for the maintenance of public security.[5]

Subsequently, during the third century B.C. and the beginning of the second century, a criminal jurisdiction was established for the control of those engaged in such politically threatening activities as violence, treason, arson, poisoning, the carrying of weapons, and the theft of state property. Tribunals and courts were instituted to deal with such cases.[6]

Thus, the criminal law which did emerge late in the Roman Republic was a device created mainly for the protection of the state itself. The protection of the rights of the individual from the state was not a concept central to Roman law. Criminal law in Rome was created by the interests that could be best satisfied through the maintenance of a strongly controlled political regime.

Political Unification and the Emergence of Criminal Law in England. In England, as in any society, a criminal law could emerge only with the parallel development of national sovereignty. The history of English law is thus related to changes in the social and political structures of the country.[7] Criminal law emerged as a specific form of law when England achieved the political unity that allowed a law to be established and administered in the name of a centralized government.

[5] Wolfgang Kunkel, *An Introduction to Roman Legal History and Constitutional History* (Oxford: Oxford University Press, 1966), p. 61.

[6] Erich S. Gruen, *Roman Politics and the Criminal Courts, 149–78* B.C. (Cambridge: Harvard University Press, 1968).

[7] Clarence Ray Jeffrey, "The Development of Crime in Early English Society," *Journal of Criminal Law, Criminology and Police Science*, 47 (March–April, 1957), pp. 647–666.

The turning point in the history of English law marked also the emergence of criminal law itself. This important change in English law began in the latter part of the eleventh century and continued throughout the twelfth. Prior to that time the territory we now know as England was divided into separate units with their own laws. These legal systems could not foster the concept of criminal law.

The law of the Anglo-Saxons was originally a system of tribal justice. Each tribe, as a group of kinsmen, was controlled by its own chief and armed warriors who met and, among other things, passed laws. Any wrong was regarded as being against or by the family; and it was the family that atoned or carried out the blood-feud if an offense occurred between kinship groups.

By the tenth century England was divided into six to eight large kingdoms. Some degree of political consolidation had come about as a result of civil wars among local tribes. The acceptance of Christianity among leaders provided not only a spiritual unity but, as found in the Roman Catholic Church, a scheme of centralized control. In the reorganization, tribal chiefs were replaced by kings who became both military leaders and landlords. As feudalism changed the organization of Saxon society, between the eighth and eleventh centuries, the blood-feud was replaced by a system of compensations. Eventually the collective responsibility of the kinship group was absorbed by the kingdom. Compensation for offenses became the domain of the king, lord, or bishop, rather than the kinship group. One of Aethelred's laws, for example, made it a breach of the king's peace to resort to the feud before compensation had been demanded from the offender or his family.[8]

It was with the Norman invasion and the reign of the Norman kings that the old tribal-feudal system of law disappeared and a new system of law emerged in England. When William conquered England in 1066, he proclaimed himself the "supreme landlord" of all England. By this move, implemented by the Domesday Survey, William redistributed the land, with the Norman nobles at the top, and placed all social relationships on a land tenure basis, under his control. In addition, William took the important step of separating state law from canon law. But the most important move taken in William's time toward the emergence of criminal law was the

[8] See F. L. Attenborough (ed.), *The Laws of the English Kings* (Cambridge: Cambridge University Press, 1922).

unification of England under one head, the "King of England."

With their administrative abilities the Norman kings developed centralized legal institutions. In order to place law under the jurisdiction of the king's government, several courts were created by the king. Writs were devised by which cases could be carried out of baronial courts into the king's courts. Itinerant judges were sent into the various "hundreds" and "shires" to administer the king's laws. By the end of the reign of Henry II (1154–1189), the law of England was in the hands of the Crown. A court of "common law" was established for the justice of all men. A new procedure and a new conception of offenses had been created.[9] Now for the first time some offenses were regarded as clearly in violation of the peace of king and country. A criminal law had emerged in England.

To be sure, criminal law in England came about for the protection of particular interests, primarily those of the king. The criminal law placed the affairs of the king's subjects under his jurisdiction. The powerful landholders and the church could no longer freely create and administer law in their own courts. Law which affected the nation was now the king's law. As supreme overlord, the king demanded the authority of his position.

But political unification, perhaps inadvertently, also benefited the interests of the common man. Men lowly placed in the land tenure system were no longer at the complete mercy of their landlords. Justice potentially was in the reach of all. Eventually in England's history, the power of the monarch diminished and finally vanished with the creation of parliamentary goverment. Today, because of this political unification in the eleventh and twelfth centuries and because of the emergence of a criminal law at the same time, a common law survives. We need not be bothered for the moment that its justice continues to be more common for some men than for others.

CRIMINAL LAW IN COLONIES AND TERRITORIES

Once criminal law emerged as concept and fact, it became a widely used means of regulating human conduct in politically organized

[9] G. O. Sayles, *Medieval Foundation of England* (London: Methuen, 1966), chap. 21. Also John W. Jeudwine, *Tort, Crime and Police in Medieval Britain* (London: Williams and Norgate, 1917), especially chaps. 7 and 8.

societies. Conceivably *all* forms of human behavior have been under the jurisdiction of criminal law, in one society or another, at one time or other. Each criminal law specified the illegality of some specific behavior. The formulation of criminal law, therefore, depends upon standards of some sort; otherwise formulation of substantive criminal laws would be impossible.

Our task is to indicate the ways in which various kinds of criminal law have been shaped by social interests in their formulation. The regulation of specific kinds of behavior will be investigated within the various institutional orders. It will be shown that the values of social groups acted as interests in the formulation of specific kinds of criminal law. The interests represented in each case are those of the social segments that have had the power to translate their values into social policy. The theory of criminal law as related to social interests can be seen to operate in several social contexts.

The formulation of criminal law in the colonies and territories of nations presents a special case of social interests in the formulation of criminal law. In such situations criminal laws are either formulated directly by the imperial nation for the control of its colonies and territories or formulated by the colonies and territories under the close supervision of the imperial nation. The social interests of the laws imposed, supervised, or inspired by imperial nations are related to the political and economic order of the imperial nation. The operation of such social interests can be seen in three settings: (1) English common law in the American colonies, (2) British law in India and Africa, and (3) American frontier law.

English Common Law in the American Colonies. The English charters for the founding of settlements in the New World provided that the laws established within the settlements should not be contrary to the laws of England. During the American colonial period, colonial statutes which were counter to the English common law could be disallowed by the Crown's Privy Council. In addition, the decisions of the provincial courts were subject to appeal by the Privy Council where any radical departure from the common law could be corrected.[10] But in spite of these provisions for the control of the American colonies, in accord with the political and economic interest

[10] Roscoe Pound, "The Development of American Law and Its Deviation from English Law," *Law Quarterly Review,* 67 (January, 1951), pp. 49–66.

of the Crown and stockholders, there were instances where innovations in law would be desirable for the colonies.

Some local conditions in America made irrelevant or impractical the legal practices of England. There were even vast differences of settlement and development within colonies which would foster divergences in the legal systems of the colonies.[11] Except for England's primary political interest in control over its colonies, the colonies were in fact relatively free to develop their own legal systems.

However, the criminal laws that developed in America did not depart substantially from English common law.[12] The interests embodied in the common law of England became the interests that were instrumental in the formulation of American criminal law. Several forces were at work, beyond the standards set by the Crown, which assured the continuance of English common law in America. One important force was in the fact that the early settlers, coming from the mother country, were deeply imbued with the ideas and traditions of the common law. Another force was an adherence to the liberal ideal of democracy. The natural law conception of man's inherent rights as a human being inspired the Declaration of Independence (1776) as it had the British Bill of Rights (1689).[13] The Lockean formula of "life, liberty and property" (later broadened to include the pursuit of happiness) served as an underlying value for American law. As another force, the English common law was exalted and perpetuated in nineteenth century America through the popularity of such codifications as Sir Edward Coke's *Institutes* and Sir William Blackstone's *Commentaries on the Laws of England*. One other force that made the interests of English common law the same as those of American law was in the attempts of American lawyers to adapt the common law to American conditions.[14] While there was considerable conflict with fellow countrymen, American lawyers

[11] Julius Goebel, Jr., "King's Law and Local Custom in Seventeenth Century New England," *Columbia Law Review*, 31 (March, 1931), pp. 416–448.

[12] See Edwin C. Surrency, "Revision of Colonial Laws," *American Journal of Legal History*, 9 (July, 1965), pp. 189–202; Elizabeth Caspar Brown, *British Statutes in American Law, 1776–1836* (Ann Arbor: University of Michigan Law School, 1964).

[13] See Carl J. Friedrich, "Rights, Liberties, Freedoms: A Reappraisal," *American Political Science Review*, 57 (December, 1963), pp. 841–854; Roscoe Pound, *The Formative Era of American Law* (Boston: Little, Brown, 1938).

[14] Perry Miller, *The Life of the Mind: From the Revolution to the Civil War* (New York: Harcourt, Brace and World, 1965), pp. 99–265.

were generally successful in asserting the legal heritage of England against provincial concerns.

All these forces combined to produce an American law which incorporated the interests of English common law. Political independence did not signify new beginnings in law. Old interests in a new setting best describes America's legal development.

British Law in India and Africa. The control of foreign colonies is in sharp contrast to the American experience. The subjects of British rule in the colonies of India and Africa were not as ready to adopt the laws of an imperial power. Native customs and traditions of India and Africa were far from amenable to the principles of English common law. Furthermore, the imposition of a single English legal system on a native colony ignored the diverse local customs within the colonies.

The importation of British law to India and Africa required a change in local customs. In India the administration of English law required, and accomplished in many instances, modifications in Hindu customary law.[15] The change was mutual, in that successful administration of English law in India also brought about changes in the English law itself.

In North India, where English law did not readily accommodate to local custom, the British legal system was used in a manipulative fashion by the local inhabitants.[16] In attempting to introduce British procedural law into the Indian courts, the British presented the Indians with a situation that involved a conflict of values between the British common law, on the one hand, and Indian customary law, on the other. The British thought that by providing an impartial judge and firm rules of court procedure cases of disputes between parties, criminal and civil, could be decided in court. But such an assumption was contrary to the values underlying the Indian caste system:

> Basic to British law is the idea of equality of the individual before the law. North Indian society operates on the reverse

[15] J. Duncan and M. Derrett, "The Administration of Hindu Law by the British," *Comparative Studies in Sociology and History,* 4 (November, 1961), pp. 10–52; Marc Galanter, "The Displacement of Traditional Law in Modern India," *Journal of Social Issues* (October, 1968), pp. 65–91.

[16] Bernard S. Cohn, "Some Notes on Law and Change in North India," *Economic Development and Cultural Change,* 8 (October, 1959), pp. 79–93.

value hypothesis: men are not born equal, and they have widely differing inherent worth. This theme or value is basic to the whole social structure and is expressed most clearly in the caste system. When Indians go into court they are supposed by definition to lose their outside statuses. It is not Thakurs and Chamars who are having a dispute, but a defendant and a complainant. The adversary system has developed to equalize the persons in court. To an Indian peasant this is an impossible situation to understand. The Chamar knows he is not equal to the Thakur. He may want to be equal, but he knows he is not. The Thakur cannot be convinced in any way that the Chamar is equal, but the court acts as if the parties in the dispute were equal.[17]

The imposition of the British legal system in North India ignored the long-established caste arrangements and community relations. Under the British system a court decision was disruptive of the network of social relationships.

The extent to which a monolithic and foreign legal system inhibits national development can be seen in the new nations of Africa. The situation is, however, paradoxical in that the English legal system provided the centralization necessary for nation-building, but at the same time hindered the development of an indigenous legal system that would best meet the needs of a new nation.

The "Africanization" of African law is a phenomenon that most African nations are now experiencing. Recently the Ghanian Parliament repealed a number of its British laws.[18] In the African colonial period the British had imposed a legal system that represented metropolitan interests. For example, the British made bigamy a criminal offense in Ghana. Ghanian customary law, however, allowed polygamy. The bigamy statute was one of the laws recently repealed.

Today the British inspired courts are in flux in the African nations. Indigenous African ideas on crime and punishment are being revived and used as sources of criminal law.[19] A distinct policy has

[17] Cohn, "Some Notes on Law and Change in North India," pp. 90–91.

[18] William Burnett Harvey, *Law and Social Change in Ghana* (Princeton: Princeton University Press, 1966), especially chap. 6; A. N. Allott, "The Changing Law in a Changing Africa," *Sociologus*, 11 (No. 2, 1961), pp. 115–131.

[19] A. St. J. Hannigan, "The Imposition of Western Law Forms Upon Primitive Societies," *Comparative Studies in Sociology and History*, 4 (November, 1961), pp. 1–9.

not yet been established regarding the extent to which native custom will be incorporated into Western-inspired law. But a law which undermines and conflicts with the values and interest of local African custom is not likely to survive intact when lawmaking is in the hands of the African nations themselves.

American Frontier Law. In the expansion of the American frontier, two legal problems naturally developed. One involved the legal status and control of the first native Americans, the Indians. The second problem, which at times was related to the first, concerned legal regulation in territories not yet with their own law.

The Crown did not recognize the sovereign right of the native Indians and acknowledged only their right of occupancy in the land.[20] In other words, without existing law, any law that was to be established in America was to be a law imposed by the Crown or by the colonial settlers according to standards set by the Crown. As the law developed, any offense against the colony by Indians outside of colonial territory was administered by tribal leaders. But for those Indians who were within the territory, cases were tried in colonial courts. The Indians who were subject to colonial law were not judged by their own customary law but according to the interests of the settlers from England.

Later a new problem arose in the formulating and administering of law in the western Indian territory. The United States federal government sent agents and legal officers into the expanding territories. One such case was the attempt of the federal government to establish law and order in the Indian Nations of Oklahoma. On May 2, 1875, Judge Isaac C. Parker arrived in Fort Smith to take over the Federal District Court of the territory. His task was to control the Indians who were against the white man and to put an end to the "outlawry" of the breed of man that has since become the western folk hero. Judge Parker fast acquired the reputation of "the hanging judge." In his twenty-one years on the bench at Fort Smith, Judge Parker heard 13,490 cases and convicted 9,454 persons, of whom 344 were tried for offenses punishable by death. Of the 344

[20] W. Stitt Robinson, "The Legal Status of the Indian in Colonial Virginia," *Virginia Magazine of History and Biography,* 61 (July, 1953), pp. 247–259.

cases, 165 were convicted and 160 of these were sentenced to the gallows. Seventy-nine persons were eventually hanged, while 2 others were killed in attempting to escape and two more died in jail awaiting execution. Judge Parker saw his mission thus:

> During the twenty years that I have engaged in administering the law here, the contest has been one between civilization and savagery, the savagery being represented by the intruding criminal class. The United States government, in its treaties from the days of Andrew Jackson, stipulated that this criminal element should be kept out of the country, but the treaties have only been made to be broken. . . . Thus this class keeps on increasing; its members marry, and the criminal population keeps ever growing larger. . . . At the present time there seems to be a criminal wave sweeping over the country, the like of which I have not yet seen before.[21]

Judge Parker, according to his sympathetic biographer, "had taken pardonable pride in eradicating lawlessness from his jurisdiction. He had taught the criminal class to fear the law and respect the rights and property of peaceful citizens, and had helped the Indian advance to a higher civilization."[22]

There was also need in the fast-growing western mining camps for some kind of order to resolve the conflicts that arose between miners and the disputes that developed over land and mining rights. There were as yet no territorial or state governments to create and administer law. In this void there developed a "local law" among the miners to regulate their own self-interests.[23] In other words, a popular sovereignty was created in the mining territory, a sovereignty which formulated and administered its own form of law. The miners' customs, or local laws, spread throughout the western territories. Eventually when states were formally established, the local laws of the miners were enacted into statute law or were incorporated into

[21] Quoted in Glenn Shirley, *Law West of Fort Smith: Frontier Justice in the Indian Territory, 1834–1896* (New York: Collier Books, 1961), p. 146.

[22] Shirley, *Law West of Fort Smith,* p. 180.

[23] For one of the few studies of law in the mining territory, see Charles Howard Shinn, *Mining Camps: A Study in American Frontier Government,* originally published 1884 (New York: Harper and Row, 1965).

the legal precedents of court decisions. The interests of the miners of the nineteenth century were formulated into laws which continue to operate in the twentieth century.

PROTECTION OF THE POLITICAL ORDER

In a sense the formulation of all criminal law is political. Formal codes and decisions are created in order that certain behaviors may be defined as criminal by groups in control of politically organized society. But, in addition, particular kinds of criminal laws are created to protect the political order of the state. These *political criminal laws* define as criminal those behaviors that are regarded as dangers or threats to the very existence of the state.

Interest in the protection of the political order is characteristic of all states. In the creation of such laws, those in positions of power attempt to preserve both the political system and their own positions within the system.

"Every political regime has its foes or in due time creates them."[24] The struggles or perceived conflicts that may take place between power holders, their foes, and the contenders for political power assume a great variety of forms. Various kinds of criminal laws may be formulated in the attempt to control or eliminate the political foe from competition. These criminal laws, as political weapons, serve to authenticate and limit the political action of those who would appear to jeopardize the stability and survival of the existing political order.

Most politically organized societies, especially those which claim to be political democracies, maintain the paradox of two opposing ideals. On the one hand, states claim the power to govern but, on the other, grant the freedom that may result in words and actions against the state. The opposing ideals are able to exist because of the unspoken agreement that "the majority agrees to tolerate the criticism and dissent of the minority (or minorities), while the minority agrees to seek power only through persuasion and political

[24] Otto Kirchheimer, *Political Justice: The Use of Legal Procedure for Political Ends* (Princeton: Princeton University Press, 1961), p. 3.

activity, not through violence."[25] Thus, in the abstract, the majority is not to persecute the minority and the minority is not to express dissent through revolution.

The boundaries and definitions of political freedom, however, are by no means constant within any society. The latitude of dissent that may be regarded as legitimate varies from one time to another. During some periods a considerable amount and degree of dissent may be tolerated, while in other periods dissent may be suppressed by means of the criminal law.

Political expression is especially restricted during periods of tension and conflict. When a political emergency is perceived, the government is likely to take actions of various sorts to protect the political order. The events that led to the American Revolution illustrate the ways in which criminal law may be used to maintain the desired political order. England as the imperial nation naturally tried to maintain its political control over the colonies. At the same time the British government was faced with other administrative problems, including administration of the territorial acquisitions elsewhere in North America and a mounting debt at home. In order to organize a more efficient administration, Britain made several demands of the colonies, such as the trade and revenue acts passed in Parliament, which resulted in a tightening of control over the colonies. Occurring simultaneously in the colonies, however, was the development of a revolutionary ideology and a new spirit of nationalism. As a result, Britain's attempt to demand more of the colonies and the Americans' growing desire for freedom of political action produced a sharp clash of interests.[26] The ultimate outcome, of course, after a series of insurrections and a war, was independence for the colonies in 1776.

One of the devices used by the British government in the colonies to establish and preserve their own political order was substantive criminal law. The British used at various times the law of treason against the colonists. The law had its origins in a statute enacted in

[25] Paul B. Horton and Gerald R. Leslie, *The Sociology of Social Problems,* 3rd ed. (New York: Appleton-Century-Crofts, 1965), pp. 632–633.

[26] This is the thesis found in Lawrence Henry Gipson, *The Coming of the Revolution, 1763–1775* (New York: Harper and Row, 1954). Also see George Adrian Washburne, *Imperial Control of the Administration of Justice in the Thirteen Colonies, 1684–1776* (New York: Columbia University Press, 1923).

the time of Edward III, making it a crime to plot or imagine the death of the king, to adhere to the king's enemies, to give them aid and comfort, or to levy war against the king. The law of seditious libel was also used to control public criticism of British efforts.

There is some debate on the question of the extent to which the British resorted to their criminal law of seditious libel to control dissent in the colonies.[27] But there is no question as to the ironical fact that each of the colonies formulated similar laws to protect its own political interests. These political criminal laws of the colonies were almost identical to the English laws that were being imposed on them.

The English common law on political crime was eventually adopted by the states and the federal government. What had seemed oppressive in the hands of the British became the law for Americans to impose on those who would appear to endanger their government. The federal government in 1798 enacted the Sedition Act, providing for the punishment of anyone who uttered or published statements against the government of the United States.[28] The law, as well as curtailing loyalty to the British, became an instrument of the Federalists in their attempt to suppress the activities (considered as pro-French) of the opposition Republican Party.[29]

The American law of treason was shaped by fears the Americans had of British loyalists during and immediately following the Revolution. Drawing upon English common law once again, the Americans formulated and utilized treason laws against those who aided the British or fled to the enemy.[30] After the Declaration of Inde-

[27] See Harold L. Nelson, "Seditious Libel in Colonial America," *American Journal of Legal History,* 3 (April, 1959), pp. 160–172; and Frederick S. Siebert, *Freedom of the Press in England, 1476–1776* (Urbana: University of Illinois Press, 1952).

[28] Leonard W. Levy, *Freedom of Speech and Press in Early American History: Legacy of Suppression* (New York: Harper and Row, 1963); James Morton Smith, "The Sedition Law, Free Speech, and the American Political Process," *William and Mary Quarterly,* 9 (October, 1952), pp. 497–511.

[29] Herbert L. Packer, "Offenses Against the State," *Annals of the American Academy of Political and Social Science,* 339 (January, 1962), pp. 77–89.

[30] See Bradley Chapin, *The American Law of Treason: Revolutionary and National Origins* (Seattle: University of Washington Press, 1964); J. Willard Hurst, "Treason in the United States," *Harvard Law Review,* 58 (December, 1944), pp. 226–272; 58 (February, 1945), pp. 395–444; and 58 (July, 1945), pp. 806–857.

pendence, the state legislatures enacted a series of anti-loyalist laws. "Test acts" compelled a declaration of loyalty from those who appeared to be indifferent or enemies of the Revolution. In addition to these acts, there were laws (1) disfranchising the loyalists or removing them from office, (2) suppressing, quarantining, and exiling loyalists, (3) providing for the crime of adhering to Great Britain, and (4) amercing, taxing, or confiscating the property and estates of loyalists.[31] In most states loyalists were legally defined as traitors.

All of the states today have criminal laws to protect subversion of the political order. Subversion, however, is not always clearly defined in the state laws, although most agree on which kinds of behavior are subversive:

> There can no doubt be general agreement that, at the very least, subversive activities include (1) the use of violent or otherwise unconstitutional means to change this country's political or economic institutions; (2) the commission of espionage, sabotage, and other crimes of stealth in behalf of foreign enemies or domestic cliques; (3) the bearing of arms against the United States, other affirmative behavior in aid of hostile forces; and (4) the entry into a conspiracy to perform these acts or the actual though unsuccessful attempt to do them. Conduct of these types is unquestionably within the reach of criminal laws in every American state.[32]

In addition to the state laws numerous federal statutes have been created to control subversive activity. The Espionage Act of 1917 made it a crime to "willfully make or convey false reports or false statements with intent to interfere with the operations or success of the military or naval forces of the United States." A 1918 amendment to the Espionage Act broadened the proscriptions in terms reminiscent of the Sedition Act of 1798. The Voorhis Act of 1940 restricted the registration of persons and organizations that act as agents of foreign powers. The Smith Act of 1940 forbade the advocacy of the overthrow of the government. The Internal Security Act of 1950 (McCarran Act) required the registration of com-

[31] Claude H. Van Tyne, *The Loyalists in the American Revolution* (New York: Macmillan, 1962), especially appendix C.

[32] Walter Gellhorn, "A General View," in Walter Gellhorn (ed.), *The States and Subversion* (Ithaca: Cornell University Press, 1952), p. 359.

munist and communist-front organizations as well as strengthened other legislation on subversion. The Immigration and Nationality Act of 1952 (McCarran-Walter Act) provided for the deportation of resident aliens because of disloyal beliefs and associates. The Communist Control Act of 1954 required the registration of Communist party members with the Attorney General. In addition to such legislation, loyalty and security programs have been initiated and black-list procedures have been established.

Political expression is an especially delicate matter in the United States. It appears that Americans, as compared to other peoples in representative governments, are particularly intolerant of social and political differences.[33] This intolerance is expressed in the denial of various civil rights to certain social and political minority groups, religious groups, racial and ethnic groups, and political dissenters of various persuasion. Numerous criminal laws have been formulated by groups in power to deal with these conditions and activities. In addition to the various acts that have been defined as subversive, recent attempts to express dissatisfaction with nuclear testing, civil defense, military build-ups, and racial discrimination have been subject to criminal action. A host of previously existing laws have been used in the suppression of dissent and protest. Demonstrators for civil rights and other causes have been arrested on such charges as disorderly conduct, breach of peace, parading without a permit, trespassing, loitering, and violation of fire ordinances. All these crimes have the common element that the offenders are pursuing values different from those of the groups that are formulating and administering criminal law.

RELIGIOUS FOUNDATIONS OF CRIMINAL LAW

Along the shores and tidewater in the vicinity of what is today Boston Harbor, a Puritan community was established in 1630. Although the Massachusetts Bay Colony was chartered as a commercial enterprise, the objectives of its settlers were clearly re-

[33] Herbert H. Hyman, "England and America: Climates of Tolerance and Intolerance," in Daniel Bell (ed.), *The Radical Right* (Garden City, N.Y.: Doubleday, 1963), chap. 12.

ligious and social. From the outset, the chief aim of the undertaking was, in Governor John Winthrop's words, the building of "a City upon a Hill," the founding of a society that would be an example of godliness to the world. Religious interests were to play a predominant role in the creation of a social and legal order in early Massachusetts.

The new colony was an extension of many of the traditions of the England from which the settlers had emigrated. But it was to be, in addition, a revision of conditions that were regarded as unjust or wrong. Puritanism itself as a religious doctrine and as a way of life had been shaped by English political ideas. Among these ideas were the beliefs that government exists to regulate imperfect man, that political leaders must be obeyed, and that the welfare of the whole is more important than that of the individual. Puritanism drew as well from the medieval imagery of piety, doom, and sin.[34] Out of these older ideas the Puritans developed a conception of the covenant. Under this conception government was viewed as originating in a compact among the people. But more than this, the power of the state was viewed as legitimate because it was a government conforming to what God had decreed. "Thus, in subjecting themselves to a state that was divinely approved, the people also subjected themselves to obedience to God."[35]

In adhering to the conception of the covenant, the word of God served as a basis for the establishment of government and society in Massachusetts Bay. The Puritans viewed themselves as being an elite chosen by God to represent Him on earth. But most important for government, they viewed the positions to which the leaders were elected in the colony as being ordained by God. Once elected, the governor and the magistrates were granted power through divine authority. As "Gods upon earth," the leaders must be obeyed in order that the covenant be kept. This idea was forcefully expressed to the Puritans when Winthrop declared that "the determination of law belongs properly to God: He is the only lawgiver, but He hath given power and gifts to man to interpret his

[34] See Perry Miller, *The New England Mind: The Seventeenth Century* (New York: Macmillan, 1939).

[35] George Lee Haskins, *Law and Authority in Early Massachusetts* (New York: Macmillan, 1960), p. 44.

laws; and this belongs principally to the highest authority in a commonwealth, and subordinately to other magistrates and judges according to their several places."[36] The logical conclusion of the covenant was rule by a few for the interests they deemed appropriate: "The government of Massachusetts was thus a dictatorship of a small minority who were unhesitantly prepared to coerce the unwilling to serve the purposes of society as they conceived it."[37]

The early history of Massachusetts Bay Colony was marked by a continuing problem about the place of law in a religious community.[38] The problem was resolved by the early settlers in the construction of a legal structure based upon Biblical authority. The Scriptures thus served as a most appropriate source for establishing a government according to God's word. In 1635 the General Court of the colony ordered work to begin on a legal code. By 1641 a brief bill of rights, known since as the Body of Liberties, was passed. Finally, in 1648, a comprehensive code of law, known as "Laws and Liberties," was adopted. The code — the first of its kind in the English-speaking world — consisted of a compilation of constitutional guarantees, provisions for the conduct of government, trade, military affairs, and the relations between church and state, as well as the substantive law of crime, tort, property, and domestic relations. At the beginning of the Code was the Epistle which dramatically related the laws of the colony to the religious principles of the Old Testament Scriptures:

> So soon as God had set up Political Government among his people Israel he gave them a body of laws for judgment both in civil and criminal causes. These were brief and fundamental principles, yet withall so full and comprehensive as out of them clear deductions were to be drawn to all particular cases in future times.[39]

The Code was a unique effort to order man's life and conduct in accordance with the ideals of Puritanism.

[36] Quoted in Richard B. Morris, *Studies in the History of American Law,* 2nd ed. (New York: Joseph M. Mitchell, 1959), p. 35.

[37] Haskins, *Law and Authority in Early Massachusetts,* pp. 44–45.

[38] See Kai T. Erikson, *Wayward Puritans: A Study in the Sociology of Deviance* (New York: John Wiley, 1966), pp. 54–64. Also see Edwin Powers, *Crime and Punishment in Early Massachusetts* (Boston: Beacon Press, 1966).

[39] Quoted in Haskins, *Law and Authority in Early Massachusetts,* p. 145.

The Biblical influence in the formulation of the law of the colony is most clearly observed in the provisions of the criminal (or capital) laws of the Code. The provisions, all punishable by death, included the crimes of idolatry, witchcraft, blasphemy, bestiality, sodomy, adultery, rape, man stealing, treason, false witness with intent to take life, cursing or smiting a parent, stubbornness or rebelliousness on the part of a son against his parents, and homicide committed with malice prepense, by guile or poisoning, or in anger or passion. Most of the provisions, as well as other enactments, were annotated by some chapter and verse from the Old Testament, and several incorporated Biblical phraseology. A comparison of a provision from the law to its counterpart in the Old Testament is illustrated in the provision regarding rebellion of the son:[40]

> *Code of 1648:* If a man have a stubborn or REBELLIOUS SON, of sufficient years and understanding (*viz*) sixteen years of age, which will not obey the voice of his Father, or the voice of his Mother, and that when they have chastened him will not harken unto them: then shall his Father and Mother being his natural parents, lay hold on him, and bring him to the Magistrates assembled in Court and testifie unto them, that their Son is stubborn and rebellious and will not obey their voice and chastisement, but lives in sundry notorious crimes, such a son shall be put to death.
>
> *Deuteronomy 21:18–21:* If a man have a stubborn and rebellious son, which will not obey the voice of his father, or the voice of his mother, and that, when they have chastened him, will not harken unto them: Then shall his father and his mother lay hold on him, and bring him out unto the elders of his city, and unto the gate of his place; And they shall say unto the elders of his city, This our son is stubborn and rebellious, he will not obey our voice; he is a glutton, and a drunkard. And all the men of his city shall stone him with stones, that he die. . . .

Other capital laws containing words, clauses, or phrases taken directly from the Old Testament have been noted:

> Thus, the witchcraft provision defined a witch as one that

[40] Quoted in Haskins, *Law and Authority in Early Massachusetts,* p. 146.

> "hath or consulteth with a familiar spirit" in terms of Leviticus 20:27 and Deuteronomy 18:11, which speak respectively of one "that hath a familiar spirit" and of "a consulter with familiar spirits." Again, it is prescribed in Leviticus 20:15 and 16 that "if a man lie with a beast, he shall surely be put to death: and ye shall slay the beast," and a similar punishment was provided "if a woman approach unto any beast, and lie down thereto;" by comparison, the bestiality law of Massachusetts states that "If any man or woman shall LYE WITH ANY BEAST, or bruit creature, by carnall copulation; they shall surely be put to death: and the beast shall be slain, and buried, and not eaten." In the same chapter of Leviticus, 20:13, it is stated that "If a man also lie with mankind, as he lieth with a woman, both of them have committed an abomination;" the colony law against sodomy prescribes that "if any man LYETH WITH MAN-KINDE as he lieth with a woman, both of them have committed abomination. . . ." In Exodus 21:16 it is declared that "he that stealeth a man, and selleth him, or if he be found in his hand, he shall surely be put to death;" in Massachusetts law, "If any man STEALETH A MAN, or Man-kinde, he shall surely be put to death." Finally, the colonial provision that "if any child, or children . . . shall CURSE, or SMITE their natural FATHER, or MOTHER: he or they shall be put to death," is paralleled by Exodus 21:15 and 17, to the effect that "he that smitteth his father, or his mother . . . And he that curseth his father, or his mother, shall surely be put to death."[41]

There can be no doubt that the religious principles of the Old Testament provided one of the cornerstones for the criminal law of the Puritans. The authority of the Bible served as a justification for the provisions of the law. The law was God's word enacted on earth.

The purpose of law for the Puritans was the accomplishment of God's will in a society bound together by a religious and political covenant. Authority of the state was thus religiously condoned. Carried to its conclusion, this meant that the welfare of the whole, rather than that of the individual, was the chief concern of the state. Law and government, therefore, have the power to coerce individuals according to the interests of the holders of power. With

[41] Haskins, *Law and Authority in Early Massachusetts,* pp. 146–147.

respect to this character of Puritan law, and in relation to our law of today: "The end of law as viewed by the colonists was less alien to our own conceptions than a first impression might suggest. In politically organized society, law operates as a restraint on individual action for the benefit of some other individual or of the group as a whole."[42]

SUNDAY LAW

Since the time that Sunday became somehow different from other days of the week, interests have been effective in guarding it through criminal law. Until fairly recent times religious interests determined the legal meaning of the Sabbath. Today, however, Sunday is receiving the protection of the law because of the influence of social and economic interests.

Sunday law, or "blue law," had its origin in the command from Mount Sinai: "Ye shall keep the Sabbath therefore; for it is holy unto you: every one that defileth it shall surely be put to death" (Exodus 31:14). The command gained legal character in A.D. 321 when Constantine, after his conversion to Christianity, issued an edict requiring all work to cease on the day that was settled by law to be the Sabbath.[43] Numerous statutes in reference to the regulation of activities on Sunday were later enacted in England. In 1237 Henry III forbade attendance at markets on Sunday; the Sunday showing of wools at the staple was banned by Edward III in 1354; in 1409 Henry IV prohibited the playing of certain games on Sunday; Henry VI proscribed Sunday fairs in churchyards in 1444 and four years later he made unlawful all fairs and markets and all showings of goods or merchandise; Sunday bodily labor was disallowed by Edward VI in the mid-sixteenth century; and various Sunday sports and amusements were restricted in 1625 by Charles I. The early English Sunday laws were thus aimed at frequenting markets, participating in commercial activity, laboring, and engaging in amusements on Sunday.

[42] Haskins, *Law and Authority in Early Massachusetts,* p. 225.

[43] For a history of Sunday law, see Abram H. Lewis, *A Critical History of Sunday Legislation from 321 to 1888* A.D. (New York: D. Appleton, 1888); and George E. Harris, *A Treatise on Sunday Laws* (Rochester, N.Y.: The Lawyers' Cooperative Publishing Co., 1892).

The American colonies wasted little time in enacting Sunday laws. The colonial Sunday laws, however, were similar to the later English statute of Charles II (29 Charles II, c. 7, 1677). The law stated:

> For the better observation and keeping holy the Lord's day, commonly called Sunday; be it enacted . . . that all the laws enacted and in force concerning the observation of the day, and repairing to church thereon, be carefully put in execution; and that all and every person and persons whatsoever shall upon every Lord's day apply themselves to the observation of the same, by exercising themselves thereon in the duties of piety and true religion, publicly and privately; and that no tradesman, artificer, and workman, laborer, or other person whatsoever, shall do or exercise any worldly labor or business or work of their ordinary callings upon the Lord's day, or any part thereof (works of necessity and charity only accepted) . . . and that no person or persons whatsover shall publicly cry, show forth, or expose for sale any wares, merchandise, fruit herbs, goods, or chattels, whatsoever, upon the Lord's day, or any part thereof. . . .

The law of Charles II thus added to the earlier statutes the concept of compulsory worship and church attendance on Sunday. The concept was evident in the 1610 statute of the colony of Virginia, which made church attendance compulsory, for both the morning and afternoon services.[44] Such laws were for the benefit of the respective churches of the colonies, just as they had been for the protection of the established church in England.

Most states today have Sunday laws among their statutes. Their substance no longer relates to church attendance, but to other diversions that are likely to occur on Sunday, such as labor, amusement, and sales. The change in the substance of Sunday law is indicated in the statutes of the state of New York. The first Sabbath law of New York, included in conditions of the Burgomaster of Amsterdam of 1656, required the Scriptures to be read in public by a hired schoolmaster. Shortly after, in 1664, the "Duke of

[44] Sunday Laws in America are discussed in Alvin W. Johnson, "Sunday Legislation," *Kentucky Law Journal,* 23 (November, 1934), pp. 131–166; and Warren L. Johns, *Dateline Sunday: U.S.A.: The Story of Three Centuries of Sunday-Law Battles in America* (New York: Taplinger, 1967).

York laws" were issued to regulate worship on Sunday. The forerunner of the present Sunday law, however, was an act of 1695 which forbade labor on Sunday. The act continued in effect until 1788, when it was adopted as part of the laws under the State Constitution. Certain revisions were made in the years 1813, 1830, and 1909, but the body of the act remained. Today the statute prohibits on Sunday certain acts "which are serious interruptions of the repose and religious liberty of the community." Thus, in New York, as in other states, there has been a shift from the law of church attendance to a law of the restriction of work on Sunday. Sunday law has become "closing" law.

The enforcement of Sunday law, needless to say, is not usually taken seriously. The laws are only sporadically enforced, and then only with considerable discretion within local settings. However dated and obsolete these laws may seem, there has been in recent times a revival in the formulation and administration of Sunday law. The current situation has been succinctly described and analyzed in the following way:

> The Sunday blue laws are unfair and seem to serve no useful function in our society today. However, due to their antiquity, they are well established and widespread, although seldom enforced. In addition to their ages, their widespread incorporation and continuation are due to a large degree to various pressure groups. Their incorporation probably had its basis in the religious pressure elements and their continuance, in the pressure groups representing the retail sellers' associations.[45]

New pressure groups with other than religious interests have been effective in renewing Sunday laws. Interests in the formulation and administration of Sunday laws have become secularized, economic rather than religious, accompanied by such rationales as relaxation, leisure, and recreation.

The action of pressure groups on Sunday legislation can be seen in recent amendments to existing statutes. The wording of the statutes has been altered to include the private interests of specific groups.[46] In 1957 the Massachusetts Sunday law was amended to

[45] Eugene P. Chell, "Sunday Blue Laws: An Analysis of Their Position in Our Society," *Rutgers Law Review,* 12 (Spring, 1958), p. 520.

[46] Chell, "Sunday Blue Laws," pp. 511–512.

allow frozen custard stands to operate on Sunday. The frozen custard lobby was able to have the ice cream sales clause expanded to permit on Sunday the sale of "frozen dessert mixes." Likewise, local pressure groups in Massachusetts were active in changing the Sunday statute to permit the selling of fishing bait on Sunday. Pressure groups in New York were also able to have the Sunday law expanded, allowing roadside stands to sell farm products.

In a similar fashion, through the efforts of the Automobile Dealers Association, several states have amended their Sunday laws in respect to the sale of automobiles on Sunday. The action was inspired by the increasing combination of the traditional Sunday pleasure drive with Sunday shopping on the superhighway. Sunday drivers were finding it convenient to purchase autos on Sunday from the automobile dealers located on the highways. This meant that the auto dealers within the city limits, out of range of the highways, could not compete with the highway auto dealers. Into this crisis stepped the Automobile Dealers Association, dominated by downtown dealers, to successfully lobby for the prohibition of the sale of autos on Sunday. A similar phenomenon has occurred in respect to the restriction of the sale of other kinds of merchandise in the large discount stores also located on the superhighways. Downtown businesses have been successful in local areas in having statutes amended or enforced in order to curb the competition of businesses advantageously located on the highway in easy access of the affluent Sunday driver.

It was on the basis of such a situation that the United States Supreme Court in 1960 heard an appeal from the Maryland Court of Appeals. The Maryland State Court had convicted and fined employees of a large department store on a highway in Anne Arundel County for selling on Sunday a looseleaf binder, a can of floor wax, a stapler, staples, and a toy. The Maryland State Court had ruled that the conduct of the employees was in violation of a Maryland statute which forbade the sale on Sunday of all merchandise, except the retail sale of tobacco products, confectioneries, milk, bread, fruit, gasoline, oils, greases, drugs, medicines, newspapers, and periodicals. After hearing the case the Supreme Court upheld (on May 29, 1961), in *McGowan v. Maryland,* the conviction of the Maryland State Court.

The principal argument upon which the Supreme Court based

its decision in *McGowan v. Maryland* was that while Sunday law originated for religious purposes today the law is maintained for secular purposes: "In the light of the evolution of our Sunday Closing Laws through the centuries, and of their more or less recent emphasis upon secular considerations, it is concluded that, as presently written and administered, most of them, at least, are of a secular rather than of a religious character, and that presently they bear no relationship to establishment of religion, as those words are used in the constitution of the United States."[47] Furthermore, the opinion continues, secular interests may be served on Sunday: "The present purpose and effect of most of our Sunday Closing Laws is to provide a uniform day of rest for all citizens; and the fact that this day is Sunday, a day of particular significance for the dominant Christian sects, does not bar the State from achieving its secular goals." In addition, it was argued that "the present purpose and effect of the statute here involved is not aid to religion but to set aside a day of rest and recreation." Finally, in regard to the issue of religious liberty, Chief Justice Warren, in writing the majority opinion, observed that Sunday law does not violate constitutional rights: "People of all religions and people with no religion regard Sunday as a time for family activity, for visiting friends and relatives, for late sleeping, for passive and active entertainments, for dining out, and the like."[48]

The Supreme Court in its decision has therefore recognized that "Sunday closing legislation no longer exclusively represents religious interests."[49] That Sunday law now represents economic interests is recognized in the Court's decision. The Court remarked that the recent Sunday laws of such states as New Jersey were reformulated because of the pressure of labor groups and trade associations. It was noted by the Court as well that modern Sunday legislation in England was promoted by such interest groups as the National Federation of Grocers, the National Chamber of Trade, the Drapers' Chamber of Trade, and the National Union of Shop Assistants.

The conclusion in reference to the theory of interests, therefore,

[47] *McGowan v. Maryland,* in 366 United States Reports (October term, 1960), p. 421.

[48] *McGowan v. Maryland,* pp. 451–452.

[49] *McGowan v. Maryland,* p. 435.

is that a criminal law may be intended for a particular interest at one time and then amended and implemented at another time for some other interest. Sunday law, while being in existence for hundreds of years, for religious reasons, was never officially negated, nor ever much enforced. But with changes in social conditions and with a shift in social interests, Sunday law has been revived and lives once again.

THE LAW OF THEFT

The creation of a particular criminal law must have its conception in some concrete setting of time and place. The development of the law of theft demonstrates that necessity. For prior to the fifteenth century there was no legal conception of theft as we know it today. It was during the fifteenth century in England that the modern law of theft was officially formulated into criminal law. The law of theft was shaped by changing social conditions, and especially by pressing social interests of the time. The definition of theft as a crime was a solution to a legal problem that arose within a particular social framework.

The decision that resulted in the legal concept of theft occurred in England in 1473, in what is known as the Carrier's Case. The case has been documented and interpreted by Jerome Hall in his book *Theft, Law and Society*.[50] The facts of the case are these: The defendant was hired to carry bales to Southampton. Instead of fulfilling his obligation, he carried the goods to another place, broke open the bales, and took the contents. The man was apprehended and charged with felony.

The most illustrious judges of the time discussed the case at length. While the defendant was finally held guilty by a majority of the judges, a legal problem of considerable portent developed during the proceedings. Before the case arose, the common law recognized no criminality in a person who came legally into possession and converted it to his own use. The reasoning of the common law had been that the owner of transported goods was responsible for protecting himself by employing trustworthy persons. There was, in the Carrier's Case, a legal problem of *stare decisis* in which the judges regarded themselves as bound by the common law.

[50] Jerome Hall, *Theft, Law and Society*, 2nd ed. (Indianapolis: Bobbs-Merrill, 1952).

Until the Carrier's Case it had been agreed that while trespass (the taking of property from one who is in possession of it) was an essential element of larceny, a person in possession of property could not commit a trespass upon that property. Therefore, since a bailee (an employee who is trusted with property) had possession, larceny could not technically be committed by such an employee. The judges, however, departed from precedent by introducing a new concept which could neither be found among the existing legal rules nor logically derived from them. For the judges held that "breaking bulk" terminated the bailment, that such property at once reverted to the possession of the bailor, and that the removal of it from the bales supplied the trespass. Hall thus observes: "By this refinement the door was opened to admit into the law of larceny a whole series of acts which had up to that time been purely civil wrongs."[51] Law was being made by judges in the Carrier's Case by the departure from and the renunciation of certain precedents of the common law.

An important question arises as to the forces that were active in the creation of a new legal concept. In his analysis of the case, Hall outlines the changes that were occurring in fifteenth century England. These changes coupled with the social conditions and the institutions of the period made convenient a change in the law of theft. To begin with, in the political realm, the courts were subservient to the wishes of Edward IV. This meant that the special interests of the Crown were protected by the courts. Among the interests of the king that received the favor of the courts were the royal commercial activities, including trade with merchants on the Continent. Edward himself was a merchant who carried on many private ventures.

The economic conditions of the period were especially important for the decision reached in the Carrier's Case. During this phase of the Renaissance a commercial revolution was taking place in England and Europe. The old feudal structure resting on an agricultural economy was giving way to a new order based on industry and trade. These economic conditions bear upon an interpretation of the Carrier's Case: "(1) the complainant was an alien merchant; (2) he had a covenant with the kings which provided safe passage

[51] *Ibid.*, p. 10.

for him and his goods; (3) the property taken is described as being within bales, and weighing twenty pounds; (4) the defendant was a carrier; (5) and he was to deliver the merchandise at Southampton."[52]

Hall thus argues that the complainant was a foreign merchant (probably Italian) whose trade was desired by the Crown. Such foreign merchants were subject to special risks: There was naturally hostility by local merchants toward foreign trade. Moreover, foreign merchants were handicapped in the transport of goods because of the uncertainty of finding trustworthy carriers who would not abscond with the goods. The king attempted to relieve the situation somewhat, issuing convenants of safe conduct through the country.

The merchandise taken by the bailee of the Carrier's Case was probably wool or cloth, or both. Such goods were usually transported in bales. Also, Southampton was a principal port for shipping these goods, serving as a port for trade with Latin countries in particular. All these deductions mean that "the interests of the most important industry in England were involved in the case."[53]

The relation of the conditions of fifteenth-century England to the decision of the Carrier's Case has been concisely summarized:

> We are now in a position to visualize the case and the problem presented to the judges as a result of the legal, political and economic conditions described above. On the one hand, the criminal law at the time is clear. On the other hand, the whole complex aggregate of political and economic conditions described above thrusts itself upon the court. The more powerful forces of the time were interrelated very intimately and at many points: the New Monarchy and the *nouveau riche* — the mercantile class; the business interests of both and the consequent need for a secure carrying trade; the wool and textile industry, the most valuable, by far, in all the realm; wool and cloth, the most important exports; these exports and the foreign trade, this trade and Southampton, chief trading city with the Latin countries for centuries; the numerous and very influential Italian merchants who bought English wool and cloth inland and shipped them from Southampton. The great forces of an

[52] *Ibid.,* p. 19.
[53] *Ibid.,* p. 31.

> emerging modern world, represented in the above phenomena, necessitated the elimination of a formula which had outgrown its usefulness. A new set of major institutions required a new rule. The law, lagging behind the needs of the times, was brought into more harmonious relationship with the other institutions by the decision rendered in the Carrier's Case.[54]

The Carrier's Case of 1473 vividly demonstrates the way in which changing social conditions and emerging social interests may bring about the formulation of a criminal law. The decision of the Carrier's Case provided the framework for the further development of the law of theft. Eventually, with the growth in banking and the use of paper currency, the law was expanded to include the act of embezzlement by clerks, officers, and the like. A Whig Parliament in the eighteenth century passed an embezzlement statute in order to protect mercantile interests. The legal protection of property has always been to the interest of the propertied segments of society.

ANTITRUST LAWS

Toward the end of the nineteenth century in the United States an antimonopoly movement emerged. This movement was accompanied by a body of doctrine which regarded the problem of monopoly as soluble only through the powers of government. Subsequent action of the federal government resulted in an innovation in criminal law, that is, the concept that the state had the responsibility of protecting the national economic order from private interests within that order. This departure from the traditional scope and purpose of the criminal law, a departure which meant that the criminal law not only protected private property but also assisted in the maintenance of a particular kind of economy, marked the creation of a new type of criminal law, administrative criminal law.

A tradition for antitrust legislation existed in the common law of England and America.[55] The common law precedents had established that certain commercial activities were to be restricted by law. Yet the common law doctrine as applied by the individual states was

[54] *Ibid.*, p. 33.

[55] See Hans B. Thorelli, *The Federal Antitrust Policy: Origination of an American Tradition* (Baltimore: Johns Hopkins Press, 1955), pp. 9–53.

not effective in controlling the monopolies that were developing in the United States. Broad interpretation by state courts of the interstate commerce clause of the Constitution and the first article of the Fourteenth Amendment allowed many corporations to expand greatly beyond state borders and to receive the protection of the federal government. Since there was no federal common law on the regulation of monopolies, the need for federal antitrust legislation was clear.

Opposition to trusts and monopolies was aroused in several segments of American society. Diverse groups, not always with compatible ideologies, agitated for antimonopoly legislation.[56] Some groups were gravely concerned with the ruthless exploitation of national resources by corporations that used them for their own profit-making ventures. Labor was hostile to powerful corporations, finding that it was at a distinct disadvantage in bargaining with the large corporations. Small businessmen feared possible surrender or ruin because of the concentration of wealth and facilities in gigantic corporations. Declining farm prices were attributed to the growth of large corporations. The Populist Party was active in supporting agrarian antagonism toward big business. Typical of the antimonopoly spirit of the period was the feeling expressed by a Granger, who related monopoly to the question of progress:

> Progress which the possessors of the good things of earth call innovation, progress the cardinal principle of this democracy of the people, will go on as all history shows. It must be through continual strife, for progress is but a contest still going on in spite of the death chants, the impenetrable armor, and the resisting spirit of self; a contest which has been going on through earth's long day, and will still go on until evening — until the mighty purposes of creation are accomplished, and the many are entitled to preeminence over the few in the view of the earth as they are now entitled in the eye of heaven. This is what the great democracy of the people demands. That is what the antimonopoly movement means.[57]

In the 1880's monopolies were attacked in the name of the theory

[56] Thorelli, *The Federal Antitrust Policy,* pp. 54–163.

[57] Quoted in Arthur P. Dudden, "Men Against Monopoly: The Prelude to Trust-Busting" *Journal of the History of Ideas,* 18 (October, 1957), p. 593.

and practice of laissez-faire economics. A challenge was presented to the long-ingrained classical economics. Influential also were individual radicals, such as Wendell Phillips and Peter Cooper, and the writings of Henry George, Edward Bellamy, and Henry Demarest Lloyd reached wide audiences. President Cleveland brought the issue to the front in a tariff message of 1887 and stressed it with even greater urgency the following year: "As we view the achievements of aggregated capital we discover the existence of trusts, combinations and monopolies, while the citizen is struggling far in the rear or is trampled to death beneath an iron heel. Corporations which should be carefully restrained creatures of the law and servants of the people, are fast becoming the people's masters."[58] That year the platforms of both major political parties pledged to oppose trusts and monopolies.

The result of the widespread opposition to monopolies from various sides was the enactment of the Sherman Act of 1890. The law, drafted primarily by Senator John Sherman of Ohio, declared that "(1) Every contract, combination in the form of trust or otherwise, or conspiracy, in restraint of trade or commerce among the several States, or with foreign nations is hereby declared to be illegal . . . (2) Every person who shall monopolize, or attempt to monopolize . . . any part of the trade or commerce among the several States, or with foreign nations, shall be deemed guilty of a misdemeanor. . . ." Thus, to combine in restraint of trade and to monopolize became public offenses. The federal government was empowered to proceed against violations of the law by criminal action.

In broad perspective, the interest to be protected in the law was the basic economic order of the nation. The aim of the supporters of antitrust legislation was not, for the most part, to alter the existing economic order, but to protect the free enterprise system. "The interest to be protected was the maintenance of a competitive economy based on private enterprise. The State did not mean to become owner or entrepreneur, but it felt compelled to use its legislative, administrative, and judicial machinery for the protection of the economic well-being of the community as a whole — as conceived

[58] Quoted in Samuel Eliot Morison and Henry Steele Commager, *The Growth of the American Republic,* vol. 2 (New York: Oxford University Press, 1950), p. 143.

by a liberal economic philosophy — and to defend it against powerful industrial and commercial interests."[59]

Further legislation and measures for the stricter enforcement of antitrust laws followed. Particular attention was given to the regulation of corporations during the administration of Theodore Roosevelt. Roosevelt's intentions were clear, to work within the framework of the capitalistic system: "In dealing with the big corporations we call trusts, we must resolutely purpose to proceed by evolution and not by revolution. . . . Our aim is not to do away with corporations; on the contrary these big aggregations are an inevitable development of modern industrialism. . . . We can do nothing of good in the way of regulating and supervising these corporations until we fix clearly in our minds that we are not attacking the corporations, but endeavoring to do away with any evil in them. We are not hostile to them; we are merely determined that they shall be so handled as to subserve the public good."[60]

The legislation and actions of the New Deal added considerably to governmental planning and regulation of the economy. Yet in spite of the antitrust legislation and enforcement since the Sherman Act of 1890, it must be cautioned that the purpose was to protect the capitalistic system from abuse, rather than to create a new type of economic order. Franklin D. Roosevelt was not the socialist the public thought and feared, but was indeed a conservative. The case has been nicely presented:

> It would be a mistake to assume that this socialization was developed entirely at the expense of private enterprise. Indeed it is certain that the New Deal did more to strengthen and to save the capitalist economy than it did to weaken or destroy it. That economy had broken down in many nations abroad, and its collapse contributed to the rise of totalitarian governments which completely subordinated business to the state. The system was on the verge of collapse in the United States during the Hoover administration, and it is at least conceivable that had that collapse been permitted to occur, it might have been followed by the establishment of an economy very different from that to which Americans were accustomed. Historically

[59] Wolfgang Friedmann, *Law in a Changing Society* (Harmondsworth, Eng.: Penguin Books, 1964), p. 161.

[60] Quoted in Morison and Commager, *The Growth of the American Republic*, vol. 2, p. 391.

> Franklin Roosevelt's administration did for twentieth-century American capitalism what Theodore Roosevelt's and Wilson's had done for nineteenth-century business enterprise: it saved the system by ridding it of its grosser abuses and forcing it to accommodate itself to larger public interests. History may eventually record Franklin D. Roosevelt as the greatest American conservative since Hamilton.[61]

The attack upon corporations, then, beginning in the latter part of the nineteenth century and continuing to the present, has not been against business but has been inspired and led by the business interest itself. Antitrust legislation was formulated and administered by and for the interests of capitalist economics.

PURE FOOD AND DRUG LAWS

The increasing responsibility of the modern state for protecting the public's welfare is reflected in recent criminal law. Only in fairly recent times has criminal law come to embody provisions for the regulation of that which is regarded by the state as important for the health and safety of the community. Criminal laws of today thus regulate such spheres of social life as employment, housing, sanitation, traffic, and the conduct of occupations and professions. Among the concerns in the protection of the public order is that of the purity and safeness of foods and drugs. The effort to control foods and drugs through criminal law is a demonstration of how the public interest may eventually be served in spite of the private interests of individual members of society.

Through the first half of the nineteenth century the United States was chiefly an agricultural nation and the problem of purity of food and safeness of drugs rested largely with the family. During this period the principle of *caveat emptor*, or "let the buyer beware," prevailed regarding any purchases. Beginning in the industrial era following the Civil War, the economy grew in complexity. As many new products were introduced and as the consumer became further removed from the producer, the standards for a person's judgment became uncertain. Because of this situation the

[61] Morison and Commager, *The Growth of the American Republic,* vol. 2, p. 630.

older attitude of *caveat emptor* was eventually replaced by another which favored the protection of the consumer and put the blame for poor food and drug standards on the manufacturer or distributor. The new value, *caveat vendor*, became reinforced in legislation, making the producer and distributor responsible for the quality of food and drugs.

With an increasing amount of food and drugs being produced and shipped, the possibilities for spoilage, adulteration, and misrepresentation were considerable. The public gradually became aware of adulteration through various bulletins and reports, the purchase of the products, and the appearance of popular books, articles, and newspaper editorials. The Division of Chemistry of the Department of Agriculture, under the direction of Dr. Harvey W. Wiley, was especially effective in defining the abuses as a threat to public welfare. Dr. Wiley's dramatic "poison squad" experiments showed that some food preservatives were harmful and dangerous. It was also shown by the Division that a thriving interstate business was being developed in the sale of patent medicines, some of which were of questionable value.

After the public became aware of dangers in the foods and drugs they were consuming, conflicts arose over a solution.[62] Various state and federal legislative measures were proposed. Much opposition to these proposals arose because of value conflicts between several interest groups. In general the conflict was between consumer and producer. The first attempts to gain passage of legislation were instigated, in true capitalistic fashion, by those interest groups desiring to protect their respective products from what they thought was unfair competition. Consequently, the early bills that were passed were concerned chiefly with one or two specific products and did not apply to the basic problem of adulteration and misrepresentation in food and drugs.

Not until the 1880's was the first federal pure food and drug legislation introduced which would be of benefit to the public. These measures, however, were defeated. In the words of one who has documented the struggle: "It and other efforts like it were defeated by a durable alliance of quacks, ruthless crooks, pious

[62] A natural history of the social problem of food adulteration is found in Donald J. Newman, "A Study of the Criminal Nature of Pure Food Law Violations," unpublished M.A. thesis, University of Wisconsin, 1952.

frauds, scoundrels, high-priced lawyer-lobbyists, vested interests, liars, corrupt members of Congress, venal publishers, cowards in high office, the stupid, the apathetic, and the duped."[63] With interests like these not much could be hoped for in the public's interest.

Over one hundred and fifty pure food and drug bills were introduced in Congress from 1880 to 1906. Most of the measures were never heard of after their introduction, and the few that were approved were of minor significance.[64] But through continued pressure from the popular press and the opinions received from congressional constituents, the apathy of Congress was overcome, and in 1906, the Federal Food and Drug Act was passed by both the House and Senate. The act declared it unlawful to manufacture in any territory, or to introduce into any state, any adulterated or misbranded food or drug. Offending products were to be seized, and criminal penalties were provided for persons found guilty of violating the provisions of the act.

The need for revision of the act, however, became apparent shortly after its passage. The absence of adequate control over advertising provided an especially serious loophole for evasion of the spirit of the law, and labeling requirements of the law were such as to permit extravagant and unwarranted therapeutic claims for a product. Also, the 1906 act contained no provisions applying to cosmetics and failed to provide measures for safe and effective health devices. In spite of amendments in 1912 (the Sherley amendment) and 1919 (the New Weight Act), the problem of impure and unsafe foods and drugs had not been effectively reformed through law.

A renewed effort was made to regulate food and drugs. During this period further awareness of the problem was provided in such popular works as Kallet and Schlink's *100,000,000 Guinea Pigs* and Lamb's *American Chamber of Horrors*.[65] Various consumer organizations were formed and consumer research groups were es-

[63] Morton Mintz, *The Therapeutic Nightmare: A Report on Prescription Drugs, the Men Who Take Them, and the Agency That Controls Them* (Boston: Houghton Mifflin, 1965), p. 41.

[64] For these and later laws, see Stephen Wilson, *Food and Drug Regulation* (Washington, D.C.: American Council of Public Affairs, 1942).

[65] Arthur Kallet, and F. J. Schlink, *100,000,000 Guinea Pigs* (New York: The Vanguard Press, 1933); Ruth deForest Lamb, *American Chamber of Horrors* (New York: Farrar and Rinehart, 1936).

tablished. After Franklin D. Roosevelt took office in 1933 a committee was appointed to draft new legislation.

A bill to correct the deficiencies of the 1906 law was introduced in 1933. As could be expected, planned attacks were launched against the bill. Particularly active in the opposition to the proposal was the organization representing the patent medicine interests, the United Medicine Manufacturers of America. The organization attempted to block the bill by engaging in a drive which involved "17 plans." Among the plans were to: "(1) secure cooperation of newspapers in spreading favorable publicity; (2) enlist all manufacturers and wholesalers to instruct customers through their salesmen; (3) secure the pledge of manufacturers, wholesalers, advertising agencies, and all other interested affiliates to address letters to Senators to gain their promise to vote against the bill; (4) line up with other organizations, such as the Drug Institute, Proprietary Association, National Association of Retail Druggists, to make a mass attack on the bill; (5) enlist the help of carton, tube, bottle, and box manufacturers; (6) ridicule organizations favoring the bill; and (7) convey by every means available — radio, newspapers, mail, and personal contact — the alarming fact that if the bill is adopted, the public will be deprived of the right of self-diagnosis and self-medication."[66]

But the public interest was to succeed, at least in concept. The Federal Food, Drug and Cosmetic Act was enacted in 1938. The act required, among other things, more effective methods for the control of false labeling and advertising. Informative, specific labeling was definitely required. False advertising of foods, drugs, and cosmetics was prohibited, with provision for more severe penalties for violation of the law. In addition, authority was established for setting standards for the identity, quality, strength, and purity of drugs. Later, in 1951, the act was amended by the passage of the Durham-Humphrey Amendment. The amendment placed stricter controls on the dispensing of drugs.

In the meantime a number of other special federal laws were enacted to govern the manufacture and marketing of particular classes of drugs (narcotics, marihuana, biologic products). Still other laws were passed to regulate such activities as the weighing,

[66] From Mintz, *The Therapeutic Nightmare*, pp. 45–46.

measuring, and mailing of foods and drugs.[67] The various federal laws were complemented by state laws which were also concerned with manufacturing, labeling, and advertising, but which in addition regulated the occupational activity of pharmacy.[68]

Continued interest in providing the public with safe and pure foods can be seen in the federal government's inquiry into the drug industry at the beginning of the 1960's. Presumably interested in the broad problem of administered prices, the Senate Subcommittee on Antitrust and Monopoly under the chairmanship of Estes Kefauver touched on such topics as the high cost of drugs, the large number of new drugs released each year, the multiple names for identical chemicals and compounds, advertising and promotion of drugs, safeness and efficacy of drugs, and violation of antitrust laws by drug manufacturers.[69] The hearings were highly critical of the amount of money drug manufacturers spend on advertising and promotion in comparison to what they spend for research. Upon the conclusion of the hearings, amid strong opposing pressure from the large pharmaceutical houses and their lobbying organizations, Congress passed in 1962 the Kefauver-Hart Drug Act. The act, however, was not successful in gaining the regulation of drug prices, but was successful in securing provisions for stricter control of drug testing, labeling, and advertising.

Although the drug act of 1962 was able to correct many abuses in the drug industry, other problems remain. Pharmaceutical interests, especially manufacturers and dispensers of drugs, continue to

[67] Thomas W. Christopher and Charles W. Dunn, *Special Federal Food and Drug Laws* (New York: Commerce Clearing House, 1954).

[68] David H. Vernon and Franklin M. Depew, *General State Food and Drug Laws* (New York: Commerce Clearing House, 1955). For a study of the formulation of occupational laws according to the interests of the occupations, pharmacy included, see Ronald L. Akers, "The Professional Association and the Legal Regulation of Practice," *Law and Society Review,* 2 (May, 1968), pp. 463–482.

[69] U.S. Congress, Senate, Subcommittee of the Committee on the Judiciary, *Hearings Before the Subcommittee on Antitrust and Monopoly,* 86th Congress, 1st and 2nd Sessions, Parts 14–22, 1959–1960; U.S. Congress, Senate, Subcommittee of the Committee on the Judiciary, *Report of the Committee on the Judiciary,* "Antitrust and Monopoly Activities, 1960," Report No. 167, 87th Congress, 1st Session, 1961; U.S. Congress, Senate, Subcommittee of the Committee on the Judiciary, *Report of the Committee on the Judiciary,* "Administered Prices: Drugs," Report No. 448, 87th Congress, 1st Session, 1961.

advertise and sell drugs according to their trade name, when prescription by generic name would be to the advantage of the public. Yet from a broad perspective we can see that since the end of the last century the public interest has been increasingly served, in spite of private interests.

SEXUAL PSYCHOPATH LAWS

Some criminal laws, not unlike our other social passions and conveniences, experience periods of increased popularity. The formulation of "sexual psychopath" laws is such an instance of fashion in law. Beginning in the later 1930's and extending into the 1950's, more than half the states enacted sexual psychopath laws. The statutes varied somewhat from one state to another, but generally defined the sexual psychopath as "one lacking the power to control his sexual impulses or having criminal propensities toward the commission of sex offenses."[70] From the standpoint of sanctions, the laws usually provided that a person diagnosed as a sexual psychopath be confined for an indefinite period in a state hospital for the insane. Why were these laws enacted during a particular period, and what social interests were involved in their formulation?

Sexual psychopath laws were in part a response to public anxiety about serious sex crimes. Like the earlier and somewhat comparable "habitual offender" laws that also swept the country, the sexual psychopath laws provided a partial solution to what was being defined as a social problem.[71] Consequently, characteristic to the American legal system, a law was created to solve a problem.

The problem of the sex offender, as defined by the public, was based on a series of propositions, most of which were false or at least questionable:

> Namely, that the present danger to women and children from serious sex crimes is very great, for the number of sex crimes is large and is increasing more rapidly than any other crime; that most sex crimes are committed by "sexual psychopaths" and

[70] See Alan H. Swanson, "Sexual Psychopath Statutes: Summary and Analysis," *Journal of Criminal Law, Criminology and Police Science,* 51 (July–August, 1960), pp. 215–235.

[71] Habitual Offender laws are discussed in Paul W. Tappan, "Habitual Offender Laws in the United States," *Federal Probation,* 13 (March, 1949), pp. 28–31.

> that these persons persist in their sexual crimes throughout life; that they always give warning that they are dangerous by first committing minor offenses; that any psychiatrist can diagnose them with a high degree of precision at an early age, before they have committed serious sex crimes; and that sexual psychopaths who are diagnosed and identified should be confined as irresponsible persons until they are pronounced by psychiatrists to be completely and permanently cured of their malady.[72]

But once the public's concern had been aroused, partly through press coverage of a few spectacular sex crimes, and partly through the diffusion of a misinformed conception of the sex offender, sexual psychopath legislation followed as the answer to the problem.

Yet the public's concern about sex offenses could not be effective in the formulation of criminal law without the organization of action groups within the community. Concrete pressure for sexual psychopath legislation was provided in most states by the organization of committees, which in most cases were guided by psychiatrists. These committees presented sexual psychopath bills to the public and to the legislatures as the most scientific and enlightened method of protecting society against dangerous sex criminals. Thus, "the psychiatrists, more than any others have been the interest group back of the laws."[73] A committee of psychiatrists and neurologists in Chicago wrote the bill that became the sexual psychopath law of Illinois. In Minnesota all the members of the governor's committee except one were psychiatrists.

The fact that the formulation of the sexual psychopath laws was predominantly in the hands of psychiatrists accounts in large measure for the substance of the laws. Since a common assertion among psychiatrists is that serious sex crimes are the result of emotional or mental pathology, or that all psychological defectives have actual or potential sexual abnormalities, it is little wonder that the sexual psychopath laws stipulated that sex offenders be handled as psychologically disturbed persons and be treated as patients. But the psychiatric interest in the formulation of sexual psychopath laws was also a matter of private economics.

The interests of psychiatrists in sexual psychopath legislation

[72] Edwin H. Sutherland, "The Diffusion of Sexual Psychopath Laws," *American Journal of Sociology,* 56 (September, 1950), pp. 142–148.

[73] *Ibid.,* p. 145.

was, nevertheless, reinforced by the more general movement which promoted the treatment of all offenders. Furthermore, professionally trained persons employed in corrections have tended to believe that emotional traits are the explanation of crime. The treatment of the criminal as a patient, therefore, was consistent with the aims of those engaged in the application of the sexual psychopath laws.

In spite of the rush to enact sexual psychopath laws, there has been a tendency not to enforce the laws. There are several reasons for the lack of enforcement of the sexual psychopath laws:

> One is that the laws were passed in a period of panic and were forgotten after the emotion was relieved by this action. A second reason is that the state has no facilities for the care and custody of sexual psychopaths; the state hospitals are already crowded with psychotic patients. A third reason is that the prosecutor and judge, anxious to make records as vigorous and aggressive defenders of the community, favor the most severe penalty available and are unwilling to look upon serious sex criminals as patients. They use the sexual psychopath laws only when their evidence is so weak that conviction under the criminal law is improbable. Finally, it is reported that defense attorneys have learned that they can stop the proceedings under this law by advising their clients to refuse to talk to the psychiatrists. The psychiatrists can make no diagnosis if those who are being investigated refuse to talk.[74]

But perhaps "the greatest saving grace has been the almost uniform lack of enforcement that has followed their enactment."[75] Basically, the sexual psychopath laws depart from some of the most fundamental conceptions of criminal law. Most important, the Anglo-American legal doctrine of *nulla crimen sine lege*, prohibiting prosecution in the absence of clearly specified substantive norms, is denied by most of the sexual psychopath statutes. Since the individual may be adjudged either without a criminal charge or without a finding of guilt, merely through the diagnosis that he is a sexual psychopath, due process considerations are ignored. Furthermore, since the concept of "sexual psychopath" is so vaguely and variously defined by psychiatrists, there is a great deal of variation in diag-

[74] Edwin H. Sutherland, "The Sexual Psychopath Laws," *Journal of Criminal Law, Criminology and Police Science,* 40 (January–February, 1950), pp. 543–554.

[75] Paul W. Tappan, "Sex Offender Laws and Their Administration," *Federal Probation,* 14 (September, 1950), p. 33.

nosis and a considerable amount of discretion in the administration of the law.

> There appears to be no agreement as to the syndromes of aberration that justify special treatment. Indeed, hospital authorities handling cases of alleged sex psychopaths committed to them by the courts discover a wide spread of psychological types — many who are normal, along with neurotics, psychotics, epileptics, feeble-minded, alcoholics, and constitutional types. Agreement among authorities is often difficult enough to attain for purposes of classifying individuals where traditional and fairly precise clinical categories are involved; consensus is impossible in the no man's land of psychopathic personality. The hazard inherent in the substantive definitions of these statutes is manifest upon inspection; the psychopathology is defined by such nondiscriminating terminology as "impulsiveness of behavior," "lack of customary standards of good judgment," "emotional instability," or "inability to control impulse." The cases adjudicated under these criteria display varied forms of personality organization and a widely assorted sexual symptomatology, a significant proportion of which is in fact normal behavior viewed from either a biological or statistical point of view.[76]

And in some jurisdictions a person may be adjudicated — according to this imprecise status of sexual psychopath — without a criminal charge being placed against the individual and without it being established that a crime has been committed. "Thus individuals who are nonpsychotic and nondefective, against whom no charge has been laid, may be confined for long periods in hospitals that lack both the space and the treatment facilities to handle them. By the simple expedient of shifting jurisdiction to civil courts, these legislators have made it possible to commit minor deviates who are not insane to psychiatric institutions where they do not belong."[77]

There is no reason to believe that similar rashes of legislation will not recur. Law has its element of fashion. The recent enactment of a drug addiction control law in the state of New York may become an example for other states. Again certain persons could be adjudicated and confined for long periods of time in institutions without the safeguards of due process. The establishment of official

[76] *Ibid.*, p. 33.
[77] *Ibid.*, p. 34.

policies in the name of the common good, and under the guise of scientific knowledge, is always a force in the formulation of certain types of criminal law.

PROTECTION OF MORALITY AND PUBLIC ORDER

Whether or not it is the proper business of criminal law to enforce moral principles, much of our criminal law is formulated and maintained for just that purpose. A great many of our criminal laws attempt to control personal behaviors that are contrary to the morals of some members of the community. Many of these criminal laws are kept on the books, without serious or uniform enforcement, because they reflect a popular sense of reprobation. The behaviors they prohibit are regarded, at least by some, as wrong and unworthy of the society. The criminal laws that aim to protect morality and public order include those which regulate various kinds of sexual conduct, prostitution, homosexuality, abortion, drinking, the use of drugs, and certain public behaviors defined by such names as "public nuisance," "loitering," "trespassing," and "vagrancy."[78]

Regulation of Sexual Conduct. Much of the concern for public order pertains to the control of sexual conduct. This concern, in Anglo-American society at least, is based on a fairly rigid conception of appropriate sexual expression. Our moral sense carries strong Puritan overtones. To be moral in America is to be *sexually* discreet.

The range of sexual conduct that is covered by law is so extensive that the law makes potential criminals of most of the adolescent and adult population.[79] One of the principal reasons for such complete control over the sexual behavior of the members of society is to protect a particular kind of family system. A great number of state laws seek to control acts which might otherwise endanger the chastity of women before marriage. There are the numerous laws in regard to rape (statutory and forcible), fornication, incest, and

[78] On public order crimes, see Marshall B. Clinard and Richard Quinney, *Criminal Behavior Systems: A Typology* (New York: Holt, Rinehart and Winston, 1967), pp. 247–269.

[79] See Morris Ploscowe, "Sex Offenses: The American Legal Context," *Law and Contemporary Problems,* 25 (Spring, 1960), pp. 217–225; Also, Gerhard O. W. Mueller, *Legal Regulation of Sexual Conduct* (Dobbs Ferry, N.Y.: Oceana Publications, 1961).

sexual deviance of juveniles. The criminal laws on adultery also exist to protect the family by preventing sexual relations outside the marriage bond.[80] The Puritans of Massachusetts Bay Colony placed such a value on sexual relations within the family that they made adultery a crime punishable by death. Other criminal laws today as in the past regulate sexual relations of family members. Through these laws the cherished monogamous family pattern is preserved.

Some of our criminal laws on sexual behavior were formulated to protect specific aspects of marriage and family life for very special interests. Several southern states, for instance, enacted laws to prevent marriages between Negroes and whites. In 1967, however, the Supreme Court ruled that an antimiscegenation statute of Virginia was unconstitutional. Such "slavery laws," held over from a bygone era, had been originally formulated to ensure the slavery status of Negroes and in more recent times have been used to maintain segregation of the races.

Another type of criminal law, also enacted at an early time in Virginia, pertained to bastardy among women of the lower ranks. This law was not only instituted for a moral purpose but was to ensure the maximum work from domestic servants. "Having paid a very high price for their labor, their masters, not unnaturally, were opposed to their entering a relationship which was quite certain to lead to interruptions in their field work, perhaps, at the very time their part in that work would be most valuable, if not wholly indispensable. Not only would the birth of children make it necessary for them to lie by for a month or more, but it might even result in their deaths, and the complete loss of the money invested by the planter in their purchase."[81] Also in the law of bastardy the blame for the offense could be placed on the servant woman who had been overpowered by the advances of her masters.

Criminal law has also been formulated to prevent the exposure of members of the society to that which is regarded by some as lewd or obscene. The Comstock Act of 1873 stands in American criminal law as a landmark in the control of obscenity. Before that time the

[80] Morris Ploscowe, *Sex and the Law* (Englewood Cliffs, N.J.: Prentice-Hall, 1951), pp. 136–164.

[81] Philip Alexander Bruce, *Social Life in Old Virginia* (New York: Capricorn Books, 1965, originally published in 1910), p. 45.

common law was not clear on the issue. In fact, obscenity was not considered to be a problem before the nineteenth century. By the middle of the nineteenth century a new concept of obscenity had emerged, given an identity by the Victorian Age.[82] The protection of woman and the young became a concern of several segments of the population. Finally, in 1873, with considerable pressure for a statutory law, the Comstock Law was enacted, providing for the censorship of literature and other printed matter which might come in the hands of the innocent.

Today well-organized interest groups, such as the National Organization for Decent Literature, continue to pressure courts and legislatures for statutes and decisions on the regulation of obscenity. A short time ago in New York moral interests were successful in having the cabaret code amended to prevent bar waitresses or barmaids from working with "their breasts or lower part of the torso uncovered."[83] The morning following the amendment the owner of a bar and her three topless waitresses, after being arrested during the night, appeared in court to answer summonses for "offending the public morals."

Prostitution, Homosexuality, and Abortion. The laws in regard to prostitution vary greatly from one country to another. In most states the act of solicitation is a misdemeanor punished by a fine or a jail sentence of one year. Repeated apprehensions may result in a strong charge of felony. In some states laws have been enacted to control not only solicitation by prostitutes but also the activities of the exploiters and customers of prostitutes. While prostitution may be defined as a crime, the conduct is frequent in all societies. The laws remain, however, as a representation of what some in society expect in the ideal moral order. But the Wolfenden Report of England perhaps best expressed the reasons for the continued legal regulation of prostitution:

> If it were the law's intention to punish prostitution *per se*, on the ground that it is immoral conduct, then it would be right that it should provide for the punishment of the man as well

[82] Henry H. Foster, Jr., "The 'Comstock Load'—Obscenity and the Law," *Journal of Criminal Law, Criminology and Police Science,* 48 (September–October, 1957), pp. 245–258.

[83] Reported in *The New York Times,* November 15, 1966, p. 49.

> as the woman. But that is not the function of the law. It should confine itself to those activities which offend against public order and decency or expose the ordinary citizen to what is offensive or injurious; and the simple fact is that prostitutes do parade themselves more habitually and openly than their prospective customers, and do by their continual presence affront the sense of decency of the ordinary citizen. In so doing they create a nuisance which, in our view, the law is entitled to recognize and deal with.[84]

Criminal penalties for homosexual acts in the United States have tended to be severe. Some states provide penalties of ten or more years imprisonment. In actuality, however, a relatively small proportion of persons are arrested for homosexual acts and when penalties are administered they tend to be lenient. While a moral connotation is still attached to homosexuality by some segments of society, the trend is toward the removal of certain homosexual acts from the list of crimes. The Wolfenden Report, after stating that the purpose of law is to protect the citizen, asserted that it is not the function of criminal law "to intervene in the private lives of citizens, or to seek to enforce any particular pattern of behavior, further than is necessary to carry out the purpose we have outlined."[85] In England the law of homosexuality was subsequently changed to allow homosexual acts privately carried out between persons twenty-one years of age and over. Similar legal reforms are currently under consideration in the United States.

Abortion has long been defined as a crime. Though a few states today allow the termination of pregnancy on broad medical grounds, most prohibit abortion except when the life of the mother is in danger. Understandably the taking of a life is a moral offense, but the question of whether or not life is taken when an abortion is performed is subject to debate. Various groups have exerted pressure to have their views represented in an appropriate abortion law.[86] Legal reform has taken place in England in part through the well-organized activities of the Abortion Law Reform Association. Similar reform proposals have been advanced in the United States.

[84] The Wolfenden Report, *Report of the Committee on Homosexual Offenses and Prostitution* (New York: Stein and Day, 1963), pp. 143–144.

[85] *Ibid.*, p. 81.

[86] See Edwin M. Schur, *Crimes Without Victims* (Englewood Cliffs, N.J.: Prentice-Hall, 1965), pp. 11–66.

The Planned Parenthood Federation has called for the drafting and adoption of a law that would recognize therapeutic abortion for psychological, eugenic, and humanitarian purposes. The American Law Institute has proposed a model abortion code with similar provisions. Such legalization schemes have been opposed primarily by the Roman Catholic Church. A solution to the problem of abortion is by no means clear. But any legal solution that will be achieved will represent the aims of the most powerful interest groups in society.

Drinking and Drunkenness. Although drinking itself is not a crime, being drunk in public view may result in a criminal arrest. Criminal laws have been formulated to handle persons who openly disturb the public order.[87] The person who drinks excessively may be apprehended simply because he is disturbing the community's sense of propriety or because his being intoxicated may lead to other acts of public nuisance or disturbance. To become intoxicated and exuberant in one's own home is proper middle class behavior. But to be drunk in public is to violate the Puritanical standards of moral strength and personal discipline.

The likelihood exists that public drunkenness will not be treated as crime in the future. A legal change has occurred already in the United States. In 1966 the United States Court of Appeals for the District of Columbia ruled that a chronic alcoholic cannot be convicted of the crime of public drunkenness. Since the defendant to a drunkenness charge "has lost the power of self-control in the use of intoxicating beverages," the court held, the defendant thus lacks necessary criminal intent to be guilty of a crime and cannot therefore be punished under the criminal law. Similar rulings and legislative measures may eventually eliminate a vast portion of criminal offenses.

The current trend in the law associated with drinking and drunkenness is in part an extension of the forces that operated in the repeal of the Eighteenth Amendment. The repeal of the constitu-

[87] Such offenders are discussed in Irwin Deutscher, "The Petty Offender: A Sociological Alien," *Journal of Criminal Law, Criminology and Police Science,* 44 (January–February, 1954), pp. 592–595; David J. Pittman and C. Wayne Gordon, *Revolving Door* (New York: The Free Press of Glencoe, 1958); and Earl Rubington, "The Chronic Drunkenness Offender," *Annals of the American Academy of Political and Social Science,* 315 (January, 1958), pp. 65–72.

tional amendment in 1933 marked the end of the "great experiment" known as Prohibition, which had been established through the Volstead Act and ratified through the Eighteenth Amendment in 1920. It has been observed that the movement to place a ban on drinking and the liquor trade was an assertion of the rural Protestant mind against the urban culture that had emerged at the end of the nineteenth century and the beginning of the twentieth.[88] Prohibition meant for a significant portion of the population the stamping out of sin in an evil society. The rural element was temporarily successful, in the enactment of prohibition legislation, but succumbed within thirteen years to the inevitable.

Within a generalized context of resentment against drinking and what it represented, specific interest groups were active in the movement that led to prohibition legislation. The Prohibition party was founded in 1869 as a third political party to deal with the problem of drinking. Later such organizations as the Anti-Saloon League and the Woman's Christian Temperance Union were founded to crusade against alcohol and the saloon. The lobbying efforts of these groups were effective in bringing about the enactment of state and local temperance legislation. The "dry" lobby groups exerted great pressure against legislators. For example, in the case of the Anti-Saloon League: "With the menace of thousands of votes cast at the next election against any legislator who dared to vote against a dry measure, the League could make the representatives of the people vote against their personal wet convictions."[89] The activities of the dry interest groups accompanied with other forces in American society at the time resulted in the formal enactment of prohibition:

> In this way, the Eighteenth Amendment and the Volstead Act became the law of the land. Through the many roots of prohibition — rural mythology, the psychology of excess, the exploited fears of the mass of the people, the findings of science and medicine, the temper of reform, the efficiency of the dry pressure groups, their mastery of propaganda, the stupidity and self-interest of the brewers and distillers, the necessary trimming of politicians, and the weakness of the elected representatives of the people — through all these channels the sap

[88] Andrew Sinclair, *Era of Excess: A Social History of the Prohibition Movement* (New York: Harper and Row, 1964).

[89] *Ibid.*, p. 105.

> of the dry tree rose until the legal prohibition of the liquor trade burst out new and green in the first month of 1920. The roots had been separate; yet they were all part of a common American seed. They combined and contributed to the strength of the whole. The Anti-Saloon League, bent on its particular reform, was the heir and beneficiary of many interactions in American life. As the drys stood on the threshold of victory at the opening of the twenties, they could see manifest destiny in the success of their cause. They seemed to be the darling army of the Lord. Behind them appeared to lie one mighty pattern and purpose. Before them hung the sweet fruits of victory.[90]

But prohibition was to fail as law as it was to fail as a noble experiment. An outdated morality could not be enforced through criminal law. Rural interests were replaced by the interests of a new social order. "The old order of the country gave way to the new order of the cities. Rural morality was replaced by urban morality, rural voices by urban voices, rural votes by urban votes. A novel culture of skyscrapers and suburbs grew up to oust the civilization of the general store and Main Street. A technological revolution broadcast a common culture over the various folkways of the land. It is only in context of this immense social change, the metamorphosis of Abraham Lincoln's America into the America of Franklin Roosevelt, that the phenomenon of national prohibition can be seen and understood. It was part of the whole process, the last hope of the declining village. It was less of a farce than a tragedy, less of a mistake than a proof of changing times."[91]

The Use of Drugs. The Harrison Act passed by Congress in 1914 had the effect of defining users of certain drugs as criminals. In technical language the Harrison Act required that all drug-handlers be registered and that the fact of securing drugs be made a matter of record.[92] But through the interpretation of the act, the court rulings in specific cases, and the enactment of supplementary laws,

[90] *Ibid.*, p. 170.

[91] *Ibid.*, pp. 5–6. Laws, such as that of prohibition, are discussed as responses to the lack of consensus on norms in Joseph R. Gusfield, "Moral Passage: The Symbolic Process in Public Designations of Deviance," *Social Problems*, 15 (Fall, 1967), pp. 175–188.

[92] Alfred R. Lindesmith, *The Addict and the Law* (Bloomington: Indiana University Press, 1965), chap. 1.

criminal sanctions were provided for the unauthorized possession, sale, or transfer of drugs. In addition to the federal statutes and rulings, the states have enacted their own antinarcotic laws. In the United States, penalties for violation of drug laws have become more severe in recent years. The possession of narcotics, for example, is now a felony instead of a misdemeanor.

Drug laws have not only defined users as criminals but have created a generalized public suspicion and fear of drug users and addicts. Today the use of any type of drug among a segment of the population — be the drug addictive or not, a narcotic drug, marihuana, or a psychedelic drug — produces a public response that almost certainly results in the call for repressive legislation. Much of this atmosphere has been created by the actions of the Federal Bureau of Narcotics. The Bureau has, in particular, been responsible for administrative decisions which have served as the basis for most of the drug legislation.[93] The Bureau of Narcotics has defined its interests as total restriction of drugs and complete enforcement of the law. These interests have become the standards by which the public now views and officially acts upon the use of drugs.

In sharp contrast to the American drug policy is the policy of Great Britain. In England drug addiction is considered a medical rather than a legal problem. The addict, therefore, is not regarded as a criminal. The Dangerous Drug Act of 1920 defined the addict as a patient who may receive drugs upon the medical discretion of a physician.[94] As a result, drug addicts in England do not have to engage in criminal activities to maintain a drug supply. Because of the British approach to drug addiction, it is now being argued, primarily by academicians, that the American policy on drug use is unsound and that in order to deal more effectively with the drug problem official policy on drugs should be changed.[95] Lindesmith

[93] See Alfred R. Lindesmith, "Federal Law and Drug Addiction," *Social Problems,* 7 (Summer, 1959), pp. 48–57; Howard S. Becker, *Outsiders: Studies in the Sociology of Deviance* (New York: The Free Press, 1963), pp. 135–146; Donald T. Dickson, "Bureaucracy and Morality: An Organizational Perspective on a Moral Crusade," *Social Problems,* 16 (Fall, 1968), pp. 143–156.

[94] Alfred R. Lindesmith, "The British System of Narcotics Control," *Law and Contemporary Problems,* 22 (Winter, 1957), pp. 138–154; Edwin M. Schur, *Narcotic Addiction in Britain and America: The Impact of Public Policy* (Bloomington: Indiana University Press, 1962).

[95] Lindesmith, *The Addict and the Law;* Schur, *Narcotic Addiction in Britain and America.*

has made several proposals: (1) antinarcotic laws should be written so that addicts do not have to violate them solely because they are addicts; (2) drug users are admittedly handicapped by their habits but they should nevertheless be encouraged to engage in productive labor even when they are using drugs; (3) cures should not be imposed upon narcotics victims by force but should be voluntary; (4) police officers should be prevented from exploiting drug addicts as stool pigeons solely because they are addicts; and (5) heroin and morphine addicts should be handled according to the same principles and moral precepts applied to barbituate and alcohol addicts because these three forms of addiction are basically similar.[96] Greater understanding of drug use and addiction is being gained. Efforts are being made to handle drug addiction as a disease and not as a criminal problem. The danger that accompanies this trend is the formulation of programs that may be both as punitive and unsuccessful as current legal practices.

The Law of Vagrancy. Vagrancy has been a crime in virtually every state in the United States. Since the state statutes have had their heritage in English law, the common law meaning of the term "vagrancy" is either stated or implied in the statutes. Accordingly, a vagrant is an idle person, beggar, or person wandering without being able to give a good account of himself. Most important to the vagrancy concept, then, is the nature of the person. "Vagrancy is the principal crime in which the offense consists of being a certain kind of person rather than in having done or failed to do certain acts."[97]

Vagrancy laws are widely used on the community level to detain various kinds of questionable and suspicious persons. The vagrancy laws and their enforcement thus are aimed at potential criminals, are used sometimes in lieu of other charges, and often are the means to rid the community of those who do not meet the standards of the respectable members.

The crime of vagrancy has been derived from early English laws

[96] Lindesmith, *The Addict and the Law,* p. 270.

[97] Forrest W. Lacey, "Vagrancy and Other Crimes of Personal Condition," *Harvard Law Review,* 66 (May, 1953), p. 1203. Also see Caleb Foote, "Vagrancy-Type Law and Its Administration," *University of Pennsylvania Law Review,* 104 (March, 1956), pp. 603–650.

which came into existence during the fourteenth century in response to changing social conditions.[98] The first full-fledged vagrancy law was enacted in 1349. The statute made a crime of giving alms to able-bodied, unemployed persons and established that such persons would be criminally punished. The law and supplementary statutes were formulated, after the Black Death and the flight of workers from landowners, for the purpose of supplying needed labor: "There is little question that these statutes were designed for one express purpose: to force laborers (whether personally free or unfree) to accept employment at a low wage in order to insure the landowner an adequate supply of labor at a price he could afford to pay."[99]

Changing social conditions in England made it unnecessary to enforce the vagrancy statutes. But by the sixteenth century, with increased emphasis on commerce and industry, vagrancy law was revived. However, because of changes in the social structure, there was a shift in the focal concern of the law from the regulation of labor to the control of criminal activities. The following summarizes the development of the law of vagrancy in early English society:

> The foregoing analysis of the vagrancy laws has demonstrated that these laws were a legislative innovation which reflected the socially perceived necessity of providing an abundance of cheap labor to landowners during a period when serfdom was breaking down and when the pool of available labor was depleted. With the eventual breakup of feudalism the need for such laws eventually disappeared and the increased dependence of the economy upon industry and commerce rendered the former use of the vagrancy statutes unnecessary. As a result, for a substantial period the vagrancy statutes were dormant, undergoing only minor changes and, presumably, being applied infrequently. Finally, the vagrancy laws were subjected to considerable alteration through a shift in the focal concern of the statutes. Whereas in their inception the laws focused upon the "idle" and "those refusing to labor" after the turn of the sixteenth century an emphasis came to be upon "rogues," "vagabonds," and others who were suspected of being engaged in

[98] William J. Chambliss, "A Sociological Analysis of the Law of Vagrancy," *Social Problems,* 12 (Summer, 1964), pp. 67–77. Also see George Rusche and Otto Kirchheimer, *Punishment and Social Structure* (New York: Columbia University Press, 1939), pp. 32–41.

[99] Chambliss, "A Sociological Analysis of the Law of Vagrancy," p. 69.

> criminal activities. During this period the focus was particularly upon "roadmen" who preyed upon citizens who transported goods from one place to another. The increased importance of commerce to England during this period made it necessary that some protection be given persons engaged in this enterprise and the vagrancy statutes provided one source for such protection by re-focusing the acts to be included under these statutes.[100]

In other words, the formulations and changes in the vagrancy statutes were the result of the efforts of powerful interest groups. "The vagrancy laws emerged in order to provide the powerful landowners with a ready supply of cheap labor. When this was no longer seen as necessary and particularly when the landowners were no longer dependent upon cheap labor nor were they a powerful interest group in society the laws became dormant. Finally a new interest group emerged and was seen as being of great importance to the society and the laws were then altered so as to afford some protection to this group."[101]

With only minor variations the vagrancy statutes remained essentially the same through the seventeenth and eighteenth centuries. The statutes were adopted by American colonies and states to serve the same purposes they were performing in English society. Today the vagrancy laws continue to provide a source of control of persons and activities regarded as undesirable in the community.

However, the vagrancy laws are currently being evaluated and questioned. One writer has stated, "The time is surely at hand to modernize the vagrancy concept or, better yet, to abandon it altogether for statutes which will harmonize with notions of a decent, fair, and just administration of criminal justice, and which will at the same time make it possible for police departments to discharge their responsibilities in a reasonable manner."[102] Along these lines, a significant change in vagrancy law has been made in the state of New York. In 1967 the New York Court of Appeals ruled unconstitutional a statute of 1788 that provided for the arrest of persons with no visible means of support.[103] The court ruled that

100 *Ibid.*, p. 76.

101 *Ibid.*, p. 77.

102 Arthur H. Sherry, "Vagrants, Rogues, and Vagabonds—Old Concepts in Need of Revision," *California Law Review*, 48 (October, 1960), p. 567.

103 Reported in *The New York Times*, July 8, 1967, pp. 1 and 9.

the law "constitutes an overreaching of the proper limitations of the police power." Furthermore, the court said that the statute has little use "other than, perhaps, as a means of harassing, punishing or apprehending suspected criminals in an unconstitutional fashion." The old statute was declared unconstitutional on the ground that it interfered with the liberty of a citizen to conduct himself as he sees fit as long as he does not interfere with the rights of others. Such repeal, which is likely to occur in other states as well, will end the use of laws of the vagrancy type to enforce community interests. Perhaps other means of maintaining public order, legal or extralegal, will be substituted for vagrancy law. But in this case at least, the forces that would protect individual rights have triumphed over those forces that would at the same time control individuals in the protection of public order.

3

Application of Criminal Definitions

CHAPTER FOUR

Enforcement of Criminal Law

Once human conduct has been abstractly defined as criminal in the criminal law, criminal definitions are concretely applied by agents of the law. Moreover, criminal definitions are applied to situations, persons, and behavior at a number of legal stages. The stages include the enforcement of the law, prosecution, court proceedings, sentencing, and finally the release of cases from the legal system. Shown in Figure 4.1 are the specific stages of the American legal system and the movement of criminal cases through the system. As indicated, the police observe or have reported to them instances which are regarded as violations of the criminal law. An arrest may then be made and a charge may be entered. During prosecution a decision is made whether to continue a case or to drop it. Through bargaining the defendant may plead guilty to a charge or may stand trial. Upon conviction the accused is sentenced. Following the completion of the sentence, cases are processed out of the legal system. The most striking feature of the legal system is the great number of alternatives available in the enforcement and administration of the criminal law.

This chapter is devoted solely to the sociology of law enforcement. Enforcement will be construed narrowly as the *arrest* of persons suspected of committing a crime. Arrest is here regarded as a distinct operational step which involves decisions to interfere with the freedom of persons suspected of criminal conduct.[1] It is one of the stages

[1] See Wayne R. LaFave, *Arrest: The Decision to Take a Suspect into Custody* (Boston: Little, Brown, 1965).

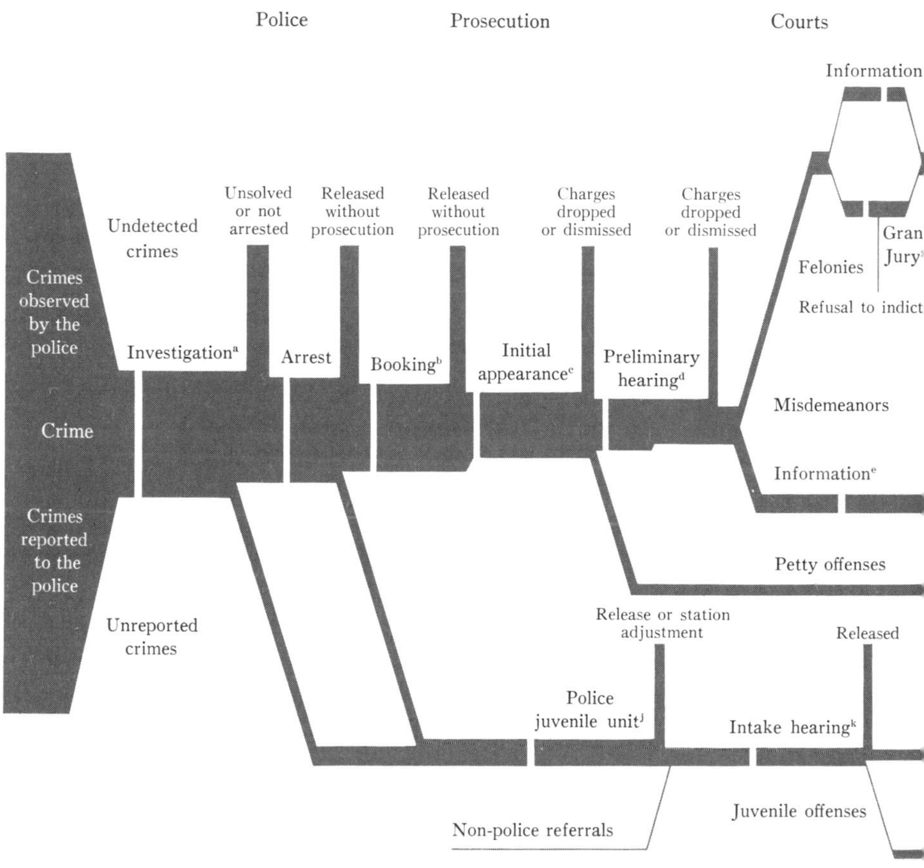

[a] May continue until trial.

[b] Administrative record of arrest. First step at which temporary release on bail may be available.

[c] Before magistrate, commissioner, or justice of peace. Formal notice of charge, advice of rights. Bail set. Summary trials for petty offenses usually conducted here without further processing.

[d] Preliminary testing of evidence against defendant. Charge may be reduced. No separate preliminary hearing for misdemeanors in some systems.

[e] Charge filed by prosecutor on basis of information submitted by police or citizens. Alternative to grand jury indictment; often used in felonies, almost always in misdemeanors.

Source: The President's Commission on Law Enforcement and Administration of Justice, *The Challenge of Crime in a Free Society* (Washington, D.C.: U.S. Government Printing Office, 1967), pp. 8-9.

FIGURE 4.1
The American Legal System

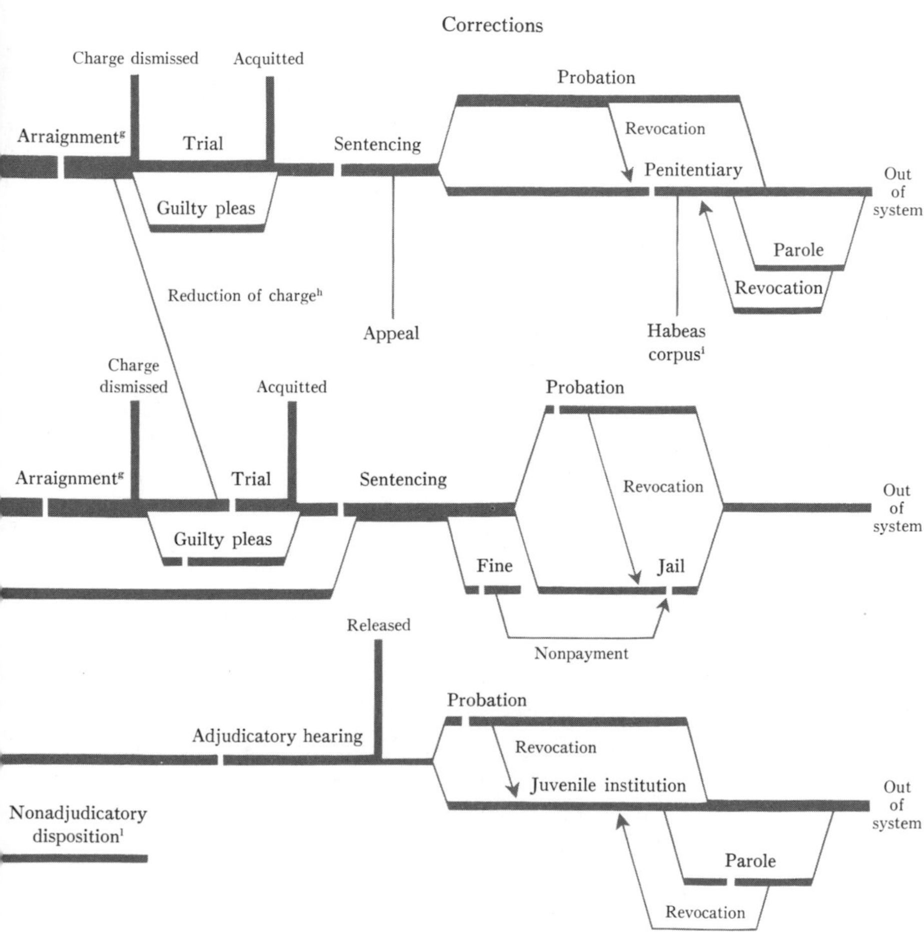

[f] Reviews whether government evidence sufficient to justify trial. Some states have no grand jury system; others seldom use it.

[g] Appearance for plea; defendant elects trial by judge or jury (if available); counsel for indigent usually appointed here in felonies. Often not at all in other cases.

[h] Charge may be reduced at any time prior to trial in return for plea of guilty or for other reasons.

[i] Challenge on constitutional grounds to legality of detention. May be sought at any point in process.

[j] Police often hold informal hearings, dismiss or adjust many cases without further processing.

[k] Probation officer decides desirability of further court action.

[l] Welfare agency, social services, counseling, medical care, etc., for cases where adjudicatory handling not needed.

at which persons and behaviors may be defined as criminal. The application of criminal definitions beyond arrest — in the course of prosecution, conviction, and sentencing — will be covered in Chapters 5 and 6.

POLICE DISCRETION

The criminal code does not provide specific instructions for the enforcement of the law. How the law is enforced is largely a matter of *discretion*. Yet it is commonly assumed that the police can and should fully enforce the criminal law by arresting all persons who violate the law. The ideal of *full enforcement* is preserved officially in formal law as well as in popular conception.[2] Criminal statutes are so stated as to imply that the duty of the police is to faithfully enforce all the laws, against everyone, in all circumstances, at all times. The common stereotype of the policeman is that of the ministerial officer whose function it is to detect crime, gather evidence, and make arrests. Police themselves tend to reinforce this conception by denying that decisions are involved in their work or that informal standards exist for making their decisions.

Full enforcement of criminal law, however, is not a realistic expectation. Numerous limitations and circumstances preclude the possibility of enforcing the law to the fullest extent. First, *procedural* restrictions prohibit the enforcement of the law beyond the lawful rights of the individual citizen. Second, *interpretational* latitude, resulting primarily from ambiguity in the wording of many statutes, permits considerable discretion as to what constitutes a criminal offense. Third, *technical* difficulties confound law enforcement, such as limitation of police time, personnel, and equipment in the detection and investigation of crime. Fourth, *organizational* demands of local police departments provide guides for both the enforcement and nonenforcement of criminal law. Fifth, *ideological* orientations or values of policemen provide a basis for selective law enforcement. Sixth,

[2] Joseph Goldstein, "Police Discretion Not to Invoke the Criminal Process: Low Visibility Decisions in the Administration of Justice," *Yale Law Journal*, 69 (March, 1960), pp. 543–594; Sanford H. Kadish, "Legal Norm and Discretion in the Police and Sentencing Processes," *Harvard Law Review*, 75 (March, 1962), pp. 904–931; Edward L. Barrett, Jr., "Police Practices and the Law—From Arrest to Release of Charge," *California Law Review*, 50 (March, 1962), pp. 11–55.

numerous *societal* pressures prevent full enforcement of some criminal laws. Included in this last category of reasons for partial enforcement are such factors as the lack of correspondence between particular criminal statutes and current norms, the failure of victims and the public to report offenses, and the harmful social consequences that might follow the enforcement of certain criminal laws. Whatever the reasons, law enforcement is a matter of decision-making. Discretion is the principal characteristic of law enforcement.

Police discretion rarely becomes known to the public. Most persons have little idea of the extent of discretionary decisions in law enforcement and little knowledge of the ways in which discretion operates. There is instead a generalized public feeling that since discretion involves personal decisions on the part of police, the operation of such discretion is totally improper in a democratic society. Solutions such as the following are currently being suggested in regard to the problem of the discretionary power of police:

> The first step is to elevate police discretion from the sub-rosa position it now occupies; the role of police as decision-makers must be expressly recognized. Then, as has been found possible with respect to other administrative agencies, the areas in which discretion properly may be exercised must be delimited, principles to govern its exercise must be established, and effective means of control must be discovered.[3]

No matter what solutions may be proposed and implemented, for our immediate purpose it is sufficient to recognize that discretion does exist and that it is basic to law enforcement. From a sociological standpoint, the purpose is to understand the operation of police discretion. At a crucial stage in the legal process persons are defined as criminal because police act in certain ways rather than in other ways.

LEGAL REGULATION OF LAW ENFORCEMENT

Law enforcement takes place within a tenuous framework of social control and legal regulation. The issue of the control of police prac-

[3] Wayne R. LaFave, "The Police and Nonenforcement of the Law," *Wisconsin Law Review,* 1962 (January–March, 1962), p. 239. Also see LaFave, *Arrest,* p. 153.

tices lays bare one of the fundamental problems of modern society: "A democracy, like all other societies, needs order and security, but it also and equally requires civil liberty. This complexity of need creates difficult theoretical and practical problems."[4] Any resolution of the conflicting demands of order and freedom can be, at best, one in which the demands are maintained in a state of tension.

The policeman is placed in the middle of the control-freedom dilemma. He is charged with the enforcement of a multitude of criminal laws and is at the same time expected to observe the rights of the individual. His decision to invoke the law is basically a decision to restrict the individual. Yet the policeman's function of control is itself regulated to ensure that the suspect receives his *legal* rights once his freedom has been restricted. That police are often charged with brutality and lawlessness reflects the difficulty of both attempting to control human conduct and providing for the protection of the rights of the individual.

Most of the law that regulates police behavior has developed from specific cases in which defendants have questioned the procedures used in their criminal convictions. Thus courts, in contrast to legislatures and executive agencies, have been the principal law-givers in the regulation of law enforcement. In recent years, primarily by default, the Supreme Court has sought to provide legal guarantees for the protection of the person against the actions of the state. Court rulings have been made in reference to a number of issues directly related to law enforcement. Decisions have been made in respect to such related matters as arrest warrants, search and seizure, interrogation, confessions, wiretapping and eavesdropping, the use of informers, and the right of counsel. As a result of the active role of the court in these matters the charge is being made that the courts are moving beyond their proper function. Courts are also being accused of laying down rules that impede law enforcement. The more enlightened criticism, however, would be that other lawmaking institutions are neglecting their function and, most of all, that the conduct of those who enforce the criminal law must be adequately regulated in a free society.[5]

[4] Jerome Hall, "Police and Law in Democratic Society," *Indiana Law Journal,* 28 (Winter, 1953), p. 162.

[5] See Herbert L. Packer, "Policing the Police," *The New Republic* (September 4, 1965), pp. 17–21.

The Supreme Court decisions on law enforcement are founded on three provisions of the Constitution. The Fourth Amendment provides: "The right of the people to be secure in their persons, houses, papers, and effects, against unreasonable searches and seizures, shall not be violated, and no warrants shall issue but upon probable cause, supported by oath or affirmation, and particularly describing the place to be searched, and the persons or things to be seized." The Fifth Amendment provides that "no person . . . shall be compelled in any criminal case to be a witness against himself, nor be deprived of life, liberty, or property, without due process of law." And the Fourteenth Amendment provides that "no state shall . . . deprive any person of life, liberty, or property without due process of law, nor deny to any person within its jurisdiction the equal protection of the laws." A number of Supreme Court decisions, particularly in recent years, have resulted from the review of criminal cases in which these constitutional guarantees have been jeopardized.[6]

One of the first constitutional tests of law enforcement practices confronted by the Supreme Court was in the *Weeks v. United States* case of 1914. In establishing the "exclusionary rule" in that case, the Court ruled that evidence obtained by illegal means must be excluded from criminal procedure. With the *McNabb v. United States* case in 1943 the Supreme Court ruled that confessions are inadmissible if obtained by federal officers during an unlawful detention. The McNabb decision was elaborated upon in 1957 in *Mallory v. United States*. The Court ruled in this case that confessions are inadmissible when they are obtained from an arrestee who has not been properly brought before a magistrate. In 1961 the Court ruled in *Mapp v. Ohio* that evidence obtained through unreasonable searches and seizures must be excluded from state and federal criminal trials. The *Gideon v. Wainwright* decision of 1963 ensured the right of counsel for defendants. The right of counsel was further specified in 1964 in

[6] Supreme Court decisions on law enforcement are discussed by, among others, Richard C. Donnelly, "Police Authority and Practices," *Annals of the American Academy of Political and Social Science,* 339 (January, 1962), pp. 90–110; David Robinson, Jr., "Massiah, Escobedo, and Rationales for the Exclusions of Confessions," *Journal of Criminal Law, Criminology and Police Science,* 56 (December, 1965), pp. 412–431; Bernard Weisberg, "Police Interrogation of Arrested Persons: A Skeptical View," *Journal of Criminal Law, Criminology and Police Science,* 52 (May–June, 1961), pp. 21–46; "A Symposium on the Supreme Court and the Police: 1966," *Journal of Criminal Law, Criminology and Police Science,* 57 (September, 1966), pp. 237–311.

Massiah v. United States and *Escobedo v. Illinois.* The decisions of 1964 provide that the accused in custody may not be questioned until the request for legal counsel has been complied with. Specific guidelines for law enforcement and minimum procedural safeguards were established in 1966 in *Miranda v. Arizona.* Cases such as these will continue to be decided by the courts as the divergent values on control and freedom continue to be defined and balanced. Moreover, legislative action as well as decisions by the courts will add to the controversial issues involved in the legal regulation of law enforcement.

Ultimately the regulation of law enforcement must come from sources other than governmental agencies. In democratic society the police themselves bear part of the responsibility for safeguarding the rights of the citizen and at the same time maintaining peace and order in the society. Police must develop a professional orientation that is sensitive to individual rights. Efficient enforcement of the law is not the sole end of the police function. Police are also responsible for a humane law enforcement policy. An argument for the development of a *legal* professionalism among police has been strongly presented:

> The needed philosophy of professionalism must rest on a set of values conveying the idea that the police are as much an institution dedicated to the achievement of legality in society as they are an official social organization designed to control misconduct through the invocation of punitive sanctions. The problem of police in a democratic society is not merely a matter of obtaining newer police cars, a higher order technical equipment or of recruiting men who have to their credit more years of education. What must occur is a significant alteration in the ideology of police, so that police "professionalization" rests on the values of a democratic legal order, rather than on technological proficiency.[7]

LAW ENFORCEMENT SYSTEMS

Globally and historically law enforcement assumes numerous forms. Even within some contemporary societies the forms of police sys-

[7] Jerome H. Skolnick, *Justice Without Trial: Law Enforcement in Democratic Society* (New York: John Wiley and Sons, 1966), pp. 238–239.

tems are varied. One of the most important distinguishing characteristics of law enforcement systems is the degree to which they are centralized within their respective states. With some obvious exceptions, democratic countries usually permit local autonomy in police administration and authoritarian states tend to centralize police control. England, Wales, and Scotland have scores of local police forces. Belgium has dual police systems for the national and local levels. In Denmark all police activities are administered by functionaries of the crown. For the most part, European countries have tended to follow the French pattern of a national police charged with overall law enforcement, maintenance of public order, and investigation of major crimes. In such countries a branch of the national police performs local duties, but routine matters are principally the responsibility of locally recruited forces. Law enforcement systems in the United States and Canada, on the other hand, consist of parallel national, state, and local police forces.

The most centralized of law enforcement systems are those organized explicitly for the purpose of political control. Governments which have maintained such systems have been known in their time as "police states." Notable examples include the Nazi Gestapo, Mussolini's ORVA, and the Soviet Union's NKVD. The FBI in the United States is actually maintained in part as a political police force, enforcing laws on subversion, espionage, and sedition.

Outside of the FBI, and a number of federal quasi-judicial agencies with law enforcement powers, the approach to law enforcement in the United States has been to avoid a centralized police force. There never has been a federal system for the control of local law enforcement. While the FBI suggests a uniform method for the reporting of crime statistics, the control of police behavior is a matter of state and local authority.

Although the British police system today is controlled to a considerable extent by the national government, whereas the American system is locally autonomous, law enforcement in the United States has its origins in English legal institutions. The organization of a police force for the purpose of detecting and arresting law violators, protecting the innocent, preventing crime, and maintaining order in the community can be traced to the development of various kinds of peace officers in England.[8] In early England, local citizens were mu-

[8] See Leon Rodzinowicz, *A History of English Criminal Law and Its Admin-*

tually responsible, through the "pledge" system, for the maintenance of law and order. Eventually local noblemen appointed constables to enforce the law. When the local areas, known as "hundreds," were grouped to form "shires," the office of the "shire-reeve" came into being. During the reign of Edward I (1272–1307) the first official police forces were established in the large towns of England. These "watch and ward" officers were charged with protecting property and arresting offenders between sunset and daybreak. In 1326 Edward II created the office of the justice of the peace to assist the sheriff in policing the country. The constable, however, remained the primary law enforcement officer in all the towns throughout England.

As long as England was a rural country the existing offices of law enforcement were adequate. But by the middle of the eighteenth century, with the growth of fairly large towns and cities, innovations in law enforcement were needed. One of the most important experiments in law enforcement was Henry Fielding's appointment of a foot patrol (later known as the "Bow Street Runners") in the Bow Street magistracy of London. However, such a small local force could not meet the law enforcement needs of the urban area. So critical had the situation become at the close of the eighteenth century that committees of the House of Commons called for a better system of protecting the public. Finally in the early years of the nineteenth century a committee of the Commons issued a report that investigated the increase in crime and urged a change in the method of policing the metropolis. Sir Robert Peel, the person responsible for the establishment of the committee, and Home Secretary, introduced a police reform bill which was passed by Parliament in 1829.[9] The Metropolitan Police Act of 1829 thus established for London a police force separate from the old constabulary system and served as the model for other cities in Great Britain.

The American colonies in the seventeenth and eighteenth centuries

---

istration from 1750 (London: Stevens & Sons, 1956), vols. 2 and 3; Alwyn Solmes, *The English Policeman 1871–1935* (London: George Allen & Unwin, 1935); William Alfred Morris, *The Medieval English Sheriff to 1300* (Manchester: University Press, 1927).

[9] J. L. Lymon, "The Metropolitan Police Act of 1829: An Analysis of Certain Events Influencing the Passage and Character of the Metropolitan Police Act in England," *Journal of Criminal Law, Criminology and Police Science,* 55 (March, 1964), pp. 141–154.

adopted the contemporary law enforcement offices of England.[10] American villages and rural areas had their night-watchmen, constables, sheriffs, and justices of the peace. Following the creation of police forces in the English cities in the early nineteenth century, American cities established their own forces. London's police plan was adopted by New York in 1844. During the next ten years similar police systems were organized in Chicago, Boston, and Philadelphia.[11] By the early 1900's most cities in the United States had unified police forces of their own.

Law enforcement in the United States today cannot be viewed as a single system. Although some 420,000 persons are employed in approximately 40,000 law enforcement agencies, the law enforcement duties vary considerably. There are at least five types of law enforcement systems in the United States, conforming roughly to the major levels of government: (1) the police agencies of the federal government; (2) the state police forces and criminal investigation agencies of the fifty states; (3) the sheriffs and deputy sheriffs in over 3,000 counties, plus a few county police forces which either duplicate the sheriffs' police jurisdiction or virtually displace it; (4) the police of a thousand cities and over 20,000 townships or New England towns, to which must be added an unknown number of magisterial districts and county districts in the south and west; and (5) the police of 15,000 villages, boroughs, and incorporated towns, together with a small number of forces serving public quasi-corporations and ad hoc districts.[12] These systems of law enforcement are interrelated in their functions and at times overlap in their jurisdictions.

Even within the various systems of law enforcement there are specific police agencies. On the federal level, for example, there are such agencies with law enforcement powers as the Federal Bureau of Investigation, the Secret Service, the Bureau of Narcotics, Post Office Inspectors, the Bureau of Internal Revenue, the Bureau of Customs,

[10] Cyrus Harreld Karreker, *The Seventeenth-Century Sheriff: A Comparative Study of the Sheriff in England and Chesapeake Colonies* (Chapel Hill: University of North Carolina Press, 1930); Julius Goebel and T. Raymond Naughton, *Law Enforcement in Colonial New York* (New York: The Commonwealth Fund, 1944).

[11] For a history of the evolution of the police force in Boston, see Roger Lane, *Policing the City: Boston, 1822–1885* (Cambridge: Harvard University Press, 1967).

[12] Bruce Smith, *Police Systems in the United States,* 2nd rev. ed. (New York: Harper, 1960).

the Immigration Border Patrol, and the Alcohol Tax Unit of the Department of the Treasury. In addition, the federal government maintains the United States Marshal as a law enforcement agent whose duty it is to preserve order in the courtroom, handle subpoena and summons, seize goods, transport prisoners, and serve as a disbursing officer.[13]

Law enforcement on the state level was not established in the United States until the first part of this century. In 1905 Pennsylvania organized the first state police force. By World War II, all states had their own police forces. Today the state police forces perform such varied functions as highway patrol, fire investigation, liquor inspection, juvenile offender arrest, and property inspection.[14] State police also provide a number of services to local police forces, including criminal identification, laboratory services, and communication services.

Outside the framework of civil law enforcement is a type of law enforcement usually obscured from public view: the *private police*. Private police agencies, such as Pinkerton's National Detective Agency, came into being in the middle of the last century when private companies desired protection that could not be afforded them by civil police. Railroads, coal companies, and iron ore companies in particular employed their own police forces to control theft and robbery, and in some cases to prevent and break strikes of workers against the companies.[15] Today private police are employed by numerous kinds of businesses, industries, and institutions. They are used by firms to guard property, apprehend thieves, investigate offenses, and to detect fraud and embezzlement. Several hundred national and local agencies are engaged in the private enforcement of criminal law. Although private police do not usually make arrests, suspects they apprehend may be turned over to civil police for official arrest and prosecution.

The discussion of law enforcement in this chapter will be devoted principally to civil law enforcement on the local level. Not only has

[13] Rita W. Cooley, "The Office of United States Marshal," *Western Political Quarterly,* 12 (March, 1959), pp. 123–140.

[14] Jack J. Preiss and Howard J. Ehrlich, *An Examination of Role Theory: The Case of the State Police* (Lincoln: University of Nebraska Press, 1966).

[15] J. P. Shalloo, *Private Police: With Special Reference to Pennsylvania* (Philadelphia: American Academy of Political and Social Science, Monograph No. 1, 1933).

most sociological research been concentrated on *local police activity,* but the majority of persons defined as criminal receive their special status from the police of the villages, towns, and cities. The principal imposers of criminal definitions at the law enforcement stage of the legal process are the police of local communities.

COMMUNITY CONTEXT OF LAW ENFORCEMENT

In a sense there are as many systems of law enforcement as there are communities. Each police department must operate within a community. To a considerable degree, then, the differences in law enforcement can be attributed to the concrete social setting in which police operate.

The role of the police in the community in relation to the duties of law enforcement has always been the source of a major dilemma. The dilemma is brought on by the issue of whether the police are to be involved in community affairs, or whether they are to be isolated from the community. Too much involvement might negate the possibilities of fulfilling the ideal of fair and impartial handling of cases, while too much isolation removes the police from an understanding of the needs of the community. A delicate balance of the alternatives is all that can be expected at best.

Certain natural forces, because of the requirements of law enforcement, contribute to the isolation of the police in any community.[16] Much of police activity involves intrusion into the private interests of the citizen. To separate from one's daily life those who are charged with the detection and arrest of one's person is a rather logical reaction to the police. This reaction is reinforced by the traditional public conception of fear and mistrust of the police. The police, in addition, provide the public with a constant reminder of the deviant aspects of human behavior. The actions of the police represent the social sanctions and degradations that may be a consequence of deviation within the community.

One other factor that tends to isolate the police is found in the organization and procedure of police work itself. The requirements

[16] John P. Clark, "Isolation of the Police: A Comparison of the British and American Situations," *Journal of Criminal Law, Criminology and Police Science,* 56 (September, 1965), pp. 307–319.

of patrol, investigation, surveillance, and the like necessitate a clear-cut separation of the police from the public in order that the functions may be fulfilled. Most of the operating policies of the police are beyond public scrutiny; that is, they are secretive and known only to the police themselves. Some forced community isolation seems necessary, because of what is expected of the police.

To view police activity solely from the standpoint of law enforcement is perhaps to miss the crux of the role of the police in the community. It may be argued that the principal function of the police is to promote peace in the community.[17] All communities operate and survive through the resolution of internal tension and conflicts. The police serve as one of the agencies that assist in maintaining some community integration and order. Through their various activities, the police bring discipline to personal disputes that arise from more basic value conflicts in the various parts of the community.

Thus, in his day-to-day activity, the policeman is both a "law officer" and a "peace officer." In a sense, however, the two functions cannot be separated. The policeman in his attempt to maintain peace in the community decides whether or not to invoke the law on the basis of the actual situation.[18] In some situations "peace keeping" may best be achieved by not making an arrest. In others an arrest may appear to be the most appropriate means of maintaining order in the community.

In part, maintaining peace in the community involves giving support to some members of the community. Many disputes that arise require human support. Even in controlling one member of the community, the policeman may be lending support to another. The supportive role of the police has been documented in a study of the calls received at the desk of a metropolitan police department.[19] In an analysis of the telephone calls, it was found that nearly half of the calls were requests for support of some kind. The calls for support were concerned with personal problems and consisted of requests for

[17] Michael Banton, *The Policeman in the Community* (London: Tavistock, 1964), p. 127.

[18] Egon Bittner, "The Police on Skid-Row: A Study of Peace Keeping," *American Sociological Review, 2* (October, 1967), pp. 699–715. Also see James Q. Wilson, *Varieties of Police Behavior* (Cambridge: Harvard University Press, 1968), pp. 16–56.

[19] Elaine Cumming, Ian Cumming, and Laura Edell, "Policeman as Philosopher, Guide and Friend," *Social Problems,* 12 (Winter, 1965), pp. 276–286.

health services (such as ambulance escorts, investigation of accidents, suicide attempts), children's problems (complaints about trespassing or destructive behavior), and the behavior of incapacitated persons. Other calls consisted of requests for assistance regarding personal disputes and quarrels, violence or protection from potential violence, and requests for assistance regarding missing persons and the behavior of youths. The policeman thus performs many actions that are not directly related to enforcement of the law per se, but are instead supportive of other aspects of the welfare of the community.

One of the most important sources of variation in the actions of police is found in the *expectations* of law enforcement in different kinds of communities. First, communities differ from one another in regard to the kinds of behavior that should receive criminal sanction. The correspondence between the criminal law and what is actually condemned may vary considerably from one community to another. Within one community, or a segment of a community, arrest of a violent spouse may be expected, while such an arrest would be entirely inappropriate in another community or segment. Second, communities differ in their norms on the seeking of assistance from the police. While one community may prescribe that complaints be made to the police, another may restrict the citizen's use of the police. Third, community attitudes toward the police vary considerably. In the villages of Great Britain the policeman is perceived as an individual known for his personal characteristics.[20] On the other hand, in the bigger towns policemen are seen more as members of a social category. Also, in some British working class neighborhoods the police are identified with the propertied classes and are at times viewed as enemies. These feelings appear to be even more marked in the industrial regions of the west of Scotland. Such community variations in attitudes toward the police have their effect both upon the use of the police by community members and upon the way in which police respond to situations in which law breaking may be involved.

Perhaps the most significant characteristic that accounts for community differences in law enforcement is the extent to which the community is homogeneous in such matters as cultural values, social class, race, and occupation. A homogeneous community tends to have fairly well defined expectations in regard to appropriate community

[20] Banton, *The Policeman in the Community,* p. 210.

behavior. The consequence for law enforcement is that the police in a homogeneous community operate as an integral part of the community, enforcement of the law being guided by the way such enforcement relates to the order of the community.

In a heterogeneous community, in comparison, the police must operate more by the formal law than by community expectations. The police in a homogeneous community may detect more law violations than those in a heterogeneous community, but the police in a homogeneous community handle the cases informally rather than through the formality of an arrest. Furthermore, in a homogeneous community, violators of the law may be referred back to the community for disposition rather than to the legal process. Invocation of the law may be the only means of maintaining order in the heterogeneous community. Thus, in the homogeneous community a wide scope of law-violating behavior is handled informally by the police, while in the heterogeneous community criminal sanctions are more readily applied to the same behaviors.

The relationship between community homogeneity and law enforcement is found in a study of the handling of juvenile cases by police in four different communities in the Pittsburgh area.[21] The research consisted of an investigation of the differential selection by the police of juvenile offenders for court appearance. It was found that there were clear differences in the rates of juvenile arrests and court referrals between the four different kinds of communities. The large industrial community ("Steel City") had a juvenile arrest rate of 37.3 per 1,000 juvenile population, in comparison to a rate of 12.4 in the residential and commercial community ("Trade City"), 34.8 in the small industrial community ("Mill Town"), and 49.7 in the well-to-do residential community ("Manor Heights"). Through the further analysis of police records and a series of interviews with police, Goldman concluded that there were indeed community differentials in the handling of juvenile cases by the police.

Several patterns of handling cases of juvenile offenders in the four communities were distinguished in the above research. The patterns appeared to be a function of the relations between the police and the community. In general, the police attempted in each community to

[21] Nathan Goldman, *The Differential Selection of Juvenile Offenders for Court Appearance* (New York: National Council on Crime and Delinquency, 1963).

reflect what they considered to be the attitudes of the community toward delinquency. Differentials in arrests according to the type of relation between the police and the community were summarized as follows: (1) "Where there exists an objective, impersonal relation between the police and the public, court referral rates will be high and there will be little discrimination with respect to seriousness of offense, race, and sex of the offender"; (2) "Where there exists a personal face-to-face relation between the police and the public, there will be more discriminations with respect to court referral of an arrested juvenile."[22] The research thus showed that law enforcement is associated with the role of the police in the specific community. Differences in the relation between the community and the police explain some of the differences in law enforcement from one community to another.

Law enforcement in rural areas seems to be especially affected by the expectations of the community and the role of law enforcement officers in the community. A study of the social role of the county sheriff has documented the nature of law enforcement in a rural area.[23] In "Star County," in southern Illinois, the sheriff was permitted (or expected) to use a great amount of discretion in law enforcement. His primary function was to conserve the peace, and peace was not always best preserved by the making of an arrest. The rule of thumb in enforcement was the principle of public safety. The conclusion that may be drawn is that a community organized on informal relations resorts to official sanctions only when other means are exhausted or are for some reason inappropriate. In rural communities, whenever possible, informal controls tend to be used in place of law enforcement. Or, law enforcement in rural communities takes place with a maximum of discretion.

In the final analysis, no matter how the community is organized, the police attempt to accomplish their job within the context of their community. This means that the police tend to select law violators not according to legal prescriptions alone but also according to how closely enforcement approximates the expectations of the commu-

[22] Goldman, *The Differential Selection of Juvenile Offenders for Court Appearance,* p. 129.

[23] T. C. Esselstyn, "The Social Role of the County Sheriff," *Journal of Criminal Law, Criminology and Police Science,* 44 (July–August, 1953), pp. 177–184.

nity.[24] Although some isolation between police and community is inevitable, the police would rather avoid public criticism and gain local acceptance. The handling of cases, the defining of persons as criminal, is more a matter of informal community relations than it is the following of abstract principles of law enforcement.

POLICE ORGANIZATION AND LAW ENFORCEMENT

The behavior of the police is greatly influenced by the organization of police departments. The application of criminal definitions in law enforcement takes place within the context of locally organized police forces. Organizational considerations are, therefore, always involved when a decision is made to enforce the criminal law.

One of the most significant organizational aspects of law enforcement is the bureaucratization of the police.[25] The bureaucratic, and quasi-military, organization of the police is characterized by a system of subordination and by a chain of command. However, although still bureaucratic, modernized police departments tend to be organized according to a centralized command system. The communications center, as the core of the modern metropolitan police department, provides the principal source of organizational structure. That is, each police department is divided into a number of separate units. These units differ from one another in the specialized occupational roles they incorporate, and are necessary because of the variety of cases dealt with by the police.

The functional divisions of police departments have been divided according to the different kinds of activities handled by the police: (1) traffic patrol and other patrol of structural disorder, involving enforcement of regulations which do not entail the moral turpitude of those who break the law; (2) street patrol (including radio cars), especially in downtown areas, to control individual offenses in public places; (3) investigative work, generally involving complaints; (4) undercover work, in which fraud is used to get inside situations

[24] William J. Chambliss and John T. Liell, "The Legal Process in the Community Setting," *Crime and Delinquency,* 12 (October, 1966), pp. 310–317.

[25] David J. Bordua and Albert J. Reiss, Jr., "Command, Control and Charisma: Reflections on Police Bureaucracy," *American Journal of Sociology,* 72 (July, 1966), pp. 68–76.

otherwise protected by the institutions of privacy; and (5) quasi-military action, in which the problem is to apply coercion to control public riot.[26] The implication of the differentiated structure within police departments is that the criminal law is selectively enforced according to the organization and normative expectations of the separate units within the police department. Each division develops and perpetuates its own unique system of law enforcement.

The "effectiveness" of the police in enforcing the law corresponds closely to the organization of police departments.[27] As documented in a study of a non-professionalized police department in an east coast city and a professionalized police department in a west coast city, the arrest rates reflect the nature of the organization of police departments.[28] Wilson found that in the non-professionalized department the members had no strong sense of urgency about police work and, hence, there were low rates of official actions with regard to offenders. In the professionalized department, however, infractions of the law were more likely to be detected and offenders were more likely to be arrested, producing a higher crime rate in the city with the professionalized police force.

The extent to which police organization and procedure can affect the rate of reported crime is also illustrated in the yearly change of crime rates within particular cities. The annual fluctuations are at times an obvious result of changes in law enforcement policy. For various reasons policy changes occur within police departments in such matters as the recording of crime. In the course of organizational change in the New York City Police Department in 1966, it was decided to change the procedure of recording crime statistics. The newly appointed Chief Inspector suggested that under the old system of recording a great number of offenses either went unrecorded or were "downgraded" in the official reports. He estimated that roughly 60 per cent of the complaints involving burglary had in the previous year been officially recorded as lesser crimes, such as

[26] Arthur L. Stinchcombe, "Institutions of Privacy in the Determination of Police Administrative Practice," *American Journal of Sociology,* 69 (September, 1963), pp. 158–159.

[27] Robert Edward Mitchell, "Organization as a Key to Police Effectiveness," *Crime and Delinquency,* 12 (October, 1966), pp. 344–353.

[28] James Q. Wilson, "The Police and the Delinquent in Two Cities," in Stanton Wheeler (ed.), *Controlling Delinquents* (New York: John Wiley, 1968), pp. 9–30; also see Wilson, *Varieties of Police Behavior,* pp. 83–139.

petty larceny, or had been given a non-criminal label, such as lost property. In order "to insure factual recording of crime statistics," the Inspector ordered that "there should be no discretion with regard to reporting a crime and no ambiguity with regard to categorizing a crime."[29] Needless to say, the burglary rate the following year climbed considerably. A new policy had been established in regard to imposing and recording criminal definitions by the police.

POLICE IDEOLOGY AND LAW ENFORCEMENT

As a result both of the role played by the police in society and the organization that comes into being in relation to that role, a special occupational ideology develops among the police:

> The policeman finds his most pressing problem in his relationships to the public. His is a service occupation but of an incongruous kind, since he must discipline those whom he serves. He is regarded as corrupt and inefficient by, and meets with hostility and criticism from, the public. He regards the public as his enemy, feels his occupation to be in conflict with the community, and regards himself to be a pariah. The experience and the feeling give rise to a collective emphasis on secrecy, an attempt to coerce respect from the public, and a belief that almost any means are legitimate in completing an important arrest. These are for the policeman basic occupational values. They arise from his experience, take precedence over his legal responsibilities, are central to an understanding of his conduct, and form the occupational concepts within which violence gains its meaning.[30]

Each policeman learns to behave appropriately according to the ideology of his occupation. During his training, the recruit gradually adopts an outlook on his work and a justification for using certain procedures and methods in the line of "duty." Furthermore, socialization of police recruits into the occupation is affected to some extent by their backgrounds. A study of the training of policemen for entry into the New York City Police Department found that police candidates tend to be drawn primarily from the lower middle class

[29] *The New York Times,* March 15, 1966, pp. 1 and 26.

[30] William A. Westley, "Violence and the Police," *American Journal of Sociology,* 59 (July, 1953), p. 35.

segment of the population.[31] The recruits considered their new source of employment to be an upward step, but at the same time were convinced that police work, in relation to other occupations, was not assigned high prestige by the general population. Because of backgrounds similar in socioeconomic status and career expectations, the recruits adapted similarly to their training. They eventually displayed, in particular, a common lack of ability to handle enforcement situations impersonally. In addition, the recruits shared the belief, which increased during their training, that the police lack the basic legal authority to effectively carry out their work.

Upon completion of academy training and assignment to a local precinct, the police rookie is called upon to face the challenge of actual duty. "His reputation is made in the next few weeks and will shadow him for the rest of his police career: no matter where or when he is transferred, a phone call will precede his arrival, reporting the evaluation that was made of his handling of his first few important cases."[32] The principal challenge to the new patrolman is the dilemma of choosing between the professional ideal of police work learned in the academy and the pragmatic approach of the precinct. The "lock-them-up" philosophy of the precinct contradicts the professional orientation toward police work learned in the academy.

> In the case of the young policeman the choice between professionalism and pragmatism is apt to depend largely on the circumstances of the case. It is, for example, no great feat for a policeman working in an upper-class neighborhood to protect the rights of his white clientele. It is much more difficult in a lower-class community. In a slum area the professional ethic loses most of the time; the civil rights of lower-class individuals do not count as much as the necessity to accomplish a staggering amount of police work as expeditiously as possible. Shifting from idealism to pragmatism, the newcomer to a lower-class precinct house enters a new reference group whose members are a little contemptuous of all the Academy represents.[33]

[31] John H. McNamara, "Uncertainties in Police Work: the Relevance of Police Recruits' Backgrounds and Training," in David J. Bordua (ed.), *The Police: Six Sociological Essays* (New York: John Wiley, 1967), pp. 163–252.

[32] Arthur Niederhoffer, *Behind the Shield: The Police in Urban Society* (Garden City, N.Y.: Doubleday, 1967), p. 52.

[33] *Ibid.*, p. 54.

It becomes obvious to the new policeman that every law on the book cannot be enforced. The rookie realizes as well that the laws are, in fact, to be enforced with considerable discretion according to the norms of his department and neighborhood.

The occupational ideology learned by the policeman is closely related to two characteristics of his day-to-day work: danger and authority. These two characteristics can lead to a description of the "working personality" of the policeman:

> The element of danger seems to make the policeman especially attentive to signs indicating a potential for violence and lawbreaking. As a result, the policeman is generally a "suspicious" person. Furthermore, the character of the policeman's work makes him less desirable as a friend, since norms of friendship implicate others in his work. Accordingly, the element of danger isolates the policeman socially from that segment of the citizenry which he regards as symbolically dangerous and also from the conventional citizenry with whom he identifies.
>
> The element of authority reinforces the element of danger in isolating the policeman. Typically, the policeman is required to enforce law representing puritanical morality, such as those prohibiting drunkenness, and also laws regulating the flow of public activity, such as traffic laws. In these situations the policeman directs the citizenry, whose typical response denies recognition of his authority, and stressed his obligation to danger. The kind of man who responds well to danger, however, does not normally subscribe to codes of puritanical morality. As a result, the policeman is unusually liable to the charge of hypocrisy. That the whole civilian world is an audience for the policeman further promotes police isolation and, in consequence, solidarity. Finally, danger undermines the judicious use of authority.[34]

The combination of danger and authority in police work frustrates any possibility of procedural regularity in law enforcement.

Through socialization and experience within the occupation, the policeman develops other personal attributes. As shown in a study of policemen in the New York City Police Department, policemen after appointment to the force tend to become cynical. "When they succumb, they lose faith in people, society, and eventually in themselves.

[34] Skolnick, *Justice Without Trial,* p. 44.

In their Hobbesian view the world becomes a jungle in which crime, corruption, and brutality are normal features of the terrain."[35] Cynicism is part of the occupational ideology of the police and is learned in the course of socialization into the occupation. Furthermore, the policeman, in addition to becoming cynical, tends to acquire an authoritarian personality during his police career. "The police occupational system is geared to manufacture the 'take charge guy,' and it succeeds in doing so with outstanding efficiency. It is the police system, not the personality of the candidate, that is the more powerful determinant of behavior and ideology."[36]

The occupational ideology of the police ultimately affects the defining of persons as criminal. While the activities of the police are governed officially by procedural law, their actual behavior conforms to their own occupational code. The policeman's view of the effect of the exclusionary rule, for example, is not that the rule has guaranteed greater protection of freedom for the citizen, but rather that it has unnecessarily complicated the task of detecting and apprehending criminals.[37] Similarly, many practices of the police are in opposition to the guarantee of due process. Actual police practices are minimally affected by legalistic considerations:

> When he (the policeman) sees a black girl and a white serviceman enter a hotel together, he assumes an act of prostitution is in the offing. To him, these are not constitutionally protected citizens, but predictable actors whose misbehavior he usually judges correctly. Sometimes, to be sure, he may be in error. The probabilities, however, are so strong, he feels, that his judgment is rarely going to be wrong.[38]

For the policeman, "due process of law is, therefore, not merely a set of constitutional guarantees for the defendant, but also a set of working conditions which, under increasingly liberal opinions by the courts, are likewise becoming increasingly arduous."[39]

Thus, because of the particular role of the police in society, specific kinds of occupational values exist among the police. As part of the occupational structure, they provide the rationale for the use of

35 Niederhoffer, *Behind the Shield,* p. 9.
36 *Ibid.,* p. 151.
37 Skolnick, *Justice Without Trial,* pp. 211–219.
38 *Ibid.,* p. 202.
39 *Ibid.,* p. 202.

harsh and oftentimes illegal methods by the police.[40] Furthermore, and with justification, the police believe that the public supports their use of such methods. The public, especially in the United States, provides the police with an implicit directive on the use of violence and other expedient methods to accomplish police goals. It may be the fate of democratic society that harsh and illegal law enforcement practices will always be supported by the public belief in submission to popular sovereignty.

THE ENCOUNTER BETWEEN POLICE AND CITIZENS

The making of an arrest takes place within a complex of social relations and personal perceptions. That which is defined as criminal is not so much behavior in obvious violation of a specific criminal law as it is a definition of circumstances that occur in the encounter between interacting parties in a concrete situation. In few cases of law enforcement is there clear evidence that a particular person is the "criminal." Usually it is only in the totality of the encounter that a decision is made to apply the label "criminal" to a person and his behavior.

The encounter can take place only when the police have been mobilized. The police tend to be mobilized through the actions of private citizens, rather than through police initiative. Thus the police may be mobilized in several ways:

> Police departments refer to incidents or complaints that originate by mobilizing police units through the communication center as *"calls-for-service," "dispatches,"* or *"runs,"* the first term referring to the citizen's call or complaint and the latter terms to the fact that a mobile unit is radio-dispatched to take the complaint. A request for police action made by a citizen personally appearing at the police station is referred to as a *"sta-*

[40] Albert J. Reiss, Jr., "Police Brutality — Answers to Key Questions," *Trans-Action,* 5 (July–August, 1968), pp. 10–19; Ellwyn R. Stoddard, "The Informal 'Code' of Police Deviancy: A Group Approach to 'Blue-Coat Crime'," *Journal of Criminal Law, Criminology and Police Science,* 59 (June, 1968), pp. 201–213. Police misconduct and brutality are documented in David Burnham, "Misconduct Laid to 27% of Police in 3 Cities' Slums," *The New York Times,* July 5, 1968, pp. 1 and 28; David Burnham, "Police Violence: A Changing Pattern," *The New York Times,* July 7, 1968, pp. 1 and 34.

> *tion complaint*" or a "*citizen station mobilization.*" All incidents arising in a field setting are commonly referred to as "*on-view*" incidents, but a distinction can be made among them. A direct, in-the-field, citizen request for police action, usually by flagging a patrol car or a call to an officer on the beat, is sometimes referred to as a "*field complaint*" or a "*citizen field mobilization.*" When an officer initiates contact and reports on an incident that occurs in his presence, it is referred to as an "*on-view*" mobilization. Any law violation occurring in an officer's presence that leads to an arrest with the officer as complainant is an "*on-view arrest.*"[41]

In respect to these types of police mobilization, it was found in a study of 5,360 mobilization situations in Boston, Chicago, and Washington, D.C., that 81 per cent of the mobilizations were dispatches, 14 per cent were on-views; and the remaining 5 per cent were citizen field mobilization. Most important, nearly three-quarters of the mobilizations consisted of some kind of police-citizen interaction.[42] In a great majority of cases, then, the police are involved in criminal defining situations because of the reporting of offenses by citizens.

The encounter of police and citizens in a situation that may potentially be defined as criminal involves playing a number of social roles. In addition to the policeman, eight citizen roles may be distinguished in the encounter: complainant, member of complainant group, offender, member of offender group, victim, member of victim group, informant, and bystander.

> A *complainant* is a person who wants police action in response to what he sees as an "offense" of some kind; e.g., a man whose car has been stolen or a woman who complains about a noisy party is a complainant. A *member of a complainant* group is a person who supports or stands with the central complainant. An *offender* is either a person who is seen or treated as a possible violator of the law or as a person who is not fulfilling role obligations or expectations that the complainant regards as "legal."

[41] Donald J. Black and Albert J. Reiss, Jr., "Patterns of Behavior in Police and Citizen Transactions," in the President's Commission on Law Enforcement and Administration of Justice, *Studies in Crime and Law Enforcement in Major Metropolitan Areas,* vol. 2, Field Surveys III (Washington, D.C.: U.S. Government Printing Office, 1967), pp. 4–5.

[42] Black and Reiss, "Patterns of Behavior in Police and Citizen Transactions," p. 17.

> The first kind of offender is represented by a person accused of a larceny, the second by a man whose wife thinks he has been negligent in fulfilling his obligations as husband or head of the household. A *member of an offender group* is a person who supports or stands with the offender. A citizen is called a *victim* who needs or requests help or a service from the police in a situation that does not involve an "offense" or possible criminal violation of any kind, e.g., a sick or accidentally injured person. A *member of a victim group* is a person who supports or is behaviorally concerned about a victim. The *informant* is a participant who gives information relative to the nature of any situation or incident but who does not support or stand with any of the more involved participants; he is, however, more than a mere guide or person who gives information only about the location of a situation. The *bystander* is nothing more than an onlooker.[43]

The outcome of the playing of these roles may be a criminal arrest.

Of the various social roles involved in the situations that may become defined as criminal, the most important are those of the policeman, the suspect, and the victim. The role of the victim in the creation of crime is not only in being the object of an offense. The *victim,* for the purpose of an arrest, may be the only person who is able to report the offense to the police. It was found in the studies for the President's Commission on Law Enforcement and Administration of Justice that in only about half the cases of victimization did the victim report the offense to the police.[44] The tendency to report or not to report varied, of course, according to the type of offense and the characteristics of the victim. But in general, victims did not report offenses to the police for several reasons. The most frequently cited reason was a resigned belief that the police could not do anything about the incident, would not catch the offender, or would not want to be bothered. Many other nonreporting victims believed that the incident was not a police matter. These victims either did not want the offender to be known to the police or thought that the incident was a private affair. Other victims simply did not want to get in-

[43] *Ibid.,* pp. 53–54.

[44] Philip H. Ennis, *Criminal Victimization in the United States: A Report of a National Survey,* President's Commission on Law Enforcement and Administration of Justice, Field Surveys II (Washington, D.C.: U.S. Government Printing Office, 1967), pp. 41–51.

volved with the police. They did not want to take the time or the trouble to report the offense. Still other victims were afraid of possible reprisal from the offender and his friends or some other kind of loss. Finally, some did not notify the police because of their own uncertainty of what ought to be done. It is not always clear whether a criminal offense has been committed or what is the proper procedure for reporting an offense. For all these reasons, possible criminal defining situations do not come to the attention of the police.

The ultimate encounter that may lead to a criminal definition is between the *policeman* and the *suspect*. The possible encounter is guided by a conflict of two opposing interests: (1) those of a person who wants to carry out certain behaviors (some of which may conceivably be in violation of the criminal law), and (2) those of the policeman who wants to prevent criminal violations and apprehend criminals. These opposing interests are responsible for the development of sets of strategies by both parties.[45] The strategies are formulated on the basis of what the one party expects of the other. Each attempts to predict the behavior of the other, at the same time attempting to reduce the opponent's ability to predict his own moves.

Once the encounter has taken place, the conflicting interests of the policeman and the suspect continue to be important in the relationship. The concern now, however, becomes not the matter of whether the two parties are to have a face-to-face encounter, but how that encounter will be conducted. It is during this confrontation that the policeman makes the decision on whether or not to impose a criminal definition through the act of arrest.

Many factors beyond the principal reason for the encounter between the policeman and the suspect enter into the arrest decision. The policeman, using a *probabilistic* model of law enforcement, looks for personal characteristics that may be indicative of criminal behavior. The outward appearance and demeanor of the suspect are obviously of interest to him in a possible arrest situation. A study of the disposition of juvenile cases showed that the decision of whether or not to bring a boy to the station — and the decision made at the station — "were based largely on cues from which the officer

[45] The game-like conception of police-suspect relations is found in Dean R. Smith, "Random Patrol: An Application of Game Theory to Police Problems," *Journal of Criminal Law, Criminology and Police Science,* 53 (June, 1962), pp. 258–263.

inferred the youth's character."[46] The cues included the youth's group affiliations, age, race, grooming, and dress. Members of known delinquent gangs, older boys, Negroes, and youths with well-oiled hair, black jackets, and soiled denims or jeans tended to receive the more serious dispositions.

But the most important cue found to be used by the police in handling juveniles was a youth's demeanor. The patrolmen themselves stated that the demeanor of apprehended juveniles was the major determinant of their decisions for 50 to 60 per cent of the cases they processed. Youths who were perceived by the police as being uncooperative were more likely to be dealt with severely than youths who were perceived as being cooperative. The researchers made the following conclusion on the demeanor of juveniles and the decisions of the police:

> The cues used by police to assess demeanor were fairly simple. Juveniles who were contrite about their infractions, respectful to officers, and fearful of the sanctions that might be employed against them tended to be viewed by patrolmen as basically law-abiding or at least "salvageable." For these youths it was usually assumed that informal or formal reprimand would suffice to guarantee their future conformity. In contrast, youthful offenders who were fractious, obdurate, or who appeared nonchalant in their encounters with patrolmen were likely to be viewed as "would-be tough guys" or "punks" who fully deserved the most severe sanction: arrest.[47]

The policeman, then, uses various symbols and behavioral cues in applying criminal definitions. The policeman maintains an image of the kind of person who is a "troublemaker" or who is likely to be a law-breaker. When the suspect lives up to this expectation, he increases the possibility of his own arrest. Furthermore, the attitude the person assumes in his relation with the policeman has consequences for the outcome of the encounter. Persons who behave antagonistically toward the police are more likely to be treated in a hostile, authoritarian, or belittling manner by the police than are other citizens.[48] The encounter between police and citizen is, indeed,

[46] Irving Piliavin and Scott Briar, "Police Encounters with Juveniles," *American Journal of Sociology,* 70 (September, 1964), p. 210.

[47] Piliavin and Briar, "Police Encounters with Juveniles," pp. 210–211.

[48] Black and Reiss, "Patterns of Behavior in Police and Citizen Transactions," pp. 33–37.

a crucial moment of interaction and assessment. Both parties are involved in jockeying for their personal fates. The result of the encounter may be the creation of a crime.

THE OFFENSE SITUATION AND SELECTIVE LAW ENFORCEMENT

The encounter of policeman and citizen takes place in a specific offense situation. The outcome is affected not only by the interactions, perceptions, and reactions of the parties, but also by the larger setting of the encounter. Offense situations may thus vary in such matters as the racial context, the objectives of the police and community in the enforcement of certain laws, and the nature of the offense. Differences in law enforcement can be affected by variations in these situations.

The Racial Context of Arrest. Considerable evidence suggests that the police have long had differential arrest policies in regard to race.[49] It is apparent that police have tended to arrest Negroes on slight evidence in comparison to the amount of evidence required to arrest whites. Furthermore, Negroes have been exposed more than others to the misuses of police power. The attitudes and policies of the police in regard to race were dramatically described by a police captain some time ago, in a Southern town, when he told a writer: "In this town there are three classes of homicide. If a nigger kills a white man, that's murder. If a white man kills a nigger, that's justifiable homicide. If a nigger kills a nigger, that's one less nigger."[50]

Official police statistics reveal that Negroes are arrested between three and four times more frequently than whites.[51] While Negroes comprise about one-tenth of the population, they constitute nearly one-third of the persons arrested for all offenses. From such figures as these it is obvious that the status of being Negro entails a greater risk of being arrested than does the status of being white. The differences in arrest rates are not, however, due entirely to the fact that

[49] See Guy B. Johnson, "The Negro and Crime," *Annals of the American Academy of Political and Social Science,* 271 (September, 1941), pp. 93–104.

[50] Cited in Banton, *The Policeman in the Community,* p. 173.

[51] See the discussion on Negro crime rates in Margin E. Wolfgang, *Crime and Race: Conceptions and Misconceptions* (New York: Institute of Human Relations Press, 1964).

Negroes may be involved more than whites in law-violating behavior, but that in similar situations Negroes are more likely than whites to be apprehended.

Selective enforcement according to racial factors results in part from long-held prejudices of individual policemen.[52] But also important is the fact that the Negro tends to fit the stereotype that police have of the criminal.[53] Through the use of certain cues, a probabilistic model of law violation, and their past experiences, the police are more likely to arrest the Negro than the white man in a similar offense situation. The extent to which police use a Negro image of the offender was shown in a survey of police officers in Philadelphia: 75 per cent of the policemen overestimated the percentage of arrests involving Negroes made in the districts to which they were assigned.[54] With such conceptions of events and offenders, a differential in law enforcement according to the racial context of the situation is to be expected.

Police and Community Objectives in the Arrest Situation. In order to accomplish certain objectives, possibly known only to the police and various community members, an arrest may be made. The situation may be such that an arrest may solve a problem that seemingly could not be resolved in any other fashion. A policeman might arrest a person who ordinarily would not be arrested in order to maintain respect for the police system.

> A police patrol stopped a car that had been traveling at 39 m.p.h. in a 30 m.p.h. zone. They decided prior to leaving the squad car that they would only issue a warning. When the deputies approached, the driver said in a sarcastic tone, "What in hell have I done now?" Because of his belligerent attitude the driver was placed under arrest.[55]

Another instance of the use of arrest to accomplish extralegal objectives is in the arrest of a person in order to maintain an image of

[52] For documentation of anti-Negro attitudes among police, according to race of police and racial composition of the police precinct, see Black and Reiss, "Patterns of Behavior in Police and Citizen Transactions," pp. 132–139.

[53] Piliavin and Briar, "Police Encounters with Juveniles," pp. 212–213.

[54] William M. Kephart, *Racial Factors and Urban Law Enforcement* (Philadelphia: University of Pennsylvania Press, 1957), pp. 88–93.

[55] LaFave, *Arrest,* p. 146.

full enforcement. This form of arrest often occurs when an offense not usually handled by arrest comes to public attention:

> The police were aware of the operation of a private card game in which there was no house "cut." Since this operation therefore qualified as mere social gambling, no action was taken against the offenders. However, the operators of the game made no attempt to conceal the operation, and it was soon apparent to the general public that the police must be aware of it. Realizing this, the police arrested the gamblers.[56]

Once an offense is widely publicized, an arrest becomes imminent.

An arrest may on occasion be made in order to detain or punish a person suspected of other criminal activity.

> The police learned of a minor property theft. As the victim was not interested in prosecution, the police, in accord with their usual policy, decided not to arrest. However, when they learned that the offender was known to the police department as a "bad actor," and that the police had been unsuccessful in obtaining his conviction for other, more serious offenses, they arrested him.[57]

In addition, an arrest may be made for a minor offense when the police suspect that a person is responsible for a relatively serious offense, but they need more time to gather sufficient evidence in order to successfully prosecute the case.

> Officers had reasonable grounds to believe that a particular man was responsible for a recent homicide. However, desiring an opportunity to conduct a prolonged in-custody investigation, they arrested him on a vagrancy charge. He was then convicted for vagrancy, and the murder investigation was continued while he served his sentence.[58]

In some situations offenders may be arrested to ensure their own safety. The drunk, in particular, may be arrested in order to protect him from the cold, because he has injured himself, or because he is likely to become a criminal victim.[59] In such a case, the person will probably be released the next morning.

[56] *Ibid.*, p. 147.
[57] *Ibid.*, p. 149.
[58] *Ibid.*, p. 151.
[59] *Ibid.*, pp. 439–449.

Arrest charges that are often used to accomplish a multitude of extralegal objectives are those of vagrancy and disorderly conduct. These arrests are not usually made for the enforcement of the respective laws but for such purposes as the banishment of unwanted persons, the prevention and control of other offenses, and the clearing of public areas.[60] Police departments may even conduct drives at certain times of the year, in the name of the enforcement of the vagrancy and disorderly conduct statutes, to get "undesirables" out of town.

Public Morals and Law Enforcement. Some forms of private conduct on occasion become the concern of the police. Criminal laws created primarily for purposes of reprobation are subject to a great amount of discretion in their enforcement. The laws are enforced only occasionally, and then only under particular circumstances. Thus, in the appropriate situational contexts the police are expected to enforce public morals through the arrest of private citizens.

In general the police are not called upon to enforce laws that regulate private conduct. Although there are laws based on moral behavior, they are not usually enforced as long as the conduct is unharmful to the persons involved and as long as the participating parties consent to the behavior. Enforcement is likely to take place however, when personal violence erupts and also when conduct becomes defined by the community as a public nuisance. Therefore, solicitation by homosexuals and prostitutes in public places may bring the police into action in the enforcement of laws on homosexuality and prostitution.[61]

Since the behavior of homosexuals in public is likely to be offensive to a large segment of the community, numerous complaints may be registered with the police. The responsibility of the police, then, becomes not so much the full enforcement of the law but the assurance of a public order that satisfies the sensibilities of community members. The public demands that the police provide the community with an inoffensive environment.

Prostitutes are usually arrested for purposes other than prosecution. The prostitutes who tend to be arrested, however, are those who

[60] Caleb Foote, "Vagrancy-Type Law and Its Administration," *University of Pennsylvania Law Review,* 104 (March, 1956), pp. 603–650.

[61] See LaFave, *Arrest*, pp. 465–470.

come to public attention, the street walkers rather than the call girls. While prostitution may be condoned in the community, as long as it does not recruit our wives and daughters, community members do not like to be reminded of the behavior. Therefore, the police are required to crack down on the girls who publicly solicit for their favors. Furthermore, the police may obtain information about other criminals from the arrest of prostitutes.[62] Most of the time, however, the objective of such arrests is the harassment of prostitutes. The harassment program may unwittingly force such prostitutes to develop, as it were, undercover techniques that are less obvious and offensive to the public.

The Enforcement of Dormant Laws. A great many of our criminal laws were created to support values that have since ceased to be important. Although the laws have remained on the books, they have in essence become dormant. On occasion, however, these laws have been enforced for brief periods. In most cases, the revival of these laws has been for purposes other than those intended in the original legal formulations. The sporadic enforcement of dormant laws represents the ultimate use of discretion in law enforcement.

The enforcement of Sunday closing laws provides one of the best examples of the sporadic enforcement of a dormant law. Sunday laws were enacted early in the history of our states, and their enforcement usually has been the responsibility of local authorities. Thus, Sunday laws are enforced according to particularistic objectives.

Furthermore, within local communities, Sunday laws, when enforced, have been enforced for diverse reasons. In New York City sporadic attempts in the enforcement of the Sunday law have been guided by different objectives. In this century alone there have been several instances of organized efforts to enforce the law on Sunday closing of business establishments. In each case, the reasons for the enforcement of the dormant law were different.

In 1924 the number of police actions in regard to Sunday closing rose 77 per cent in New York over the previous year. Responsible for the sudden enforcement policy was the agitation of a group of citizens known as the Lord's Day Alliance. The Alliance crusaded for the enforcement of Sunday law primarily on religious grounds. The

[62] Skolnick, *Justice Without Trial,* pp. 96–109.

following year the arrest rate for being open on Sunday declined to its regular low level. Then in 1938 another campaign for the enforcement of Sunday law was launched in the Flatbush section of Brooklyn. The campaign, under the direction of the Flatbush Chamber of Commerce, was motivated by the civic interests of local businessmen in keeping a law-abiding image for the community.

The increased enforcement of the Sunday law in 1954 in the Bedford-Stuyvesant area of Brooklyn was prompted by a campaign for better working conditions. A union, the American Federation of Retail Kosher Butchers, began the campaign in an attempt to abolish forced work on Sunday by management. In the next year, this time on Manhattan's West Side, the police responded to pressures by unions which were organizing the car wash industry in the area. The police reacted by acting upon any business establishment that was open on Sunday. One of the last police crackdowns on Sunday openings was in August of 1962 in the upper Broadway area. Behind the drive, which lasted one week, was the attempt of the large chain-store supermarkets to have the small neighborhood stores closed on Sundays.

The enforcement of Sunday closing laws illustrates the extent to which discretion is used in enforcing dormant laws. Furthermore, their enforcement is prompted by pressure on police by diverse interests to accomplish various objectives.

Political Protest and Law Enforcement. One other example of law enforcement in a particular context is the role of the police in situations involving political protest. In such situations the police are used by those who hold power to resolve value conflicts in favor of the dominant interests of the society. The use of the police to control political protest clearly shows the extent to which the police are the representatives of the powerful interests of the society. Law enforcement in this context consists of the selective application of criminal definitions on those who protest against the established government in ways that are regarded by the government as illegitimate. Behavior that is regarded by the government as illegitimate may, consequently, be defined as criminal.

The very emergence of the police in the last century was a response to conditions of unrest and mass protest. In several democratic countries in the nineteenth century the elite were able to organize police for the purpose of protecting their interests.[63] The police were able not only to control the various forms of protest against politically organized society, but served as well to divert the hostility of the protesters from the elites to the police themselves. Protest in many cases, as today, was deflected from the original issues to protests against the power of the police. In this fashion, the interests of the powerful in society are not only protected but are also given support by the existence of the police.

Political protest almost by definition is regarded as a threat and danger to the existing government. The police become involved in such situations not only for the express purpose of maintaining peace, but also to preserve the status quo of the government. Actions of the police in such situations serve to punish the protesters as much as to keep order. In fact, police intimidation and brutality have been evident in many instances of political protest by citizens. In the "race riots," in particular, much of the violence that has occurred has been either prompted or initiated by the police.[64] In many other cases of protest and in demonstrations of various kinds, the only violence has been that which the police have inflicted on the participants. The only illegalities in situations of protest may be those committed by the police themselves.[65] But since criminal definitions are imposed by the police, they are not likely to be the ones defined as criminals.

The federal government, especially, resorts to the use of the police to protect its own interests. In the name of national security, laws have been created and enforced in order to protect the government from perceived threats. The scare of communism in this century in the United States resulted in the arrest of thousands of persons under a host of laws especially enacted for that purpose or under laws that may be conveniently enforced for the same purpose.[66] Whether

[63] Allan Silver, "The Demand for Order in Civil Society: A Review of Some Themes in the History of Urban Crime, Police, and Riot," in Bordua (ed.), *The Police,* pp. 1–24.

[64] Allen D. Grimshaw, "Actions of Police and the Military in American Race Riots," *Phylon,* 24 (Fall, 1963), pp. 271–289.

[65] See Joseph C. Mouledoux, "Political Crime and the Negro Revolution," in Marshall B. Clinard and Richard Quinney, *Criminal Behavior Systems: A Typology* (New York: Holt, Rinehart and Winston, 1967), pp. 217–231.

[66] See Robert K. Murray, *Red Scare: A Study of National Hysteria, 1919–1920* (Minneapolis: University of Minnesota Press, 1965); William Preston,

dubious methods such as harassment have been used or whether arrests have been made, police have been used to protect and help preserve the interests of the government and the interests of those who benefit from the status quo.[67] In situations of political protest the police are required to enforce the law according to the interests of those in power. Such is to be expected, since the police are, after all, agents of the government.

Jr., *Aliens and Dissenters: Federal Suppression of Radicals, 1903–1933* (Cambridge: Harvard University Press, 1963).

67 See Jerome H. Skolnick, *The Politics of Protest* (New York: Ballantine, 1969), especially pp. 241–292.

CHAPTER FIVE

Administration of Criminal Justice

Justice is an ideal that abstractly pervades the value systems of most human societies. The American colonists, imbued with the liberal thought of the European enlightenment, made justice the basis of democratic government. The Massachusetts Bill of Rights of 1780 captured the essence of the ideal: "It is essential to the preservation of the rights of every individual, his life, liberty, property, and character, that there be an impartial interpretation of the laws and the administration of justice." A similar notion of justice was written into the Declaration of Independence and the Bill of Rights.

In symbolic form, justice weighs all men impartially on her scales. She represents our ideal of equality between all parties and classes. Law is thus to be administered according to an ideal, not according to the experiences of everyday life. Yet the administration of justice is full of devices for individualizing the application of criminal law. The complicated machinery of the judicial system involves a series of mitigating practices whereby cases are necessarily individualized according to numerous extralegal factors.[1] However, the very structure of the judicial system tends to obscure from public view the operation of the criminal law. Partly by design, the decision-making activities of the judicial system are hidden behind the "purple curtain" of the law. The fiction of

[1] Roscoe Pound, *An Introduction to the Philosophy of Law* (New Haven: Yale University Press, 1954), chap. 3.

judicial objectivity is obscured by a system that administers the law according to its own rules.

From an idealistic standpoint, it is useful to analyze the administration of criminal law in reference to the concept of justice. Even from a standpoint of scientific inquiry, the concept of justice is appropriate. Whether or not we always maintain an explicit image of the good and the beautiful, our sociological interest in the administration of criminal law is directed to a goal that is consistent with — and aided by — considerations of justice: How is the criminal law actually administered? From personal experience we know that the criminal law is not administered uniformly. To understand the processes involved in the administration of the criminal law is thus our immediate interest. Nevertheless, in our moments of idealism, we are investigating the differentials in the administration of justice. Whether we use the phrase "administration of criminal law" or "administration of justice," our interest is a sociological investigation of the processes that result in the application of criminal definitions.

POLITICALITY OF JUSTICE

The administration of justice, contrary to common belief, is not "above politics" but is by its very nature political. That is, the administration of criminal law is political in that public policy is being made. The political nature of the judiciary is inherent in government itself. Wherever decisions are made — and that is what the judiciary is about — politics necessarily serves as the basis of the process.

In addition to being political in the general sense of policy making, the judicial system is a creature of the political community in more specific ways. The courts, for instance, are an essential part of the local political structure. To begin with, the kinds of criminal cases that enter the courts are influenced by the character of community politics. The prosecuting attorney, an elected official and often the key figure in the local political machine, determines according to his discretion what law is being violated. His actions result in either the release of suspects or their indictment; and if suspects are indicted, the prosecutor decides the character of the charge. Still later in the process, the fate of the accused depends upon the discretion of the judge, also an appointed or locally elected official. The extent to which the local political system and the administration of criminal laws are related is indicated in conclusions reached by two political scientists:

> Thus, elected officials sensitive to the political process charge, prosecute, convict, and sentence criminal defendants. This means that such decisions are made in response to cues from the political structure; thereby the political system provides channels by which local claims and local interests can influence judicial outcomes. In this way, the judiciary helps create the conditions necessary for the re-election of court officials or for their frequent promotion to higher offices in the state or nation. In short, criminal prosecutions provide opportunities for the political system to affect judicial decisions and for the judicial process to provide favors which nourish political organizations.[2]

The politicality of local criminal justice is shaped considerably by the structure of the American party system. Political leadership in the country is dispersed among the political parties. Because of the decentralized nature of the parties, local politics is influenced by party considerations. Party leaders use the judiciary as a source of patronage. Elected judges usually owe their office to favors rendered to a political party. Specific party concerns inevitably enter into the content of public policy, including the decisions made in respect to criminal matters.

Since the judiciary is the focus of significant power, it is one of the principal points at which the claims of interest groups are aimed.[3] Because courts serve as the arena where the conflicting claims of diverse groups are presented and resolved, some control over the courts is desired by the interest groups affected by judicial decisions. Interest groups utilize every resource at their command to ensure that decisions of the courts are made in the protection of their interests.

Because the judiciary operates within a fairly routinized legal

[2] Herbert Jacob and Kenneth Vines, "The Role of the Judiciary in American State Politics," in Glendon Schubert (ed.), *Judicial Decision-Making* (New York: The Free Press of Glencoe, 1963), p. 250.

[3] David B. Truman, *The Governmental Process* (New York: Alfred A. Knopf, 1951), chap. 15; Harmon Zeigler, *Interest Groups in American Society* (Englewood Cliffs, N.J.: Prentice-Hall, 1964), chap. 11.

structure, interest groups must rely primarily upon indirect means to gain access to the decision-making process. These indirect methods may be classified into three categories: (1) those influencing the selection of judges, (2) those influencing the content of decisions, and (3) those maximizing or minimizing the effects of decisions as they are implemented.[4] By such methods, interest groups are able to have criminal statutes interpreted in their favor. The application of criminal definitions at the judicial level is largely a matter of selective interpretations of the law that favor the interests of some while negating the interests of others. Under the adversary system of justice, there is little compromise: someone wins while someone else loses.

The politicality of justice is by no means the sole result of the conflict between diverse interest groups. The political nature of the administration of criminal law is also affected by the interests of the government itself. In every society the wielders of governmental power use the criminal law to legitimate their assertions and the criminal courts to maintain their domination. Opposing political viewpoints and actions may be suppressed through the use of the courts by the government. Through various forms of the *political trial,* political foes may be eliminated from political competition.[5] In addition, the judicial system may be used by governments to repress certain groups in the society. Judges in the American south, for example, have tended to consistently make decisions that would maintain the domination of the white man over the black. In South Africa, the ruling minority has been able to successfully subjugate the rest of the population in large part by their use of the criminal courts. In these cases and others, the judiciary maintains the interests of the established government.

DISCRETION AND DECISION-MAKING IN THE JUDICIAL PROCESS

Justice is political because the administration of criminal law involves making decisions. Furthermore, whenever decisions are

[4] Jack Peltason, *Federal Courts in the Political Process* (New York: Doubleday, 1955), p. 29.

[5] Otto Kirchheimer, *Political Justice: The Use of Legal Procedure for Political Ends* (Princeton: Princeton University Press, 1961), p. 46.

made, discretion necessarily occurs. Judicial decision-making without the exercise of discretion is inconceivable.

Within the judicial process a number of types of decisions are made at various stages. Once a case is admitted to the judicial system, after an arrest, a series of decisions are made regarding the fate of the suspect. Some cases, on the basis of the decision reached during the first judicial appearance, may be removed entirely from the judicial system. The other cases, however, move sequentially from one stage to another before going out of the system. At each stage, the decision reached by certain officials limits the alternatives for the decisions in the subsequent stages.

Following the arrest, then, the suspect is usually brought before a court official (the magistrate) to determine the nature of the case. A preliminary hearing may follow to establish "probable cause." A decision is also made on the detention of the suspect, including the possible setting of bail. Between the time of the first judicial appearance and the indictment, the prosecution decides what charges to press or whether to press charges at all. Once formal charges are made, pretrial proceedings are established during the arraignment. Decisions are reached regarding such matters as the time of trial, the use of the plea, challenge of the formal charge, the nature of the evidence, and the defendant's mental or physical capacity. If a trial takes place, rather than a settlement through guilty plea proceedings, decisions are made by judge and jury in the courtroom. In arguing their cases, the prosecuting attorney and the lawyer for the defense make innumerable strategic decisions. The decision to convict the accused and the decision to impose a particular sentence are the consequences of the decisions made from the time of the arrest.

The fate of the convicted person is still problematic to some extent, however, in that an appellate review may alter previous decisions. But most likely the convicted person must continue within the judicial system until the time when officials make decisions regarding his release. From the time the suspect enters the judicial process, the decisions of others determine whether or not he will be defined as criminal.

As in the use of discretion by the police, the boundaries of discretion in the administration of criminal law are not clearly defined. Obviously judicial decisions are not made uniformly. Decisions are made according to a host of extralegal factors, including the age of the offender, his race, and social class.

Perhaps the most obvious example of judicial discretion occurs in the handling of cases of persons from minority groups. Negroes, in comparison to whites, are convicted with lesser evidence and sentenced to more severe punishments. In a study of 821 homicides in several counties of North Carolina between 1930 and 1940, it was found that the fewest indictments were made when whites killed Negroes and the highest proportion when Negroes killed whites.[6] The courts tended to regard the slaying of a white by a Negro as almost prima facie evidence of guilt, while the murder of a Negro by a white was believed to require mitigating circumstances such as provocation. Furthermore, prisoner statistics show that in most states Negroes are committed to prison longer than are whites for the same types of offenses.[7]

Another source of variation in judicial decision-making is found in the great variety of judicial systems. In the United States there are fifty-two separate court jurisdictions, consisting of the judicial systems of the fifty states, the District of Columbia, and the federal government. Furthermore, within the state jurisdictions there are several forms of courts, variously known as "police" courts, "special sessions" courts, and "quarter" courts. Some courts deal with minor criminal violations of local laws and ordinances and others with more serious offenses. While these courts have specialized functions, considerable confusion results from the overlapping of their jurisdictions.

The federal judicial system is also composed of several types of courts with diversified activities and functions. In addition, there are the federal circuit courts which are divided according to the geographical areas of the country. Because of the complexity and diversity of the judiciary in the United States, variations in judicial

[6] Harold Garfinkel, "Research Note on Inter- and Intra-Racial Homicides," *Social Forces,* 27 (May, 1949), pp. 369–381. Also see Thorsten Sellin, "Race Prejudice in the Administration of Justice," *American Journal of Sociology,* 41 (September, 1935), pp. 212–217.

[7] *National Prisoner Statistics,* "State Prisoners: Admission and Releases, 1964" (Washington, D.C.: Federal Bureau of Prisons, 1965). Also see Henry Allen Bullock, "Significance of the Racial Factor in the Length of Prison Sentence," *Journal of Criminal Law, Criminology and Social Science,* 339 (January, 1962), pp. 411–417.

decision-making are to be expected. The administration of the criminal law cannot be uniform, but necessarily involves the use of localized discretion in the course of individualized justice.

PROSECUTION AND NONTRIAL ADJUDICATION

By popular conception, the focal point of the administration of justice consists of the court trial, where the fate of the accused is decided by twelve of his peers. Not only is this conception incorrect about the *way* in which persons are convicted, but it is misleading in the implication that adjudication consists *only* of the decision of the judge or jury to convict or acquit. As we have seen, several judicial stages necessarily precede a trial. But it is most significant that in these pretrial proceedings the majority of criminal cases never reach the stage of the criminal trial. The decision to impose a criminal definition is usually made in the *pretrial* proceedings by *nontrial* adjudication.

Upon arrest, or following the issuance of a summons or on-the-spot citation, the suspect is supposed to be brought promptly before a magistrate, who reads the warrant to the suspect.[8] If the offense is a minor one, triable by the magistrate, a summary trial may be held immediately. If the offense is more serious, not triable by the magistrate, the purpose of the initial appearance is more limited. The suspect will be given the opportunity of having a preliminary hearing to determine if there is sufficient evidence to justify being held for possible trial. If he waives a preliminary hearing, he is then bound over to a court of trial jurisdiction.

The principal function of the first judicial appearance is not, however, to determine whether there is sufficient evidence for trial. Neither the prosecuting attorney nor the defense lawyer is ready at this point to determine whether probable cause exists. The principal function of the first appearance is to provide for the defendant's release, pending further judicial proceedings. While release is a constitutional right, the bail procedure of temporarily forfeiting money for freedom has resulted in a number of unjust practices.

[8] See Frank W. Miller and Frank J. Remington, "Procedures Before Trial," *Annals of the American Academy of Political and Social Science,* 339 (January, 1962), pp. 111–124.

Ideally the only criterion for the determination of the amount of bail is the amount necessary to ensure the reappearance of the defendant. In practice, however, the bail system discriminates against those who cannot afford to pay the bail fee, fosters a shady bail-bond business, and promotes the use of questionable judicial procedures in the setting of bail.[9] Recent alternatives to the bail system, such as pretrial parole, are eliminating the deficiencies of bail, at the same time providing for both the constitutional release of the defendant and the assurance of his return for subsequent judicial processing.[10]

Arraignment and the Plea. In some jurisdictions the suspect is arraigned immediately after being booked at the police station, thus bypassing the appearance before a magistrate. Whether arraignment is the first judicial appearance or a later one, the arraignment proceeding consists of an appearance before a judge of the trial court. There the judge reads the charge to the defendant and informs him of his right to counsel. The initial charge is based either upon the "information" or "indictment," depending upon the procedures used in the jurisdiction. Some jurisdictions rely upon a grand jury to return an indictment for felony cases with charges for misdemeanors being based on information filed by the prosecuting attorney.

Whatever procedure is used for reaching a charge, the judge then asks the defendant to plead to the charge. The defendant may plead guilty, not guilty, or may stand mute. With the permission of the judge, he may also have the option of pleading *nolo contendere,* which is the same as a plea of guilty except that it cannot be used as an admission in subsequent civil suits. If the defendant pleads guilty, the judge will ordinarily enter a judgment of conviction, postponing the sentence until a presentence investigation can be made by the probation department. If the defendant stands mute, the judge will enter a plea of not guilty, and a trial will follow. If

[9] Caleb Foote, "The Bail System and Equal Justice," *Federal Probation,* 23 (September, 1959), pp. 43–48; Frederic Suffet, "Bail Setting: A Study of Courtroom Interaction," *Crime and Delinquency,* 12 (October, 1966), pp. 318–331; Ronald Goldfarb, *Ransom: A Critique of the American Bail System* (New York: Harper and Row, 1965).

[10] Charles E. Ares, Anne Rankin, and Herbert Sturz, "The Manhattan Bail Project: An Interim Report on the Use of Pre-Trial Parole," *New York University Law Review,* 38 (January, 1963), pp. 67–95.

the plea of the defendant is not guilty, the judge asks whether the defendant desires a jury trial or whether he prefers to be tried by the judge without the presence of a jury. A plea of not guilty places the burden on the state to prove every element of the offense beyond a reasonable doubt.

Guilty Plea Negotiation. Important as the trial is as an ideal in the administration of justice, it is far from the most commonly used method of convicting and acquitting defendants. Roughly 90 per cent of criminal convictions are based on pleas of guilty which are adjudicated without a trial.[11] Estimates on the percentage of cases disposed of by guilty pleas, however, are difficult to establish because of such matters as variations in use from one jurisdiction to another, fluctuations from time to time, and variations according to the kinds of crime being tabulated. Nevertheless, the statistics in Table 5.1 indicate the extent to which guilty plea convictions are used in the general trial jurisdictions of several states.

TABLE 5.1
Guilty Plea Convictions in Several States
(1964 statistics unless otherwise indicated)

State	*Total convictions*	*Guilty pleas*	
		Number	*Percentage*
California (1965)	30,840	22,817	74.0
Connecticut	1,596	1,494	93.9
District of Columbia (yr. end. June 30, 1964)	1,115	817	73.3
Hawaii	393	360	91.5
Illinois	5,591	4,768	85.2
Kansas	3,025	2,727	90.2
Massachusetts (1963)	7,790	6,642	85.2
Minnesota (1965)	1,567	1,437	91.7
New York	17,249	16,464	95.5
U.S. District Courts	29,170	26,273	90.2
Average			87.0

Source: President's Commission on Law Enforcement and Administration of Justice, *Task Force Report: The Courts,* Washington, D.C.: U.S. Government Printing Office, 1967, p. 9.

[11] See Donald J. Newman, *Conviction: The Determination of Guilt or Innocence Without Trial* (Boston: Little, Brown, 1966), pp. 3–4.

Our judicial system has come to depend upon the use of the guilty plea. If all criminal cases were to receive a trial upon a plea of not guilty, the courts simply could not handle the case load. There are not enough, and conceivably could never be enough, judges, prosecutors, and defense attorneys to operate a system in which most defendants would go to trial.

The judicial necessity of guilty pleas has given rise to the practice commonly known as "plea bargaining." A substantial portion of guilty pleas result from negotiations between the prosecutor and defense lawyer or between the prosecutor and the defendant. In addition to managing the case load, the negotiated plea accomplishes other purposes.

> As the term implies, plea negotiation involves an exchange of concessions and advantages between the state and the accused. The defendant who pleads guilty is treated less severely than he would be if he were convicted of the maximum charge and assessed the most severe penalty. At the same time, he waives his right to trial, thereby losing his chance, no matter how slight, for outright acquittal. The state, at the relatively small cost of charge reduction leniency, gains the numerous administrative advantages of the guilty plea over a long, costly, and always uncertain trial. In this way the negotiated plea in a real sense answers two important objectives of criminal justice administration: the individualization of justice and the maintenance of the guilty plea system.[12]

The negotiated guilty plea is thus a compromise conviction reached by the state and the accused for the benefit of both.

Having studied this informal conviction process, Newman reported in an article that plea bargaining occurred in more than half the felony cases studied.[13] During the process the accused, directly or through an attorney, offered to plead guilty providing the charge was reduced in kind or degree, or exchanged for a specific type or length of sentence. The subsequent conviction agreements followed several patterns according to the types of bargains involved:

[12] *Ibid.*, p. 77.

[13] Donald J. Newman, "Pleading Guilty for Considerations: A Study of Bargain Justice," *Journal of Criminal Law, Criminology and Police Science*, 46 (March–April, 1956), pp. 780–790.

1. *Bargain Concerning the Charge.* A plea of guilty was entered by the offenders in exchange for a reduction of the charge from the one alleged in the complaint. This ordinarily occurred in cases where the offense in question carried statutory degrees of severity such as homicide, assault, and sex offenses. This type was mentioned as a major issue in twenty percent of the cases in which bargaining occurred. The majority of offenders in these instances were represented by lawyers.

2. *Bargain Concerning the Sentence.* A plea of guilty was entered by the offenders in exchange for a promise of leniency in sentencing. The most commonly accepted consideration was a promise that the offender would be placed on probation, although a less-than-maximum prison term was the basis in certain instances. All offenses except murder, serious assault, and robbery were represented in this type of bargaining process. This was by far the most frequent consideration given in exchange for guilty pleas, occurring in almost half (45.5 percent) of the cases in which any bargaining occurred. Again, most of these offenders were represented by attorneys.

3. *Bargain for Concurrent Charges.* This type of informal process occurred chiefly among offenders pleading without counsel. These men exchanged guilty pleas for the concurrent pressing of multiple charges, generally numerous counts of the same offense or related violations such as breaking and entering and larceny. This method, of course, has much the same effect as pleading for consideration in the sentence. The offender with concurrent convictions, however, may not be serving a reduced sentence; he is merely serving one sentence for many crimes. Altogether, concurrent convictions were reported by 21.8 percent of the men who were convicted by informal methods.

4. *Bargain for Dropped Charges.* This variation occurred in about an eighth of the cases who reported bargaining. It involved an agreement on the part of the prosecution not to press formally one or more charges against the offender if he in turn pleaded guilty to (usually) the major offense. The offenses dropped were extraneous law violations contained in, or accompanying, the offense alleged in the complaint such as auto theft accompanying armed robbery and violation of probation where a new crime had been committed. This informal method, like bargaining for concurrent charges, was reported

chiefly by offenders without lawyers. It occurred in 12.6 percent of cases in which bargaining was claimed.[14]

Although most of the remainder of the sample pleaded guilty without considerations, in many of these cases the attorneys probably bargained, or attempted to bargain, without successfully achieving a conviction compromise.

The interactions and perceptions of the prosecutor and the defense are critical in the negotiation of a guilty plea. A student of the guilty plea process observed that the prosecutor (district attorney) and the defense (public defender) develop during their interactions a common orientation to the alteration of charges.[15] The negotiators are not able, for purposes of a suitable reduction in charge, to refer to a statutory definition of a particular offense, since the penal code does not provide the reference for deciding the correspondence between the conduct of the offender and the legal category. In the charge of burglary, for example, the prosecutor and defense negotiate about a nonstatutory type of "burglar." The reduction of a burglary charge to a charge of petty theft is accomplished because the negotiators are able to regard the reduction as reasonable and consistent with the kinds of behaviors that are normally associated with the specific charge. During their interaction and repeated negotiations, then, the prosecutor and defense develop unstated guides for reducing original charges to lesser charges.

Plea bargaining takes place between the prosecutor and the accused or his defense for reasons more immediate than those of the individualization of justice and the maintenance of the judicial system.[16] The decision to reduce the charge is often made because the prosecutor realizes that his evidence is probably insufficient for conviction at trial. In other cases reduction may be necessary because of the reluctance of complainants, victims, or witnesses to testify. The prosecutor at other times may suggest a reduction in charge because he believes that the judge or jury is unlikely to convict the defendant. Judges themselves in some cases may favor

[14] *Ibid.*, p. 787.

[15] David Sudnow, "Normal Crimes: Sociological Features of the Penal Code in a Public Defender Office," *Social Problems*, 12 (Winter, 1965), pp. 255–276.

[16] Newman, *Conviction,* pp. 67–75, 105–130, 177–187.

charge reduction to avoid the necessity of imposing the mandatory sentence (either maximum or minimum) associated with the original charge. A parole sentence may only be possible if the original charge is reduced to a lesser charge. On the other hand, whatever the bargaining agreement, the judge may acquit the defendant for a number of reasons that grow out of an interest in individualized justice and judicial maintenance. Acquittals are made because (1) the conduct is regarded as a minor violation, (2) the offender is viewed as unaccountable for his behavior, (3) the conduct is considered normal to the subculture of the defendant, (4) the conduct is a matter of private morality, (5) specialized treatment may be deemed more appropriate than punishment, (6) restitution is otherwise made to the victim, and (7) the judge disagrees with the purpose of the law or with the law enforcement effort.[17]

Whether the judge convicts according to the plea negotiated by the prosecutor and defense or acquits the defendant, he obviously has a personal interest in the outcome of each case. Technically the judge is not suppossed to enter into the bargaining. However, by subtle cues and not so subtle demands, the judge has an influence on the negotiation of pleas. The advantages of plea negotiation for the judge have been indicated in a study of "Metropolitan Court":

> According to the ideology of the law, the judge is required to be not only impartial but active in seeking out and preserving the rights of all offenders. Nevertheless, he also has a vested interest in a high rate of negotiated pleas. He shares the prosecutor's earnest desire to avoid the time consuming, expensive, unpredictable snares and pitfalls of an adversary trial. He sees an impossible backlog of cases, with their mounting delays, as possible public evidence of his "inefficiency" and failure. The defendant's plea of guilty enables the judge to engage in a social-psychological fantasy — the accused becomes an already repentant individual who has "learned his lesson" and deserves lenient treatment. Indeed, as previously indicated, many judges give a less severe sentence to a defendant who has negotiated a plea than to one who has been convicted of the same offense after a trial.[18]

[17] *Ibid.*, pp. 152–172, 188–196.

[18] Abraham S. Blumberg, *Criminal Justice* (Chicago: Quadrangle Books, 1967), p. 65.

Whatever may be the reason for the negotiation of a guilty plea, be it the vested interest of the prosecutor, the defense, the judge, or an interest further removed, the resulting conviction is a criminal definition. Guilty plea negotiation ultimately amounts to the creation of crime.

THE CRIMINAL LAWYER IN THE ADVERSARY SYSTEM

Underlying the administration of criminal justice in the United States is the adversary principle. In the adversary system of criminal justice, opposing parties — the state and the accused — are engaged in a public battle. The game is one of black and white; one side must be entirely correct and the other all wrong. One side wins when the judgment is made in its favor. Furthermore, there are rules and procedures to guide the battle throughout its course. The adversary principle is a basic part of the American system of criminal justice.

The adversary system requires a number of specific occupational roles for its functioning. As such, criminal justice is bureaucratically organized.[19] That is, the system of criminal justice is composed of distinct legal work roles with specified duties and obligations. Each position is defined in itself and in relation to the others. Expectations of performance in respect to the administration of criminal law regulate the occupational behavior of persons that occupy the work roles. The principal roles in the organization of the judicial system are those of the prosecutor, the defense attorney, and the judge. In separate ways, each is engaged in a process which results in the defining of persons and behaviors as criminal.

The judge acts on the basis of evidence and arguments presented by the prosecuting and the defense attorneys. He finds the defendant guilty or innocent, sometimes by referring to the decision of a jury, and then imposes a sentence. The prosecutor's role, how-

[19] *Ibid.* For other observations on the social organization of the administration of criminal justice, see Jerome H. Skolnick, "Social Control in the Adversary System," *Journal of Conflict Revolution,* 11 (March, 1967), pp. 52–70. On the juvenile court, see Aaron V. Cicourel, *The Social Organization of Juvenile Justice* (New York: John Wiley, 1968).

ever, is more critical in the early stages of the judicial process. As the representative of the state, the prosecutor has the authority to determine whether an alleged offender should be charged and the authority to obtain a conviction through guilty plea negotiation. He has the responsibility of presenting the state's cases in court, that is, of prosecuting the accused. His skill as a trial lawyer is important in the conviction of the defendant. The prosecutor also has an influence on the arrest practices of the police, the volume of cases in the courts, and the number of offenders referred to the correctional system.[20] By definition of his legal role, the prosecutor is engaged in a continuous battle against the accused and their defending lawyers.

Legal Representation of the Accused. The right of the accused to be represented by legal counsel has been assured in the Sixth Amendment to the Constitution, and is essential to the adversary system of criminal justice. An individual forced to answer to a criminal charge needs the assistance of one who understands the legal system and who will protect the defendant's legal rights. The defendant is not likely to understand the legal system, largely because of its planned obscurity. In order for a judicial system to be effective and efficient, counsel for the defendant is necessary. Furthermore, an adversary system of justice depends upon vigorous challenges to the state's accusations.

When and how to assure or provide legal counsel for the accused has been the vital issue in the adversary system. Through the establishment of various procedures, in part inspired by rulings of state supreme courts and the United States Supreme Court, defendants are either entitled or required to have legal counsel from the moment of arrest. Likewise, through a recent Supreme Court decision in the *Gault* case, the jurisdictional rights of counsel have been expanded to include juvenile delinquency proceedings.

In providing for counsel, several schemes have been instituted to ensure (in theory at least) that defendants are represented by

[20] For a discussion of the responsibilities of the prosecutor as outlined in state statutes, see Duane R. Nedrud, "The Career Prosecutor," *Journal of Criminal Law, Criminology and Police Science,* 51 (September–October, 1960), pp. 343–355. Also see President's Commission on Law Enforcement and Administration of Justice, *Task Force Report: The Courts* (Washington, D.C.: U.S. Government Printing Office, 1967), pp. 72–79.

legal counsel.[21] The types of legal representation include (1) court appointed counsel, as in the legal aid system, (2) the public defender system, whereby the state provides permanent lawyers to defend the accused, and (3) lawyer reference plans, in which private or public agency lawyers are made known to defendants. The availability of these and other forms of legal representations varies from one jurisdiction to another. Also, and most important for the conviction process, the outcome of cases depends to some extent on the kind of legal counsel the defendant receives.[22]

That criminal justice is differently administered according to social class is at least vaguely realized by most persons. Since the poor are accused of criminal behavior more often than members of other classes, their dependence upon legal service is crucial. However, legal services are the most inadequate for the class which requires legal assistance the most. The poor are least likely to use lawyers; when they do they usually have access to the least competent lawyers, and the legal counsel with which they are provided is generally of limited character. Surveys from several states indicate that about two out of three lower class families have never employed a lawyer, compared with about one out of three upper class families.[23] The few private attorneys who are available to the poor tend to be the least well trained and, because of the insecurity of their practice, are likely to succumb to temptations to exploit clients.[24]

To supplement private legal representation, special agencies and procedures, such as legal aid societies and the defender system,

[21] Albert P. Blaustein and Charles O. Porter, *The American Lawyer: A Summary of the Survey of the Legal Profession* (Chicago: University of Chicago Press, 1954), pp. 64–96.

[22] Differences in the outcomes of criminal cases according to type of legal representation are reported in Lee Silverstein, *Defense of the Poor in Criminal Cases* (Chicago: American Bar Foundation, 1965); Dallin H. Oaks and Warren Lehman, "Lawyers for the Poor," *Trans-Action*, 4 (July–August, 1967), pp. 25–29; Laura Banfield and C. David Anderson, "Continuances in the Cook County Criminal Courts," *University of Chicago Law Review*, 35 (Winter, 1968), pp. 259–316. Differences in juvenile cases are reported in Edwin M. Lemert, "Legislating Change in the Juvenile Court," *Wisconsin Law Review* (Spring, 1967), pp. 421–448.

[23] Jerome E. Carlin and Jon Howard, "Legal Representation and Class Justice," *UCLA Law Review*, 12 (January, 1965), pp. 382–383.

[24] Jerome E. Carlin, *Lawyers' Ethics: A Survey of the New York City Bar* (New York: Russell Sage Foundation, 1966), pp. 71–73.

have extended legal services to the poor. Nevertheless, it appears that indigents are not provided with legal services adequate to their needs. The ultimate result is higher rates of conviction and severer sentences for the poor.

> With respect to the representation of criminal defendants, there is considerable evidence to suggest that neither the assigned counsel nor public defender system as now constituted is capable of providing adequate service to the indigent accused. A large proportion of poor defendants (particularly in misdemeanor cases) are not represented at all. Moreover, when counsel is provided he frequently has neither the resources, the skill nor the incentive to defend his client effectively; and he usually enters the case too late to make any real difference in the outcome. Indeed, the generally higher rate of guilty pleas and prison sentences among defendants represented by assigned counsel or the public defender suggest that these attorneys may actually undermine their clients' position.[25]

Career Patterns in the Practice of Criminal Law. Lawyers who represent criminal defendants on a private basis tend to be engaged in a particular type of legal practice. They also tend to have distinct career patterns. Both tendencies affect the way in which such lawyers handle criminal cases.

More than half the lawyers practicing in cities in the United States are self-employed. The other half are either employed in firms or as lawyers in corporations, governmental legal departments, and legal aid societies.[26] The individual practitioner (or "solo" lawyer) differs sharply from those engaged in the other types of legal practice. It was found in a comparison of individual practitioners and firm lawyers in Detroit that solo lawyers more often came from minority, religious-ethnic, entrepreneurial, and working class homes, had inferior educations, and experienced chaotic work histories.[27] In addition to their special backgrounds, individual practitioners tend to restrict their practices to those residual matters that the large law

[25] Jerome E. Carlin, Jon Howard, and Sheldon L. Messinger, "Civil Justice and the Poor: Issues for Sociological Research," *Law and Society Review,* 1 (November, 1966), p. 56.

[26] 1958 Supplement to *Lawyers in the United States: Distribution and Income* (Chicago: American Bar Foundation, 1959), pp. 54–55.

[27] Jack Ladinsky, "Careers of Lawyers, Law Practice, and Legal Institutions," *American Sociological Review,* 28 (February, 1963), pp. 47–54.

firms have not pre-empted. Their practice, as found in Chicago, includes the following matters:

> (1) matters not large enough or remunerative enough for the large firms to handle — most general work for small to medium-sized businesses and corporations, the smaller real estate transactions (for individuals or small businesses), and estate matters for middle-income families; (2) the undesirable cases, the dirty work, those areas of practice that have associated with them an aura of influencing and fixing and that involve arrangements with clients and others that are felt by the large firms to be professionally damaging. The latter category includes local tax, municipal, personal injury, divorce, and criminal matters.[28]

Thus, the lawyers who privately handle the criminal cases of lower and working class defendants tend to be individual practitioners. Moreover, they are likely to be engaged in a diversified legal practice in which the handling of criminal cases is only an occasional affair. Their practice of law generally centers around the local police court or the traffic court and tends to be ethnic and neighborhood oriented. The following quotation from a solo lawyer in Chicago illustrates the way in which diverse legal matters are related for the individual practitioner:

> I handle some small criminal cases. This year I had one case, an indictment in felony court, a bench trial. The rest would be either police court — up to the preliminary hearing, getting charges reduced to misdemeanors, and so on — assault and battery, domestic problems, mostly drunks and disorderlies, assaults, etc. Neighborhood stuff. So many domestic relations cases come out of the police court; after representing them in the police court, you get them dismissed for divorce.[29]

The individual practitioners who do specialize in criminal law practice must maintain regular sources of case referral. These lawyers depend upon close relations with bondsmen, policemen, and community leaders for business. The competition for criminal cases among solo lawyers who specialize in criminal law produces a legal

[28] Jerome E. Carlin, *Lawyers on Their Own: A Study of Individual Practitioners in Chicago* (New Brunswick, N.J.: Rutgers University Press, 1962), pp. 17–18.

[29] *Ibid.*, pp. 105–106.

practice that is based more on sharp business practices than the pursuance of criminal justice.

The difference between lawyers with criminal practices and those with civil practices has been documented in a study of the careers of a sample of lawyers in five cities.[30] This study compared criminal lawyers and civil lawyers on such characteristics as social origins, choice of legal career, preparation for law, adjustment to legal practice, and reasons for entering the particular field of legal practice. It was found that the criminal lawyers, in comparison to the civil lawyers, tended to have relatively low socioeconomic backgrounds, had less professional training, had difficulty getting established, were solo practitioners engaged in an entrepreneurial career, and were not especially satisfied with criminal practice.

On the basis of the characteristics of the criminal lawyers, the study distinguished between two types of criminal law careers. In the first type,

> the attorney did not choose to enter criminal law, but rather he accepted criminal cases as they came his way in the process of establishing a practice or as a supplement to a meager practice in civil law. From the standpoint of the legal profession, these lawyers are among the least successful, and accordingly one may judge their morale to be correspondingly low. The second type of criminal lawyer is one who often chose this field, but in any case he enjoys the drama and thrill of those accused of crime. He may achieve considerable success; lacking this, he is compensated by his intense absorption in the work.[31]

Only about one-fourth of the criminal lawyers can be placed in the second type of criminal law career. Of course, some criminal lawyers do not fit into either of the two types, including the successful ones who do not have a welfare orientation and those who strongly identify with the welfare of their clients but whose careers may be described as failures. Nevertheless, the majority of practitioners of criminal law can be described as either those who have failed to establish a successful practice and therefore accept criminal cases as a way of enlarging a legal practice, or those who relish the excite-

[30] Arthur Lewis Wood, *Criminal Lawyer* (New Haven: College & University Press, 1967), pp. 34–67.

[31] *Ibid.*, p. 238.

ment of criminal work and feel that their practice secures justice for those accused of crime.

Behavior and Ethics of Criminal Lawyers. All lawyers are subject to the normative controls of their occupation. Among these controls are standards that proscribe behavior considered unethical by society in general, such as cheating, bribery, and stealing. Additional standards deal with professional problems, such as relations among colleagues, methods of obtaining business, and conflicts of interests. Lawyers differ in the extent to which they conform to these standards. Ultimately the legal assistance the client receives is influenced by the behavior and ethics of the lawyer that handles the case.

On the ethical conduct of lawyers, in a study of a sample of New York City bar members it was found that various characteristics of the lawyers' practice influence violation of professional standards.[32] Among other things, it revealed that because of the instability of their practice, lawyers with low status clients are subject to far more temptations, opportunities, and client pressure to violate professional ethics than are lawyers with high status clients. Also influencing the ethical conduct of the lawyers is the court setting in which the lawyer operates and the constraints provided by the lawyer's work group. Conformity to professional norms and ethics thus depends greatly on the location of the lawyer within the structure of the legal profession.

For the lawyer engaged in criminal practice, professional norms cover several areas: "(1) confidentiality of the attorney-client relationship; (2) affective or emotional neutrality with respect to the merits of the case, while at the same time service in the interests of the client; and (3) participation in procedures in which a professional as opposed to a personal relationship is maintained with other participants — the police, the bondsman, the prosecutor and the judge."[33] The behavior of the defense lawyer is especially complicated by the fact that he is confronted with conflicting claims. Because of his legal role, the defense attorney must act as a mediator between the client and judicial agents. The professional conduct of the criminal lawyer, therefore, is related to the way in which he

[32] Carlin, *Lawyers' Ethics,* pp. 165–182.
[33] Wood, *Criminal Lawyer,* p. 93.

manages the conflicting claims imposed by the adversary system of justice.

The great majority of defendants handled by criminal lawyers are actually guilty of some offense. Because of his precarious position, the defendant is subject to considerable manipulation by his attorney, and his case tends to become guided by the personal interests of the lawyer. Finally, the lawyer's handling of the defendant's case is affected by the bureaucratic structure of the court: "In the sense that the lawyer in the criminal court serves as a double agent, serving higher organizational rather than professional ends, he may be deemed to be engaged in bureaucratic rather than private practice."[34] In this way, criminal law practice is actually bureaucratic practice, because of the enmeshment of the lawyer and his client in the authority and discipline of the judicial system. Strategies and decisions affecting the application of criminal definitions are made within the boundaries established by the adversary system of justice.

THE CRIMINAL TRIAL AND THE JURY

The adjudication of the accused may eventually take place in a criminal trial. When negotiation between the various legal agents has failed to result in the defendant's plea of guilty, or when the defendant pleads not guilty without any attempt at bargaining, a criminal trial will provide the setting for the further enactment of the drama of imposing a criminal definition. While variations occur in the operation of a trial, a trial generally follows a number of steps.[35] The arraignment and plea may be followed by: (1) the selection of the jury, (2) the prosecutor's and defense's opening statements, (3) presentation of the state's and the defense's evidence, (4) prosecutor's and defense's arguments to the jury, (5) prosecutor's rebuttal, (6) judge's instructions on the law, (7) rendition of the jury verdict, and (8) imposition of a sentence.

[34] Abraham S. Blumberg, "The Practice of Law as Confidence Game: Organizational Cooptation of a Profession," *Law and Society Review,* 1 (June, 1967), pp. 15–39.

[35] Robert E. Knowlton, "The Trial of Offenders," *Annals of the American Academy of Political and Social Science,* 339 (January, 1962), pp. 125–141.

It is obvious that not all of these steps are included in any trial. It may be decided that the defendant will be tried before a judge or panel of judges, rather than by a jury. Various motions for change in procedure may be entered during the trial. Decisions may be made in regard to the waiving of statements, evidence, and testimony. Motions may be made by the defense for a new trial or to hold immediate judgment. Following the sentence, the case may be appealed to a higher court, or upon a charge of the denial of due process there may be further litigation. In other words, the final conviction depends upon a host of decisions and actions once the defendant reaches the trial stage.

Extralegal Considerations in the Criminal Trial. According to popular conception the criminal trial is symbolic of justice in America. This conception is based on the notion that justice is rationally dispensed. The assumption is that persons involved in the judicial process — lawyers, defendants, witnesses, jurors, judges — base their statements, arguments, and judgments on facts and according to the rules of law. All parties are supposedly engaged in pursuit of the "truth" about the case. Such a conception of the criminal trial ignores both the nature of the actions of men and the organizational constraints imposed by the judicial system itself. The criminal trial may be most profitably analyzed as a system of human actions that entails perceptions and behaviors the like of which are found in any social situation. The persons involved in the trial are acting according to their own pasts, their present perspectives, and their future expectations; and their actions are oriented to the behavior of others.

> In a sense the courtroom may be viewed as a microcosm of the larger social world in which human beings exist, act, and interact. That the action reconstructed in court and the action-process of reconstruction are meaningful and purposive, that they involve subjective as well as objective meanings, and that they significantly hinge on human goals, purposes and motives becomes at once apparent. If some juridical writers envisage a mere mechanical application of formalized law, the participants in the ordinary court trial of a criminal case are involved in more mundane practices.[36]

[36] Edwin M. Schur, "Scientific Method and the Criminal-Trial Decision," *Social Research,* 25 (Summer, 1958), p. 178.

The combative nature of the criminal trial ensures that judicial actions are social and extralegal rather than logical deductions from abstract principles. As a substitute for private brawls, the modern criminal trial places parties in opposing camps. The adversary system of justice promotes a "fight" method rather than a "truth" method of trying cases.[37]

In other words, the criminal trial nominally is a process of constructing a reality — a social reality. Objective facts are not gathered in a criminal trial, but decisions are reached on "evidence" that is meaningful to the interacting and conflicting participants. Subjectivity enters into the arguments of the attorneys, the testimony of the witnesses, the deliberations of jurors, and the actions of the judge. All the actors involved in the drama are reacting subjectively to the actions of each other. The decisions reached during the trial, including the decision that ultimately defines the defendant as a convicted criminal, are made by men as social beings. That is to say, though the criminal trial is not an exercise in fact finding and logical deduction, it is a product of human action. Could something else be expected?

Testimony and Witnesses. The testimony of various types of witnesses is used by both sides — the prosecution and the defense — to argue the merits of their respective positions. Of particular concern to the defense attorney is the decision on whether or not to put the defendant on the stand as a witness in his own behalf. The decision of the defense is usually based on speculation about how the jury will react to the performance of the defendant. Also, the defense will be reluctant to place a defendant on the witness stand who has a prior criminal record.[38] Though procedurally a previous conviction should not be considered as evidence of guilt on another charge, the defendant with a previous conviction is especially vulnerable to probing by the prosecuting attorney. The use of the defendant as a witness is of strategic importance in the criminal trial.

Both the prosecution and defense will utilize any witness who may favorably shape the opinions of the judge and jury members.

[37] Jerome Frank, *Courts on Trial: Myth and Reality in American Justice* (Princeton: Princeton University Press, 1949), chap. 6.

[38] Arnold S. Trebach, *The Rationing of Justice* (New Brunswick, N.J.: Rutgers University Press, 1964), pp. 172–173.

Such witnesses, however, tend to be placed in an insecure position.[39] In spite of procedures to guarantee his protection, the witness is subject to pressures from the public, the press, and personal contacts. He may eventually suffer repercussions from his testimony. The witness is most dramatically subjected to harassment during the opposition's cross-examination in the courtroom. Little wonder that the "facts" provided by witnesses are selective and subjective, rather than objective as commonly supposed.

Among the testimony that may be included in the adjudication of the accused is the testimony of the so-called "experts." Criminal procedure today relies especially upon the testimony of the psychiatrist. Most states provide for observation of defendants suspected of mental disorders. On the basis of a judge's decision to accept evidence provided by a psychiatrist, the accused may be judged incompetent to stand trial and then be committed indefinitely to a mental hospital.

During the criminal trial, the psychiatrist, in responding to the *M'Naghten* test of insanity, is asked to make a judgment as to the responsibility and, in essence, the guilt or innocence of the defendant.[40] In jurisdictions that have rules of the *Durham* type, the psychiatrist may describe the mental state of the defendant entirely in psychiatric language. The psychiatrist thus has a crucial role in the criminal trial of today because of the information he can supposedly provide in regard to the legal concept of the defendant's responsibility.

The power of the psychiatrist in the criminal trial, because of the questionable nature of his practice, has been seriously criticized in recent years. A person charged with a criminal offense may be denied the right to trial as a result of the pretrial psychiatric examination.[41] In other words, psychiatrists are engaged in putting people away without the guarantee of a trial. Such "putting away" may

[39] See Rudolph E. Morris, "Witness Performance Under Stress: A Sociological Approach," *Journal of Social Issues,* 13 (November 2, 1957), pp. 17–22; Israel Gerver, "The Social Psychology of Witness Behavior With Special Reference to Criminal Courts," *Journal of Social Issues,* 13 (November 2, 1957), pp. 23–29.

[40] Seymour L. Halleck, "A Critique of Current Psychiatric Roles in the Legal Process," *Wisconsin Law Review* (Spring, 1966), pp. 379–401. Also see Abraham S. Goldstein, *The Insanity Defense* (New Haven: Yale University Press, 1967).

[41] Thomas S. Szasz, *Psychiatric Justice* (New York: Macmillan, 1965).

actually be inspired by adversaries who do not want the would-be defendant around.

To illustrate this point, Szasz describes the case of a filling station operator in Syracuse, New York, who had been pressed by real estate developers to sell his property for the development of a shopping center on the site. When agents of the developers attempted to erect a sign on the property, the enraged operator fired warning shots from a rifle into the air. He was arrested but was never brought to trial. On the recommendation of the prosecuting attorney, the filling station operator was ordered to undergo psychiatric examination to determine his fitness to stand trial. He was held incapable and was committed to a state mental hospital. Still in a hospital after ten years, the filling station operator had already served more time than he would have spent in prison had he been tried and convicted. Whatever criticism one wants to direct at the use of psychiatric evidence, the fate of the defendant may be directly affected by the testimony of "experts."

Trial by Jury. Trial by a jury stands as the cornerstone of American criminal justice. In practice, trial by jury in the United States accounts for about 80 per cent of criminal jury trials in the world today.[42] However, the jury trial is the mode of conviction for only a small fraction of criminal prosecutions in the United States. Of those cases which are tried, nearly half are tried without a jury. Only about one in seven felony prosecutions ends in a trial by jury.

The relatively small use of the jury trial for criminal conviction is accounted for by (1) legal restrictions on the right of trial by jury, (2) the decision of the prosecution and defense to settle by guilty plea conviction, and (3) the choice of the defendant to be tried before a judge without a jury.[43] Although the Sixth Amendment to the Constitution guarantees the right to trial by jury, the states specify the kinds of offenses that will be tried by a jury. Under the laws of most states, a jury trial may be denied for such minor offenses as traffic violation, disorderly conduct, petty gambling, public drunkenness, and prostitution.

Beyond the stipulations of the state laws, trial by jury is a choice

[42] Harry Kalven, Jr. and Hans Zeisel, *The American Jury* (Boston: Little, Brown, 1966), p. 13.
[43] *Ibid.*, pp. 14–17.

that is left open to the defendant. Whether to be prosecuted without a trial or to be tried with the waiver of a jury, depends upon the strategy worked out by the defendant and the various legal actors. The decision to avoid a jury trial varies considerably according to the nature of the offense and local custom. About 90 per cent of forgeries are prosecuted through guilty pleas, but only about 30 per cent of murders are prosecuted in such a way. When trials are used for murder, the jury is waived only about 15 per cent of the time, whereas for forgery the jury is waived about 50 per cent of the time. Furthermore, local variations in the waiver of jury are marked. In Wisconsin, the jury is waived in approximately three-fourths of criminal cases; in Utah it is waived in only about 5 per cent of the cases.[44]

While the jury trial is not used as frequently as commonly assumed, it nevertheless exerts an important influence on American criminal justice. The trial operates as a control on the judicial administration of cases that are not tried by a jury.

> It has become something of a commonplace to read the statistics on the impact of guilty pleas and jury waivers as gravely reducing the significance of the jury and transferring its power largely to the prosecuting attorney in the bargaining over guilty pleas. But we saw at every stage of this informal process of pre-trial dispositions that decisions are in part informed by expectations of what the jury will do. Thus, the jury is not controlling merely the immediate case before it, but the host of cases not before it which are destined to be disposed of by the pre-trial process. The jury thus controls not only the formal resolution of controversies in the criminal case, but also the informal resolution of cases that never reach the trial stage. In a sense the jury, like the visible cap of an iceberg, exposes but a fraction of its true volume.[45]

Once the decision has been made to try the defendant before a jury, numerous social factors enter into the way in which the jury operates in arriving at a decision on the defendant's guilt or innocence. The prosecutor and defense are well aware that jurors' backgrounds and personal characteristics influence the way in which jurors respond to the evidence and arguments presented in the trial.

[44] *Ibid.*, pp. 19–30.
[45] *Ibid.*, pp. 31–32.

In selecting the jury, during the *voir dire* examination, the attorneys attempt to choose jurors who will make decisions favorable to the respective sides of the case. For each attorney, a trial may be won or lost during the empaneling of the jury. The composition of the jury is thus an important factor in determining the kind of definition that will be imposed on the defendant.

Defendants are supposedly tried by a representative body of the citizenry, at least such is the stereotype. However, social and economic biases are present in the methods by which jurors are selected. The result is that the lower occupational groups tend to be systematically excluded from juries in the United States.[46] Furthermore, and important for our purpose, the unrepresentative character of the jury affects the way in which juries deliberate and arrive at decisions about the innocence or guilt of the defendant.

The sources of bias in jury deliberation have been commented on in several studies of jury behavior. On the basis of a study of mock jury deliberations, it was found that foremen tend to be selected according to their social position in the larger community.[47] The incidence of selection was three and a half times as great among proprietors as among laborers. In addition, only one-fifth as many women were made foremen as would be expected by chance. The role of foreman is particularly important in jury deliberation because of the foreman's opportunity to change the opinion of the individual jurors according to his own views.[48]

The social status and sex of the individual jurors appear to be related to the extent to which they participate in jury deliberations and influence the overall decision of the jury. From the studies of mock juries it has been found that men and persons of higher social status, in comparison to women and persons of lower social status, have higher participation rates and greater influence in jury deliberations.[49] Men of the upper occupational groups tend to act more

[46] W. S. Robinson, "Bias, Probability, and Trial by Jury," *American Sociological Review,* 15 (February, 1950), pp. 73–78.

[47] Fred L. Strodtbeck, Rita M. James, and Charles Hawkins, "Social Status in Jury Deliberations," *American Sociological Review,* 22 (December, 1957), pp. 713–719.

[48] William Bevan, Robert S. Albert, Pierre R. Loiseaux, Peter N. Mayfield, and George Wright, "Jury Behavior as a Function of the Prestige of the Foreman and the Nature of His Leadership," *Journal of Public Law,* 7 (Fall, 1958), pp. 419–449.

[49] Strodtbeck, James, and Hawkins, "Social Status in Jury Deliberations,"

in jury deliberation than any other type of juror. Women and persons of the lower occupational groups, on the other hand, when they do participate, tend to react to the contributions of the others.

Thus, the ability of jury members to influence the decisions of others is in part a function of the social status and sex of the jurors. Furthermore, jurors also differ according to the kinds of things they focus on during the deliberation. In general, as found in another mock jury study, jurors spend about half their time exchanging experiences and opinions either directly or indirectly related to the trial. About a quarter of the time is spent on procedural matters, about 15 per cent is spent on review of the facts of the case, and about 8 per cent on the court instructions.[50] The more educated give relatively more emphasis to procedure and instructions, the less educated place greater emphasis on testimony, personal and daily life experiences, and opinions based on the trial rather than on procedure and instruction. The same researcher found that in insanity trials lower class jurors are more likely to favor the defendant. Women jurors, on the other hand, are more sympathetic toward the defendant than men, but are likely to qualify their verdict according to the nature of the offense.[51]

In the end, the verdict reached by the jury may not be the same as the one the trial judge would have rendered. The extent to which the verdicts of juries and judges differ has been extensively researched.[52] This study investigated and analyzed a sample of 3,576 cases of actual jury verdicts and the matching hypothetical verdicts of the judges involved in the cases. The major finding of the research was that the judge and jury *agreed* in 75.4 per cent of the trials. More specifically, the judges and juries agreed to acquit in 13.4 per cent of the cases and to convict in 62.0 per cent. In the trials in which the judges and juries disagreed, the disagreement was predominantly in one direction: the jury was more likely than the judge to acquit. The jury acquitted when the judge would have convicted in 16.9 per cent of the cases. In contrast, the jury con-

---

pp. 713–719; also see Fred L. Strodtbeck and Richard D. Mann, "Sex Role Differentiation in Jury Deliberations," *Sociometry,* 19 (March, 1956), pp. 3–11.

[50] Rita M. James, "Status and Competence of Jurors," *American Journal of Sociology,* 64 (May, 1959), pp. 536–570.

[51] Rita James Simon, *The Jury and the Defense of Insanity* (Boston: Little, Brown, 1967), pp. 98–119.

[52] Kalven and Zeisel, *The American Jury,* esp. pp. 55–65.

victed when the judge would have acquitted in 2.2 per cent of the cases. In other words, the juries were more lenient that the judges in 16.9 per cent of the cases and less lenient than the judges in 2.2 per cent of the cases. Practically, this means that when the defense decides to bring the case before a jury, the defendant fares better on the average 14.7 per cent of the times than he would have in a bench trial. The defense strategy in reference to the type of trial, in other words, plays an important part in determining the probability of a criminal conviction.

JUDICIAL SENTENCING

Following the conviction of the defendant, a decision must be made regarding the sanction that will be attached to the newly ascribed status of "criminal." The specification of the sanction, a process known as *sentencing*, involves the manipulations and discretions of a number of persons. In some jurisdictions the type and length of sentence are determined by the jury. In other jurisdictions sentencing is the responsibility of an administrative board. But in most jurisdictions in the United States the judge assigns the sentence.[53]

However, even when sentencing is the province of the judge, other persons participate in the decision-making process. Many states provide for a presentence investigation of the convicted defendant. The decision to proceed with such an investigation depends upon the discretion of the defense attorney and to some extent upon the maneuvers of the prosecutor and the judge. The presentence investigation is then made by persons in the probation department attached to the court. The report, which covers the defendant's personal and social background, his criminal record, and his mental and physical condition, includes the probation department's recommendations for sentencing. With the report and recommendations in hand, the judge imposes a sentence. But as shown in a study of the relation between presentence reports and dispositions, in most cases judges sentence according to the recommendations of the probation department.[54] Although the final sen-

[53] See Paul W. Tappan, "Sentencing Under the Model Penal Code," *Law and Contemporary Problems,* 23 (Summer, 1958), pp. 528–543.

[54] Robert M. Carter and Leslie T. Wilkins, "Some Factors in Sentencing Policy," *Journal of Criminal Law, Criminology and Police Science,* 58 (De-

tencing decision may belong to the judge, the decisions of others are crucial in the actual disposition.

The sentence imposed by the judge must fall within the limits provided by the penal law. The codes of penal law contain an elaborate classification of crimes with corresponding penalties graded according to seriousness of the crime. Within the boundaries of penal law, however, judges may exercise a great deal of discretion in deciding upon a sentence. A range of alternative sentences and lengths of sentences are available to the judge for any given crime.

Furthermore, recent legal innovations, especially the indeterminate sentence and probation, have increased the discretionary possibilities of sentencing. In addition, the movement toward individualizing treatment has provided both a rationale and justification for the use of discretion in sentencing convicted offenders.

The fact that sentencing practices of judges vary is easy to illustrate with sentencing statistics. A study of sentences assigned in nearly 7,500 criminal cases handled by six judges over a ten-year period in a county in New Jersey reported that the judges differed considerably in the frequency, length, and types of sentences they assigned to convicted offenders.[55] The diversity of the sentencing tendencies of the judges was even more marked when the sentences were analyzed according to the type of crime.

An explanation for the varied sentencing practices may be found in the backgrounds and attitudes of the judges. Some indication of the relation of various background and attitudinal characteristics of judges to their decisions is provided in research on the judicial decisions of a sample of state and federal supreme court judges.[56]

---

cember, 1967), pp. 503–514. Also see Robert M. Carter, "The Presentence Report and the Decision-Making Process," *Journal of Research in Crime and Delinquency,* 4 (July, 1967), pp. 203–211; Trebach, *The Rationing of Justice,* pp. 178–187.

[55] Frederick J. Gaudet, "The Difference Between Judges in Granting Sentences of Probation," *Temple Law Quarterly,* 19 (April, 1946), pp. 471–484; Frederick J. Gaudet, "Individual Differences in Sentencing Tendencies of Judges," *Archives of Psychology,* 32 (1938); Frederick J. Gaudet, G. S. Harris, and C. W. St. John, "Individual Differences in Penitentiary Sentences Given by Different Judges," *Journal of Applied Psychology,* 8 (October, 1934), pp. 675–680.

[56] Stuart S. Nagel, "Judicial Backgrounds and Criminal Cases," *Journal of Criminal Law, Criminology and Police Science,* 53 (September, 1962), pp. 333–339.

TABLE 5.2

Average Sentences in Months, by Offense and Judicial Circuit, of Federal Prisoners Received from the Courts into Federal Prison

(fiscal year ended June 30, 1966)

Judicial circuit	*Narcotics laws*	*Forgery*	*Immi-gration*	*Liquor laws*	*Stolen motor vehicles*	*Other offenses*
1st Circuit (Me., Mass., N.H., R.I., P.R.)	45.8	13.7	13.7	4.0	26.5	31.8
2nd Circuit (Conn., N.Y.)	64.2	18.2	9.2	14.9	25.2	23.8
3rd Circuit (Del., N.J., Penn., V.I.)	33.1	24.8	12.0	25.8	36.2	51.7
4th Circuit (Md., N.C., S.C., Va., W. Va.)	51.6	20.4	24.0	15.0	34.1	34.3
5th Circuit (Ala., Fla., Ga., La., Miss., Tex.	63.9	28.7	12.2	14.0	32.6	36.2
6th Circuit (Ken., Mich., Ohio, Tenn.)	69.6	24.4	17.6	16.2	30.4	49.3
7th Circuit (Ill., Ind., Wis.)	58.6	33.7	18.3	14.8	35.4	45.1
8th Circuit (Ark., Iowa, Minn., Mo., Neb., N.D., S.D.)	66.5	32.7	5.2	16.1	35.0	45.1
9th Circuit (Alaska, Ariz., Cal., Hawaii, Idaho, Mont., Nev., Ore., Wash., Guam)	58.7	31.3	8.2	8.4	40.9	53.0
10th Circuit (Colo., Kans., N.M., Okla., Utah, Wyo.)	73.9	36.0	7.4	19.4	37.5	45.4

Source: Figures from U.S. Department of Justice, Federal Bureau of Prisons, *Statistical Report Fiscal Year 1966* (Washington, D.C., 1967), pp. 46–47.

Each judge was given a decision score representing the proportion of times he favored the defense. Judges who tended to be more defendant-minded were likely to be Democrats rather than Republicans, non-members rather than members of the American Bar Association, non-former prosecutors rather than former prosecutors, Catholics rather than Protestants, and relatively liberal as measured by off-the-bench attitudes. Therefore, because of certain attributes, judges tend to make particular kinds of judicial decisions.

The decisions of judges also vary on a geographical basis. Ecological variations in sentencing statistics seem to indicate that the sentencing behavior of judges is normatively regulated and that the normative patterns differ from one region to another. In Table 5.2 are shown the average sentences assigned to persons convicted of federal crimes and committed to federal institutions. Even federal judges appear to be bound by local customs in sentencing persons who violate federal laws. For the convicted offender, the sentence he receives depends to some extent on the sentencing patterns of the jurisdiction in which he is tried and sentenced.

To show that judges differ in their sentencing practices is not necessarily to criticize judicial sentencing. The principal matter for our purpose is that defendants are differently defined and handled according to a process that consists of factors beyond the behavior of those who are criminally defined. Sentencing itself must be regarded as a process in which a series of decisions are made, decisions that are necessarily based on the operation of discretion by various legal agents.

These sentencing decisions probably are made within the framework provided by the law, including the nature of the crime and the offender's prior criminal record.[57] Nevertheless, within the boundaries of the law there is the opportunity for decisions to be made on the basis of social or extralegal considerations. The criminal sanctions that are ultimately imposed on the convicted defendant are influenced by such extralegal matters as the nature of the judges who assign the sentences, the norms that regulate sentencing, the social organization of the judiciary, the activities of the attorneys, and the responses and cues provided by the defendant himself. Sentencing could not take place any other way. Sentencing, like all social actions, is a human endeavor.

[57] Edward Green, *Judicial Attitudes in Sentencing* (London: Macmillan, 1961).

CHAPTER SIX

Penal and Correctional Administration

The application of criminal definitions is not completed with the sentencing of the convicted offender. Once a sentence has been decided upon, it must be administered. The administration of the sentence involves the same types of processes that operate in all other stages of applying criminal definitions. Thus, administration of the sentence is influenced by such community and organizational factors as community expectations, public reaction, and the occupational organization and ideology of the legal agents. Ultimately, within this social and cultural framework, the fate of the criminally defined is determined by the evaluations of those assigned the task of administering criminal sentences.

Conceptually and practically the administration of the criminal sentence can be divided into orientations that emphasize either the punishment or the treatment of offenders. The legal policies themselves provide a general orientation to the administration of sentences, and differ from one jurisdiction to another in the relative emphasis placed on penal and correctional objectives. It is in the administration of sentences that the fulfillment of these orientations becomes evident.[1]

A major development in the system of criminal justice in the United States has been the growing emphasis on correction. Over

[1] Research on the punishment-treatment orientation of several jurisdictions is found in Norman S. Hayner, "Correctional Systems and National Values," *British Journal of Criminology*, 3 (October, 1962), pp. 163–175.

the last fifty years probation and parole have been used increasingly, the juvenile court was created, treatment and prevention programs were developed, and treatment was established within the prison. All these signal the rise of "the rehabilitative ideal."[2] However, the results of this rise have not been as humanitarian in outcome as intended. In fact, the schemes resulting from the rehabilitative ideal have often led to an increase in penal measures. Many of the original aims of the ideal have been debased and practices have been instituted which conflict with individual rights. As a consequence, in the administration of criminal sentences the separate orientations of punishment and treatment have not been as disparate as might have been expected.

Whatever the general objectives of penal and correctional policy, the criminal sentence may be served and completed in a number of ways. The convicted offender may be placed on probation, imprisoned, given therapy, educated, executed, or paroled. Or attempts may be made to prevent criminal offenses through the establishment of community prevention programs. These efforts will be discussed in relation to the social reality of crime.

ORGANIZATION AND SUPERVISION OF PROBATION

The sentencing of an offender may consist of a prescribed period of probation supervised by agents of the state. The satisfactory completion of the probationary period depends on the offender's "good behavior" and conformity to the stipulated conditions of probation. The removal of the convicted offender from the status of "criminal" depends in the end on the actions and recommendations of the probation officer.

The decisions of probation officers are made within the broader context of the organization of the probation system. Currently the administration of probation is "involved in a transitional period of organizational conflict as a consequence of moving from a politically

[2] Francis A. Allen, "Criminal Justice, Legal Values and the Rehabilitative Ideal," *Journal of Criminal Law, Criminology and Police Science,* 50 (September–October, 1959), pp. 226–232. For a discussion of the possible infringement of the constitutional and civil rights of prisoners who are made to participate in therapy programs, see David Sternberg, "Legal Frontiers in Prison Group Psychotherapy," *Journal of Criminal Law, Criminology and Police Science,* 56 (December, 1965), pp. 446–449.

oriented to a professionally career-oriented service."[3] Increasingly, officers with a professional orientation are being drawn from the field of social work. These more recent workers contrast with the older, politically oriented officers. Though the professionally oriented workers are humanitarian and liberal in ideology, recognizing the dignity of the human personality, the older workers, drawing ideological support from a conservative middle-class philosophy of life, act as paternal counselors to the offender. The professionally oriented officers, trained in the casework approach, believe in promoting the welfare of the community by aiding the offender, while the politically oriented officers, relying on their own common sense and experience, attempt to protect the community from the offender.

The administration of probation, therefore, is beset by a conflict between the different types of officers and a subsequent struggle for the control of probation agencies. Moreover, the *decisions* of the probation officers are affected by these organizational problems. Because of several incompatible role obligations in his occupation, the officer has difficulty in making consistent and satisfactory decisions. The officer trained in social work finds that his acquired skills have not equipped him to deal with authoritative and punitive demands. These officers demonstrate a great deal of disagreement and confusion about the proper way to supervise cases.[4] Many regard some surveillance and enforcement activities as inappropriate responsibilities. The officer without training in social work, on the other hand, discovers that he lacks the knowledge and ability to understand the personal needs of the offenders he is supervising. Most probation officers, therefore, whatever their occupational orientation, experience some kind of conflict in their work.

Aside from the personal inconveniences that the officers experience, those who are ultimately affected by the organization of probation are the persons on probation. The divergent orientations to probation work directly affect the ways in which probationers

[3] Lloyd E. Ohlin, *Sociology and the Field of Corrections* (New York: Russell Sage Foundation, 1956), p. 45.

[4] See Lloyd E. Ohlin, Herman Piven, and Donnell M. Pappenfort, "Major Dilemmas of the Social Worker in Probation and Parole," *National Probation and Parole Journal,* 11 (July, 1956), pp. 211–225; Dale E. Van Lanengham, Merlin Taber, and Rita Dimants, "How Adult Probation Officers View Their Job Responsibilities," *Crime and Delinquency,* 12 (April, 1966), pp. 97–108; Seymour Z. Gross, "Biographical Characteristics of Juvenile Probation Officers," *Crime and Delinquency,* 12 (April, 1966), pp. 109–116.

are handled. "Competing philosophies and working principles within the agency result in the inconsistent handling of cases and produce frustrations on the part of the workers which, in turn, affect the counseling and disposition of problem cases."[5] As has been true for the offender throughout the processing of his case, his fate is decided as much by the problems and actions of others as by his own volitions.

In maintaining surveillance over the offender, the probation officer makes crucial decisions about the probationer's behavior. Probation can be successfully completed only when the terms stipulated in the sentence have been met to the satisfaction of the probation officer — or of any other legal agents who may come in contact with the probationer. If the probationer should be suspected of violating the terms of probation, his probationary status can be revoked. When such a case occurs, the probation officer recommends whether or not probation should be revoked. In many jurisdictions the decision is made during a judicial hearing.[6] At that time the probation officer can testify that the probationer has violated probation and can, in addition, offer an appropriate course of action. Officers tend to differ among themselves in the kinds of decisions they make in revocation proceedings.[7] The differences in recommendations are related to the personal characteristics and orientations of the officers, the extenuating circumstances of the cases, the role relations of the officers and the offenders, and the involvement of other legal agents in the cases. Again, decisions that directly determine the offender's future are made by others, and are influenced by extralegal considerations.

SOCIAL ORGANIZATION OF PENAL CUSTODY

However diverse the rationale, the "prison exists as a dramatic symbol of society's desire to segregate the criminal."[8] And once the

[5] Ohlin, *Sociology and the Field of Corrections*, p. 47.

[6] Ronald B. Sklar, "Law and Practice in Probation and Parole Revocation Hearings," *Journal of Criminal Law, Criminology and Police Science*, 55 (June, 1964), pp. 175–198.

[7] John P. Reed and Charles E. King, "Factors in the Decision-Making of North Carolina Probation Officers," *Journal of Research in Crime and Delinquency*, 3 (July, 1966), pp. 120–128.

[8] Gresham M. Sykes, *The Society of Captives: A Study of a Maximum Security Prison* (New York: Atheneum, 1965), p. 18.

prisons are populated with criminals, the primary task becomes that of custody. To provide for the secure maintenance of inmates is thus the major objective in the administration of the prison.

> The prison wall, that line between the pure and the impure, has all the emotional overtones of a woman's maidenhead. One escape from the maximum security prison is sufficient to arouse public opinion to a fever pitch and an organization which stands or falls on a single case moves with understandable caution. The officials, in short, know on which side their bread is buttered. Their continued employment is tied up with the successful performance of custody and if society is not sure of the priority to be attached to the tasks assigned the prison, the overriding importance of custody is perfectly clear to the officials.[9]

The internal order of the prison is maintained by the strict control of inmates and the rigid satisfaction of all functions and personnel within the prison. The prison, as a "system of total power," is an organization unto itself, an organization that is relatively unaffected by external events and in which social control is paramount.[10] A distinct caste-like division is maintained between those who rule and those who are ruled. Furthermore, operation of the prison requires several, often contradictory, internal hierarchic organizations.

> The structure of prisons provides for three principal hierarchies — devoted to *keeping, using,* and *serving* inmates — but not for the integration of their divergent purposes. The separate organizations concerned with keeping and with serving inmates, for example, are not merely overlapping, but have entirely different and partly contradictory purposes.[11]

Each type of organization, in turn, promotes a particular kind of relationship between the staff and the inmates and a specific pattern of authority, communication, and decision-making. However, the

[9] *Ibid.,* p. 18.

[10] See Erving Goffman, "On the Characteristics of Total Institutions," in Donald R. Cressey (ed.), *The Prison: Studies in Institutional Organization and Change* (New York: Holt, Rinehart and Winston, 1961), pp. 15–106; Sykes, *The Society of Captives,* pp. 40–62.

[11] Donald R. Cressey, "Limitations on Organization of Treatment in the Modern Prison," in Richard A. Cloward, *et al., Theoretical Studies in Social Organization of the Prison* (New York: Social Science Research Council, 1960), pp. 79–80.

persons most affected by the divergent organizations of the prison are the inmates. Differences in the handling of the inmates' affairs are in large measure the result of the organizational problems inherent in the prison.

Administration of the prison can be best understood if we recognize the pressures exerted by groups that are attempting to achieve conflicting objectives. These "correctional interest groups" determine the ways in which prison policy is established and administered.[12] Among these interest groups are some that operate within the prison, such as the groups that make up the staff (administrative staff, custodians, professional workers) and the inmate population. Interest groups that operate outside of the prison include welfare agencies, educational groups, religious organizations, various kinds of legal agents, and leaders of political parties. The numerous inconsistencies and contradictions in prisons are due to the activities of these groups. The unique organization that is the prison is a result of the convergence of competing groups that define their interests according to the ways in which prisons are operated.

The objective of custody creates its own form of communication and decision-making within the prison. In an authoritarian fashion, a social order is imposed upon the inmates by the administrators. The conditions of such an order are maintained by a rigid system of communication. A massive body of regulations from above is passed on to those below. Decision-making occurs at the top of the administrative structure and is communicated through well defined channels of authority. At the bottom of the chain of command, that is, among the inmates, decision-making is kept at a minimum. "Inmates are officially permitted to make only those types of decisions which prior study by administrators has shown to be of no danger to community safety."[13]

The requirements of a custodial regime present the inmate with a personally frustrating situation. Being used to achieving goals, the prisoner finds that it is virtually impossible to realize these goals

[12] Lloyd E. Ohlin, "Conflicting Interests in Correction Objectives," in Cloward, *et. al., Theoretical Studies in Social Organization of the Prison,* pp. 111–129.

[13] Donald R. Cressey, "Prison Organizations," in James G. March (ed.), *Handbook of Organizations* (Chicago: Rand McNally, 1965), p. 1044. Also see Richard McCleary, "Communication Patterns as Bases of Systems of Authority and Power," in Cloward, *et al., Theoretical Studies in Social Organization of the Prison,* pp. 49–77.

within the prison. The inmate is deprived of basic liberties, goods and services, heterosexual relationships, and autonomy.[14] Imprisonment is painful. Not only are the physical deprivations overwhelming, but the withdrawal of the many commonly assumed freedoms is an attack against the foundations of the prisoner's sense of being.

The pains of imprisonment cannot be easily removed by the inmate:

> Unable to escape either physically or psychologically, lacking the cohesion to carry through an insurrection that is bound to fail in any case, and bereft of faith in peaceful innovation, the inmate population might seem to have no recourse but the simple endurance of the pains of imprisonment. But if the rigors of confinement cannot be completely removed, they can at least be mitigated by the patterns of social interaction established among the inmates themselves. In this apparently simple fact lies the key to our understanding of the prisoner's world.[15]

The social world of prisoners, however imperfect that society may be, is an uneasy solution to the rigors of penal custody.

The inmate society is composed of a number of related social roles, which are structured by the ideology of the inmate code. The chief tenets of the code are, roughly: (1) Do not interfere with the interests of other inmates; (2) Refrain from arguments and quarrels with fellow inmates; (3) Do not exploit or take advantage of one another; (4) Maintain integrity in the face of privation; and (5) Do not side with the custodial authorities.[16] Inmate society, in prison argot, orders and classifies inmates by their orientations to the maxims of the code. The *rat* is an inmate who violates the norm proscribing the betrayal of a fellow inmate; the *merchant* exploits his fellows by manipulation; and the *tough* quarrels with other prisoners. The *square John* or *center man* makes the mistake of allying with officials. The role that most nearly fulfills the norms of the inmate code is that of the *right guy,* the *real con,* or the *real man.* This epitomizes what it is to be the ideal inmate, as judged

[14] Sykes, *The Society of Captives,* pp. 63–83.

[15] *Ibid.,* p. 82.

[16] Gresham M. Sykes and Sheldon L. Messinger, "The Inmate Social System," in Cloward, *et al., Theoretical Studies in Social Organization of the Prison,* pp. 5–9.

by fellow inmates. But all the social roles are important for an understanding of the inmate society, for they establish patterns of social interaction among inmates.[17] Only by this interaction, within a society of the inmates' own creation, can the rigors of imprisonment be made bearable.

The extent to which prisoners conform to the inmate culture and oppose the expectations of the prison staff varies according to a number of factors. An early study observed that most inmates gradually assimilate aspects of the prison culture.[18] This assimilation has been called "prisonization," suggesting that inmates increase their commitment to the prison culture with the *length* of time they serve in the prison. Using another temporal conception, it was more recently found that conformity to expectations of the prison staff also depends on the length of time *remaining* to be served.[19] Wheeler showed that inmates tend to follow an adaptive U shaped pattern of conformity. That is, in the early and late phases of incarceration inmates conform to staff expectations, whereas those in the middle phase deviate from such expectations. Further research by others has specified these relationships. It has been found that the temporal effect of the inmate code on administrative expectations varies according to the social characteristics of the inmate, the type of crime committed by the offender, the experiences the inmate has had prior to imprisonment, and the social role the inmate plays in the inmate society.[20] Also, there is evidence that inmates in a prison oriented primarily to custody are less likely to become committed to prison objectives than inmates who are in a treatment-oriented prison.[21] All these findings support the position

[17] Sykes, *The Society of Captives,* pp. 84–108.

[18] Donald Clemmer, *The Prison Community* (New York: Rinehart, 1940), pp. 294–320.

[19] Stanton Wheeler, "Socialization in Correctional Communities," *American Sociological Review,* 26 (October, 1961), pp. 697–712.

[20] See, in particular, Peter G. Garabedian, "Social Roles and Processes of Socialization in the Prison Community," *Social Problems,* 11 (Fall, 1963), pp. 139–152; Daniel Glaser, *The Effectiveness of a Prison and Parole System* (Indianapolis: Bobbs-Merrill, 1964), pp. 548–583; Charles Wellford, "Factors Associated with Adoption of the Inmate Code: A Study of Normative Socialization," *Journal of Criminal Law, Criminology and Police Science,* 58 (June, 1967), pp. 197–203.

[21] David Street, "The Inmate Group in Custodial and Treatment Settings," *American Sociological Review,* 30 (February, 1965), pp. 40–55.

taken here, namely that the social organization of custody affects the administration of penal and correctional policy.

A final consideration in this administrative setting involves the relationship between inmates and the prison staff. Although the social organization of the prison is composed of an inmate system and an administrative system, prison organization also contains an informal system of inmate-staff relations. Both inmates and staff find it necessary to establish patterns of interaction in order to secure their separate interests. Successful operation of the inmate society requires a certain amount of cooperation from the staff. Likewise, the interests of the prison staff can be achieved only with the cooperation of the inmates. In a sense, there is a "corruption of authority" among the members of the prison staff.[22] The guard, for example, under pressure to maintain a smoothly running cell block, ignores breaches of prison rules in return for manageable conduct by the inmates. The informal inmate-staff system is thus a response to the insurmountable difficulties of maintaining strict control in a custodial institution. Informal patterns, not specified in prison regulations, are essential to the administration of penal and correctional policy within the confines of custody.

ADMINISTRATION OF INSTITUTIONAL TREATMENT

The modern prison is based on a paradox: it is designed to punish inmates and at the same time reform them by nonpunitive measures. The paradox is a logical outcome of earlier practices.

> Even the first prison used some nonpunitive measures believed to have a reformative effect on prisoners, such as haphazard religious and secular education, and exhortations in the name of God, mother, and country. An important characteristic of Elmira, the first American "reformatory," established in 1876, was provision of educational classes and vocational training, which were believed to be reformative. Yet this reformatory was constructed as a maximum-security *penal* institution, and the educational and vocational efforts at rehabilitation were made in that setting. The conflicting punitive and treat-

[22] Gresham M. Sykes, "The Corruption of Authority and Rehabilitation," *Social Forces,* 34 (March, 1956), pp. 257–262.

> ment conceptions of reformation thus became institutionalized, for almost all prisons in the United States have followed the Elmira pattern.[23]

Because of the basic incompatibility of punishment and treatment, rehabilitating the offender within the punitive setting is either difficult, at best, or impossible. The inherent contradictions in the achievement of both goals are many.[24] From the standpoint of the inmate, it is contradictory to put an offender into a custodial institution against his own will, and, at the same time, expect him to be willing to enthusiastically participate in a treatment program. Similarly, there is the difficulty of expecting staff members of an institution to enforce and administer conflicting goals. Furthermore, the implementation of punishment and treatment requires diverse kinds of organizational arrangements. And theoretically, punitive restriction is incompatible with rehabilitation theory. Attempts at treatment, nevertheless, continue to be pursued vigorously within the prison.

Some of the most important concrete problems that arise in institutional treatment involve the relation of staff members to one another, the relationships of the inmates, and the interaction between staff members and inmates. The staff in charge of treatment is faced with the problem of getting the respect of the inmates while the inmates are also being required by other staff members to obey elaborate regulations. The regulations themselves are restrictive, and their violation results in penalties and even harsher restrictions. The therapeutic staff must maintain the restrictions while simultaneously offering the potential for inmate self-expression. This hypocritical behavior on the part of the therapeutic staff understandably receives little respect from the inmates. Further, the attempts of the therapeutic staff to administer treatment conflicts with the objectives of the custodial staff.[25] Not only are the goals

23 Cressey, "Limitations on Organization of Treatment in the Modern Prison," pp. 85–86.

24 See Donald R. Cressey, "Contradictory Directives in Complex Organizations: The Case of the Prison," *Administrative Science Quarterly,* 4 (June, 1959), pp. 1–19; Johan Galtung, "Prison: The Organization of Dilemma," in Cressey (ed.), *The Prison,* pp. 107–145.

25 See Gene G. Kassebaum, David A. Ward, Daniel M. Wilner, and Will C. Kennedy, "Job Related Differences in Staff Attitudes Toward Treatment in a Women's Prison," *Pacific Sociological Review,* 5 (Fall, 1962), pp. 83–88; Joseph C. Mouledoux, "Organizational Goals and Structural Change: A Study of the

of the therapeutic staff and the custodial staff contradictory, but the implementation of their goals requires divergent actions. The therapeutic and custodial staffs view one another's daily activities as being at cross-purposes.

> Custodial workers are concerned with maintaining control and this concern is reflected in their priorities of action in a given situation as well as in the considerations they express in planning and supervising inmates' activities. On the other hand, treatment personnel tend to be concerned with mitigating the psychological or interpersonal problems of inmates. Conflict engendered by these different priorities is exacerbated because custodial and treatment workers, by virtue of their different responsibilities, are also frequently confronted in a different manner by inmates. These workers thus develop different conceptions of the inmates and each staff group becomes convinced of the correctness of its view and derides that of the other.[26]

In addition, the relationships that the inmates develop among themselves affect the implementation of treatment programs. As we have seen, inmates are forced to form their own social system in response to the pains of imprisonment. This inmate system, in turn, affects the way in which treatment is administered. In particular, the participation of inmates in treatment programs is influenced by their involvement in the inmate system. Inmates who are highly committed to the inmate system are less likely to participate meaningfully in a treatment program.[27] Imprisonment makes an inmate

---

Organization of a Prison System," *Social Forces,* 41 (March, 1963), pp. 283–290; George H. Weber, "Conflicts Between Professional and Non-Professional Personnel in Institutional Delinquency Treatment," *Journal of Criminal Law, Criminology and Police Science,* 48 (June, 1957), pp. 26–43; Stanton Wheeler, "Role Conflict in Correctional Communities," in Cressey (ed.), *The Prison,* pp. 229–259; Mayer W. Zald, "Power Balance and Staff Conflict in Correctional Institutions," *Administrative Science Quarterly,* 7 (June, 1962), pp. 22–49.

[26] Irving Piliavin, "The Reduction of Custodian-Professional Conflict in Correctional Institutions," *Crime and Delinquency,* 12 (April, 1966), pp. 125–134.

[27] See Daniel Glaser and John R. Stratton, "Measuring Inmate Change in Prison," in Cressey (ed.), *The Prison,* pp. 381–392; Clarence Schrage, "A Preliminary Criminal Typology," *Pacific Sociological Review,* 4 (Spring, 1961), pp. 11–16; Charles R. Tittle and Drollene P. Tittle, "Structural Handicaps to Therapeutic Participation: A Case Study," *Social Problems,* 13 (Summer, 1965), pp. 75–82.

system necessary, and the inmate system creates its own problems for the administration of institutional treatment.

The ability of a treatment program to be administered with any success in an institutional setting varies according to the ideology and structure of the prison. Although all prisons are punitive in that their inmate populations are confined against their wills, coupled with the fact that physical confinement produces social and psychological deprivations, prisons do differ in the manner in which they balance punitive and treatment goals. Some prisons are primarily oriented and arranged for the rehabilitation of the inmates, while other prisons devote most of their attention to the punitive custody of prisoners.

There is considerable evidence to indicate that the ideological orientation and structure of the prison determine the administration of institutional treatment programs. In one study, the organization of six institutions for male delinquents was examined.[28] The institutions differed in the relative emphasis placed on punishment and treatment. The findings showed that the treatment-oriented institutions varied systematically from those which were custodial-oriented in such characteristics as power distribution, departmental structure, role definition, organizational conflict, and systems of social control. It was also found that the staff attitudes toward inmates differed in the two types of institutions. All these factors were shown to influence the effectiveness of treatment within the institutions. Similarly, other research has shown that in treatment-oriented institutions inmates are more positive toward the prison goals and that inmate leaders often serve as coordinators and interpreters for administrative policies.[29] Whether the institution is basically oriented to treatment or custody determines the potential for the administration of treatment programs.

[28] David Street, Robert D. Vinter, and Charles Perrow, *Organization for Treatment* (New York: The Free Press, 1966). Also see Mayer N. Zald, "Organization Control Structures in Five Correctional Institutions," *American Journal of Sociology,* 68 (November, 1962), pp. 335–345.

[29] Bernard B. Berk, "Organizational Goals and Inmate Organization," *American Journal of Sociology,* 71 (March, 1966), pp. 522–534. Also see Street, "The Inmate Group in Custodial and Treatment Settings," pp. 40–55; Richard M. Stephenson and Frank R. Scarpitti, "Argot in a Therapeutic Correctional Milieu," *Social Problems,* 15 (Winter, 1968), pp. 384–395.

Whatever the orientation of the prison, some form of treatment is usually attempted. A host of treatment "techniques" have been designed and administered with the aim of changing criminals into noncriminals. The punitive-oriented prisons have tended to rely on clinical techniques, working with individual inmates in some form of counseling or psychotherapy. Treatment-oriented prisons, on the other hand, have tended to implement programs based on a group-relations principle, attempting to change the attitudes and behavior of inmates through the manipulation of social relationships.[30] Recent developments in institutional treatment have involved a modification of the custodial setting in which treatment is administered. Included in these recent developments are work release programs outside of the prison, halfway houses where offenders receive residential treatment while they also work or attend school, and community treatment centers where offenders attend daily sessions but live at home.[31]

Nevertheless, the effectiveness of institutional treatment is questionable: "Prisons are highly successful as a means of incapacitating persons for a period of time, but their successes in deterring them from becoming recidivists or repeaters is much less."[32] Others have similarly reached the conclusion that "the success of imprisonment as a means of reformation is very slight."[33] After a review of

[30] The theoretical background of the "group-relations principle," is discussed in Donald R. Cressey, "Social Psychological Foundations for Using Criminals in the Rehabilitation of Criminals," *Journal of Research in Crime and Delinquency,* 2 (July, 1965), pp. 49–59. For a discussion of specific programs, see Lloyd W. McCorkle, "Group Therapy in the Treatment of Offenders," *Federal Probation,* 16 (December, 1952), pp. 22–27; Lloyd W. McCorkle and Richard Korn, "Resocialization Within Walls," *Annals of the American Academy of Political and Social Science,* 293 (May, 1954), pp. 88–98.

[31] Arthur Pearl, "The Halfway House: The Focal Point of a Model Program for the Rehabilitation of Low Income Offenders," in Frank Reisman, Jerome Cohen, and Arthur Pearl (eds.), *Mental Health for the Poor* (New York: The Free Press, 1964), pp. 497–508; Lamar T. Empey and Jerome Rabow, "The Provo Experiment in Delinquency Rehabilitation," *American Sociological Review,* 26 (October, 1961), pp. 679–695; President's Commission on Law Enforcement and Administration of Justice, *Task Force Report: Corrections* (Washington, D.C.: U.S. Government Printing Office, 1967), pp. 38–44.

[32] Marshall B. Clinard, *Sociology of Deviant Behavior,* 3rd ed. (New York: Holt, Rinehart and Winston, 1968), p. 792.

[33] Edwin H. Sutherland and Donald R. Cressey, *Principles of Criminology,* 7th ed. (Philadelphia: J. B. Lippincott, 1967), p. 542.

several sources of available statistics, it was observed that a large proportion of prisoners return to prison.[34] Furthermore, and more specifically, approximately 55 per cent of persons received into state and federal prisons and reformatories have had previous experience with institutional rehabilitation. More recent evidence shows, however, that the prison may be more effective in rehabilitation than previously indicated. An analysis of several follow-up studies of inmates released from various prisons reaches the conclusion that reimprisonment rates actually vary between 20 and 40 per cent for different correctional systems.[35] In addition, it is argued, the criminal career of the offender is reversed during prison experience and at least 90 per cent of the inmates released from the federal prison system seek legitimate careers for a month or more after they leave prison.[36]

Some of the variations in reimprisonment rates can be accounted for by the ways in which treatment programs are implemented in various prisons. Variations are also influenced by the structure of the respective inmate populations, the selective use of probation, and the policies of probation and parole officers.[37] In regard to differences in prison populations, some persons have strongly presented the case that some types of prisoners are better risks for rehabilitation than others. Treatment methods used with one type of inmate could be less effective with others.[38] More recently, an elaborate typology of criminal careers was proposed, along with associated treatment strategies for each type.[39] Group therapy or milieu forms of therapy are recommended for semiprofessional property offenders, drug addicts, joyriders, aggressive rapists, and certain other types. Intensive psychiatric treatment is suggested for nonviolent sex offenders, incest cases, male homosexuals, violent sex offenders, and psychopathic assaultists. A program of minimal treatment is recommended for statutory rapists and for "one-time loser" property or

[34] George B. Vold, "Does the Prison Reform?" *Annals of the American Academy of Political and Social Science,* 293 (May, 1954), pp. 42–50.

[35] Daniel Glaser, *The Effectiveness of a Prison and Parole System* (Indianapolis: Bobbs-Merrill, 1964), pp. 13–35.

[36] *Ibid.,* pp. 475–487.

[37] *Ibid.,* pp. 13–35.

[38] George B. Vold, *Theoretical Criminology* (New York: Oxford University Press, 1958), pp. 296–304.

[39] Don C. Gibbons, *Changing the Lawbreaker: The Treatment of Delinquents and Criminals* (Englewood Cliffs, N.J.: Prentice-Hall, 1965), pp. 228–282.

personal offenders. The implication is that inmate recidivism rates will be lowered when treatment programs are related to the needs of particular types of offenders.

Another reason for the inconclusive evidence on recidivism is the lack of systematic postrelease information and reliable follow-up studies of inmates, which results in part from the underdevelopment of rehabilitation theories. Correctional workers, in addition, have not been trained in the skills necessary for evaluative research. But more important, persons engaged in administering institutional treatment have vested interests which foster particular kinds of programs. A negative evaluation of a program might mean personal loss for those associated with the program.

> Precise research on the "success" of either general programs of crime control or more specific methods of correction furnishes information which is the basis for public esteem and professional reputation, as well as information about the correctional technique being evaluated. These two are very different. Personal and organizational needs supplement the societal needs being met by administration and utilization of various correctional techniques. For example, by utilizing or advocating use of particular techniques in correctional work, a person may secure employment and income, good professional reputation, prestige as an intellectual or scholarly authority, the power stemming from being the champion of a popular ideology, and many other personal rewards. An agency organized around administration of a technique may fill such needs for dozens, even hundreds, of employees, and may itself have more general, organizational needs for survival. Hence, evaluative research results which would show that the technique is ineffective and would, thereby, seriously threaten the agency or the personnel must be avoided if possible.[40]

Regardless of the variations in the effectiveness of institutional treatment, we are left with the question of why some inmates *do not* return to prison. The argument usually advanced is that those who do not return have been rehabilitated *because of* specific treatment they have received in prison. But perhaps some persons do not return to prison *in spite of* institutional treatment. It might be

[40] Donald R. Cressey, "The Nature and Effectiveness of Correctional Techniques," *Law and Contemporary Problems,* 23 (Autumn, 1958), p. 758.

suggested that some ex-prisoners never return because of circumstances they encounter upon their release. This is the basis of the argument that most of those who return to prison have not been able to find legitimate opportunities during the first crucial weeks of their release.[41] Those who remain outside of prison most often find themselves in situations where it is no longer necessary to engage in criminally defined activity or are able to avoid criminal definitions in some other way. If this is so, the prison is virtually useless as a rehabilitative agency. Rather, it serves as a holding device while the inmate ages and society changes. Time itself can create new circumstances for the offender. Following this argument, the prison should at least be a humane place of caretaking. But, as implied above, custody (by definition) cannot be humane. Meaningful community and personal activity, much of it not currently regarded as "work," would be a much better alternative to penal custody and institutional treatment. "Rehabilitation" as an explicit objective would be better relegated to penological history.

ADMINISTRATION OF CAPITAL PUNISHMENT

Several administrative means are used for releasing inmates from the prison. The original sentence may be modified by the executive in the form of pardon, commutation, or amnesty. Other prisoners are released merely through the expiration of their sentences. In such cases, the expiration date is fixed by the legislature, or on an indeterminate sentence, an administrative board decides upon the date of release within the minimum and maximum limits established by the court.

But the final and fatal solution to the removal of the prisoner is either by execution or by death from other causes while in prison. Some prison deaths are the result of the mistreatment of inmates. These deaths aside, primarily because the public has little knowledge about them, the administration of capital punishment can be considered as the most consequential aspect of the application of criminal definitions.

That death, as a legal sentence, is subject to human discretion

[41] Glaser, *The Effectiveness of a Prison and Parole System*, pp. 487–496.

seems rather absurd. But, since the death sentence is a provision of law and an administrative action, discretion operates in decision-making. To begin with, variations are found in the decision to make capital punishment a sentencing alternative. At the end of 1967 capital punishment was legally provided for in all but nine jurisdictions.[42] Among these jurisdictions variations occur in the number and types of crimes that are subject to the death penalty. In addition, states differ in their stipulations as to whether the death penalty is mandatory upon conviction.[43] Alabama provides capital punishment for sixteen offenses, with the mandatory sentence for assault by a person serving a life sentence. California has provisions for six capital crimes, with the mandatory sentence for train wrecking, assault by a lifer, perjury, and treason. More generally, most of the states with capital punishment provisions specify murder and kidnaping as capital offenses. Rape and treason are subject to the death penalty in about half the capital punishment states. Other states have scattered capital provisions for such offenses as robbery, arson, dueling, illegal use of explosives, attempt on the life of the executive, and lynching. Most of the variations result from differences in regional and local customs. Although it may be true that death is a private affair, legally lives are taken by the wills and actions of others.

The extent of discretion involved in the administration of capital punishment is obvious from a view of execution statistics. Historically, the number of executions has been decreasing. Between 1900 and 1966 there have been approximately 7,126 executions in the United States.[44] But since 1930, when statistics began to be systematically compiled, executions have declined from an annual average of 167 during the 1930's to an annual average of 27 during the

[42] Bureau of Prisons, "Executions 1930–1967," *National Prisoner Statistics*, No. 42, Washington, D.C., 1968, pp. 30–32.

[43] See Robert H. Finkel, "A Survey of Capital Offenses," in Thorsten Sellin (ed.), *Capital Punishment* (New York: Harper & Row, 1967), pp. 22–31; Leonard D. Savitz, "Capital Crimes as Defined in American Statutory Law," *Journal of Criminal Law, Criminology and Police Science*, 46 (September–October, 1955), pp. 355–363.

[44] Bureau of Prisons, "Executions 1930–1967," p. 8; and Hugo Adam Bedua, "Introduction: The Laws, the Crimes, and the Executions," in Hugo Adam Bedua (ed.), *The Death Penalty in America* (Garden City, N.Y.: Doubleday, 1964), p. 35. Also see Thorsten Sellin, "Executions in the United States," in Sellin (ed.), *Capital Punishment*, pp. 31–35.

first seven years of the 1960's. Though there were 199 executions in 1935, there were 15 executions in 1964, 7 in 1965, and only 2 in 1967. Nevertheless, even with the decrease in executions, at the end of 1967, 435 persons were under sentence of death waiting time in the death rows of state and federal prisons.

There have always been regional variations in executions. As shown in Table 6.1, approximately 60 per cent of the executions between 1930 and 1967 occurred in the south.[45] Of the executions between 1930 and 1967, 2,306 were in the southern states, 608 in the northeastern states, 509 in the western states, and 403 in the north central states. These regional variations are also evident according to executions for *types* of offenses. Of the 455 executions for rape, 443 took place in the south. Less than 1 per cent of the executions in the northeastern region were for rape, whereas rape accounted for 15 per cent of the executions in the southern region.

Execution patterns also prevail regarding the *race* of execution victims. Review of the execution statistics for the years 1930–1967 shows that 54 per cent of those executed were Negroes.[46] For rape, in particular, the vast majority of those executed, 89 per cent, were Negroes. These figures indicate that capital punishment is highly discriminatory. Although the disproportional percentage of Negroes executed, compared to the proportion of Negroes in the general population, reflects lower class and racial involvement in violence, this disproportion *also* indicates the greater willingness of jurisdictions to apply the death penalty to Negroes than to whites convicted of similar crimes. Lower class persons from the discriminated-against racial and ethnic groups have a greater risk of being executed than their counterparts in crime.

The discriminatory (or discretionary) character of execution operates at several stages preceding the final execution. Not only are Negroes and lower class persons more likely than others to be convicted for committing similar crimes, but they are more likely to be given a death sentence rather than some alternative sentence. Further, once Negroes and lower class persons are placed on death row, their sentences are less likely to be commuted.

The person or group of persons responsible for commutation of execution sentences have grave discretionary powers. The authority

[45] Bureau of Prisons, "Executions 1930–1967," pp. 10–11.
[46] *Ibid.*, p. 10.

TABLE 6.1
Executions in the United States, 1930–1967

Region and state	*All offenses*	*Murder*	*Rape*	*Armed robbery*	*Kid-naping*	*Other offenses*
UNITED STATES	3,859	3,334	455	25	20	25
NORTHEAST	608	606	—	—	2	—
N.H.	1	1	—	—	—	—
Vt.	4	4	—	—	—	—
Mass.	27	27	—	—	—	—
Conn.	21	21	—	—	—	—
N.Y.	329	327	—	—	—	2
N.J.	74	74	—	—	—	—
Penn.	152	152	—	—	—	—
NORTH CENTRAL	403	393	10	—	—	—
Ohio	172	172	—	—	—	—
Ind.	41	41	—	—	—	—
Ill.	90	90	—	—	—	—
Iowa	18	18	—	—	—	—
Mo.	62	52	10	—	—	—
S.D.	1	1	—	—	—	—
Neb.	4	4	—	—	—	—
Kan.	15	15	—	—	—	—
SOUTH	2,306	1,824	443	23	5	11
Del.	12	8	4	—	—	—
Md.	68	44	24	—	—	—
D.C.	40	37	3	—	—	—
Va.	92	71	21	—	—	—
W. Va.	40	36	1	—	3	—
N.C.	263	207	47	—	—	9
S.C.	162	120	42	—	—	—
Ga.	366	299	61	6	—	—
Fla.	170	133	36	—	1	—
Ky.	103	88	10	5	—	—
Tenn.	93	66	27	—	—	—
Ala.	135	106	22	5	—	2
Miss.	154	130	21	3	—	—
Ark.	118	99	19	—	—	—
La.	133	116	17	—	—	—
Okla.	60	54	4	1	1	—
Tex.	297	210	84	3	—	—
WEST	509	496	—	—	7	6
Mont.	6	6	—	—	—	—
Idaho	3	3	—	—	—	—
Wyo.	7	7	—	—	—	—
Colo.	47	47	—	—	—	—
N.M.	8	8	—	—	—	—
Ariz.	38	38	—	—	—	—
Utah	13	13	—	—	—	—
Nev.	29	29	—	—	—	—
Wash.	47	46	—	—	1	—
Ore.	19	19	—	—	—	—
Cal.	292	280	—	—	6	6

Source: Adapted from Bureau of Prisons, "Executions 1930–1967," *National Prisoner Statistics,* No. 42, Washington, D.C., 1968, pp. 10–11.

and procedures for granting clemency vary considerably from one jurisdiction to another. They can be generally classified as:

> (1) a board alone; (2) a board alone, with the governor sitting as a member; (3) a board alone, the governor sitting as a member with grant, conditional on his being in the majority; (4) the governor, empowered to act only if a board makes a favorable recommendation (governor can overrule, denying commutation); (5) the governor with the advice and consent of an executive council, an elected body. Under the Federal Constitution the President alone has the power to abrogate a death sentence, derived from the power to grant reprieves and pardons.[47]

These pardoning authorities, in turn, hold differing philosophies about their responsibilities and use various criteria in making their decisions. Among the facts that these authorities consider are the nature of the crime, the character of the trial, the mental and physical condition of the offender, and rehabilitation possibilities.[48] But also important in their decisions are such extralegal considerations as the publicity surrounding the case, political pressures, precedents in other cases, and personal views on capital punishment. Once a person is placed in death row, life is dependent upon the personal problems of others.

The operation of selective factors in commutation and execution has been documented in research. Examination of the records for capital offenders in North Carolina showed that of the persons committed to North Carolina's death row since 1909, the sentences of whites were commuted more often than the sentences of Negroes. Sixty-two per cent of the Negroes committed to death row were executed, compared to 43.8 per cent of the whites waiting for execution. Also, inmates who went to the death chair tended to have less education and more menial jobs than those who were granted clemency.[49]

Similarly, it was found that of condemned inmates executed in Pennsylvania since 1914, significantly more Negroes than whites

[47] Solie M. Ringold, "The Dynamics of Executive Clemency," in Sellin (ed.), *Capital Punishment,* p. 227.

[48] See Elkan Abramowitz and David Paget, "Executive Clemency in Capital Cases," *New York University Law Review,* 39 (January, 1964), pp. 136–189.

[49] Elmer H. Johnson, "Selective Factors in Capital Punishment," *Social Forces,* 36 (December, 1957), pp. 165–169.

were included.[50] After finding that certain characteristics distinguished the executed inmates from those who had their execution orders commuted, such as the kind of counsel received during the trial, the researchers established that the race of the offender was the most important factor determining whether or not a person waiting execution was executed or granted clemency. It was concluded that "Negroes have not received equal consideration for commutation of the death penalty."[51] Such findings and conclusions illustrate not only that research in the administration of penal and correctional policy can uncover and explain the workings of the law, but also that such research has implications for legal reform.

Despite questions raised in the administration of capital punishment, popular arguments continue to be advanced for retaining statutory provisions for the death penalty. The principal arguments refer to (1) the death penalty as a deterrent to crime, (2) the certainty of punishment when the death penalty is prescribed, and (3) the financial economy of capital punishment.[52] On the first argument, the preponderance of evidence indicates that capital punishment does not act as a deterrent. This conclusion is based on a number of observations and researches that have demonstrated, first, that murder rates have remained constant despite trends away from the use of capital punishment; second, that where one state has abolished capital punishment and another has not, the murder rate is no higher in the abolition state than in the retention state; and, third, that the possible consequences of the act of murder are not considered by the murderer at the time of the offense.[53]

[50] Marvin E. Wolfgang, Arlene Kelly, and Hans C. Nolde, "Comparison of the Executed and the Commuted Among Admissions to Death Row," *Journal of Criminal Law, Criminology and Police Science,* 53 (September, 1962), pp. 301–311.

[51] *Ibid.,* p. 311.

[52] Sutherland and Cressey, *Principles of Criminology,* pp. 346–353.

[53] William J. Chambliss, "Types of Deviance and the Effectiveness of Legal Sanctions," *Wisconsin Law Review* (Summer, 1967), pp. 704–707. Evidence substantiating these conclusions is presented in Frank E. Hartung, "Trends in the Use of Capital Punishment," *Annals of the American Academy of Political and Social Science,* 284 (November, 1952), pp. 8–19; Leonard D. Savitz, "A Study in Capital Punishment," *Journal of Criminal Law, Criminology and Police Science,* 49 (December, 1958), pp. 338–341; Karl F. Schuessler, "The Deterrent Influence of the Death Penalty," *Annals of the American Academy of Political and Social Science,* 284 (November, 1952), pp. 54–62; Thorsten Sellin, "Capital Punishment," *Federal Probation,* 15 (September, 1961), pp. 3–11; Thorsten Sellin, *The Death Penalty* (Philadelphia: The Amercian Law Institute, 1959).

The second major argument in favor of capital punishment, the certainty of punishment, is negated by the fact that the death penalty is seldom imposed. Witnesses are less willing to testify and juries are less willing to convict when the penalty is the possibility of death rather than some other.[54] In regard to the third argument, the financial economy of the death penalty, the fact is that the per capita cost for execution is more than that for imprisonment.[55] Trials of capital cases tend to be more costly and time consuming than trials for other cases. In addition, the maintenance costs for inmates in death row are higher than for inmates in the rest of the prison. Thus capital punishment does not perform the functions claimed by its most vociferous advocates.

Although the capital punishment debate continues, the demise of the death penalty as a provision and as an actuality is imminent. Capital punishment is "an archaic custom of primitive origin that has disappeared in most civilized countries and is withering away in the rest."[56]

> If an intelligent visitor from some other planet were to stray to North America, he would observe, here and there very rarely, a small group of persons assembled in a secluded room who, as representatives of an all-powerful sovereign state, were solemnly participating in deliberately and artfully taking the life of a human being. Ignorant of our customs, he might conclude that he was witnessing a sacred rite somehow suggesting a human sacrifice. And seeing our great universities and scientific laboratories, our mental hospitals and clinics, our many charitable institutions, and the multitude of churches dedicated to the worship of an executed Savior, he might well wonder about the strange and paradoxical workings of the human mind.[57]

PAROLE DECISIONS AND SUPERVISION

But the major form of release from prison is parole. Sixty-five per cent of the inmates released from state and federal institutions are

[54] Herbert B. Ehrmann, "The Death Penalty and the Administration of Justice," *Annals of the American Academy of Political and Police Science,* 284 (November, 1952), pp. 73–84.

[55] Sutherland and Cressey, *Principles of Criminology,* pp. 352–353.

[56] Thorsten Sellin, "The Inevitable End of Capital Punishment," in Sellin (ed.), *Capital Punishment*, p. 253.

[57] *Ibid.,* p. 253.

discharged by parole or some form of mandatory supervision.[58] In principle, parole is the conditional release of an offender who has served a portion of his sentence in a penal or correctional institution. The parole decision is made by the members of a parole board. Such boards may be staffed by personnel of an institution or by members of a statewide board of parole. In some jurisdictions the parole boards have the authority to administer parole as well as to grant it.

The wide range of discretion in the paroling of offenders is made obvious by a review of the statistics on parole releases from state prisons. As shown in Table 6.2, the differences in the use of parole by the various states are vast. To take the extremes, 100 per cent of the first releases from New Hampshire and Washington were by parole, whereas only 12.3 per cent of the first releases from Wyoming were by parole. The variations result from differences in both state penal laws and in the organization and administration of parole within the states.

The person most obviously affected by variations in parole practice is the offender. His future is settled by the decisions made by others. And as the President's Commission on Law Enforcement and Administration of Justice has argued, the decisions are not made adequately and fairly:

> Except for sentencing, no decision in the criminal process has more impact on the convicted offender than the parole decision, which determines how much of his maximum sentence a prisoner must serve. This again is an invisible administrative decision that is seldom open to attack or subject to review. It is made by parole board members who are often political appointees. Many are skilled and conscientious, but they generally are able to spend no more than a few minutes on a case. Parole decisions that are made in haste and on the basis of insufficient information, in the absence of parole machinery that can provide good supervision, are necessarily imperfect decisions. And since there is virtually no appeal from them, they can be made arbitrarily or discriminatorily.[59]

[58] See Bureau of Prisons, "Prisoners in State and Federal Institutions for Adult Felons, 1966," *National Prisoner Statistics,* No. 43, Washington, D.C., 1968, p. 28.

[59] President's Commission on Law Enforcement and Administration of Justice, *The Challenge of Crime in a Free Society* (Washington, D.C.: U.S. Government Printing Office, 1967), p. 12.

TABLE 6.2

Inmates Released on Parole from State Prisons, 1966

(Includes conditional releases under mandatory supervision)

State	*Total releases*	*Percentage of total releases*
N.H.	117	100.0
Wash.	1,391	100.0
Kan.	1,199	98.2
Utah	337	93.5
Ohio	4,642	93.4
Cal.	7,766	90.7
Wis.	1,866	89.0
Hawaii	168	88.7
N.Y.	7,602	87.3
Mich.	4,108	85.2
Penn.	2,633	84.7
Nev.	234	84.2
N.J.	2,918	83.1
Conn.	1,114	80.7
Ind.	2,186	78.8
Me.	587	78.5
Vt.	237	78.5
N.D.	152	78.3
Colo.	1,612	76.5
W. Va.	678	76.0
Ill.	3,396	73.9
Minn.	974	72.5
Ark.	1,123	71.0
Mass.	1,327	66.6
U.S.	87,640	65.8
D.C.	693	65.7
Idaho	241	63.5
La.	1,741	63.1
Ia.	1,085	61.4
Mont.	435	59.8
Ga.	2,728	51.3
N.M.	457	51.2

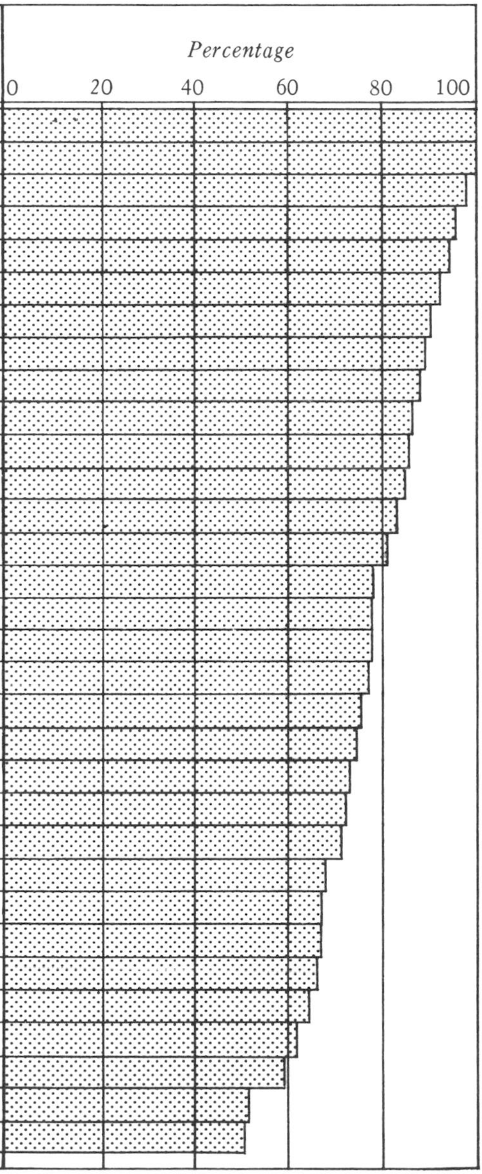

Percentage

0 20 40 60 80 100

TABLE 6.2
(continued)

State	*Total releases*	*Percentage of total releases*
Ariz.	633	50.1
Ala.	2,198	47.5
Va.	1,827	47.3
Miss.	863	45.0
N.C.	2,722	44.5
R.I.	127	44.1
Fla.	2,899	42.5
Ken.	1,340	42.3
S.D.	411	41.8
Del.	204	39.7
Ore.	1,030	38.7
Tenn.	1,558	37.2
Tex.	5,824	35.7
Md.	4,190	35.5
Mo.	1,955	35.5
S.C.	1,323	32.8
Neb.	780	27.7
Okla.	1,822	17.3
Wyo.	187	12.3

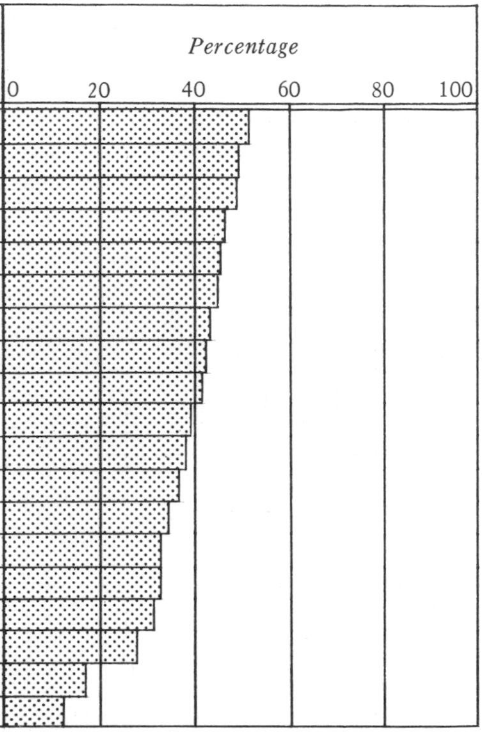

Source: Adapted from Bureau of the Prisons, "Prisoners in State and Federal Institutions for Adult Felons, 1966," *National Prisoner Statistics*, No. 43, Washington, D.C. 1968, pp. 28-29.

To say the least, decisions to release prisoners on parole are not always made according to the interests of the offender. Though much descriptive and predictive information is available on prospective parolees, decisions are often made intuitively. In addition, parole boards develop informal procedures for processing cases.[60] These procedures provide guides for decision-making. Parole decisions thus tend to be based on such characteristics as the original length of sentence rather than the individualities of each case. Inmates, when they are paroled, are likely to be released according to

[60] Some information on parole board decision-making is found in Don M. Gottfredson and Kelley B. Ballard, Jr., "Differences in Decisions Associated with Decision Makers," *Journal of Research in Crime and Delinquency*, 3 (July, 1966), pp. 112–119.

decisions made early in the prisoner's incarceration rather than in respect to the inmate's prognosis for a successful parole. Such procedures, combined with the nature of parole board compositions and the haste with which decisions must be reached, are the basis for the decision to parole prisoners.

Once parole has been granted, the satisfactory completion of the parole period is related to variations in the regulation and supervision of parole. Nationally, the average parole period for offenders is 29 months. Regionally the variations are considerable: 31 months in the east and northeast, 20 months in the midwest and plains, 28 months in the border south, 37 months in the south, and 24 months in the west.[61] Furthermore, state averages for the parole period range from less than 12 months to over 84 months.

The administration of parole is not dependent on regional variations alone. Parole supervision is also influenced by the relationship between the parolee and the parole officer. One of the principal duties of the parole officer is to observe the parolee's behavior, especially to determine if the parolee is violating the conditions of parole or any other regulations and laws.[62] Such parole conditions generally forbid unauthorized association with persons having a criminal record, and seek to control behavior in such areas as drinking, employment, and mobility. Parolees usually must obtain permission to change their residence, to travel to another area, to marry, or to purchase certain items. In practice the parole officer

61 President's Commission on Law Enforcement and Administration of Justice, *Task Force Report: Corrections,* p. 187.

62 Considerable research exists on the violation of parole and parole prediction, primarily from the standpoint of the characteristics and behavior of the parolee. See, for example, Dean V. Babst, Don M. Gottfredson, and Kelley B. Ballard, Jr., "Comparison of Multiple Regression and Configural Analysis Techniques for Developing Base Expectancy Tables," *Journal of Research in Crime and Delinquency,* 5 (January, 1968), pp. 72–80; Robert E. Clark, "Size of Parole Community as Related to Parole Outcome," 57 (July, 1951), pp. 43–47; Daniel Glaser, "A Reconsideration of Some Parole Prediction Factors," *American Sociological Review,* 19 (June, 1954), pp. 335–341; Lloyd E. Ohlin, *Selection for Parole: A Manual of Parole Prediction* (New York: Russell Sage Foundation, 1951); Jerome H. Skolnick, "Toward a Developmental Theory of Parole," *American Sociological Review,* 25 (August, 1960), pp. 542–549. For a discussion of some of the problems and issues in parole prediction, see Charles W. Dean and Thomas J. Duggan, "Problems in Parole Prediction: A Historical Analysis," *Social Problems,* 15 (Spring, 1968), pp. 450–459.

uses a great deal of discretion in supervising the parolee. But ultimately decisions made during the interaction between the officer and the parolee determine when, whether, and how parole will be completed.

The parole officer has a difficult role to perform.[63] He is expected to supervise and assist the parolee and, at the same time, to protect the community from the ex-prisoner. He must fulfill the authoritarian function of representing the state, but must simultaneously be oriented to the rehabilitation of the offender. As a middleman, or as a person who plays the role of "stranger," the parole officer must elicit the participation of the parolee and of the members of the community in integrating the parolee into community life. The role that the parole officer plays is both a handicap and a resource in accomplishing these diverse tasks.

The dual considerations of protecting the public and helping the parolee have given rise to different types of performance by parole officers, oriented in various degrees to these demands.[64] Some parole officers emphasize both control and assistance (the "paternal" officers), while others pay little attention to either (the "passive" officers). Others emphasize assistance but not control (the "welfare" officers). Finally, some emphasize control but not assistance (the "punitive" officers). Each officer style has a different way of perceiving and evaluating parolees. The fate of the offender is thus determined to a large extent by the type of parole officer who happens to be assigned to him.

PREVENTION PROGRAMS IN THE COMMUNITY

Some programs attempt to prevent or reduce the occurrence of crime and delinquency. Such approaches are generally directed toward the larger environment. Instead of dealing with the individuals, circumstances and conditions beyond individuals are the focus of attention. Or, when individuals are considered, they are dealt

[63] Elmer H. Johnson, "The Parole Supervisor in the Role of Stranger," *Journal of Criminal Law, Criminology and Police Science,* 50 (May–June, 1959), pp. 38–43.

[64] Glaser, *The Effectiveness of a Prison and Parole System,* pp. 429–442.

with according to their larger social environment. Prevention programs, therefore, are usually located within community or neighborhood. Most of these have been directed toward preventing juvenile offenses. The administration of such programs is related to the scope and comprehensiveness of environmental change.

One of the first community-centered prevention programs, and the most limited in scope, was the Cambridge-Somerville Youth Study.[65] In the late 1930's in that area of Boston, 325 boys under twelve years of age were selected to receive preventive treatment. A matched group of the same size was selected as a control. Several community agencies cooperated in the program. The general program consisted of counseling, guidance for the family, medical and academic assistance, and recreational activities. The control group was given none of these services. At the end of the experimental period, in 1945, the two groups were compared for their contact with legal authorities. It was found, to the chagrin of the many persons involved, that the offense records of the two groups were similar; 27.7 per cent of the treatment group members had appeared in court for offenses, compared to 26.1 per cent of the control group. Still later, in 1956, a follow-up study traced the adult lives of the two groups.[66] As before, it was found that as many treated boys as control boys had been convicted of crimes in later years. The number of crimes committed was also similar for the two groups. The study can be commended for testing an assumption about the potentialities of one kind of prevention program, but the results are not pleasant for those who would change individuals through only limited change in social conditions.

A step beyond the casework approach to prevention are the programs that involve participant work with *street corner groups*. Such efforts are sometimes referred to as "detached worker" programs, indicating that a social worker is detached from the local agency. Workers are assigned to make contact with gangs in the community with the ultimate objective of changing the attitudes and behavior patterns of the members.

[65] Edwin Powers and Helen L. Witmer, *An Experiment in the Prevention of Delinquency—the Cambridge-Somerville Youth Study* (New York: Columbia University Press, 1951).

[66] Joan and William McCord, "A Follow-up Report on the Cambridge-Somerville Youth Study," *Annals of the American Academy of Political and Social Science*, 322 (March, 1959), pp. 89–96.

One of the earliest projects of this kind was conducted in New York.[67] From 1947 to 1950 trained workers were attached to several street gangs in central Harlem. In their association with the gangs, the workers attempted, with some reported success, to redirect the activity of gangs from fighting, stealing, sex offenses, marihuana smoking, and so forth to organized athletics, block parties, movie programs, camping trips, and the like. This approach was expanded by the New York City Youth Board to include work with gangs in several of the city's high delinquency areas.[68] A more recent but similar project was the YMCA-sponsored program in Chicago.[69] The success of the program is uncertain, but the research associated with it has been rewarding.

A project somewhat wider in scope operated in Boston from 1954 to 1957.[70] Attempting to reduce juvenile offenses in a lower class area, the Boston Delinquency Project included efforts to improve the coordination of community agencies and to improve the family system. But the primary objective was shifting the values of street corner groups from an emphasis on law-violating behavior to an emphasis on law-abiding behavior. In attempting to accomplish this goal, project field workers established and maintained contact with approximately 400 youths who were members of some 21 corner groups. The evaluative results of the project are mixed. Apparently the project had a "negligible impact" on the law-violating behavior of the gang members.[71] Nevertheless, it was successful in other ways. In particular, local community organization was improved. It is even possible that the project will have delayed effects in preventing delinquency.

Instituting a prevention program within an area of the city usually creates or brings to the surface conflict among city agencies. A post-mortem of the prevention project in Boston documented the

[67] Paul L. Crawford, Daniel I. Malamud, and James R. Dumpson, *Working with Teen-age Gangs* (New York: Welfare Council of New York City, 1950).

[68] New York City Youth Board, *Reaching the Fighting Gang* (New York: New York City Youth Board, 1960).

[69] James F. Short, Jr., and Fred L. Strodtbeck, *Group Process and Gang Delinquency* (Chicago: University of Chicago Press, 1965).

[70] Walter B. Miller, "Preventive Work with Street-Corner Groups: Boston Delinquency Project," *Annals of the American Academy of Political and Social Science, 322* (March, 1959), pp. 97–106.

[71] Walter B. Miller, "The Impact of a 'Total-Community' Delinquency Control Project," *Social Problems,* 10 (Fall, 1962), pp. 168–191.

conflicts that occurred in the administration of the project.[72] About a dozen public and private organizational groups maintained an interest in the city's handling of crime and delinquency. The principal public agencies were the municipal government, the recreation department, the police department, the courts, the public schools, and the state youth corrections division. The major private groups were medical and psychiatric clinics, social work agencies, churches, universities, and various special cause groups, such as ethnic associations and crime prevention societies. Each of these groups had its own philosophy on such matters as the etiology of delinquency, the appropriate disposition of the delinquent, the proper organization and procedures for prevention, and the necessary qualifications for personnel in delinquency programs. Conflicts in these areas took place both *between* and *within* the agencies, resulting in a lack of coordination and a blocking of efforts in the administration of the city's prevention program. The respective agencies, in other words, acted as special interest groups to have their vested interests satisfied. Hence, prevention programs tend to have as a major (unstated) objective the satisfaction of the interests of those who administer the programs.

But some prevention programs do include within their scope the reorganization and development of the whole *community*. The rationale of such programs is that criminally defined behavior is a reflection of the larger social and cultural milieu and that in order to bring about change in behavior patterns the structure of the entire community must be altered. Furthermore, a basic procedure for implementing these programs is encouraging the leadership and participation of the people in the community. In other words, instead of outsiders' imposing their will and techniques upon the inhabitants, the residents themselves determine or help determine what changes are to be made in their community. Finally, the success of these programs does not necessarily depend upon the reduction of delinquent and criminal activity. Behavior patterns may eventually be changed. But in the meantime, improvements in the

[72] Walter B. Miller, "Inter-Institutional Conflict as a Major Impediment to Delinquency Prevention," *Human Organization,* 17 (Fall, 1958), pp. 20–23. Further documentation of the various groups involved in delinquency prevention is found in Robert M. MacIver, *The Prevention and Control of Delinquency* (New York: Atherton Press, 1966).

lives of the residents and in the social climate of the community are much more important.

The Chicago Area Project, beginning about 1930, has been the best known of these programs in community development.[73] The project began in three slum areas in Chicago and eventually expanded to other areas of the city. Under the direction of Clifford R. Shaw, the Area Project was based on sociological assumptions of human behavior and community organization. Basically, the implementation of the project was founded on the observation that people support and participate in only those enterprises in which they have a meaningful role. The first phase of the project required a knowledge of the area and its population. Local residents were encouraged to become the developers and administrators of the programs. Following this, residents developed services and organizations to meet the welfare needs of the community. The aims and methods of the Chicago Area Project were summarized as follows:

> (1) It emphasizes the development of a program for the neighborhood as a whole. (2) It seeks to stress the autonomy of the local residents in helping to plan, support, and operate constructive programs which they may regard as their own. (3) It attaches special significance to the training and utilization of community leaders. (4) It confines the efforts of its professional staff, in large part, to consultation and planning with responsible neighborhood leaders who assume major roles in the actual development of the program. (5) It seeks to encourage the local residents to utilize to the maximum all churches, societies, clubs, and other existing institutions and agencies, and to coordinate these in a unified neighborhood program. (6) Its activities are regarded primarily as devices for enlisting the active participation of local residents in a constructive community enterprise, for creating and crystallizing neighborhood sentiment on behalf of the welfare of the children and the social and physical improvement of the community as a whole. (7) It places particular emphasis upon the importance of a continuous, objective evaluation of its effective-

[73] Solomon Kobrin, "The Chicago Area Project — A 25-Year Assessment," *Annals of the American Academy of Political and Social Science,* 322 (March, 1959), pp. 19–29.

> ness as a device for reducing delinquency, through constructive modification of the pattern of community life.[74]

From all evaluations of the Area Project, it is evident that residents of low-income areas have been able to organize themselves to promote their own communal interests.[75] Also, though precise measurement is not possible, apparently delinquent and criminal activity has been reduced through efforts in community development. But more essential, whatever has been accomplished has been primarily by self-determination and democratic participation.[76]

For some time Saul Alinsky has argued that the prevention of crime and delinquency is part of a larger program of institutional reorganization.[77] His program is not aimed specifically at prevention, but toward the eradication of unemployment, disease, inadequate housing, demoralization, and other aspects of social deterioration. Alinsky advocates the formation of "people's organizations" in the community. His program, variously known as Back of the Yards Project, People's Organization, and Industrial Areas Foundation, differs from the Chicago Area Project in several important ways:

> First, the membership is wider; each local organization, such as a church, a union, an industry, a club, is represented. Second, the primary purpose is the development of groups composed of persons who are interested in their own welfare and are organized for political action to improve their welfare. Third, the ultimate aim is the development of a nation-wide federation of people's organizations, involving millions of people; through such a federation powerful political influence could be exerted.[78]

[74] Clifford R. Shaw and Jesse A. Jacobs, "The Chicago Area Project: An Experimental Community Program for Prevention of Delinquency in Chicago," Chicago: Institute for Juvenile Research, undated. Quoted in Clinard, *Sociology of Deviant Behavior,* p. 738.

[75] Kobrin, "The Chicago Area Project — A 25-Year Assessment"; Anthony Sorrentino, "The Chicago Area Project After 25 Years," *Federal Probation,* 23 (June, 1959), pp. 40–45; Helen L. Witmer and Edith Tufts, *The Effectiveness of Delinquency Prevention Programs,* U.S. Children's Bureau Publication No. 350 (Washington, D.C.: U.S. Government Printing Office, 1954), pp. 11–17.

[76] The community development approach has since been expanded and applied in the Delhi Project, by Marshall B. Clinard, *Slums and Community Development: Experiments in Self-Help* (New York: The Free Press, 1966).

[77] Saul D. Alinsky, *Reveille for Radicals* (Chicago: University of Chicago Press, 1946).

[78] Sutherland and Cressey, *Principles of Criminology,* p. 697.

It is the element of political power in the hands of the people that makes this program more radical than most others. Because government officials must approve programs and appropriate funds, such programs have tended to remain as proposals.

Through the years, as we have seen, prevention programs have gradually evolved into ideas based on community development, institutional reorganization, and political involvement. The project that best represents the culmination of these ideas is Mobilization for Youth, a project located in a 67 block area on the Lower East Side of New York. Beginning in the early 1960's, Mobilization for Youth was founded on the theoretical proposition that obstacles to economic and social betterment are chiefly responsible for crime and delinquency among low-income groups.[79] The stated objectives of the project were "(1) to increase the employability of youths from low-income families, (2) to improve and make more accessible training and work preparation facilities, (3) to help young people achieve employment goals equal to their capacities, (4) to increase employment opportunities for the area's youth, and (5) to help minority group youngsters overcome discrimination in hiring."[80]

A number of fairly orthodox remedies were designed to implement job training and work projects for the unemployed youth and young adults. Specific programs included a youth job center, an urban youth service corps, on-the-job training, reading clinics, preschool education, and guidance counselors. But the rest of the project, the community action portion, has been devoted to more unorthodox procedures. Among these are a staff of lawyers for welfare clients, a housing unit which collects data on landlord violations, and a group of organizers who advise and assist the poor to collectively change their lives.

Thus, Mobilization for Youth is distinguished from many other contemporary programs by the organization of the poor for social protest and human betterment. The main hope of the project, according to one of the principal staff members, is to "organize the unaffiliated — to overturn the status quo and replace it with a higher

[79] See Richard A. Cloward and Lloyd E. Ohlin, *Delinquency and Opportunity: A Theory of Delinquent Gangs* (New York: The Free Press, 1960).

[80] *Action on the Lower East Side,* Program Report: July, 1962–January, 1964 (New York: Mobilization for Youth, Inc., 1964).

level of stability, without delinquents, alcoholism or drug addiction."[81] It is this political aspect that has gotten the project into trouble with government officials. The FBI has conducted an investigation of those who have engaged in organized action; newspapers have charged the project with subversion; the files of the project have been confiscated; and federal and local funds have been questioned and altered. To provide the poor with services and assistance from above has been the traditional way of doing things. It is regarded as subversive when the poor attempt to change the social pattern of their poverty. Welfare is legitimate oppression, political action by the poor is anarchy.

Fear of the more radical aspects of Mobilization for Youth is also imbedded in the potential of a widespread movement among the poor. Such a movement could alter the American economic system.

> If a movement of welfare recipients should, in fact, take form and gather strength, the ghetto and the slum will have yielded up a new political force. And it is conceivable that such a force could eventually be turned to the objective of procuring federal legislation for new programs of income redistribution (such as a guaranteed minimum income) to replace a welfare system that perpetuates poverty while it strips men of their fundamental rights as citizens.[82]

Indeed, programs of crime and delinquency prevention today have wide and significant implications.

REMOVAL OF CRIMINAL DEFINITIONS

The law giveth, and the law taketh away. Because of the criminal law and its administration, persons are defined as criminal. Crime as a definition of one's status, then, can be withdrawn just as it is given — by legal means. For most who have been convicted and sentenced,

[81] Quoted in Murray Kempton, "When You Mobilize the Poor," *The New Republic* (December 5, 1964), p. 12.

[82] Richard A. Cloward and Richard M. Elman, "Advocacy in the Ghetto," *Trans-Action,* 4 (December, 1966), p. 33. Also see Richard A. Cloward and Frances Fox Piven, "The Weight of the Poor: A Strategy to End Poverty," *The Nation* (May 2, 1966), pp. 510–517.

punished, or treated, criminal status is temporary. The decisions that others eventually make will officially convert the criminal into a noncriminal.

No matter what legal means are used, removal of the criminal definition from the offender is not usually completely accomplished. Even when the legal definition of criminal is removed, the repercussions of once being defined as criminal linger on in many ways. Upon conviction for a crime, an offender automatically loses a variety of rights and privileges. Unless these rights and privileges are restored by some formal procedure upon release from the legal system, they may be permanently forfeited. In addition, the criminal record of the offender will be with him for the rest of his life.

Hence, convicted persons are subject to numerous disabilities and disqualifications quite apart from the sanction imposed in the sentence.[83] A number of civil rights — rights possessed by other persons by fact of citizenship — are lost by those persons convicted of felonies and certain misdemeanors. Most state statutes and constitutions provide for deprivation of some rights upon criminal conviction. Some states provide for the blanket loss or suspension of civil rights, including the right to vote, to hold public office, to sue, to enter into contracts, to inherit property, to testify, and to serve as a juror. Where statutes make provisions for the restoration of rights, it is often unclear what rights are restored and what disabilities and disqualifications remain. Moreover, the period of time for which rights are to be forfeited may depend upon the sentence. The law is complex and confusing in such matters.

In addition to the loss of numerous civil rights, convicted persons are usually prohibited from participating in other activities regulated by the government. They may be barred from obtaining professional, occupational, and business licenses, or from other kinds of employment. The procedures for restoring such privileges are not always clear. The restoration statutes usually restore only certain rights, leaving restoration of particular privileges to the discretion of various regulatory agencies.

In spite of legal efforts to remove the definition of "criminal" from the convicted person, and regardless of the provisions for restoring rights and privileges, the effects of a criminal conviction

[83] See President's Commission on Law Enforcement and Administration of Justice, *Task Force Report: Corrections,* pp. 82–92.

are likely to be felt throughout the lifetime of a person. The application of a criminal definition may in fact have the ultimate effect of creating within the person self-definitions by which he lives the rest of his life. The defining of persons as criminal may provide the definers with behaviors that may be similarly defined in the future. But for the time being, the application of a criminal definition is the creation of a crime.

4

Development of Behavior Patterns in Relation to Criminal Definitions

CHAPTER SEVEN

Societal Organization and the Structuring of Behavior Patterns

No behavior is criminal until it has been so defined through recognized procedures of the state. In this sense, "criminal behavior" differs from "noncriminal behavior" only according to the definition that has been created by others. It is not the quality of the behavior, but the nature of the action taken against the behavior that gives it the character of criminality.

All behavior may be understood in reference to the organization of society. Depending on the structural location in society, certain behaviors may at times be defined as criminal, may be regarded some of the time as law-abiding, or may be the behavior that is involved in defining others as criminal. Although the contents of the actions differ, all the behaviors represent the *behavior patterns* of certain segments of society. Hence, persons who create criminal definitions and persons who become defined as criminal act in reference to *normative systems* learned in relative social and cultural settings.

The task is to provide a perspective of society that allows an understanding of crime in relation to the organization of society, a perspective that includes the behaviors of both those who are defined as criminal and those who do the defining. Basic to such a perspective are the assumptions that, first, behavior becomes structured in a segmented society and that, second, some segments impose their order on others by formulating and applying criminal definitions. That which is defined as criminal in any society is relative to particular behavior patterns within the society and to the segments of society that formulate and apply the criminal definitions.

SEGMENTAL ORGANIZATION OF SOCIETY

The organization of society may be conceived according to two fundamentally different principles of social organization. The subsequent types of organization are based on the homogeneity and the heterogeneity of society.

> In the homogeneous type, a common system of values possesses it members, so that they tend to behave similarly in similar situations. In the heterogeneous type this common system still maintains its hold upon individuals. But free standing groups have developed, which are largely emancipated from the common conscience in respect to conditions with which they are especially concerned. The groups develop a value system specific to themselves and eccentric to the common system. There is thus a societal condition in which all persons tend to behave similarly in certain similar situations, and differently in certain other situations.[1]

Analyses of crime have usually been based on the homogeneous conception of society. The lack of consensus, consequently, has been regarded as a condition of "social disorganization" in society. Crime, following this conception, has been viewed simultaneously as an indicator and a product of social disorganization. However, when crime is viewed from the heterogeneous perspective, a very different theoretical approach develops.

The theory of the social reality of crime is formulated according to the assumption that society is characterized by a heterogeneity of organization. Underlying this theory of crime is a conception which, for consistency, I will refer to as the *segmental organization of society*. This conception is in sharp contrast to the *singular,* one-value system, conception of society. The two opposing conceptions are diagrammed in Figure 7.1. It can be seen that in addition to the homogeneous and heterogeneous assumptions of organization, the singular and segmental conceptions of social organization refer to the formulation and application of criminal definitions in society.

In the singular conception of society, crime must necessarily occur

[1] Frank E. Hartung, "Common and Discrete Values," *Journal of Social Psychology,* 38 (August, 1953), p. 3.

FIGURE 7.1
The Singular and Segmental Conceptions of the Organization of Society

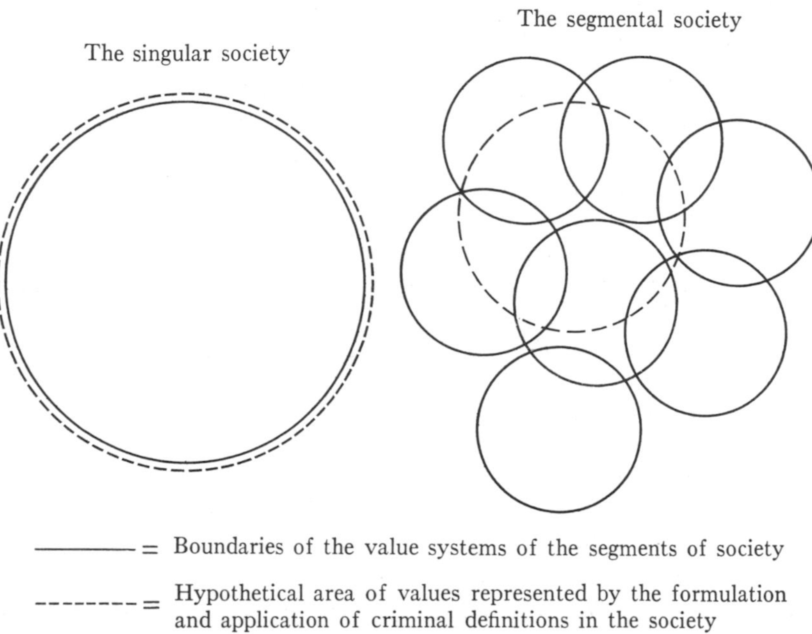

——— = Boundaries of the value systems of the segments of society

- - - - = Hypothetical area of values represented by the formulation and application of criminal definitions in the society

outside of any value system, since all persons within the society by definition conform to one value system. Furthermore, the singular conception is static, not allowing for conflict or change within the system. But most important, the singular conception assumes that the criminal definitions of the society represent the entire system rather than any part of it. Any occurrence outside of the singular society must be either deviant or criminal.

According to the segmental conception of society, on the other hand, crime as a phenomenon occurs within a society and is, indeed, an integral part of the organization of that society. The numerous segments of society, each with its own value system, are variously related to the criminal definitions of the society. For example, some values of a segment may be incorporated into some of the criminal laws, whereas other values are not represented in criminal laws. In some segments all the values are represented by all the criminal laws. Some segments have none of their values represented in the formulation, enforcement, and administration of criminal laws in the society.

Finally, in their relationship to one another, the segments of such a society may or may not have overlapping values. But since few segments have complete mutual agreement on all their values, most are in conflict with one another to some extent. Therefore, the criminal laws of the society and their enforcement and administration are a consequence of the conflict and associated distribution of power between the segments. The segmental society is thus a dynamic society and, it may be added, one that provides for a meaningful explanation of crime.

BEHAVIOR PATTERNS AND PROBABILITY OF CRIMINAL DEFINITIONS

All persons, whether or not they are at times defined as criminal, act in reference to normative patterns learned in their social and cultural settings. Since society is segmentally organized, a variety of normative systems may serve as points of reference for personal behavior. Yet, because persons are differentially located in society in reference to the various segments, learning of behavior is selective. The content of one's learning is dependent to a great extent upon his position in society. Each segment of society provides its own patterns for appropriate behavior. Therefore, learning of behavior is structured and selective, or there are *differential learning structures* in segmentally organized society.

In the search for an understanding of criminal behavior, Sutherland may be credited with the most systematic formulation of the learning of behavior patterns.[2] His argument was that persons acquire patterns of criminal behavior in the same way in which they acquire patterns of lawful behavior — by interaction with other persons in a process of communication. The content of the learning includes techniques of committing offenses as well as the specific direction of motives, attitudes, and rationalizations. The specific di-

[2] Edwin H. Sutherland, *Principles of Criminology,* 3rd ed. (Philadelphia: J. B. Lippincott, 1939).

rection of motives and rationalizations, in turn, is learned in reference to favorable or unfavorable definitions of the law. It follows, from Sutherland's proposition of "differential association," that a person becomes delinquent or criminal because of an excess of definitions favorable to violation of the law over those unfavorable to violation of the law. In composite form, the theory of differential association postulates that "criminal behavior has as its necessary and sufficient conditions a set of criminal motivations, attitudes, and techniques, the learning of which takes place when there is exposure to criminal norms in excess of exposure to corresponding anticriminal norms during symbolic interaction in primary groups."[3]

The learning of criminal behavior patterns is not random, but is structured according to a person's selective exposure to situations in which both criminal and anticriminal behavior patterns are present. *Rates* of criminal behavior can thus be explained by Sutherland's concept of "differential social organization."

> . . . [I]n a multi-group type of social organization, alternative and inconsistent standards of conduct are possessed by various groups, so that an individual who is a member of one group has a high probability of learning to use legal means for achieving success, while an individual in another group learns to accept the importance of success and to achieve it by illegal means. Stated in another way, there are alternative educational processes in operation, varying with groups, so that a person may be educated in either conventional or criminal means of achieving success.[4]

Therefore, the likelihood that a person will engage in criminal behavior is dependent upon his relative exposure to various kinds of norms and, similarly, the extent to which categories of persons engage in criminal behavior is related to the structure of criminal and anticriminal behavior patterns in an area or portion of society.

This theory of the learning of criminal behavior has been described more recently as differences in access to types of "opportunity"

[3] Melvin L. De Fleur and Richard Quinney, "A Reformulation of Sutherland's Differential Association Theory and a Strategy for Empirical Verification," *Journal of Research in Crime and Delinquency,* 3 (January, 1966), p. 7.

[4] Donald R. Cressey, "Epidemiological and Individual Conduct: A Case from Criminology," *Pacific Sociological Review,* 3 (Fall, 1960), p. 55.

structures. In the formulation, persons are located in two opportunity structures — legitimate and illegitimate. Such opportunities are conceived of as both learning and performance:

> Our use of the term "opportunities," legitimate or illegitimate, implies access to both learning and performance structures. That is, the individual must have access to appropriate environments for the acquisition of the values and skills associated with the performance of a particular role, and he must be supported in the performance of the role once he has learned it.[5]

Accordingly, the learning and performance of the criminal role, as with the conventional role, depends upon patterned relationships through which values and skills are transmitted.

Whenever criminal behavior has been viewed according to learning structures, whether in the theory of differential association or in the reformulations, it has been assumed that there are behavior patterns which are objectively "criminal." Such an assumption is fallacious when held up against the theory of the social reality of crime, since according to this theory, behaviors and behavior patterns are neither criminal nor noncriminal. All behaviors are commonly *social,* and they become criminal only when they have been officially defined as such by authorized agents of the state. Without such defining, all behaviors are in a sense "criminal," since all could conceivably be prosecuted under some law.

In the theory of the social reality of crime we may refer, however, to the *probability* that particular behaviors may be defined as criminal by legal agents. Similarly, considering particular behavior patterns, we may refer to the probability that when they are followed they will lead to the application of a criminal definition.

Because society is segmentally organized, because criminal laws represent the values of only some segments in society, and because learning structures differ in the content of behavior patterns, persons and behaviors are subject to differentials in the probability of being defined as criminal. Only a *probability terminology* allows us to speculate about the likelihood that particular persons or behaviors will become criminal, that is, become defined as criminal. It may be

[5] Richard A. Cloward and Lloyd E. Ohlin, *Delinquency and Opportunity: A Theory of Delinquent Gangs* (New York: The Free Press of Glencoe, 1960), p. 148.

suggested that persons who learn the behavior patterns of the segments of society not represented in the formulation and application of criminal laws are more likely to act in ways that will be defined as criminal than those who learn the behavior patterns of the segments that formulate and apply criminal definitions. All behaviors are *social*, with varying probabilities that they will become defined as criminal, depending on their location in the segmental organization of society.

STRUCTURING OF BEHAVIOR PATTERNS

So the problem is not explaining "criminal behavior," but explaining the development of behavior patterns that have relative probabilities of being defined as criminal. The question raised by the problem is: What are the structural sources of such behaviors? Generally, all structural sources are important to the extent that criminal definitions will be imposed on the behaviors produced by the sources.

The bulk of criminology consists of research and writing on the causes of "criminal behavior." For my purpose, this material can be reinterpreted as the *structural sources of the behaviors that may become defined as criminal.* A host of sources might be considered, but I will concentrate on what may be conceptualized as three general types of social structures that serve as the basis for patterning criminally defined behavior: (1) the age-sex structure, (2) the social class structure, and (3) the ethnic-racial structure. All three are related to the segmental organization of society. The probability that particular behaviors will both exist and be defined as criminal depends on the location of persons in the various structures of society.

Age-Sex Structure. In the official statistics on crime, contact with agents of the law follows a fairly consistent pattern according to the age and sex of the persons who are defined as criminal. The following questions may be asked: What are the behavioral variations according to age and sex status? How do behaviors become structured according to age and sex? And how are criminal definitions related to these behaviors?

For all categories of criminal offenses, taken collectively, the age of maximum criminality is in later adolescence and young adulthood. The largest proportion of persons arrested by the police are between the ages of 18 and 24. In regard to the sex factor, males become involved in offenses several times as often as females. The rate of arrest of males is now about ten times that for females.[6] In general, then, the risks of being defined as criminal are much higher for young persons and for males.

The differences in criminal liability according to age and sex can be viewed as the behavioral variations of those defined as criminal. Persons under 25 years of age, when arrested, tend to be charged with vandalism, auto theft, burglary, arson, larceny, liquor law violations, robbery, buying and receiving stolen property, and forcible rape. On the other hand, arrests for drunkenness, gambling, driving under the influence of alcohol, fraud, embezzlement, and vagrancy tend to be among persons over 25 years of age. The percentage of persons under 25 who are arrested thus varies considerably from one offense charge to another. For the year 1967, 90 per cent of the arrests for vandalism involved persons under 25, while only 15.2 per cent of the arrests for gambling consisted of persons under 25 years of age.[7]

The difference in criminal liability according to sex is similarly striking when we consider the kinds of offenses. Some are disproportionately male offenses and others are much less likely to involve males. In accordance with the arrest figures for offenses in general, for the year 1965, 7.4 males were arrested for every woman arrested. In the same year, the sex ratios (number of men for every woman) for selected offenses varied as follows: a sex ratio of 25.9 for burglary, 23.1 for auto theft, 18.1 for robbery, 15.4 for vandalism, 11.8 for gambling, 9.5 for vagrancy, 6.8 for disorderly conduct, 5.7 for sex offenses, 4.7 for murder, 3.9 for fraud, 3.5 for larceny, and 1.1 for runaways.[8]

To what extent can we assume that these arrest situations reflect behavioral variations according to differences in age and sex? Do official criminal statistics reflect the behavioral variations of the age groups and the sexes, or are the statistics only indicators of selective law enforcement? Studies of the self-reporting of behavior provide a

[6] For the variations in arrest statistics according to such characteristics as sex and race, see Federal Bureau of Investigation, *Uniform Crime Reports — 1967* (Washington, D.C.: United States Government Printing Office, 1968).

[7] Federal Bureau of Investigation, *Uniform Crime Reports — 1967,* p. 123.

[8] Walter C. Reckless, *The Crime Problem,* 4th ed. (New York: Appleton-Century-Crofts, 1967), pp. 99–100.

partial answer. Of juveniles, it has been found that (1) self-reported delinquency is extensive and variable, (2) the variations in the kinds of reported delinquencies are similar to variations in the official arrest figures, (3) boys report a much higher proportion of delinquencies than girls, and (4) institutionalized juvenile delinquents rank much higher than high school students in seriousness of involvement in delinquent behavior.[9] In a similar fashion, studies of the self-reporting of behavior among adults indicate that the general population is engaged in activities that could be defined as criminal and that, in addition, men are involved in behaviors that could be criminally defined more than are women.[10] The issue, therefore, becomes one of understanding the structuring of behavioral variations according to age and sex. Related to this is the ultimate matter of accounting for the defining of the behaviors as criminal according to age and sex in segmentally organized society.

The behavioral patterns of youth are in large measure the result of the very location of youth in the age structure. Though social class accounts for some of the variations in behavior among youths, the fact of growing up in relation to elders has a considerable influence on the kinds of behavior pursued by youths. Adolescent gangs, which engage in many activities that may be defined as delinquent or criminal, can be explained as an attempt by adolescents to gain the status not granted them by adults.[11] As a consequence of age grading in the larger society, gang membership and associated activities fill the status gap between childhood and adulthood. Delinquent activity naturally results when a society does not provide meaningful functions for adolescents.[12] Activities that have a high probability of being defined as delinquent or criminal are to be expected when an age group is not provided with any other meaningful means of involvement and fulfillment.

Since adolescence is a time for experimentation, for establishing an identity, activities of a high delinquency or criminal potential may

[9] James F. Short, Jr. and F. Ivan Nye, "Extent of Unrecorded Juvenile Delinquency: Tentative Conclusions," *Journal of Criminal Law, Criminology and Police Science,* 49 (November–December, 1958), pp. 296–302.

[10] James S. Wallerstein and Clement J. Wyle, "Our Law-Abiding Law-Breakers," *Probation,* 25 (April, 1947), pp. 107–112.

[11] See Herbert A. Bloch and Arthur Niederhoffer, *The Gang: A Study of Adolescent Behavior* (New York: Philosophical Library, 1958).

[12] Paul Goodman, *Growing Up Absurd* (New York: Random House, 1960).

be the only solution available for establishing that identity.[13] Although such problems of identity are critical for both sexes, they are qualitatively different for boys and girls. Some adolescent version of the adult male role must be achieved by the young male adolescent, whereas girls must attempt some kind of a solution that corresponds to the adult female role. Both the male and female attempts at identity result in different patterns of adolescent behavior. Hence, boys tend to steal, destroy property, or engage in fighting in an attempt to achieve power, prestige, and wealth. On the other hand, girls tend to become involved in those illicit sexual and related activities that are possible given the nature of the female role.[14] The sex roles of the adult world thus serve as general models for the creation of youthful activities that may, in turn, become defined as delinquent or criminal by adults.

As juveniles advance in the age structure of society, they learn to behave in more "adult" ways. The behavior patterns learned and pursued in adulthood have varying probabilities of being defined as criminal. The extent to which the behaviors become in fact so defined depends to a considerable degree on the careers developed by the respective adults, which will be examined in Chapter 8. The development of "criminal" careers is in part a function of personal experiences in contact with agents of the law.

A good part of the difference between adult male and female involvement in criminally defined activity is a consequence of the generalized adult sex roles in society. Men are expected to be active and aggressive; women are expected to be more passive. Each role leads to differing kinds and amounts of behavior that may be criminally defined. Furthermore, men are afforded greater opportunity to engage in the forms of activity — including the making of a gainful living — which may result in behaviors that have high potentials of being defined as criminal.

[13] See Erik H. Erikson, *Childhood and Society* (New York: W. W. Norton, 1950); Edgar Z. Friedenberg, *The Vanishing Adolescent* (New York: Dell & Company, 1962).

[14] Delinquency in relation to sex roles is discussed in Ruth Morris "Female Delinquency and Relational Problems," *Social Forces,* 43 (December, 1964), pp. 82–89; Albert J. Reiss, Jr., "Sex Offenses: The Marginal Status of the Adolescent," *Law and Contemporary Problems,* 25 (Spring, 1960), pp. 309–334; John C. Ball and Nell Logan, "Early Sexual Behavior of Lower-Class Delinquent Girls," *Journal of Criminal Law, Criminology and Police Science,* 51 (July–August, 1960), pp. 209–214.

Whatever the nature or amount of particular behaviors, the reason that they are criminal is that they are so defined by others. While the behaviors that provide the objects for criminal definition can be explained by the location of persons in the age-sex structure of society, the application of criminal definitions must be explained by the location of the persons and behaviors in reference to the expectations of the segments that enforce and administer the criminal law. Those behaviors that violate the sensibilities and interests of the powerful segments of society are the behaviors that have a high probability of being defined as criminal.

Social Class Structure. The official statistics on crime consistently indicate an over-representation of persons from the lower class. Studies of American communities have likewise shown that the lower class is most vulnerable to law enforcement and judicial action. In one New England town it was found that the lower classes accounted for about 90 per cent of the arrests over a seven-year period.[15] From such figures, it can be safely concluded that members of the lower class, in comparison to members of the middle and upper classes, have the greatest probability of being arrested and convicted for their behaviors.

Some recent evidence has accumulated to question, among juveniles at least, the existence of a disproportionate amount of illegal activity in the lower class. In one study comparing institutionalized juveniles and the self-reported behavior of a sample of high school students, it was found that 50 per cent of the boys in a training school for delinquents were from the lowest of four categories of socioeconomic status; however, when the high school boys reported their behaviors, only 13 per cent of delinquent activities were reported among boys of the lowest socioeconomic status.[16] Such studies tend to show that behavior that may be defined as criminal is more

[15] W. Lloyd Warner and Paul S. Lunt, *The Social Life of a Modern Community* (New Haven: Yale University Press, 1941). Similarly, see August B. Hollingshead, *Elmtown's Youth* (New York: John Wiley, 1949).

[16] F. Ivan Nye, James F. Short, Jr., and Virgil J. Olson, "Socio-economic Status and Delinquent Behavior," *American Journal of Sociology,* 63 (January, 1958), pp. 381–389. For related findings, see Ronald L. Akers, "Socio-Economic Status and Delinquent Behavior: A Retest," *Journal of Research in Crime and Delinquency,* 1 (January, 1964), pp. 38–46; Robert A. Bentler and Lawrence J. Monroe, "Social Correlates of Early Adolescent Theft," *American Sociological Review,* 26 (October, 1961), pp. 733–743.

evenly distributed throughout the class structure than is indicated by the official statistics on juvenile delinquency.

Therefore, it may be argued that such conduct is distributed throughout the social class structure, but that the lower class nevertheless has the greatest risk of officially being defined as delinquent or criminal. Furthermore, I contend that lower class members, in comparison to members of the other classes, are involved in behavior patterns that automatically have a greater probability of being officially handled as criminal. Lower class persons are more likely to engage in activities that result in charges of drunkenness, assault, disorderly conduct, burglary, and robbery. Middle and upper class persons, on the other hand, tend to be involved in activities that, although they may conceivably be defined as criminal, are not traditionally dealt with through criminal sanction. Although criminal laws cover such middle class behaviors as fraud, falsification of records, evasion of taxes, misuse of funds, malpractice, and so forth, these behaviors are not usually handled by traditional criminal procedures. Thus, I argue that the behavior patterns of the social classes are qualitatively different and that these patterns are subject to differing probabilities of being defined as criminal. How, then, can the varying behavior patterns of the social classes be explained in relation to criminal definitions?

The behavior patterns of each social class are learned during the childhood of each member. In addition to the behavior patterns associated with each class, the members of some social classes develop behavior patterns in response to the problems of growing up in a class structure. Some, depending upon their experiences in early life, their later circumstances, and their confrontation with the law, continue in a style of life that includes behaviors that have a high probability of being defined as criminal. For some other persons, a "criminal" career may be the culmination of a personal history that took shape in the class structure.

For the *lower class* child, especially for the boy, growing into adulthood involves gradually learning the cultural traditions of the lower class. The problem for the boy in the "hard core" lower class, however, is that as he matures, he has to cope with a female dominated household.[17] The adolescent street gang, accordingly, is the social mechanism for becoming a male adult in the lower class.

[17] Walter B. Miller, "Lower Class Culture as a Generating Milieu of Gang Delinquency," *Journal of Social Issues,* 14 (November 3, 1958), pp. 5–19.

The learning of the lower class structure involves an emphasis on the "focal concerns" of trouble, toughness, smartness, excitement, fate, and autonomy. In following these cultural patterns, within the context of the adolescent gang, lower class boys engage in activities that may well become defined as delinquent or criminal. Thus, lower class behavior readily and automatically becomes criminal in reference to the legal standards that embody the cultural patterns of another class.

Growing up in the *working class,* a cut above the lower class, presents its own problems for the working class boy, who is faced with the problem of adjusting to middle class standards.[18] Working class boys have learned the cultural patterns of one class but are assessed, particularly in the schools, by middle class standards that emphasize ambition, self-reliance, postponement of immediate satisfaction, good manners, wholesome recreation, control of physical aggression, and respect for property. Since working class boys do not fare well when assessed according to the "middle class measuring rod," they seek a solution by creating a "delinquent subculture." The "subculture" that they form or join may be in opposition to middle class values.[19] The solution for the working class boy then consists of a way of life that, being in opposition to the standards of the middle class, prescribes behaviors that have a good probability of being defined as delinquent or criminal.

For *middle class* youths, activity that can be defined as delinquent or criminal may result from following the practices of the middle class itself. Some of the behaviors of middle class youths, which may be in conflict with the law, are in fact a logical extension of values held by most middle class adults. Some middle class youths make use of the "subterranean values" of the middle class, allowing these values to serve as a code for everyday behavior rather than reserving them only for leisure-time activity.[20] For most persons growing up in

[18] Albert K. Cohen, *Delinquent Boys: The Culture of the Gang* (New York: The Free Press of Glencoe, 1955).

[19] Critiques of the theory of the "delinquent subculture" are found in David J. Bordua, "Delinquent Subcultures: Sociological Interpretations of Gang Delinquency," *Annals of the American Academy of Political and Social Science,* 338 (November, 1961), pp. 119–136; John I. Kitsuse and David C. Dietrick, "Delinquent Boys: A Critique," *American Sociological Review,* 24 (April, 1959), pp. 208–215.

[20] David Matza and Gresham M. Sykes, "Juvenile Delinquency and Subterranean Values," *American Sociological Review,* 26 (October, 1961), pp. 712–719.

the middle class, the values of the middle class need not necessarily be rejected in order to permit their violation. Rather, "techniques of neutralization" may be learned as motivation and rationalization for behavior that is at odds with middle class (and usually legal) standards.[21] At any rate, middle class youths, and also youths of the upper class, engage in behaviors that may be defined as delinquent or criminal, but the probability that such behavior will ever appear in the official statistics of delinquency and crime is relatively slight.

The conclusion about the interaction of social class, the structuring of behavior patterns, and criminal definitions is clear. Each social class has or develops its own behavior patterns, many of which may be defined as delinquent or criminal. But, since the formulation, enforcement, and administration of criminal law are based on a particular conception of appropriate behavior, primarily the standards of the middle class, official rates of delinquency and crime differ considerably from one social class to another. The probability that a person will be defined as criminal, therefore, is affected by his location in the class structure.

Ethnic-Racial Structure. The statistics on race and crime indicate that, in accordance to their proportion in the population, Negroes are arrested between three and four times as frequently as whites. Although Negroes comprise about one-tenth of the population in the United States, they account for nearly a third of the arrests for all offenses.[22] Similarly, drawing from judicial and prison statistics, Negroes have higher rates of conviction and imprisonment than whites. Hence, the status of being a Negro, in comparison to being white, involves a much greater risk of being arrested, convicted, and imprisoned. The probability of being defined as criminal thus varies according to one's location in the racial structure.

Also see Ralph W. England, Jr., "A Theory of Middle Class Juvenile Delinquency," *Journal of Criminal Law, Criminology and Police Science,* 50 (March–April, 1960), pp. 535–540; Harold L. Myerhoff and Barbara G. Myerhoff, "Field Observations of Middle Class 'Groups,'" *Social Forces,* 42 (March, 1942), pp. 328–336.

[21] Gresham M. Sykes and David Matza, "Techniques of Neutralization: A Theory of Delinquency," *American Sociological Review,* 22 (December, 1957), pp. 664–670.

[22] See Marvin E. Wolfgang, *Crime and Race: Conceptions and Misconceptions* (New York: Institute of Human Relations Press, 1964), pp. 31–35.

Furthermore, there are differences in the kinds of behaviors for which Negroes and whites are arrested. Of all the arrests in 1967 for the various offense categories, Negroes absolutely outnumbered whites in arrests for the offenses of murder, forcible rape, robbery, aggravated assault, prostitution, and gambling.[23] Likewise, Negro arrests made up more than half of the arrests for such offenses as stolen property, other assaults, carrying weapons, and possession of narcotics. Whites, on the other hand, tended to approach their proportion in the population only for such offenses as negligent manslaughter, arson, fraud, embezzlement, vandalism, drunkenness, drunken driving, disorderly conduct, and vagrancy. Thus, not only are the crime rates of Negroes higher than those of whites, the offenses for which Negroes and whites are arrested vary widely.

Differences in the crime rates of various ethnic and nationality groups are also evident.[24] And, as with the variations according to race, differences in the rate of crime are found in the types of offenses among different ethnic groups. Italian immigrants in the United States have had high rates of homicide and low rates of drunkenness, whereas Irish immigrants have tended to have lower rates of homicide and much higher offense rates for drunkenness. Also, though the immigrants themselves have tended to have offense patterns similar to those of the home country, their children have tended to be arrested for offenses characteristic of the areas in which they have settled. In addition, the extent to which the crime rate of the ethnic and nationality groups conforms to that of the native whites varies with the time the groups have been in the United States.[25] Finally, younger members of ethnic and racial groups take on the crime rates of the native whites more than do the older members.

Location in the ethnic-racial structure, therefore, presents a man with different perspectives. On the one hand, he is provided with the behavior patterns of his ethnic, nationality, or racial group. On

[23] Federal Bureau of Investigation, *Uniform Crime Reports — 1967*, pp. 126–128.

[24] For a discussion of these rates, see Donald R. Cressey, "Crime," in Robert K. Merton and Robert A. Nisbet (eds.), *Contemporary Social Problems*, 2nd ed. (New York: Harcourt, Brace and World, 1966), pp. 153–155.

[25] C. C. Van Vechten, "The Criminality of the Foreign-Born," *Journal of Criminal Law, Criminology and Police Science*, 32 (July–August, 1941), pp. 139–147.

the other hand, he confronts the behavior patterns of the other groups. Consequently, the respective groups respond to the normative patterns of their own group, but also assimilate the behavior patterns of the areas in which they reside. Furthermore, especially among Negroes, a person's behavior may be shaped by his reaction to the position he has been assigned. Much of the behavior of Negroes represents a reaction to subordination, economic insecurity, denial of employment opportunities, restricted participation, and discrimination.[26] That which becomes defined as criminal may be an honest attempt to create an existence that, ideally, is assured in the American dream.

Each group, then, develops its own behavior patterns in reference to its position in the ethnic-racial structure of society. While the behavior patterns consequently differ from one position to another, their criminality is determined not by the nature of the behavior itself but by the fact that persons in other positions, through the use of the legal resources of the state, define the behavior as criminal.

ECOLOGY OF BEHAVIOR PATTERNS AND CRIMINAL DEFINITIONS

When rates of crime and delinquency are viewed according to their geographical or ecological distribution, regularities become apparent. In general, although there are variations from one offense category to another, crime rates in the United States tend to be higher in some states than in others, higher in urban areas than in rural areas, higher in larger cities than in smaller cities, and higher in the center of cities than in the areas further removed from the center.[27] Moreover, the high rates of crime and delinquency tend

[26] See Guy B. Johnson, "The Negro and Crime," *Annals of the American Academy of Political and Social Science,* 271 (September, 1941), pp. 93–104; Earl R. Moses, "Differentials in Crime Rates Between Negroes and Whites Based on Comparisons of Four Socio-Economically Equated Areas," *American Sociological Review,* 12 (August, 1947), pp. 411–420.

[27] For a discussion of such variations in offense rates, see Edwin H. Sutherland and Donald R. Cressey, *Principles of Criminology,* 7th ed. (Philadelphia: J. B. Lippincott, 1966), pp. 183–199. Critiques of the ecological approach in criminology can be found in Terrence Morris, *The Criminal Area* (London: Routledge & Kegan Paul, 1958); Judith A. Wilks, "Ecological Correlates of Crime and Delinquency," in President's Commission on Law Enforcement and Administration of Justice, *Crime and Its Impact — An Assessment* (Washington, D.C.: U.S. Government Printing Office, 1967), pp. 138–156.

to be found in areas characterized by lower class, non-white populations living under substandard physical conditions.

Though such regularities can be explained in any number of ways, I argue that ecological areas serve as structures for learning behavior patterns and for pursuing particular behaviors. Whether or not these behaviors are criminal, however, depends upon the decisions of others. Therefore, crime rates are ecologically distributed in accordance to the probability that certain behaviors, learned and pursued within the respective areas, will be criminally defined. The geographical variations in offense rates may thus be investigated in terms of the ecology of behavior patterns and criminal definitions.

Regional Variations. The amounts and types of crime vary considerably from one region to another in the United States. An early study found that particular offenses displayed a gradient pattern throughout the country.[28] It was found that murder was concentrated in the southeastern states, with a gradient to the north and west, and that robbery was concentrated in the mid-central states, with decreasing rates on either side of an axis running through the center of the United States. Essentially the same patterning of offenses was found several years later.[29] In the later study, it was found that some offenses show more of a regional concentration.

The regional variation in crime rates can be readily observed in the annual reports of offenses known to the police in the United States. On the basis of the 1967 report, the East South Central region had the lowest total crime rate, and the Pacific region had the highest.[30] In the specific offense categories, the South Atlantic region had the highest murder rate (9.6 per 100,000 population) and the highest aggravated assault rate (191.1). The Pacific region had the highest rate of forcible rape (21.8) and burglary (1308.4), while the Middle Atlantic region had the highest robbery rate (141.5) and New England had the highest auto theft rate (471.5). On the other hand, New England had the lowest rates in

[28] Stuart Lottier, "Distribution of Criminal Offenses in Sectional Regions," *Journal of Criminal Law, Criminology and Police Science,* 29 (September–October, 1938), pp. 329–344.

[29] Lyle W. Shannon, "The Spatial Distribution of Criminal Offenses by States," *Journal of Criminal Law, Criminology and Police Science,* 45 (September–October, 1954), pp. 264–274.

[30] Federal Bureau of Investigation, *Uniform Crime Reports — 1967,* pp. 62–67.

the country for murder (2.4), forcible rape (6.3), robbery (37.0), and aggravated assault (58.1), and the East South Central region had the lowest rates of burglary (532.3), larceny (334.9), and auto theft (192.4).

Variations in these regional crime rates can be explained by different structuring of behavior patterns, with relative probabilities of being defined as criminal, according to regions of the country. There are, first, regional variations in normative systems and behavior patterns. In the south a tradition of violence, including prescriptions on the use of weapons, accompanied by a code of personal honor, provides the background for behavior patterns that have a good chance of being defined as criminal.[31] In addition, the relation of whites and blacks in the south leads to personal conflict both within the two segments and between blacks and whites.

Second, opportunity for certain activities varies according to region. The high rate of property offenses in the west is in part a result of the casual style of living, the openness of the region, and the availability of property.[32] Opportunities for activities that may be variously defined as burglary, robbery, larceny, and theft thus vary from one region to another. Finally, regions differ in expectations of enforcement and administration of criminal law. Behavior patterns vary regionally, therefore, in both the conduct that may be criminally defined and the behaviors that result in the defining of conduct as criminal.

Community Variations. One of the most consistent findings in the ecology of crime is that overall crime rates are higher for urban than rural areas and that overall rates tend to increase with size of city.[33] Urban areas usually have higher rates for all major offenses, with the exception of murder. Hence, the greatest differences in rates between rural and urban areas are for crime against property, with the differences being less apparent for crimes against the person. The rates for all categories of offenses tend to increase progressively with each category of city size.

[31] See Walter C. Reckless, *The Crime Problem,* 3rd ed. (New York: Appleton-Century-Crofts, 1961), pp. 69–70.

[32] See Wilks, "Ecological Correlates of Crime and Delinquency," pp. 150–151.

[33] See Federal Bureau of Investigation, *Crime in the United States — 1967,* pp. 100–101.

Differences in offense rates between rural and urban areas can be accounted for by basic differences in the learning and opportunity structures of the two areas. In rural areas, as observed in several studies, there is a comparative absence of behavioral norms and social processes that are conducive to the development of behaviors that may be defined as criminal.[34] Similarly, gang activity in rural areas is relatively limited. The possibilities for learning techniques and motivations for committing criminally defined activities are not as readily available in rural areas as in urban areas.

Furthermore, opportunities for carrying out such property offenses as robbery, burglary, larceny, and auto theft are much greater in urban than in rural areas, and they become even more prevalent in large cities. In such ways, then, urban areas (especially the larger cities) provide the cultural and structural environments for the development of behavior patterns that may result in criminally defined activities.

Variations Within Cities. Studies over several decades have documented fairly consistent patterns in crime and delinquency rates within the boundaries of American cities. Research by members of the "Chicago school," in particular, established that the highest offense rates generally occur in the low rent areas near the center of the city and that the rates decrease with increasing distance from the city center.[35] In addition, such studies have shown that the relative rates of crime and delinquency tend to be maintained within the respective areas of the city in spite of changes in the population of the areas.

[34] Marshall B. Clinard, "The Process of Urbanization and Criminal Behavior," *American Journal of Sociology,* 48 (September, 1942), pp. 202–213; William P. Lentz, "Rural and Urban Differentials in Juvenile Delinquency," *Journal of Criminal Law, Criminology and Police Science,* 47 (September–October, 1956), pp. 331–339; Theodore N. Ferdinand, "The Offense Patterns and Family Structures of Urban, Village, and Rural Delinquency," *Journal of Criminal Law, Criminology and Police Science,* 55 (March, 1964), pp. 86–93; John P. Clark and Eugene P. Wenninger, "Socio-Economic Class and Area as Correlates of Illegal Behavior Among Juveniles," *American Sociological Review,* 27 (December, 1962), pp. 826–834; Richard Quinney, "Structural Characteristics, Population Areas, and Crime Rates in the United States," *Journal of Criminal Law, Criminology and Police Science,* 57 (March, 1966), pp. 45–52.

[35] Clifford R. Shaw and Henry D. McKay, *Delinquent Areas* (Chicago: University of Chicago Press, 1929); Clifford R. Shaw and Henry D. McKay, *Juvenile Delinquency and Urban Areas* (Chicago: University of Chicago Press, 1942).

The distribution of offense rates tends to be related to social characteristics of areas within cities. From several sources we conclude that offense rates of areas are related to the economic, family, and racial composition of the areas. In Baltimore, it was found that delinquency rates of census tract areas were associated with the percentage of owner-occupied housing and the ratio of nonwhites to whites.[36] Similar findings have emerged from studies of the distribution of offense rates in Washington, D.C., Detroit, and Indianapolis.[37] Using somewhat different modes of analysis and theoretical assumptions, others have found similar variables to be related to the ecology of crime and delinquency in Seattle, San Diego, and Lexington, Kentucky.[38] While such findings continue to accumulate, it is important to account for the relationships between social characteristics of areas and their offense rates. One meaningful explanation may be the different kinds of learning and opportunities in the areas. The learning of and the opportunity to engage in behavior patterns differ from one area to another.

Behavior patterns that may be in conflict with legal definitions necessarily develop within ecological areas of the city. Initially such behavior among adolescents may be inspired by no more insidious purpose than that of adventure and recreation. Thrasher found some time ago in his classic studies of gangs in parts of Chicago that children, in forming play groups, engage in activities that may be defined as illegal.[39] In time, conflict with other groups in the neighborhood and contact with other values may bring the

[36] Bernard Lander, *Toward an Understanding of Juvenile Delinquency* (New York: Columbia University Press, 1954).

[37] Charles V. Willie and Anita Gershenovitz, "Juvenile Delinquency in Racially Mixed Areas," *American Sociological Review,* 29 (October, 1964), pp. 740–744; David J. Bordua, "Juvenile Delinquency and Anomie," *Social Problems,* 6 (Winter, 1958–1959), pp. 230–238; Ronald J. Chilton, "Continuity in Delinquency Area Research: A Comparison of Studies for Baltimore, Detroit and Indianapolis," *American Sociological Review,* 29 (February, 1964), pp. 71–83.

[38] Calvin F. Schmid, "Urban Crime Areas: Part II," *American Sociological Review,* 25 (October, 1960), pp. 655–678; Kenneth Polk, "Juvenile Delinquency and Social Areas," *Social Problems,* 5 (Winter, 1957–1958), pp. 214–217; Richard Quinney, "Crime, Delinquency and Social Areas," *Journal of Research in Crime and Delinquency,* 1 (July, 1964), pp. 149–154.

[39] Frederick M. Thrasher, *The Gang* (Chicago: University of Chicago Press, 1927). Also see William F. Whyte, *Street Corner Society* (Chicago: University of Chicago Press, 1943).

members to engage in a variety of activities including stealing from stores, robbery, and aggressive acts against other gangs.[40] Violent gang activity may become a collective response of adolescents in lower class slums to the problems of living in such areas of the city.

The diversity of cultural traditions within ecological areas, and the juxtaposition of the traditions, appears to be important in the development of the types and amounts of criminally defined activities. In an area where adult activity is fairly stable and organized, adolescent behavior tends to take on the same qualities.[41] On the other hand, where adult patterns are not so integrated, juvenile activities (some of which may be defined as delinquent) tend to be unorganized and more violent.

In an extension of this formulation, it has been suggested that different types of adolescent "subcultures" emerge in relation to the integration of "criminal" and "noncriminal" patterns of the neighborhood.[42] Where adult patterns are integrated, the subcultures of adolescents will be "criminal" and the gangs will engage in theft, extortion, and similar activities in order to achieve status and income. In unintegrated areas, characterized by transiency and instability, "conflict" subcultures develop. Where neither criminal nor noncriminal traditions are available to youth, a "retreatist" subculture centering on drug use and sensual experiences will emerge. Whatever the utility of such a conceptualization, different behavior patterns develop within areas of the city according to the social and cultural structure of those areas.[43]

[40] Lewis Yablonsky, *The Violent Gang* (New York: The Free Press of Glencoe, 1962); Harold W. Pfantz, "Near-Group Theory and Collective Behavior: A Critical Reformulation," *Social Problems,* 9 (Fall, 1961), pp. 167–174.

[41] Solomon Kobrin, "The Conflict of Values in Delinquency Areas," *American Sociological Review,* 16 (October, 1951), pp. 653–661.

[42] Cloward and Ohlin, *Delinquency and Opportunity,* pp. 161–186.

[43] For further empirical works to support this position, see Irving Spengel, *Racketville, Slumtown, Haulburg: An Exploratory Study of Delinquent Subcultures* (Chicago: University of Chicago Press, 1964); Irving Spengel, "Male Young Adult Criminality, Deviant Values, and Differential Opportunities in Two Lower Class Negro Neighborhoods," *Social Problems,* 10 (Winter, 1963), pp. 237–250; Albert J. Reiss, Jr. and Albert Lewis Rhodes, "The Distribution of Juvenile Delinquency in the Social Class Structure," *American Sociological Review,* 26 (October, 1961), pp. 720–732. For an example of cross-cultural variations, see Lois B. De Fleur, "Ecological Variables in the Cross-Cultural Study of Delinquency," *Social Forces,* 45 (June, 1967), pp. 556–570.

Areas within the city differ in their structuring of behavior patterns and in the presence of opportunities for engaging in behaviors that may be criminally defined. Thus, crime rates tend to vary from neighborhood to neighborhood, depending on the opportunities for the pursuit of particular activities.[44] The opportunities for committing each type of crime depend on the availability of such targets as safes, cash registers, personal possessions, and other persons and are reflected in the rates for each type of offense. Rates for burglary, robbery, and larceny are highest in areas that have a high proportion of business and commercial activity. Likewise, rates of auto theft are highest where a great deal of space is devoted to parking. Rates of forcible rape are highest in areas with a high proportion of resident females, and rates of murder and assault are highest where many personal victims are available.

All behavior patterns, then, develop within concrete ecological areas. However, the patterns that develop are relative to one another not only in content but also in the probability that they will be defined as criminal. According to the perspective provided here, the forms and amounts of crime in any community are the product of the conflict between the behavior patterns of the community and the patterns represented by those who are formulating and applying criminal definitions. And, since the nature and extent of this conflict varies ecologically, rates of crime are differentially distributed according to ecological areas.

GENERAL CULTURAL THEMES IN SEGMENTAL SOCIETY

In spite of the variations in normative systems and behavior patterns from one social or ecological segment to another, some *general cultural themes* pervade all segments. Diversity in a society does not mean that no cultural themes will be shared by all segments. Any society, in a sense, contains its own prescriptions for crime. Although laws may define some activities as criminal, the same society may contain cultural themes that are conducive to the violation of these laws. Such themes are evident in American

44 Sarah L. Boggs, "Urban Crime Patterns," *American Sociological Review*, 39 (December, 1965), pp. 899–908.

society, making some behavior patterns that may be defined as criminal a consistent part of the American way of life.

Conformity to the law has never been an overwhelming obsession in America. Local laws were established for governing the conduct of the members of the early settlements, but behavior outside the settlements was largely a matter of personal discretion. The frontier experience called for an individuality that made each man a law unto himself. The western frontier, especially, became a haven for activities which, if pursued elsewhere, would probably have been dealt with by means of the criminal law.[45] But the frontier became an area of "lawlessness" not so much because of the definitions imposed on the conduct but because there was no law to enforce and administer. The behavior patterns that developed in the frontier context and the corresponding attitudes toward authority that supported the behavior patterns remain today as part of our cultural heritage.

The dynamic character of the American experience produced a "criminogenic" culture in still other ways. Although they certainly do not explain variations in specific behavior patterns, with varying probabilities of criminal definition, cultural themes that appeared in America did stress success, power, status, prestige, competition, and exploitation.[46] Success in the competitive struggle came to be evaluated in terms of money and material wealth. Pecuniary success was established as the measure of most men, being extolled as the major goal throughout the population, with less emphasis being placed on the means by which the goal was to be achieved.[47] The choice of paths to success, however, continues to depend upon differences in the normative systems of the respective segments of society.

At the same time that an open society was creating cultural themes conducive to law violation, other values were being affirmed that were in opposition to those which might lead to criminally defined activity. A basic American hypocrisy thus became en-

[45] See Mabel A. Elliott, "Crime and the Frontier Mores," *American Sociological Review,* 9 (April, 1944), pp. 185–192.

[46] Donald R. Taft, *Criminology,* 3rd ed. (New York: Macmillan, 1956), pp. 336–343. Milton L. Barron, *The Juvenile in Delinquent Society* (New York: Alfred A. Knopf, 1960), pp. 199–221.

[47] Robert K. Merton, *Social Theory and Social Structure* (New York: The Free Press, 1957), pp. 131–160.

grained. On the one hand, a Puritan ethic prohibited indulgence in certain activities, such as gambling, drinking, prostitution, and drug use, and on the other, a way of life grew around those who appreciated such indulgences. The contradiction and paradox today has been described as follows:

> It would seem that the vast majority of Americans today would like to have their proverbial cake and eat it, too, by theoretically affirming values which they hold dear, and, at the same time, reserving for themselves a certain leeway in realizing wishes which may not always correspond to these values. As a result, law and a high degree of lawlessness exist side by side, and moralists and gangsters complement each other.[48]

Not only have illicit behaviors been made illegal by criminal law, but criminal organizations have been established to satisfy the activities that we want both prohibited and fulfilled.

The economic system that developed in America also contains its own cultural themes conducive to particular kinds of behavior patterns. A capitalist economy, based on competition and free enterprise, promotes an ethic that stresses the rightness of any activity that is pursued in the interest of one's business or occupational activity. Consequently, otherwise "respectable" members of society engage in activities that have been criminally defined by various laws, but which are not considered by them or most of the public as criminal.[49] Such business and occupational activities as misrepresentation in advertising, fraudulent financial manipulations, illegal rebates, misappropriation of public funds, fee splitting, and fraudulent damage claims are regarded as little more than the American way of doing business. In spite of recent legislation and administrative rulings, that which is done in the name of business

[48] Robert K. Woetzel, "An Overview of Organized Crime: Mores Versus Morality," *The Annals of the American Academy of Political and Social Science*, 347 (May, 1963), p. 8.

[49] See, in particular, Edwin H. Sutherland, *White Collar Crime* (New York: Holt, Rinehart and Winston, 1949); Marshall B. Clinard, *The Black Market: A Study of White Collar Crime* (New York: Holt, Rinehart and Winston, 1952); Richard Quinney, "The Study of White Collar Crime: Toward a Reorientation in Theory and Research," *Journal of Criminal Law, Criminology and Police Science*, 55 (June, 1964), pp. 208–214; Gilbert Geis, "White Collar Crime: The Heavy Electrical Equipment Antitrust Cases of 1961," in Marshall B. Clinard and Richard Quinney, *Criminal Behavior Systems: A Typology* (New York: Holt, Rinehart and Winston, 1967), pp. 139–151.

and gainful employment tends to be beyond public and legal reproach.

The rationale for one of the most entrenched criminal activities in the United States, organized crime, is consistent with the free enterprise system of business. Organized crime, like legitimate business, attempts to achieve maximum returns with a minimum of expenditure by efficient organization and management. It is therefore an integral part of our culture, being closely tied to such factors as the profit motive, indifference to public affairs, general disregard for law, laissez-faire economics, and questionable political practices.[50] Furthermore, organized crime has become a normal way of achieving success for members of a number of groups in society. It has served as an appropriate activity for late-arriving immigrant groups and has become closely associated with the neighborhood politics of these groups.[51] Organized crime thus receives considerable support in the United States because of its relationship with legitimate business patterns.

> One basic fact stands out from the details of this discussion, namely that organized crime must be thought of as a natural growth, or as a development adjunct to our general system of private profit economy. Business, industry, and finance all are competitive enterprises within the area of legal operations. But there is also an area of genuine economic demand for things and services not permitted under our legal and social codes. Organized crime is the system of business function in the area. It, too, is competitive, and hence must organize for its self-protection and for control of the market.[52]

Although the formulation and enforcement of criminal laws may assist in the control of such crime, the integration of organized crime into American culture prevents any serious control of the activity.

The relationship between cultural themes and criminally defined activities can also be seen in the American emphasis on violence. The

[50] Alfred R. Lindesmith, "Organized Crime," *Annals of the American Academy of Political and Social Science,* 217 (September, 1941), pp. 76–83.

[51] Daniel Bell, "Crime as an American Way of Life," *Antioch Review,* 13 (June, 1953), pp. 131–154; Digby Baltzell, *The Protestant Establishment* (New York: Random House, 1964), pp. 49, 215–216.

[52] George B. Vold, *Theoretical Criminology* (New York: Oxford University Press, 1958), p. 240.

emphasis, though considerable, is nevertheless characterized by ambivalence.[53] We are afraid of violence, protecting ourselves by whatever means possible, yet we are fascinated by it, supporting its coverage in the mass media and condoning it when applied to others in our own interest or in the interest of our group or nation. That violence is qualified does not negate it as an important American cultural theme. Violence that becomes defined as criminal is obviously distributed unevenly throughout society.[54] Violence that occurs in the interest of the dominant segments of society is, however, legitimized violence. Assault and murder used on others in war, in military operations, in policing riots, and in the controlling of actions conceived as politically subversive are not defined as criminal.[55] Such uses of violence are patriotic and as American, as one black leader has noted, as cherry pie. Violence, wherever it originates and however it is promoted in our society, becomes culturally diffused throughout the society as a cultural theme that affects the lives of us all.

Finally, we must recognize that the general cultural themes are *mediated* by the respective segments of society. The effects of the cultural themes consequently vary from one segment to another.

[53] William A. Westley, "The Escalation of Violence through Legitimation," *Annals of the American Academy of Political and Social Science,* 364 (March, 1966), p. 125.

[54] See Robert C. Bensing and Oliver Schroeder, *Homicide in an Urban Community* (Springfield, Ill.: Charles C Thomas, 1960); Henry Allen Bullock, "Urban Homicide in Theory and Fact," *Journal of Criminal Law, Criminology and Police Science,* 45 (January–February, 1955), pp. 565–575; Gilbert Geis, "Violence and Organized Crime," *Annals of the American Academy of Political and Social Science,* 364 (March, 1966), pp. 86–95; Thomas F. Pettigrew and Rosalind B. Spier, "Ecological Structure of Negro Homicide," *American Journal of Sociology,* 67 (May, 1962), pp. 621–629; David P. Pittman and William Handy, "Patterns in Criminal Aggravated Assault," *Journal of Criminal Law, Criminology and Police Science,* 55 (December, 1964), pp. 462–470; Austin L. Porterfield, *Cultures of Violence* (Fort Worth, Texas: Leo Potishman Foundation, 1965); Marvin E. Wolfgang and Franco Ferracuti, *The Subculture of Violence: Towards an Integrated Theory in Criminology* (London: Tavistock, 1967).

[55] Allen D. Grimshaw, "Actions of Police and Military in American Race Riots," *Phylon,* 24 (Fall, 1963), pp. 271–289; Philips Taft, "Violence in American Labor Disputes," *Annals of the American Academy of Political and Social Science,* 364 (March, 1966), pp. 127–140; Westley, "The Escalation of Violence Through Legitimation," pp. 120–126; Marvin E. Wolfgang, "A Preface to Violence," *Annals of the American Academy of Political and Social Science,* 364 (March, 1966), pp. 1–7.

The general themes have different influences among the segments because, first, the themes are more strongly shared by some segments, and second, the normative systems and opportunity structures of the segments provide varying possibilities for fulfilling the cultural themes. The general culture is thus mediated in a segmental society.

Nevertheless, behavior patterns themselves are neither criminal nor noncriminal. They are merely behavior patterns, and their criminality is determined by the actions of others, who act according to other behavior patterns. Criminality is a construct, beyond the quality of specific behaviors, that is formulated and applied by the power segments of society. The observer, knowing the organization of the society, may evaluate behavior patterns by their relative probability of being defined as criminal. However, the behaviors themselves are criminal only when they are so defined by those who represent other patterns of behavior. Crime is created in a segmental society.

CHAPTER EIGHT

Action Patterns of the Criminally Defined

Behavior becomes patterned only by the conduct of individual persons. But once behavior patterns have become established with some regularity within the segments of society, individuals are provided with a framework for personal action. That framework is, nevertheless, tenuous, since behavior patterns and associated normative systems are never static but are always emerging and changing. Yet it is within such a context that individuals construct their own patterns of meaningful social action. These *personal action patterns*, though continually developing, provide a source of personal identity and serve as the basis for social behavior. In short, personal action patterns are the essence of a life that is both human and social.

The development of action patterns gives behavior a substance in relation to criminal definitions. The following questions are thus raised in an investigation of the action patterns of the criminally defined: What is the role of the self in the development of personal action patterns? How are these patterns socially acquired? How do they develop in response to criminal definition? And, finally, how are the personal action patterns of the criminally defined organized into systems of behavior? All these questions refer to the probability that persons will be defined as criminal in a segmental society.

ACHIEVEMENT OF SELF

Each person is an object unto himself. That is, man has a conception of himself, communicates with himself, and acts toward himself.[1] By regarding himself as a separate and distinct entity, a person is able to act in a world that he simultaneously creates, confronts, and interprets. He thus acts on the basis of how he experiences his world. Action, then, is conduct that is personally constructed by the actor. For each person, action is pursued according to the personal meaning attached to that action and, furthermore, according to the personal interpretation of the actions of others.

A person's self-conception, as an image of what he means to himself and how he acts with reference to himself, is always in a process of formation. In this process, persons place themselves into categories with which they can identify, such as age, sex, occupation, ethnic group, and social class.[2] Moreover, actions themselves give an identity to a person. On the basis of his own constructions and decisions, man is ever becoming.

The achievement of any sense of self, however temporary, is crucial to all human beings. But the ease with which self-conceptions can be formed varies from one time to another and from one contemporary social situation to another. For men in some situations at particular times, the achievement of self-identity is especially problematic.

> In every age men ask in some form the questions: Who am I? Where do I belong? The degree of awareness and the kind of emphasis with which these questions are asked vary at different periods. Times of swift change and social dislocation bring them to the fore, against the background of whatever personal hopes and social harmonies an earlier period has cultivated.[3]

Hence, the achievement of self is critical for persons confronted with external environments that defy ready interpretation. Similarly, situations that frustrate expectations and aspirations promote

[1] George H. Mead, *Mind, Self, and Society* (Chicago: University of Chicago Press, 1934); Herbert Blumer, "Sociological Implications of the Thought of George Herbert Mead," *American Journal of Sociology,* 71 (March, 1966), pp. 535–544.

[2] Tamotsu Shibutani, *Society and Personality: An Interactionist Approach to the Social Psychology* (Englewood Cliffs, N.J.: Prentice-Hall, 1961), pp. 224–225.

[3] Helen M. Lynd, *On Shame and the Search for Identity* (New York: Harcourt, Brace and World, 1958), p. 13.

a crisis in self-identity. But since each man seeks a meaningful existence, some solution must be achieved.

Situations that persons find undesirable or difficult of interpretation may lead to the formation of self-conceptions that take as their reference opposition to the established order. It may not be unusual, therefore, to find that actions that result from such attitudes become defined by those in power as criminal. A great deal of the traditionally defined criminal behavior has been a response of individuals and groups to situations regarded as inadequate for the attainment of specific aspirations.[4] Calculated violation of the law may be a rational solution to socially structured and perceived problems. Protest and resistance against unjust conditions and policies may be most appropriately pursued through activities that violate criminal laws.[5]

Today, especially, violation of the law represents more than mere social deviance. Much of criminally defined activity is actually *political* behavior. Actions against the law are becoming ideological in orientation, being directed to the restructuring of the social and political order. When persons and groups of persons attempt to achieve desired goals by means of actions against the established order, the representatives of that order are likely to respond by formulating and applying criminal definitions.

Actions are a part of the process of the development of a self,

[4] On delinquency, for example, see Albert K. Cohen, *Delinquent Boys* (New York: The Free Press of Glencoe, 1955); Harold W. Pfantz, "Near-Group Theory and Collective Behavior: A Critical Reformulation," *Social Problems*, 9 (Fall, 1961), pp. 167–194; John P. Clark and Eugene P. Wenninger, "Goal Orientations and Illegal Behavior Among Juveniles," *Social Forces*, 42 (October, 1963), pp. 49–59; Delbert S. Elliott, "Delinquency and Perceived Opportunity," *Sociological Inquiry*, 32 (Spring, 1962), pp. 216–227; Judson R. Landis and Frank R. Scarpitti, "Perceptions Regarding Value Orientation and Legitimate Opportunity: Delinquents and Non-Delinquents," *Social Forces*, 44 (September, 1965), pp. 83–91; Gerald Maxwell, "Adolescent Powerlessness and Delinquent Behavior," *Social Problems*, 14 (Summer, 1966), pp. 35–47.

[5] Marshall B. Clinard and Richard Quinney, *Criminal Behavior Systems: A Typology* (New York: Holt, Rinehart and Winston, 1967), pp. 177–189; Irving Louis Horowitz and Martin Liebowitz, "Social Deviance and Political Marginality: Toward a Redefinition of the Relation Between Sociology and Politics," *Social Problems*, 15 (Winter, 1968), pp. 280–296; Richard Quinney, "A Conception of Man and Society for Criminology," *Sociological Quarterly*, 6 (Spring, 1965), pp. 119–127.

and, during this process, actions become patterned. For many, the action patterns that are formed have a fairly high probability of being defined by others (and perhaps by self) as criminal. But in expressing such actions, persons develop self-conceptions. Criminally defined behavior, like any other behavior, has meaning to the actors and is pursued in the achievement of self.

The role of the self in the development of action patterns which may be defined as criminal or delinquent has been explored in an investigation that extended over several years. The researchers examined the *self-concepts* of young teen-age boys to determine whether or not variations in conceptions of self account for specific patterns of behavior. The initial study consisted of an exploration and description of the responses of 125 "good" boys, nominated by their teachers and substantiated by official records as nondelinquent, to a battery of self-evaluation items. The researchers reported that the 125 boys portrayed themselves as law-abiding and obedient.

> Specifically, the vast majority defined themselves as being stricter about right and wrong than most people, indicated that they attempted to keep out of trouble at all costs and further indicated that they tried to conform to the expectations of their parents, teachers, and others. The nominees did not conceive of themselves as prospects for juvenile court action or detention, and they stated that their participation in such activities as stealing had been minimal and that their friends were either entirely or almost completely free of police and juvenile court contact.[6]

In subsequent research the authors reported that the "bad" boys had self-concepts that consisted of perceptions of getting into trouble, having friends who were in trouble, disliking school, expecting to go to jail, and so on.[7] Follow-up studies of the "good" and "bad" boys indicated that the earlier self-conceptions were predictive of later behavior, a much greater proportion of boys with "poor" con-

[6] Walter C. Reckless, Simon Dinitz, and Ellen Murray, "Self Concept as an Insulator Against Delinquency," *American Sociological Review,* 21 (December, 1956), p. 745.

[7] Walter C. Reckless, Simon Dinitz, and Barbara Kay, "The Self Component in Potential Delinquency and Potential Non-Delinquency," *American Sociological Review,* 22 (October, 1957), pp. 566–570.

cepts of self having juvenile court records than boys with "good" self-conceptions.[8] On the basis of these findings the authors have proposed that the nature of the concept of self insulates youths in high delinquency areas from involvement in delinquency.

> In our quest to discover what insulates a boy against delinquency in a high delinquency area, we believe we have some tangible evidence that a good self-concept, undoubtedly a product of favorable socialization, veers slum boys away from delinquency, while a poor self-concept, a product of unfavorable socialization, gives the slum boy no resistance to deviancy, delinquent companions, or delinquent subculture. We feel that components of the self-strength, such as a favorable concept of self, act as an inner buffer or inner containment against deviancy, distraction, lure, and pressures.[9]

Such research clearly supports the position that self-conceptions and action patterns are interdependent.[10] Yet, the research noted above requires some reinterpretation to take into account the theory of the social reality of crime. I argue that *both* those who engage in behavior that is not usually defined as criminal or delinquent ("good" boys) and those who engage in behavior that has a high probability of being defined as criminal or delinquent ("bad" boys) are involved in meaningful social actions. Their respective self-conceptions and actions are personally appropriate. Only from the perspective of the standards of others can self-conceptions and actions be evaluated positively or negatively, as "appropriate" or "inappropriate," "good" or "bad." A boy's affirmative answer to a question such as the possi-

[8] Frank R. Scarpitti, Ellen Murray, Simon Dinitz, and Walter C. Reckless, "The 'Good' Boy in a High Delinquency Area: Four Years Later," *American Sociological Review,* 25 (August, 1960), pp. 555–558; Simon Dinitz, Frank R. Scarpitti, and Walter C. Reckless, "Delinquency Vulnerability: A Cross Group and Longitudinal Analysis," *American Sociological Review,* 27 (August, 1962), pp. 515–517.

[9] Walter C. Reckless and Simon Dinitz, "Pioneering with Self-Concept as a Vulnerability Factor in Delinquency," *Journal of Criminal Law, Criminology and Police Science*, 58 (December, 1967), pp. 515–523.

[10] Other research on self-conceptions of offenders includes Leon F. Fanin and Marshall B. Clinard, "Differences in the Conception of Self as a Male Among Lower and Middle Class Delinquents, *Social Problems,* 13 (Fall, 1965), pp. 205–214; John W. Kinch, "Self-Conceptions of Types of Delinquents," *Sociological Inquiry,* 32 (Spring, 1962), pp. 228–234; James F. Short, Jr. and Fred L. Strodtbeck, *Group Process and Gang Delinquency* (Chicago: University Press, 1965), pp. 140–184.

bility that he will appear in juvenile court is not necessarily the basis of an "inappropriate" or a "poor" self-concept, but is more a personal prediction of future events based on past experience.[11] From the perspective of each person, all action patterns, no matter how others evaluate the patterns, are personally meaningful. Behavior that may become defined as criminal by others is behavior that is pursued in the process of the achievement of self.

ASSOCIATION, IDENTIFICATION, AND COMMITMENT

Each person constructs his own "reality world," his own view of himself and all that is about him. However, it is only as he participates in the worlds of others that he is able to develop his own world. In other words, by occupying space with others in a social setting, we share a common symbolic environment.

> While the reality world of each individual is his and his alone, it does, of course, have many aspects in common with the reality worlds of other people. The extent to which our reality worlds are alike seems to depend on the extent to which we have shared similar experiences and similar purposes.[12]

Shared meanings are provided for most persons by membership in some kind of social group. According to *reference group* terminology, social groups furnish members with a frame of reference for the organization of perceptions and experiences.[13] Persons act, then, in reference to the perspectives of their groups. Furthermore, the actions of persons are in part an attempt to preserve and enhance social status within their groups. Consequently, an explanation of variations in the behavior of persons may be sought in the context of group experiences.

[11] See Michael Schwartz and Sandra S. Tangri, "A Note on Self-Concept as an Insulator Against Delinquency," *American Sociological Review*, 30 (December, 1965), pp. 922–926; Sandra S. Tangri and Michael Schwartz, "Delinquency Research and the Self-Concept Variable," *Journal of Criminal Law, Criminology and Police Science,* 58 (June, 1967), pp. 182–190.

[12] Hadley Cantrel, *The Politics of Despair* (New York: Basic Books, 1958), p. 17.

[13] See, for example, Tamotsu Shibutani, "Reference Groups as Perspectives," *American Journal of Sociology,* 60 (May, 1955), pp. 562–569; Ralph H. Turner, "Role Taking, Role Standpoint, and Reference Group Behavior," *American Journal of Sociology,* 61 (January, 1956), pp. 316–328.

The theory of *differential association* provides such an explanation of "criminal" behavior.[14] In this view, all persons acquire their behavior during associations with others. Some, however, become criminal because the substance of their associations involves an excess of definitions favorable to the violation of the law. The theory of differential association is thus an extension of the basic theoretical perspective of the socialization process that occurs in the context of primary groups.[15] The learning of "criminal" behavior patterns is not fundamentally different from other socialization during which the individual is differentially exposed to various norms regarding some socially significant form of behavior.

The problem in the theory of differential association, however, has been not so much theoretical as empirical. Few systematic guides are provided for empirical verification of the theory. Moreover, the theory was formulated at such a high level of abstraction that it has not been possible to test it with empirical data. At best, it has been subject only to partial testing through research on the variables of association, including the frequency, duration, priority, and intensity of association. On the basis of these limited studies, nevertheless, it has been shown that persons who associate with delinquents (however defined) report more or engage in more alleged delinquent behavior than those who associate with others.[16]

Although the general principle of differential association probably holds for much of what is defined as delinquent and criminal, variations in the theory can be expected in concrete situations. In order to explore and explain these variations, the theory can be reformulated according to the logical and explanatory relations of such conceptual units as "criminal behavior," "symbolic interaction,"

[14] Edwin H. Sutherland, *Principles of Criminology*, 4th ed. (Philadelphia: J. B. Lippincott, 1947), pp. 1–9.

[15] See Melvin L. De Fleur and Richard Quinney, "A Reformulation of Sutherland's Differential Association Theory and a Strategy for Empirical Verification," *Journal of Research in Crime and Delinquency*, 3 (January, 1966), pp. 1–22.

[16] See Albert J. Reiss, Jr. and A. Lewis Rhodes, "An Empirical Test of Differential Association Theory," *Journal of Research in Crime and Delinquency*, 1 (January, 1964), pp. 5–18; James F. Short, Jr., "Differential Association and Delinquency," *Social Problems*, 4 (January, 1957), pp. 233–239; James F. Short, Jr., "Differential Association as a Hypothesis: Problems of Empirical Testing," *Social Problems*, 8 (Summer, 1960), pp. 14–25; Harwin L. Voss, "Differential Association and Reported Delinquent Behavior: A Replication," *Social Problems*, 12 (Summer, 1964), pp. 78–85.

"primary groups," "selective pattern of exposure," "crime-related learning," and so on.[17] In turn, if the theory is to be empirically tested, each unit must be divided into further subclasses of elements. Testable hypotheses can then be derived from the possible relations between the various subclasses of the conceptual units. That is, separate hypotheses of differential association can be derived and tested regarding such matters as the nature of the offense, the kind of interaction involved, the characteristics of the primary groups, and the type of normative exposure. I suspect that when some of the derived hypotheses are empirically tested, the role of association in development of personal action patterns in relation to criminal definitions will not only be supported, but will be strengthened by specification according to different types of social situations.

As the above strategy indicates, there is more to the learning of criminally defined behavior than simple association with other persons. Not only are other processes involved, but association itself is a complex process. Recognizing the complexity of the association process, the theory has been reconceptualized by an imagery of role playing.[18] The concept of differential association must first be replaced by that of *differential identification.* All persons, accordingly, identify with others, that is, view their own behavior from the perspective of other persons. Moreover, most persons identify with both "criminal" and "noncriminal" persons, by direct association, by reference to criminal roles portrayed in mass media, or as a negative reaction to forces opposed to crime. "The theory of differential identification, in essence, is that a person pursues criminal behavior to the extent that he identifies himself with real or imaginary persons from whose perspective his criminal behavior seems acceptable."[19] Thus, in the reconceptualization, persons who engage in criminally defined behavior identify with and consequently direct

[17] This strategy for empirical verification is proposed in De Fleur and Quinney, "A Reformulation of Sutherland's Differential Association Theory and a Strategy for Empirical Verification," pp. 17–21.

[18] Daniel Glaser, "Criminality Theories and Behavioral Images," *American Journal of Sociology,* 61 (March, 1956), pp. 433–444.

[19] Glaser, "Criminality Theories and Behavioral Images," p. 440. Empirical support for the theory of differential identification is found in Victor Matthews, "Differential Identification: An Empirical Note," *Social Problems,* 15 (Winter, 1968), pp. 376–383.

their actions toward persons who are behaving similarly. All factors are important in the theory of differential identification to the extent that they affect the choice of the others from whose perspective one views his own behavior. Our choices vary, and so accordingly do our behaviors.

According to the perspective developed thus far, the individual engages in behavior, some of which may be defined as criminal or delinquent, rationally and voluntarily. In any situation the individual acts according to his own evaluation of the situation and according to his reference to others. In the language of learning theory, social actions may be conceptualized as *operant* behavior, that is, behavior which is emitted in the presence of given conditions and maintained by its consequences. In other words, the behavior is stimulated by the expectation of a particular response. Most social behaviors are operant in nature, ranging from such forms as handshaking and sexual behavior to wearing clothing and driving a car. Social relations are maintained by the consequences they produce for the interacting parties. So it is that criminally defined behavior is also operant behavior. "Criminal behavior is maintained by its consequences, both material and social."[20] The criminally defined behaves in order to produce a personally desired effect, whether it is the acquisition of money, sexual gratification, or the removal of another person.

The concept of operant behavior as it applies to criminally defined behavior has been employed in a thorough revision of the theory of differential association.[21] Each proposition of the theory was reformulated according to the principle that behavior is a function of its past and current environmental consequences. Furthermore, the authors employed the related concept of *reinforcement* — that actions are repeated on the basis of the consequences of the behavior to the actor. They suggest, among other things, that criminal behavior is learned according to the principles of operant conditioning and that a person engages in those behaviors which have been most highly reinforced in the past. Consequently, some persons engage in criminally defined behavior because such behavior has been

[20] C. R. Jeffery, "Criminal Behavior and Learning Theory," *Journal of Criminal Law, Criminology and Police Science*, 56 (September, 1965), p. 300.

[21] Robert L. Burgess and Ronald L. Akers, "A Differential Association-Reinforcement Theory of Criminal Behavior," *Social Problems*, 14 (Fall, 1966), pp. 128–147.

more highly reinforced than other behavior. Personal action patterns, some of which may be defined as criminal, thus develop in reference to the responses of others. Actions are utilitarian, being pursued and repeated for their personal consequences.

The decision of whether or not to engage in behavior that has a high probability of being defined as criminal is based on the person's consideration of the likely consequences of his course of action. When confronted with a situation that may be resolved through actions that may be criminally defined, a person may evaluate the consequences of one form of action over another. Among the considerations that affect a person's decision to act in a particular way is his *commitment* to contingency interests.[22] That is, he may consider the consequences of some line of action for interests only indirectly associated with the present situation. Acting persons may have "commitments to conformity": ". . . not only fear of the material deprivations and punishments which might result from being discovered as an offender but also apprehension about the deleterious consequences of such a discovery on one's attempts to maintain a consistent self-image, to sustain valued relationships, and to preserve current and future statuses and activities."[23] Thus persons with strong commitments to law-abiding behavior are not likely to engage in actions that have a high probability of being defined as criminal. The consequences would not be to their advantage.

But for most, commitment to the legal code, specific laws in particular, is not a stable and constant matter. Persons tend to vary in their commitments during their lives and, furthermore, qualify their commitments according to the immediate context of their actions. Delinquents *drift* between various standards of conduct. "The delinquent transiently exists in a limbo between convention and crime, responding in turn to the demands of each, flirting now with one, now the other, but postponing commitment, evading decision. Thus, he drifts between criminal and conventional action."[24]

Flexibility in commitment to standards represented by the law is

[22] Howard S. Becker, "Notes on the Concept of Commitment," *American Journal of Sociology,* 66 (July, 1960), pp. 32–40.

[23] Scott Briar and Irving Piliavin, "Delinquency, Situational Inducements, and Commitment to Conformity," *Social Problems,* 13 (Summer, 1965), p. 39.

[24] David Matza, *Delinquency and Drift* (New York: John Wiley, 1964), especially pp. 27–30.

possible through the *neutralization* of legal norms. Delinquents, especially, temporarily employ "techniques of neutralization" to lessen the control of legal norms on their actions.[25] Persons violating the law are thus able at the same time to maintain some commitment to the standards of the law. Hence, actions defined as either criminal or delinquent do not necessarily represent commitment to violation itself, but are more likely episodic actions that are calculated to produce certain consequences for the actors.

Persons behave then, in reference to the anticipated consequences of their actions. The consequences that they desire are those which are socially learned. It is in the context of group association and identification that they act. Their commitments to some group rather than others, and their shifts in such commitments, are always problematic. But given one's past behavior, his present concerns, and future hopes, all actions are rationally conceived for their possible ramifications. Whether the actions may become defined as criminal by others may or may not be one of the considerations of the person when he acts in a concrete situation.

PERSONAL ACTION PATTERNS AS RESPONSES TO CRIMINAL DEFINITION

Personal actions are symbolic both for the actors and the respondents. As interaction continues between parties, or as the actor confronts similar situations, the meanings of personal actions become more firmly established. Eventually persons develop patterns of actions in reference to their interactions with others. An important process in the development of such patterns consists of the *social reactions* of others. It is in the reactions of others that one learns to regard himself in a particular way. What a person becomes, including how he behaves, will depend in large measure on the way he has been and continues to be assessed and defined by others.

The reactions of others are directed in large measure toward the

[25] Gresham M. Sykes and David Matza, "Techniques of Neutralization: A Theory of Delinquency," *American Sociological Review,* 22 (December, 1957), pp. 664–670.

control of personal actions.[26] These social reactions to behavior come from various sources. Generally, social reaction is found, on the one hand, in the informal judgments of others in face-to-face encounters and, on the other hand, in the organized formal control of private or public agencies. Both forms of reaction provide social definitions of a situation. The actions of some persons are singled out for special consideration by others during social reaction.

Although social reaction operates as social control, it is at the same time a source of *definitional conferral* that produces in persons the actions that are the object of control. That is to say, as others react negatively to the actions of a person, that person begins to take unto himself the definitions the others have conferred upon him. This self-definition according to the definitions of others was pointed out some time ago in a discussion of community reactions to juvenile behavior. A community may react to a juvenile's adventurous behavior by eventually defining the boy himself as bad. The boy then responds by accepting the definition and acting in reference to it.

> From the community's point of view, the individual who used to do bad and mischievous things has now become a bad and unredeemable human being. From the individual's point of view there has taken place a similar change. He has gone slowly from a sense of grievance and injustice, of being unduly mistreated and punished, to a recognition that the definition of him as a human being is different from that of other boys in his neighborhood, his school, street, community. This recognition on his part becomes a process of self-identification and integration with the group which shares his activities. It becomes, in part, a process of rationalization; in part, a simple response to a specialized type of stimulus. The young delinquent becomes bad because he is defined as bad and because he is not believed if he is good. There is a persistent demand for consistency in character. The community cannot deal with people whom it cannot define. Reputation is this sort of public definition.[27]

[26] See Edwin M. Lemert, *Social Pathology* (New York: McGraw-Hill, 1951), pp. 54–72; Alexander L. Clark and Jack P. Gibbs, "Social Control: A Reformulation," *Social Problems,* 12 (Spring, 1965), pp. 398–415.

[27] Frank Tannenbaum, *Crime and the Community* (New York: Columbia University Press, 1938), pp. 17–18.

In such fashion, a person tends to become the thing he is described as being.

Defining a person in negative terms, therefore, plays a part in the person's definition of himself and in his subsequent actions. A person may channel his efforts toward behaviors that have a high potential of criminality because he has been defined as being deviant in some way. Accordingly, much of the research and writing on the physical characteristics of offenders can be reinterpreted as social definitions. The various physical stereotypes of the criminal, for example, may in many instances characterize specific offenders, but the relationship is not so much genetic as it is a self-fulfillment of others' perceptions and definitions. It may well be that some offenders conform to Lombroso's "stigmata" of overly small or large head, asymmetry of face, ears of unusual size, receding chin, and so forth.[28] However, persons with such characteristics are not savage "throwbacks," but are more likely than persons with "normal" characteristics to be defined by others as deviant (both physically and socially), more likely to be officially defined as criminal, and more likely to engage in the behaviors consistent with the status they have been assigned.

Similarly, an overly high proportion of the noted outlaws of the west may have had red hair.[29] Yet, being red-headed did not genetically make such men criminals. Rather the social definitions of others prescribed red-headed men as deviant, thus making the consequences true. In the same way we may accept the findings that delinquents tend to be mesomorphs (muscular, athletic, and aggressive).[30] Boys of such appearance and temperament are probably more likely than other boys to be recruited into juvenile gangs and to engage in behaviors that may readily be defined as delinquent. Physical characteristics are first socially defined, then

[28] Cesare Lombroso, *Crime: Its Causes and Remedies* (Boston: Little, Brown, 1911). Also see E. A. Hooton, *Crime and the Man* (Cambridge: Harvard University Press, 1937). For more recent research and interpretation, see Raymond J. Corsini, "Appearance and Criminality," *American Journal of Sociology,* 65 (July, 1959), pp. 49–51.

[29] Hans von Hentig, "Redhead and Outlaw," *Journal of Criminal Law, Criminology and Police Science,* 38 (May–June, 1947), pp. 1–6.

[30] William H. Sheldon, *Varieties of Delinquent Youth: An Introduction to Constitutional Psychiatry* (New York: Harper & Row, 1949). Also see Sheldon and Eleanor T. Glueck, *Physique and Delinquency* (New York: Harper & Row, 1956).

self-defined in relation to social reactions, and subsequently shape the patterning of personal actions. The whole interacting process of physical characteristics, social reactions, and personal action is dramatically illustrated in the case of Richard Speck, the slayer of eight Chicago nurses in the summer of 1966. When finally arrested, Speck, who had been described as physically and personally unattractive, was identified through the tattoo on his arm — which read, "Born to raise hell."

The extent to which personal action patterns develop in response to the social reactions of others depends on the degree to which the person accepts and adjusts to his assigned role. The concept of "secondary deviation" is useful in conceptualizing the transition that may occur in a person's self-conception and behavior as he is confronted with social reactions. According to the concept, the deviance imputed to a person remains "primary deviation" to that person as long as it is rationalized or otherwise dealt with as a socially acceptable role. As a person continues his actions, and as social reactions are repeated and strengthened, deviation becomes secondary.

> Secondary deviation refers to a special class of socially defined responses which people make to problems created by the societal reaction to their deviance. These problems are essentially moral problems which revolve around stigmatization, punishments, segregation, and social control. Their general effect is to differentiate the symbolic and interactional environment to which the person responds, so that early or adult socialization is categorically affected. They become central facts of existence for those experiencing them, altering psychic structure, producing specialized organization of social roles and self-regarding attitudes. Actions which have these roles and self attitudes as their referents make up secondary deviance.[31]

The person develops such a stance toward himself and others because his identity and actions are organized around the facts of the deviance that others have imputed to him.

The definition of a person as "criminal" is the extreme form of stigmatization. Criminal conviction — even confrontation with the police and judicial prosecution — produces modifications in a man's identity and actions. The "criminalization of deviance" may thus

[31] Edwin M. Lemert, *Human Deviance, Social Problems, and Social Control* (Englewood Cliffs, N.J.: Prentice-Hall, 1967), pp. 40–41.

force those engaged in particular kinds of behavior to redefine themselves and their actions.[32] Furthermore, such public branding tends to lead a person to new situations and activities. The development of a new style of life, in turn, increases the probability of further criminal definition. It is through social reaction, then, in the form of criminal definition, that crime is again created and perpetuated.

BEHAVIOR SYSTEMS OF THE CRIMINALLY DEFINED

Within the legal structure of society and the relation of the segments of society to that structure, personal action patterns develop with different probabilities of criminality. For *analytical* purposes, these criminality-related action patterns may be divided into *types of behavior systems*. The task thus becomes one of describing and analyzing specific forms of action patterns that develop in the course of criminal definition.

The division of criminally defined behavior into types of behavior systems is based on various aspects of the person and his behavior. The characteristics of behavior systems most important for our study are the *career* of the person in regard to criminally defined activity and the *group support* he receives from his actions. The career of the offender consists of the extent to which criminally defined behavior is a part of his life organization. Also included are his conception of self, his identification with crime, and his progression in activities that may be defined as criminal. Group support consists of the extent to which the person's criminally defined behavior is supported by the norms of the group or groups to which he belongs. Included are the differential association of the person with behavior patterns that have varying probabilities of being defined as criminal, his social roles, and his integration into various social groups.

On the basis of such characteristics, a typology of behavior systems in relation to criminal definitions has been constructed.[33] It is composed of eight types of "criminal" behavior systems: (1) vio-

[32] See Edwin M. Schur, *Crimes Without Victims* (Englewood Cliffs, N.J.: Prentice-Hall, 1965), pp. 5–7.

[33] The following typology of behavior systems was constructed in Clinard and Quinney, *Criminal Behavior Systems: A Typology*.

lent personal, (2) occasional property, (3) occupational, (4) political, (5) public order, (6) conventional, (7) organized, and (8) professional. Each behavior system contains behavior patterns that have a fairly high probability of being defined as criminal, because of the legal structure. The action patterns of persons that may be criminally defined can be analyzed according to these eight types of behavior systems.

Violent Personal Offense Behavior. Most who engage in acts that that may be defined as murder, assault, or forcible rape do not immediately identify themselves as criminals or regard crime as a part of their lives. Their actions tend, rather, to be the consequence of a social encounter in which two or more parties conceive of violence as an appropriate solution to an interpersonal problem. But since criminal sanctions for such actions are relatively certain and severe, persons convicted of a violent personal offense are likely, in time, to conceive of themselves as criminal.

Persons who act in a personally violent way in a specific situation are not likely to be involved with the law in other parts of their lives.[34] Of those offenders who do have an arrest record, a large proportion have been arrested for actions against another person. One study, in fact, concluded that "the analysis of crimes of violence according to their factual substance shows that most of the crime is not committed by criminals for criminal purposes but is rather the outcome of patterns of social behavior among certain strata of society."[35] Therefore, we conclude from extensive evidence, that actions that result in personal violence are responses to interpersonal situations rather than the result of a career in criminally defined activity.

[34] See David J. Pittman and William Handy, "Patterns in Criminal Aggravated Assault," *Journal of Criminal Law, Criminology and Police Science,* 55 (December, 1964), pp. 462–470; Richard A. Peterson, David J. Pittman, and Patricia O'Neal, "Stabilities in Deviance: A Study of Assaultive and Non-Assaultive Offenders," *Journal of Criminal Law, Criminology and Police Science,* 53 (March, 1962), pp. 44–49; Marvin E. Wolfgang, *Patterns in Criminal Homicide* (Philadelphia: University of Pennsylvania Press, 1958); John L. Gillin, *The Wisconsin Prisoner* (Madison: University of Wisconsin Press, 1946); Menachem Amir, "Patterns of Forcible Rape," in Clinard and Quinney, *Criminal Behavior Systems,* pp. 60–75.

[35] F. H. McClintock, *Crimes of Violence* (New York: St. Martins Press, 1963), p. 57.

> Most murders and aggravated assaults represent a response, growing out of social interaction between one or more parties, in which a situation comes to be defined as requiring the use of violence. Generally in order for such an act to take place, all parties must come to perceive the situation as one requiring violence. If only one responds in a dispute, it is not likely to become violent; likewise, if only one of the disputants is accustomed to the use of violence, and the other is not, the dispute is likely to end only in a verbal argument. On the other hand, when a cultural norm is defined as calling for violence by a person in social interplay with another who harbors the same response, serious altercations, fist fights, physical assaults with weapons, and violent domestic quarrels, all of which may end in murder, may result. In the process of an argument, A and B both define the initial situation as a serious threat, B then threatens A physically, A threatens B, and B then threatens A. By circular reaction, the situation can then rapidly build up to a climax in which one takes serious overt action, partly because of fear. Consequently, the victim, by being a contributor to the circular reaction of an argument increasing in its physical intensity, may precipitate his own injury or death.[36]

Because of the presence of interaction between persons in a situation of violence, the *victim* is a crucial agent in the action that is taken. Victims, in other words, tend to precipitate their own victimization. A study of homicide found that one in four criminal homicides were instigated in this way, in that the victim first showed or used a deadly weapon or struck a physical blow.[37] Not included in this figure were homicides that involved the victim's use of vile names, his infidelity, or his failure to live up to expectations, such as failure to pay a debt. Similarly, the victim's role was found to be important in aggravated assault.[38] The researchers reported that nearly three-quarters of the cases of assault studied had been preceded by verbal arguments, including family arguments and disputes that arose in a public place. The victim of rape, as well, has much to do with the fact that she is raped. A large proportion of

[36] Clinard and Quinney, *Criminal Behavior Systems,* p. 27.

[37] Wolfgang, *Patterns in Criminal Homicide,* p. 252.

[38] Pittman and Handy, "Patterns in Aggravated Assault," p. 467.

rape victims either behave submissively or agree to sexual relations before defining the consequences as rape.[39]

The existence of previous interpersonal relationships between murderers and their victims has been documented in a number of studies. In a study of New Jersey murders, classified according to victim-offender relationships and the situations in which the murders took place, it was found that about two-thirds of the murders grew out of some altercation with acquaintances, sex rivals, relatives, or mistresses.[40] Likewise, a Philadelphia study found that approximately two-thirds of the criminal homicides took place between persons who had a previous interpersonal relationship.[41] In 28 per cent of the cases the victim was a close friend of the murderer, in 25 per cent a family relative, and in 14 per cent an acquaintance. A study of Wisconsin murders showed a similar proportion of victims who had a previous relationship with the offender.[42] In addition, studies in other countries have also revealed the importance of interpersonal relationships in criminal homicide: Nearly 80 per cent of the homicides in a London study were committed against relatives or a well known acquaintance; an Indian study indicated that most murders occur within the same caste and frequently involve a husband and wife; and a Danish study revealed that the murderer's victim was a relative or an acquaintance in nine out of ten cases and that strangers were seldom the victims.[43] Needless to say, most of the violent behaviors that end in a criminal definition occur within a specific, and personally meaningful, social context.

In a broader sense, beyond the immediate interpersonal context of personal offenses, persons vary in the extent to which they engage in violent behavior and in their perceptions of violence as an alternative to interpersonal problems. Evidence indicates that the

39 Amir, "Patterns in Forcible Rape," pp. 67–69.

40 E. Frankel, "One Thousand Murderers," *Journal of Criminal Law, Criminology and Police Science,* 29 (January, 1939), pp. 687–688.

41 Wolfgang, *Patterns in Criminal Homicide,* p. 207.

42 Gillin, *The Wisconsin Prisoner,* p. 60.

43 McClintock, *Crimes of Violence,* p. 238; Edwin D. Drivers, "Interaction and Criminal Homicide in India," *Social Forces,* 40 (December, 1961), pp. 153–158; Kaare Svalastoga, "Homicide and Social Contact in Denmark," *American Journal of Sociology,* 62 (July, 1956), pp. 37–41.

use of violence varies socially and culturally in respect to a person's geographical residence, social class, occupation, race, sex, and age.[44] Hence, violence against another person appears to be differently institutionalized in the various segments of society. In the final analysis, the extent to which a person engages in violent personal actions that may be defined as criminal depends upon his location in society, and consequently, upon his exposure to particular social norms.

Occasional Property Offense Behavior. For those who only occasionally engage in an offense against property and who are seldom defined as criminal, there is little identification with crime and little attempt to integrate such activity into a way of life. Their law-violating actions are not sophisticated in technique or skill of commission. Most of these persons have little knowledge about the world of crime or the vocabulary of crime. Thus, because of the sporadic nature of their actions and the infrequency of contact with criminal definitions, such persons do not conceive of themselves as criminals and do not usually associate with those who engage more regularly in activity that may be criminally defined.

Occasional shoplifters, as contrasted with professionals, do not conceive of themselves as criminals or regard their activities as crimes.[45] Generally they are respectable employed persons or housewives, "pilfering" only occasionally for their own use. They rationalize their actions on the basis that the things they take are of modest price and belong to large department stores than can absorb the loss. Few of these persons have criminal records.

Likewise, the major portion of check forgeries are committed by persons who have no record of such activity.[46] In a study of "naive" check forgery, it was found that such persons do not usually come from an area of high delinquency or crime and that they do not associate with criminally defined persons. The naive check forger,

[44] See Ronald H. Beattie and John P. Kenney, "Aggressive Crimes," *Annals of the American Academy of Political and Social Science,* 365 (March, 1966), pp. 73–85. Also see Franco Ferracuti and Marvin E. Wolfgang, *The Subculture of Violence: Towards an Integrated Theory in Criminology* (London: Tavistock Publication, 1967).

[45] Mary Owen Cameron, *The Booster and the Snitch: Department Store Shoplifting* (New York: The Free Press of Glencoe, 1964).

[46] Edwin M. Lemert, "An Isolation and Closure Theory of Naive Check Forgery," *Journal of Criminal Law, Criminology and Police Science,* 44 (October, 1953), pp. 296–307.

rather, tends to be socially isolated. But, in a difficult situation, forgery is personally perceived as an available alternative.

A similar lack of commitment to crime as a part of one's life is reported in a study of young rural offenders who occasionally engage in property offenses.[47] It was found that (1) their law-violating behavior did not start early in life, (2) they exhibited little knowledge of criminal techniques, (3) such activity was not pursued as a means of livelihood, and (4) they did not conceive of themselves as criminals. Rather than identifying with crime, the offenders considered themselves as "reckless" and unattached to traditional ways. They were mobile, referred to their behavior as "fast," and engaged in law-violating activity as an adventure.

The occasional property offender has little long-term social or cultural support for his behavior. Although several persons may be collectively involved in acts of vandalism, the behavior that takes place is more the result of an immediate interactional situation than a product of any kind of subculture.[48] Vandalism tends to be a spontaneous outgrowth of concrete situations of group interaction. Each interactive response by a participant builds the intensity of actions of other participants until a focus develops and a group act of vandalism occurs. For the moment at least, each participant has a feeling of excitement and a sense of involvement in a group. One has to have something.

Occupational Offense Behavior. Persons who violate criminal laws in the course of their occupational activity do not conceive of themselves as criminals but as "respectable" citizens. The fact that the offender is a member of a legitimate occupation also makes it difficult for others to conceive of occupational offenders as being real criminals. Consequently, because of the lack of public disapproval of occupational offenders, persons who violate laws that regulate occupational activity are not likely to incorporate a criminally defined role into their life organizations.

The maintenance of a noncriminal self-concept is one of the principal elements in the occupational offender's development of action

[47] Marshall B. Clinard, "Rural Criminal Offenders," *American Journal of Sociology,* 50 (July, 1944), pp. 38–45.

[48] Andrew L. Wade, "Social Processes in the Act of Juvenile Vandalism," in Clinard and Quinney, *Criminal Behavior Systems,* pp. 94–109.

patterns. This process has been observed in a study of embezzlers, which concluded that persons engage in such behavior only when they are able to apply to their own conduct verbalizations which allow them to adjust their concepts of themselves as trusted persons with their concepts of themselves as users of entrusted funds or property.[49] The trust violators thus defined the situation by rationalizations which enabled them to regard their violations as essentially noncriminal. They rationalized that their behavior was merely "borrowing," that it was justified by the presence of a nonsharable problem which could be resolved by violating their position of trust.

The respectable backgrounds of occupational offenders have been shown in several studies. A study of prosecuted cases of price and rationing violations during World War II found that less than one violator in ten had a criminal record.[50] In studies of other occupational offenders, it has been shown that the overwhelming majority of the offenders reside in the most desirable areas of the city.[51] Similarly, the respectability of the defendants involved in the 1961 criminal antitrust case in the heavy electrical equipment industry was described by a reporter as "middle-class men in Ivy League suits — typical businessmen in appearance, men who would never be taken for lawbreakers."[52] One of the defendants, a General Electric vice-president who was eventually sentenced to prison, was earning $135,000 a year. His background has been summarized as follows:

> He had been born in Atlanta and was 46 years old at the time he was sentenced to jail. He had graduated with a degree in electrical engineering from Georgia Tech, and received an honorary doctorate degree from Sienna College in 1958, was

49 Donald R. Cressey, *Other People's Money* (New York: The Free Press of Glencoe, 1953).

50 Marshall B. Clinard, *The Black Market: A Study of White Collar Crime* (New York: Holt, Rinehart and Winston, 1952), p. 295.

51 Frank E. Hartung, "A Study in Law and Social Differentiation, as Exemplified in Violations of the Emergency Price Control Act in the Detroit Wholesale Meat Industry," unpublished Ph.D. dissertation, University of Michigan, 1949, p. 221; and Richard Quinney, "Retail Pharmacy as a Marginal Occupation: A Study of Prescription Violation," unpublished Ph.D. dissertation, University of Wisconsin, 1962, p. 261.

52 Quoted in Gilbert Geis, "White Collar Crime: the Heavy Electrical Equipment Antitrust Cases of 1961," in Clinard and Quinney, *Criminal Behavior Systems*, p. 140.

> married, and the father of three children. He had served in the Navy during the Second World War, rising to the rank of lieutenant commander, was a director of the Schenectady Boys Club, on the board of trustees of Miss Hall's School, and not without some irony, was a member of Governor Rockefeller's Temporary State Committee on Economic Expansion.[53]

The importance of group association and group support in the violation of occupational laws was indicated in a study of the criminal decisions rendered against seventy large corporations.[54] Occupational violations appeared to be normative in some businesses, and some persons, if isolated from other norms, learned motives, techniques, and rationalizations favorable to violation of law. Several factors isolate businessmen from unfavorable definitions of illegal activity, including the lenient coverage of such violations in the mass media and the lack of severe criticism by government officials. Furthermore, businessmen associate chiefly with other businessmen, both at work and in their social activities. Similar conclusions of the association with certain behavior patterns and the isolation from others have been reached in a study of the violation of labor relations laws and trade practices laws in a number of manufacturing firms.[55]

A person's commitment to the norms favorable to violation within an occupation or business depends upon the roles he plays in his work. The significance of the role structure of an occupation and the orientation of the members to the roles has been shown in a study of prescription violation among retail pharmacists.[56] Because the occupation of a pharmacist is structured according to two divergent occupational roles — professional and business — pharmacists experience the problem of adapting to one of several "occupational role organizations." The types of role organizations, in turn, differ in the extent to which they produce tendencies toward violating pre-

[53] Geis, "White Collar Crime," p. 147.

[54] Edwin H. Sutherland, *White Collar Crime* (New York: Holt, Rinehart and Winston, 1949).

[55] Robert A. Lane, "Why Businessmen Violate the Law," *Journal of Criminal Law, Criminology and Police Science,* 44 (August, 1953), pp. 151–165. Also see Clinard, *The Black Market,* pp. 298–313.

[56] Richard Quinney, "Occupational Structure and Criminal Behavior: Prescription Violation by Retail Pharmacists," *Social Problems,* 11 (Fall, 1963), pp. 179–185.

scriptions. Pharmacists who are oriented to a professional role are bound by a system of occupational control which includes guides for compounding and dispensing prescriptions. The business oriented pharmacists, on the other hand, are interested in the general business goal of monetary gain, subscribing to the popular belief in business that self-employment carries with it independence and freedom from control. The professional norms, as incorporated in the prescription laws, exercise little control over the occupational behavior of the pharmacists who are oriented to the business role. Thus, it was found that violations occur most frequently among business pharmacists and least often among professional pharmacists, with pharmacists who are oriented to both roles and pharmacists who are not oriented to either role being intermediate in frequency of violations. It was therefore concluded that prescription violation is related to the structure of the occupation and the "differential orientation" of retail pharmacists to the roles within the occupation.

Political Offense Behavior. An increasing amount of criminally defined behavior consists of action patterns that are pursued in the attempt to protest, express beliefs about, or alter in some way the social structure. Such political activities are variously named by the authorities of the state: treason, sedition, espionage, sabotage, war collaboration, military draft evasion, and civil disobedience. The actions — whether they violate laws created for the suppression of such behavior or laws created for other purposes (such as loitering and parading without a permit) — are regarded by political authorities as detrimental to the state and its institutions. Certain behaviors, therefore, become defined as criminal because the political actions of some persons are regarded by the authorities as politically threatening to the structure of the state.

The political behaviors that may result in criminality are many and varied. Nevertheless, characteristics are shared by those who are defined as political offenders. Most do not engage in criminally defined activity as a full-time career. Persons who commit political crimes do not usually conceive of themselves as criminals and do not identify with crime. They violate the law only when such action seems to be the most appropriate means for achieving certain ends. The ends, to the actor, are not strictly personal but are deemed desirable for the larger society. The behavior is regarded by the offender as symbolic of a higher purpose. Such persons carry on their criminally defined activities in pursuit of an ideal.

Thus, political offenders are usually committed to a larger social order.

> The social order they have in mind, however, may differ from the existing order. It is because of their commitment to something beyond themselves and conventional society that they are willing to engage in criminal behavior. Persons who occasionally engage in political crime are interested in their society, but at times find it lacking in important ways. They may then sever their commitment to the society in place of a social order which could exist. The social order to which they are committed may be a modification of the one that exists or may possibly be an entirely new order. Nevertheless, the existing society always serves as a reference point for political offenders.[57]

During political socialization and experience, persons develop a conception about the relative legitimacy of political institutions. In general, a political system is viewed as legitimate when the authority and objectives of those in control are respected and when the available procedures in the political process are believed to be adequate. Furthermore, persons regard a political system as legitimate or illegitimate according to the way in which the values of the system correspond to their own. Groups that do not share these values are more likely to question the legitimacy of the system at times. Such groups are likely to engage in political behaviors ("extremist politics") which may be defined as criminal. Their political actions may be of a variety either to the "right" or to the "left" of what is regarded as politically traditional in a society.[58]

[57] Clinard and Quinney, *Criminal Behavior Systems,* p. 180.

[58] For some of the research and writing on political offense behavior, see Ralph S. Brown, *Loyalty and Security* (New Haven: Yale University Press, 1958); Karl O. Christiansen, "Collaborators with the Germans in Denmark During World War II," in Clinard and Quinney, *Criminal Behavior Systems,* pp. 231–246; Arnold Foster, "Violence on the Fanatical Left and Right," *Annals of the American Academy of Political and Social Science,* 364 (March, 1966), pp. 141–148; Joseph C. Mouledoux, "Political Crime and the Negro Revolution," in Clinard and Quinney, *Criminal Behavior Systems*, pp. 217–231; Robert K. Murray, *Red Scare: A Study in National Hysteria, 1919–1920* (Minneapolis: University of Minnesota Press, 1965); Herbert L. Packer, "Offenses Against the State," *Annals of the American Academy of Political and Social Science,* 339

The pursuit of illegal activities during political action is not regarded as an important consideration by most political offenders. For such persons the violation of a particular criminal law actually represents an appeal to a higher norm, possibly even an appeal to the federal law. The person who is viewed by the authorities and the public as disloyal to his country is nevertheless being true to higher loyalties.[59] Such persons are conscientiously following norms and values which differ from those of the political majority.

The intensity of group support received by political offenders varies, of course, from one kind of political activity to another. But the fact that such activity has group support is evident in almost all forms of criminally defined political activity. Nearly all those prosecuted for conscientious objection during World War II were members of groups and organizations committed to peace and opposition to war.[60] Such religious groups as the Society of Friends, Jehovah's Witnesses, Mennonites, and Church of the Brethren provided support for those who opposed military service on religious grounds. The philosophical objectors, those not basing their objections on religious grounds, also found group support for their actions. They were united by such organizations as the Pacifist Research Bureau, the War Resisters League, and the National Council Against Conscription. Some of these groups, and many new groups, continue to provide support and assistance for opposition and resistance to the draft and to military service.

The social nature of political offenses varies according to not only the extent and means of group support but also such social characteristics as the size of the supporting group or organization, the cohesiveness of the group, formality of organization, duration of the group, geographical dispersion of the members, and patterns of leadership.[61] Also, the groups to which political offenders belong

---

(January, 1962), pp. 77–89. William Preston, Jr., *Alien Dissenters: Federal Suppression of Radicals, 1903–1933* (Cambridge, Mass.: Harvard University Press, 1963).

[59] See Robin M. Williams, *American Society* (New York: Alfred A. Knopf, 1960), pp. 379–380; Mabel A. Elliott, *Crime in Modern Society* (New York: Harper & Row, 1951), pp. 179–197; Morton Grodzins, *The Loyal and Disloyal: Social Boundaries of Patriotism and Treason* (Chicago: University of Chicago Press, 1956).

[60] Mulford Q. Sibley and Ada Wardlow, *Conscientious Objectors in Prison, 1940–1945* (Ithaca, N.Y.: Pacifist Research Bureau, 1945), chap. 1.

[61] See Lemert, *Social Pathology,* pp. 175–235.

differ greatly in their aims and their ideologies. Finally, the forms of political criminality differ in the techniques and tactics used by the members: oratory, face-to-face persuasion, writing and propaganda, nonviolent action, passive resistance, demonstrations, sit-ins, marches, strikes, suicide, and guerrilla warfare. All these actions may become defined as criminal during the attempt to achieve political goals.

Public Order Offense Behavior. The largest proportion of crime consists of violations against public order. Included among these behaviors, which may be criminally defined in various ways, are prostitution, homosexual relations, and drug addiction. In most of the behaviors no real injury is suffered by another person. Rather, the behaviors violate the sense of order in the community. And as the community reacts to the behavior of public order offenders, these persons tend to become segregated from community life and may begin to play the criminal role.

Prostitutes are introduced to their activity by those who are closely associated with prostitution. But once a person becomes committed to prostitution as part of a life organization, a further period of apprenticeship is necessary in order to ensure some success in prostitution. For the call girl, in particular, a culture must be learned which includes a philosophy as well as techniques of operation.

> The structure of the apprenticeship period seems quite standard. The novice receives her training either from a pimp or from another more experienced call girl, more often the latter. She serves her initial two to eight months of work under the trainer's supervision and often serves this period in the trainer's apartment. The trainer assumes responsibility for arranging contacts and negotiating the type and place of the sexual encounter.
>
> The content of the training pertains both to a general philosophical stance and to some specifics (usually not sexual) of interpersonal behavior with customers and colleagues. The philosophy is one of exploiting the exploiters (customers) by whatever means necessary and defining the colleagues of the call girl as being intelligent, self-interested and, in certain important respects, basically honest individuals. The interpersonal techniques addressed during the learning period consist primarily of "pitches," telephone conversations, per-

> sonal and occasionally sexual hygiene, prohibition against alcohol and dope while with a "john," how and when to obtain the fee, and specifics concerning the sexual habits of particular customers. Specific sexual techniques are very rarely taught. The current sample included a considerable number of girls who, although capable of articulating this value structure, were not particularly inclined to adopt it.[62]

Because prostitutes encounter a duality of social values regarding their behavior — values that stigmatize such activity and values that support it — self-conceptions tend to be both ambivalent and subject to change.[63] Yet, since prostitutes can rationalize their behavior by reference to the value of commercial success, an appropriate self-image can be maintained. In addition, a prostitute is able to sustain her role by interaction with other prostitutes and with those who associate with prostitutes. A specialized language, an argot, also provides a sense of group solidarity for prostitutes.[64] Furthermore, contact with the law through repeated arrests strengthens the self-conceptions of prostitutes and reinforces the rationalizations that they have for their actions.

Homosexuality, whether or not it is defined as criminal in some way, involves learning a social role. The role is learned in association with others and includes the defining of oneself as a homosexual. The self-conception as a homosexual is also derived from the negative reactions of others in the community. The homosexual may, in turn, seek more and more associations within the world of homosexuality. Thus, social pressures tend to push persons along a progression of stages of homosexual behavior, although some individuals do not necessarily progress to the final stages and others may still maintain contact with the rest of the community.

> 1. The first stage usually occurs in the late teens or early twenties. As his friends start to go out with girls and eventually marry, the homosexual finds other interests and drifts away from their company. Sometimes he is scarcely aware of his

[62] James H. Bryan, "Apprenticeships in Prostitution," *Social Problems,* 12 (Winter, 1965), p. 294.

[63] Norman R. Jackman, Richard O'Toole, and Gilbert Geis, "The Self-Image of the Prostitute," *Sociological Quarterly,* 4 (Spring, 1963), pp. 150–161.

[64] David W. Maurer, "Prostitutes and Criminal Argots," *American Journal of Sociology,* 44 (January, 1939), pp. 546–550.

homosexual tendencies or has not come to terms with them, but gradually he becomes conscious of his isolation. Many young homosexuals have described their dismay when they have discovered that the sort of things which interest their friends hold no appeal for them.

2. Thus the young homosexual finds he is driven away from the company of ordinary men and women at just the time when he most needs their help. As he loses his friends he begins to regard himself as an outcast. He finds to his dismay that will-power and self-control are not the answer to his problem. The more extrovert homosexual will soon pass through this second stage and quickly make friends with other homosexuals. But others lead lonely lives, plagued by feelings of guilt and accepting the role of the social isolate.

3. At the third stage the young man meets other homosexuals and begins to go to their meeting places and joins a homosexual group. Some of them soon tire of this opportunity to mix in a group of like-minded individuals, but others accept the chance eagerly. Here a homosexual can feel at ease because he does not have to hide his true inclinations. Indeed, this is such a relief that much of the talk in these groups is about sex. It is here that the two worlds conflict. He must make sure that his friends from the other world do not meet his friends from the homosexual group. He has to explain his absences from the other world, think up convincing stories, and learn to lead two lives. Some homosexuals resolve this dilemma by moving on to the fourth stage.

4. At this last stage the homosexual way of life monopolizes his interests and absorbs all his time. He gives up his efforts to resolve the conflicts between the outside world and the homosexual way of life. He moves exclusively in a homosexual group and adopts a hostile attitude towards all those not in the group. He has, in fact, adopted all the characteristics of an introverted minority group.[65]

A large proportion of homosexuals have developed stable homosexual relationships and a style of life centering around the homosexual role. These are the confirmed homosexuals, most of whom never come to the attention of the police. These persons, as shown in one study, tend to start their homosexual relations with other

[65] Michael Schofield, *Sociological Aspects of Homosexuality: A Comparative Study of Three Types of Homosexuals* (Boston: Little, Brown, 1965), p. 181.

boys before the age of seventeen, eventually developing long-standing relations with men.[66] They establish special meeting places for their associations as they become segregated from the rest of the community. Consequently, a homosexual "subcommunity" is created. The homosexual community has its "own status symbols and mythology, and may provide the same kind of social and psychological support that a family group provides for other people."[67]

Persons who use drugs do not necessarily conceive of themselves as criminals. But in recent times, with the emphasis the Federal Bureau of Narcotics has placed on the sale and possession of drugs and with the subsequent legislation and administrative rulings, drug users have found that their action is criminally defined. The legal and public stigmatizing of the drug user has thus tended to force the user to define his own drug using actions as criminal, although the rest of his action patterns may not be so defined.

Most persons are initiated into the use of drugs by association with friends or acquaintances. They start experimenting with drugs out of curiosity as to their effects and, ultimately, to conform to the expectations of their group.[68] Some adolescents in slum areas take drugs for the "kick," as something to heighten and intensify the present moment of experience, and to differentiate their lives from the routine daily life of the "square."[69] For many of these, however, continual drug use requires a change in reference group orientation and association. As one researcher has stated, the person who progresses in drug use not only learns to appreciate the effects of drug use to the fullest, but shifts his group and ideological commitments:

> Moving along the career line toward confirmed use depends upon the user's having a positive physical response to heroin and learning how to enjoy the effects of "the high." Once the

[66] *Ibid.*, pp. 100–143.

[67] *Ibid.*, p. 183. Also see Maurice Leznoff and William A. Westley, "The Homosexual Community," *Social Problems*, 3 (April, 1956), pp. 257–263; Gordon Westwood, *A Minority: A Report on the Life of the Male Homosexual in Great Britain* (London: Longmans, Green, 1960), pp. 83–86.

[68] Julius Klein and Derek L. Phillips, "From Hard to Soft Drugs: Temporal and Substantive Changes in Drug Usage Among Gangs in a Working-Class Community," *Journal of Health and Social Behavior*, 9 (June, 1968), pp. 139–145.

[69] Harold Finestone, "Cats, Kicks, and Color," *Social Problems*, 5 (July, 1957), pp. 3–4.

> user finds pleasure in drug use and prefers his dreamy state to the action world of non-using friends, he disengages himself from the usual routines of the stand-up cat ideology and learns to believe in a new ideology that is consistent with the pleasurable effects of heroin. The speed with which the new drug user disengages himself from his former reference group depends upon the way the members adhere to the ideology of the stand-up cat.[70]

Beyond the fact of drug use itself, the social context and the personal meaning of drug use vary considerably. The observations above apply primarily to drug use among lower class adolescents. However, with the rise of the "hippie" phenomenon other patterns have emerged. In a study of drug use among hippies in the Haight-Ashbury section of San Francisco, it was found that two patterns of drug use exist in the same area, a "head" pattern consisting of those who use LSD ("acid" users) and a "freak" pattern, those who inject Methedrine ("speed shooters").[71] Each recruits a different kind of person and is accompanied by a different style of life.

Yet another pattern of drug use is found among college students. A study of drug use (primarily marijuana) among college students found that the students who used drugs adhered to what might be characterized as a "hang-loose" ethic.[72] That is, drug use tends to occur among those students whose behavior, attitudes, and self-images represent an opposition to the traditional, established order. A sequence of events associated with drug use among college students has been suggested:

> Adherence to the "hang-loose" ethic is more likely to occur among certain predisposed personality types (i.e., rebellious, cynical) and in certain social sub-groups (i.e., males, non-religious); such adherence is likely to lead to a favorable attitude toward smoking marijuana both for its "high" effects and its symbolism of rebellion against authority; this favorable attitude will be supported by other students who also

[70] Harvey W. Feldman, "Ideological Supports to Becoming and Remaining a Heroin Addict," *Journal of Health and Social Behavior,* 9 (June, 1968), p. 138.

[71] Fred Davis with Laura Munoz, "Heads and Freaks: Patterns and Meanings of Drug Use Among Hippies," *Journal of Health and Social Behavior,* 9 (June, 1968), pp. 156–164.

[72] Edward A. Suchman, "The Hang-loose Ethic and the Spirit of Drug Use," *Journal of Health and Social Behavior,* 9 (June, 1968), pp. 146–155.

> embrace the "hang-loose" ethic and engage in similar overt and covert expressions of rejection of the established order. Finally, given this climate of opinion and behavior, the smoking of marijuana becomes almost a "natural" act for many students far removed from the public's current efforts to define it either as a legal or a health problem.[73]

With increasing dependence on drugs and association with other drug users, persons involved in some patterns of drug use tend to progress into the role of drug addict. Their addiction finds support in an elaborate set of group norms that center around what one writer has called a "survival system."[74] The system furnishes the addict with the justification and the ideology for dependence on drugs. Addicted persons then recruit new members in order to sell them drugs to support their own habit. There is also defensive communication, with its own argot for drugs, supplies, and drug users, which must be learned by the initiates. Through a "neighborhood warning system" addicts provide mutual protection against arrest by the police. Because of the illegality of drug sales, addicts depend upon a complex distribution network for securing their drugs. In order to secure drugs, addicts often have to violate laws in other ways.[75] Finally, then, imposing criminal definitions on drug users and drug addicts not only defines their possession of drugs as criminal but promotes other actions that may be criminally defined. As unintended as these consequences may be, the criminal law has its own capacity for producing personal action patterns.

Conventional Offense Behavior. Some persons who are defined as delinquent during adolescence continue into adulthood with action

[73] *Ibid.,* pp. 153–154. For research on other patterns of drug use, see John C. Ball, "Two Patterns of Narcotic Drug Addiction in the United States," *Journal of Criminal Law, Criminology and Police Science,* 56 (June, 1965), pp. 203–211; Alfred R. Lindesmith, *Opiate Addiction* (Bloomington: Indiana University Press, 1947); Charles Winick, "The Use of Drugs by Jazz Musicians," *Social Problems,* 7 (Winter, 1959–1960), pp. 240–254.

[74] Seymour Fiddle, "The Addict Culture and Movement into and out of Hospitals," in Senate Committee on the Judiciary, Subcommittee to Investigate Juvenile Delinquency, *Hearings,* Part 13 (Washington, D.C.: U.S. Government Printing Office, 1963), p. 3156.

[75] See Harold Finestone, "Narcotics and Criminality," *Law and Contemporary Problems,* 22 (Winter, 1957), pp. 69–85; John O'Donnell, "Narcotic Addiction and Crime," *Social Problems,* 13 (Spring, 1966), pp. 374–385; Schur, *Crime Without Victims,* pp. 120–168.

patterns that become criminally defined. Such a career usually involves early experience with a juvenile gang. The members learn social roles and achieve status by participating in gang activities. They continuously learn techniques and rationalizations for their behavior. Gradually such persons move from petty to more serious offenses — from truancy, destruction of property, and street fighting to auto theft, robbery, and burglary. By the time they are young adults they are likely to have an extensive record of contact with the law, including experiences with the police, juvenile authorities, courts, reformatories, and possibly prisons. These experiences add to the person's sophistication in criminally defined activities and to his conception of himself as a criminal.

The progression from early juvenile gang activity to adult conventional offense behavior has been observed in several studies. In a study of Negro armed robbers it was found that the offenders had a history of arrests:

> An early patterning of stealing from their parents, from school, and on the street; truancy, and suspension or expulsion from school; street fighting, association with older delinquents, and juvenile delinquent gang memberships, all were usually evident in their social backgrounds. When compared with the men in the other criminal categories, it was found that there was more destruction of property in their delinquent activities, and there were more frequent fights with schoolmates, male teachers, and delinquent companions. There was a higher incidence of "mugging" and purse snatching. They had more often been the leaders of delinquent gangs, and they claimed they were leaders because of their superior size and physical strength.[76]

A similar career in juvenile gang activity has been called the "semiprofessional property criminal." These offenders represent the usual outcome of patterns of gang delinquency, because "many juvenile gang offenders continue in criminality as semi-professionals."[77]

[76] Julian B. Roebuck and Mervyn L. Cadwallader, "The Negro Armed Robber as a Criminal Type: The Construction and Application of a Typology," *Pacific Sociological Review,* 4 (Spring, 1961), p. 24.

[77] Don C. Gibbons, *Changing the Lawbreaker* (Englewood Cliffs, N.J.: Prentice-Hall, 1965), p. 105. For further documentation of the progression from juvenile offenses to adult conventional offenses, see Harold S. Frum, "Adult Criminal Offense Trends Following Juvenile Delinquency," *Journal of Criminal*

Most of the behaviors included in conventional offenses, whether juvenile or adult, are related to property in one way or another. As a person progresses in conventional offenses, he engages in these actions to supplement or completely make a living. When offense behavior has thus become a part of one's life organization a whole complex of factors is involved, including personal commitment to crime, self-conception, social reactions, and further continuance in a life of crime.

> As juvenile offenders progress into conventional career crime, they become more committed to crime as a way of life and develop a criminal self-conception. Because of repeated offenses, and because of subsequent arrests and convictions, conventional offenders eventually identify with crime. For occasional property offenders who pursue criminal activity only sporadically, there is vacillation in self-conception. But for conventional criminals who regularly commit offenses and who are continually isolated from law-abiding segments of society, a criminal self-conception is virtually inescapable. In addition, because property offenders are dealt with rather severely before the law, through arrest and sentencing, such offenders readily come to regard themselves as criminals. The criminal record is a constant reminder that the person has been stigmatized by the society. The record may provide a vicious circle whereby the offender, once stigmatized, often cannot enter into law-abiding society and must continue in a life of crime.[78]

One of the occupational hazards of the conventional offender is the *risk* of being detected, arrested, and convicted. But because conventional offenders develop some skill and organization in their activities, they are able to minimize the chances of being criminally defined.[79] As indicated by criminal statistics, only about a quarter of property offenses (and only those *known* to the police) are cleared

---

Law, Criminology and Police Science, 49 (May–June, 1958), pp. 29–49; Clifford R. Shaw, Henry D. McKay, and James F. McDonald, *Brothers in Crime* (Chicago: University of Chicago Press, 1938).

[78] Clinard and Quinney, *Criminal Behavior Systems,* p. 321.

[79] Observations on risk-taking among offenders are found in Edwin M. Lemert, "Social Structure, Social Control, and Deviation," in Marshall B. Clinard (ed.), *Anomie and Deviant Behavior* (New York: The Free Press of Glencoe, 1964), pp. 73–75; Daniel S. Claster, "Comparison of Risk Perception Between Delinquents and Non-Delinquents," *Journal of Criminal Law, Criminology and Police Science,* 58 (March, 1967), pp. 80–86.

by arrest. For many career offenders, then, the often-quoted adage that "crime does not pay" is a myth maintained by and for law-abiding members of society.

When criminal offenses are pursued as a means of livelihood with some success, other ways of living are not readily observed, understood, or desired by the offender. Furthermore, the excitement and notoriety of a criminal career may be more rewarding than the prospects of hard work, responsibility, and monotony provided by a respectable, law-abiding career. Also, association and involvement with other offenders provides a group consciousness that makes movement to a law-abiding life less comprehensible and desirable.

Why some conventional offenders discontinue their criminally defined activities in their mid-twenties or early thirties is, therefore, the problem to be explained: "It is much easier to determine why offenders continue in criminal careers than it is to understand what makes them quit."[80] It may be that as a person grows older he tends to lose touch with his earlier associates because of marriage and family responsibilities. Such a change in life style is probably more important in breaking an offense pattern than are the many attempts at rehabilitation. Because of certain external factors, then, a person may find that a law-abiding career may hold greater personal possibilities than a career which has the potential of being periodically defined as criminal.

Organized Offense Behavior. Some persons violate criminal laws or become defined as criminal by participating in business enterprises that are organized for making economic gain illegally. The persons involved in such activity variously occupy positions within a hierarchical system of specifically defined relationships with mutual obligations and privileges. At the top of the hierarchy are the powerful leaders, the "lords" of the underworld, who make the important decisions and run the organization. A middle echelon of gangsters, henchmen, and lieutenants carry out the commands of the leaders. At the bottom are persons marginally associated with organized crime — narcotics peddlers, prostitutes, bookies, runners — who deal directly with the public.

The hierarchic structure of organized crime, with its diversity of

[80] Walter C. Reckless, *The Crime Problem*, 3rd ed. (New York: Appleton-Century-Crofts, 1961), p. 164.

personnel, makes generalization about the careers of its members difficult. Many persons in organized crime, especially those lower in the hierarchy, have careers similar to that of the conventional offender.[81] They tend to have a life history of association with juvenile gangs and a long series of delinquent and criminal offenses. Instead of ending their careers in their early twenties, however, they have continued their activities in association with persons in organized crime.

The juvenile gang of the slum produces the adult "gangster" who uses strong-arm methods and is employed for his talents by illegal organized groups. Such persons usually come from large cities, frequently have long criminal records of armed robberies, and conceive of themselves as "tough." Those who are successful in organized crime sometimes become its leaders. Organized crime may thus provide persons with the opportunity for a lifetime career in illegal activity.

Progression into organized crime increasingly isolates the offender from conventional society. Though there are variations according to the person's location within the hierarchy, most organized offenders are committed to the world of crime. Most of their activities are in continuous violation of the law. But by a process of justification, based in part on a contempt for the rest of society, they are able to maintain an appropriate self-image. Underworld leaders may, however, choose to live segmented lives, retiring to the seclusion of pseudo-respectability.[82] Their commitment, nevertheless, remains with the world of crime, where they receive their prestige, power, and are provided with a luxurious way of life.

Throughout their careers persons in organized crime associate regularly with other offenders. These associations and the support received from them are provided by the very nature of organized crime. That is, the crime syndicate which is organized to maintain a large-scale business enterprise for the coordination and control of products and services, ensures the association of persons involved in similar illegal activities. A description of this organization of

[81] See Reckless, *The Crime Problem,* p. 203; Solomon Kobrin, "The Conflict of Values in Delinquency Areas," *American Sociological Review,* pp. 653–661; Gus Tyler, "The Roots of Organized Crime," *Crime and Delinquency,* 8 (October, 1962), pp. 325–338.

[82] See Virgil W. Peterson, "The Career of a Syndicate Boss," *Crime and Delinquency,* 8 (October, 1962), pp. 339–354.

common illegal activity has recently been provided.[83] According to the report, the core of organized crime today consists of twenty-four groups (or "families"), which operate as criminal cartels in large cities across the country. In the internal structure of each of these groups, membership varies from as many as 700 men to as few as 20. Each family is structured according to a number of well defined positions. Outside the structure of the family is the "commission," which is a combination of legislature, supreme court, board of directors, and arbitration board for the coordination of the entire family system. The commission is composed of the bosses of the most powerful families and varies from nine to twelve men. The balance of power of this nationwide council currently rests with the leaders of the five families of New York, which is considered the headquarters of the entire operation of organized crime in the United States.

Finally, organized crime must be viewed in its relationship to the legal system. The existence of organized crime, in fact, depends on the way in which the criminal law is enforced and administered. In order to continue its operations, organized crime must maintain some amount of immunity from the law. This immunity is achieved in several ways.

> First, the leaders of organized crime are not usually arrested and prosecuted because they stay behind the scenes of operation. Gangland activity cannot be readily traced to its leaders. Second, persons lower in the hierarchy of organized crime, if arrested, are likely to be released by action from their superiors. Such release and avoidance of prosecution and punishment are assured through what is popularly known as the "fix." For various reasons, persons not directly involved in criminal activity contribute to the protection of organized criminals. Law enforcement officials, judges, doctors, businessmen, and others may at times provide needed services for the protection of organized criminals.
>
> A third way in which organized crime may acquire immunity is by gaining political power through contribution to polit-

[83] President's Commission on Law Enforcement and Administration of Justice, *The Challenge of Crime in a Free Society* (Washington, D.C.: U.S. Government Printing Office, 1967), pp. 191–196. Also see Robert T. Anderson, "From Mafia to Cosa Nostra," *American Journal of Sociology,* 71 (November, 1965), pp. 302–310.

> ical organizations. Elected officials may owe their election to organized criminals. Furthermore, regular "payoffs" to officials provide protection for organized crime. Thus, on a permanent basis, organized crime may be immune to law enforcement through political graft and corruption. Fourth, because organized crime provides the public with illicit and desired services, such as prostitution, gambling and narcotics, a certain amount of immunity from arrest and prosecution results from public toleration of organized crime.
>
> A fifth means of immunity is found in the functioning of the law itself. Existing laws and enforcement procedures have not been especially successful in coping with organized crime. The survival and continuance of organized crime is possible because legal action is kept at a minimum. Lack of effective legislation and weak law enforcement are, in turn, a reflection of public toleration of organized crime in the United States.
>
> Finally, through the infiltration of legitimate business, organized crime is able to evade the law. Organized crime today often operates behind the facade of legitimate business, obscuring its operation and making its detection difficult. Also, in the case of racketeering, organized crime escapes the law because intimidated businessmen must contend with reprisal if a report is made. In addition, organized crime and legitimate business may mutually assist one another, as in the regulation of prices of given commodities or through the enforcement of labor contracts. . . . The interdependence of the underworld of crime and the upperworld of business assures the maintenance of both systems. Mutual assistance, accompanied by public espousal of the profit motive under almost any arrangement, provides considerable assurance of immunity for organized crime.[84]

Thus, organized crime is maintained, and the offenders within the organization are assured of their way of life, by the relationship of organized crime to the administration of criminal law.

Professional Offense Behavior. Some persons, remaining outside organized crime, spend the majority of their time in illegal activities. They engage in specialized offenses, all of which are directed toward economic gain. By means of skill and elaborate

[84] Clinard and Quinney, *Criminal Behavior Systems*, pp. 386–387.

techniques, they are able to acquire considerable sums of money by "professional" thievery or fraud. Their activities include pickpocketing, shoplifting, sneak-thieving from stores, stealing from jewelry stores by substituting articles, stealing from hotel rooms, and miscellaneous rackets, such as passing illegal checks and extorting money from others engaged in illegal behavior. These activities are carried out for the most part without being detected by the offender. In the unusual cases when they are apprehended, professional offenders generally find ways to have the charge dropped.

Of all the types of offenders, professionals have the most highly developed careers in crime. In addition to being more skilled in their activity, they are able to operate without violence and strong-arm tactics. Regarding themselves as professionals, they tend to avoid other types of offenders and associate primarily with one another. Furthermore, professional offenders tend to come from better economic backgrounds than do the conventional and organized offenders. Many start in legitimate employment as salesmen, hotel clerks, waiters, or bellboys.[85] They may continue to engage in legitimate employment until they have progressed so that their entire livelihood can be achieved through illegal means.

The professional offender is likely to begin his career in illegal activities at a relatively late age. Once he is engaged in professional offenses, however, he tends to continue in them for the rest of his life.

> The con man begins his special career at a much older age than other criminals, or perhaps it is better said that he continues his criminal career at a time when others may be relinquishing theirs. Unemployment occasioned by old age does not seem to be a problem of con men; age ripens their skills, insights, and wit, and it also increases the confidence they inspire in their victims. With age the con man may give up the position of the roper and shift to being an inside man, but even this may not be absolutely necessary. It is possible that cultural changes outmode the particular con games older men have been accustomed to playing and thereby decrease their earnings some-

[85] See Edwin H. Sutherland, *The Professional Thief* (Chicago: University of Chicago Press, 1937), pp. 21–25.

> what, but this seems unlikely. We know of one con man who is seventy years of age and has a bad heart, but he is still as effective as he ever was.[86]

The longevity of the professional offender results, of course, in part from the fact that very few are ever arrested, tried, convicted, or sentenced to prison.

Professional offenders develop a philosophy of life to justify their actions and to enhance their self-images. Basic to this philosophy is the belief that all men are actually dishonest. They also justify their behavior by the belief that all persons would violate the law if they had the skill and opportunity. As Joseph "Yellow Kid" Weil, a successful confidence man, said of himself:

> The men I fleeced were basically no more honest than I was. One of the motivating factors in my action was, of course, the desire to acquire money. The other motive was a lust for adventure. The men I swindled were also motivated by a desire to acquire money, and they didn't care at whose expense they got it. I was particular. I took money only from those who could afford it and were willing to go in with me in schemes they fancied would fleece others.[87]

The professional offender can thus justify his own behavior by the conduct of his victim, who, after all, has been willing to participate in an illegal act. Such rationalizations are shared and supported by professional offenders in their association with one another.

The importance of group associations among professional offenders is indicated in the way in which persons are recruited into that world. Recognition by other professional offenders is the essential quality.[88] Without such recognition, no amount of knowledge and experience can provide the offender with the qualifications for a successful career built around the social role of the professional offender.

Included in the procedure of acquiring recognition by established professional offenders are two necessary elements: selection and tutelage. Selection takes place as professional offenders come in

[86] Lemert, *Social Pathology,* pp. 323–324.

[87] Joseph R. Weil and W. T. Brannon, *"Yellow Kid" Weil* (Chicago: Ziff-Davis, 1948), p. 293.

[88] Sutherland, *The Professional Thief,* pp. 197–228.

contact with other offenders (amateur thieves, burglars), with persons on the fringes of crime (pimps, "fences"), or with persons engaged in legitimate occupations. The contracts are made in places where professional offenders are working, in jails, or in places of leisure-time activities. Selection, which must be by mutual agreement between established and prospective professionals, is followed by a probationary period in which the neophyte learns the skills, techniques, attitudes, and values of the professional offender. In addition, he assimilates standards of group morality, such as honesty among professionals and not to inform on others. Gradually he becomes acquainted with other professional offenders. He eventually acquires the special language or argot by which members communicate with one another.[89] On the basis of such knowledge and expertise, the person develops action patterns in a world he shares with fellow professional offenders.

There is some indication that professional offense behavior may be changing as other changes are taking place in society.

> At the end of the last century, persons and organizations that were the victims of professional crime, especially of forgery, established as a reaction to professional crime a number of schemes which subsequently brought about a change in the organization and operation of professional crime. The establishment of the bankers' associations, the creation of merchants' protective agencies, and improvements in police methods made the risks of organized professional forgery exceedingly great. Also important to the decline of professional forgery has been the increasingly widespread use of business and payroll checks as well as personal checks. Because of these reactions the systematic check forger no longer has to resort to criminal associates or to employ the more complex procedures used in past decades. Thus, it can be seen that professional crime, as is true of other types of crime, is related to the structure of society. As society and the reaction to crime change, so do the organization and operation of the types of crime.[90]

[89] David W. Maurer, *The Big Con* (New York: Signet Books, 1962); David W. Maurer, *Whiz Mob* (New Haven: College and University Press, 1964).

[90] Clinard and Quinney, *Criminal Behavior Systems,* p. 436. Regarding these changes, see Edwin M. Lemert, "The Behavior of the Systematic Check Forger," *Social Problems,* 6 (Fall, 1958), pp. 141–149. Other studies of professional offenders are found in Cameron, *The Booster and the Snitch;* Ted Polsky, "The Hustler," *Social Problems,* 12 (Summer, 1964), pp. 3–15; Julian B. Roebuck,

PERSONAL MEANING OF ACTION

Each man seeks a meaningful existence. In abstraction the possible paths to man's existential salvation are many. But each person is bound by the social space he occupies in his own time in history. The alternatives that are at his command are limited. A man's horizons are set by his perceptions of the possibilities of being human and by the opportunities that are structured about him.

The action patterns that persons develop for themselves are solutions to the multiple problems of being socially human. Each person's actions, including a patterning of self-images and overt behaviors, are shaped by his relationships with others. It is within a socially structured environment, with the help of his friends (and others), that a person creates a meaningful life for himself.

The substance of a person's action is problematic. Though the content of the actions is shaped by the social and cultural location of the person in society, actions are ultimately the product of each individual. But the name that will be given the behavior is also an enterprise of others. And the names tend to be simplistic — like "good" or "bad," "virtuous" or "sinful," "law-abiding" or "criminal."

I have maintained throughout this chapter that personal actions are meaningful to the actors and that the actions are constructed in part through the reactions of other persons. The person may, consequently, develop a way of behaving — including a supporting style of life — that takes its reference from criminal definitions. Criminal definitions not only provide behavior with the quality of criminality, but also assist in living a life.

"The Negro Number Man as a Criminal Type: The Construction and Application of a Typology," *Journal of Criminal Law, Criminology and Police Science,* 54 (March, 1963), pp. 48–60; Julian B. Roebuck and Ronald C. Johnson, "The 'Short Con' Man," *Crime and Delinquency,* 10 (July, 1964), pp. 235–248; Edwin M. Schur, "Sociological Analysis of Confidence Swindling," *Journal of Criminal Law, Criminology and Police Science,* 48 (September–October, 1957), pp. 296–304.

5

Construction of Criminal Conceptions

CHAPTER NINE

Public Conceptions of Crime

Man constructs his own reality. And with the help of others, he creates a social world. The construction of this world is related to the knowledge man develops, the ideas to which he is exposed, and the manner in which he selects and interprets information to fit the world he is shaping. Man behaves, then, in reference to his conceptions of reality.

Included in man's social reality are conceptions about crime. Wherever the concept of crime exists, images are communicated in society about the meaning of crime, the nature of the criminal, and the relationship of crime to the social order. *Criminal conceptions* are thus constructed and diffused throughout society by various means of communication. For purposes of analysis, conceptions of crime can be discussed according to (1) social reaction to crime, (2) the diffusion of criminal conceptions, (3) social types in the world of crime, (4) public attitudes toward crime, and (5) public attitudes toward the control of crime. All these issues in the construction of criminal conceptions affect the development of criminal definitions and behavior patterns in a society.

SOCIAL REACTION TO CRIME

The reaction of the public to crime is both a product of the social reality of crime and a source in the construction of conceptions of crime. On the one hand, social reactions to crime are a consequence of the reality the public has constructed in regard to crime. Persons react in specific ways to the occurrence of criminally defined activity, to the enforcement and administration of the law, and to the treatment of the offender. Without a social reality of crime, there would be no reaction to crime. But, on the other hand, the reactions that are elicited in response to crime are at the same time shaping the social reality of crime. As persons react to crime, they develop patterns for the responses of the future.

In spite of the often spontaneous quality of personal responses to crime, reaction to crime takes place in a social and cultural context. That is to say, social reaction to crime is socially structured and is patterned according to a system of norms. All societies have a variety of *reactive norms* that prescribe the appropriate reactions for particular situations and specify how and by whom the reactions are to be administered.[1] For many areas of human activity both *legal* and *extralegal* reactions are prescribed. The violation of a particular criminal law, for example, is accompanied by a set of appropriate formal sanctions. The formal sanctions are, in turn, administered through procedures established by law. The same violation is likewise subject to extralegal sanctions, including such public reactions as stigmatization of the offender and denial of employment.[2] Moreover, social reactions are normatively patterned according to such contingencies as the type of offense, the personal and social characteristics of the offender, the social location of the offense, and the degree to which the offense violates other social norms. All these affect the manner and the regularity with which reactions (both legal and extralegal) will be practiced. Thus, social reactions, like all other forms of behavior, are to be understood according to their social patterning and cultural regulation.

The reactive norms within any society are not generalized for the entire society, but vary considerably from one segment to another. Extralegal prescriptions, in particular, vary throughout a population according to such social characteristics as the age, sex, ethnicity,

[1] See Alexander L. Clark and Jack P. Gibbs, "Social Control: A Reformulation," *Social Problems,* 12 (Spring, 1965), pp. 402–406; Jack P. Gibbs, "Sanctions," *Social Problems,* 14 (Fall, 1966), pp. 152–154.

[2] See Richard D. Schwartz and Jerome H. Skolnick, "Two Studies of Legal Stigma," *Social Problems,* 10 (Fall, 1962), pp. 133–142.

religion, and social class of the reactors.[3] Among the legal reactions are specific prescriptions in the criminal codes of the respective political units. But the legal codes provide alternative reactions for any offense. Because of the latitude of prescriptions, the patterns of legal reaction differ from one kind of criminal case to another, varying in such matters as the types of sanctions utilized and the consistency with which the reactions are imposed and administered. Hence, social reactions, whether legal or extralegal, are not socially monolithic in either their cultural prescription or their actual patterning. Variations in social reactions are to be sought and explained as reflecting the segmental organization of society.

From the perspective of the individual, responses to crime are influenced by *knowledge* about crime and *perceptions* about the meaning of crime. The attitudes of persons toward such matters as criminal behavior, law enforcement, and the handling of offenders are affected by the kinds and amounts of knowledge they have about these matters. Persons differ greatly in their knowledge about the existence and substance of laws in the society.[4] Reaction to all that is associated with crime initially rests upon knowledge about crime. Likewise, perception of the crime phenomenon underlies any social reaction to crime. How a person perceives crime provides a framework for his own understanding of and subsequent reaction to crime.

> Attitudes to crime and criminals then, vary, not so much in terms of the intrinsic nature of the criminal act, but in terms of the likelihood of the act being an established part of the observer's own social world. Crime is in the last analysis what the other person does. What I do, if it is against the law, is susceptible to redefinition through rationalization. Even if the observer is unlikely to commit the particular crime in question, his attitude to it will be conditioned by a degree of modification which may result in either a lenient tolerance or a

[3] In respect to variations in social reactions regarding homosexuals, see John I. Kitsuse, "Societal Reaction to Deviant Behavior: Problems of Theory and Method," *Social Problems,* 9 (Winter, 1962), p. 256.

[4] Torgny T. Segerstedt, "A Research into the General Sense of Justice," *Theoria,* 15 (1949), pp. 323–338. Also see Frederick Beutel, *Some Potentialities of Experimental Jurisprudence as a New Branch of Social Science* (Lincoln: University of Nebraska Press, 1957).

> punitive rejection, depending upon how far the crime threatens the observer, or the group to which they all belong.[5]

Perception precedes a response of any kind.

Criminal conceptions are gradually constructed. The social reactions of today must be viewed within a cultural framework that has developed *historically*. With this in mind, it has been suggested that the early Puritan image of deviation continues to be reflected in many of our modern reactions to crime.[6] For the Puritans in Massachusetts Bay, crime was an act against the symmetry and orderliness of nature itself. The criminal, in keeping with the Puritans' theological doctrine, was relegated to a category of permanent misfits who were predestined to oppose the social order by engaging in unacceptable activities. As a result of these attitudes the Puritans developed a "deployment pattern" in regard to crime and deviance:

> To characterize the New England deployment pattern in a word, we may say (1) that the Puritans saw deviant behavior as the special property of a particular class of people who were more or less frozen into deviant attitudes; and (2) that they generally thought it best to handle the problem by locking these people into fairly permanent deviant roles. Puritan theories of human development began with the assumption that men do not change a great deal as they mature or are exposed to different life experiences, and in this sense the settlers of the Bay had little faith in the promise that men might "reform" or overcome any pronounced deviant leanings. A person's character, like his social estate, is fixed by the preordained pattern of human history, and if he should somehow indicate by his surly manners and delinquent ways that he is not a very promising candidate for conversion, the community was not apt to waste many of its energies trying to change him or mend his character. In a very real sense, he belonged to a deviant "class" and was not expected to improve upon that condition.[7]

The Puritan heritage is still very much a part of our public and legal reaction to crime. Our image of the criminal is predicated on a

[5] Terence Morris, "The Social Toleration of Crime," in Hugh J. Klare (ed.), *Changing Concepts of Crime and Its Treatment* (Oxford: Pergamon Press, 1966), pp. 33–34.

[6] Kai T. Erikson, *Wayward Puritans: A Study in the Sociology of Deviance* (New York: John Wiley, 1966).

[7] *Ibid.*, pp. 196–197.

belief in the irreversibility of human nature. Strengthened by positivistic assumptions in our criminology, we tend in our social reactions to place the criminal in a class by himself.

> Now, as then, we leave few return routes open to people who try to resume a normal social life after a period of time spent on the community's boundaries, because most of us feel that anyone who skids off into the more severe forms of aberrant expression is displaying a serious defect of character, a deep blemish which cannot easily be erased. We may learn to think of such people as "sick" rather than "reprobate," but a single logic governs both of these labels, for they imply that nothing less than an important change of heart, a spiritual conversion or a clinical cure, can eliminate that inner seed which leads one to behave in a deviant fashion.[8]

DIFFUSION OF CRIMINAL CONCEPTIONS

Once a society has a generalized criminal mythology, conceptions of crime are diffused throughout the population. The *diffusion* of criminal conceptions simultaneously involves the *construction* of conceptions of crime among individuals and groups. This mutual process is accomplished in a number of ways. All the means which facilitate construction of conceptions, however, are mediated by the social context of diffusion and by the interpersonal relations associated with the adoption of criminal conceptions.

Among the most important agents in the diffusion of criminal conceptions are the media of mass communication. Crime coverage in the newspapers, television, and movies affect a person's estimate of the frequency of crime as well as the interpretations that he attaches to crime. Research has shown that a special reality is presented in the newspapers in respect to crime. In one study, it was found that the amount of crime news in each of four Colorado newspapers varied independently of the amount of crime in the state as reflected by crime statistics.[9] Persons were then asked, in a public opinion poll, to estimate the amount of crime in the state. The results indicated

[8] *Ibid.*, pp. 204–205.

[9] F. J. Davis, "Crime News in Colorado Newspapers," *American Journal of Sociology,* 57 (January, 1952), pp. 325–330.

that public opinion about crime tended to reflect trends in the amount of crime news rather than the actual crime rates. Coverage of crime in the newspapers created a conceptual reality that was meaningful to the public in spite of any other social reality of crime.

Moreover, the mass media provide varying and often divergent portrayals of crime. Perusal of different newspapers in the same city on the same day is enough to illustrate that one's construction of a conception of crime depends upon which newspaper he happens to read. One of the most striking examples is a comparison of two newspapers in New York City that have considerably different orientations to news presentation: the New York *Daily News* and *The New York Times*. In a content analysis of the two newspapers, it was found that over three months the *Daily News* presented nearly twice as many items about juvenile delinquency as did the *Times*.[10] In front-page coverage, the *Daily News* carried four stories for each one displayed in the *Times*. Furthermore, there were differences between the two papers in the emotionality with which the news items were presented. Differences were seen, especially, in the terminology and phraseology of the headlines of the two papers. Typical of the *Daily News* headlines were: "Cops Nab Two In Cat-Mouse Roof Top Chase," "Stolen Kiss Traps Robber of Girl In Hall," "Hunt Two Boy Bullies Who Killed Lad," "Thugs Finger A Fingerman," and "Beer Gets Guv's Girl Canned From College." The headlines from the *Times*, in comparison, were mild and unemotional: "Museum Theft Laid To Delinquents," "Third Slain In Youth Violence," "Youth Crime Rise Is Held Magnified," and "Three Fires Set In Bronx School."

Thus public conceptions of crime and delinquency are constructed and diffused on the basis of "news" presentations. Specific conceptions are shaped by what is considered to be news about the subject of crime. Since the press is one of the chief dispensers of information about crime, conceptions of crime and delinquency are influenced by the newspaper coverage to which one is exposed. A recent portrayal of the crime problem in the *Daily News*, for instance, as shown in the cartoon (page 283) dramatically presents an image of crime for the Sunday viewer.

[10] Rita Bachmuth, S. M. Miller, and Linda Rosen, "Juvenile Delinquency in the Daily Press," *Alpha Kappa Delta*, 30 (Spring, 1960), pp. 47–51.

STREET WALKER

© 1969 New York News Syndicate

The style and content of much of the media represent a continual preoccupation with crime. For the many persons who find this sort of coverage to their liking, the real world is a selective one, a crime-centered one. Not only is attention focused on crime, but the more sensational and adventuresome aspects of crime are portrayed. The routine nature of the major portion of crime is also neglected. Coverage of crime in the mass media, therefore, is not only selective but is a distortion of the everyday world of crime. But such is the stuff from which reality worlds are constructed for much of the population.

The effect of the coverage of crime in the mass media has been a topic for considerable speculation and research.[11] Many educators, social observers, and parents have worried about the possible effects of the depiction of crime and violence in the media. It is not my purpose here, however, to survey and evaluate the many arguments and findings. I have no doubt of the selective nature of the coverage of crime in the mass media. Likewise, I am convinced that crime as presented in the media affects the recipient's attitudes and behavior. I am also certain that in some cases persons are "tried" by the press before their cases are decided in a court of law.[12] But, first, the relationship that I perceive between exposure to media and the attitudes and behaviors of persons is on a more general level. That is, public conceptions of crime are created in part by the images of crime in the mass media. And, second, the relationship must be viewed along with the mediating forces of social context and interpersonal relations.

Recent research on mass communications has confirmed that the possible effects of the mass media are mediated by interpersonal networks of communication and by such contextual matters as integration in social groups and membership in various kinds of groups.[13] Personal contacts in a social context influence one's interpretation of the content of the mass media. Moreover, mass communication, in

[11] Much of the research is reviewed in Joseph T. Klapper, *The Effects of Mass Communications* (New York: The Free Press of Glencoe, 1960), pp. 135–165.

[12] See Alfred Friendly and Ronald L. Goldfarb, *Crime and Publicity: The Impact of News on the Administration of Justice* (New York: Vintage Books, 1968).

[13] See Elihu Katz, "The Two-Step Flow of Communication: An Up-to-Date Report of an Hypothesis," *Public Opinion Quarterly,* 21 (Spring, 1957), pp. 61–78; John W. Riley, Jr. and Mathilda White Riley, "Mass Communications

working through mediators, reinforces existing conceptions. The social nature of exposure to mass media, therefore, influences the nature and impact of the portrayal of crime in mass communication.

The implication of the above idea is that exposure to such images affects individuals differently according to their past experiences and their present associations. In particular, it appears that persons who are involved in patterns of criminally defined activity are more likely to be influenced by crime portrayals than persons not so involved.[14] On an even more subtle level, however, the effect of exposure to crime in the mass media may not be significant until a personal problem or a particular social condition presents itself. Exposure in the past may thus furnish a future alternative for action.

Certainly we can convincingly argue that mass communications are socially mediated. Nevertheless, there would be nothing to mediate if a particular image did not exist in the mass media in the first place. Mass communications *do* make a difference. My argument, reinterpreting the thesis of the effects of mass media, is that a specific kind of crime coverage in the media provides the source for building criminal conceptions. A conception of crime is presented in the mass media. That conception, diffused throughout the society, becomes the basis for the public's view of reality. Not only is a symbolic environment created within the society, but personal actions take their reference from that environment. Indeed, the construction of a conceptual reality is also the creation of a social reality of actions and events.

SOCIAL TYPES IN THE WORLD OF CRIME

All the nuances of crime cannot be vividly communicated. In communication, images must be simplified, sharpened, and reduced to their essentials. Thus, in order to facilitate the diffusion of conceptions of crime, *stereotypes* of crime and criminals are created. Of-

---

and the Social System," in Robert K. Merton, Leonard Broom, and Leonard S. Cottrell, Jr. (eds.), *Sociology Today* (New York: Basic Books, 1959), pp. 537–578; Everett M. Rogers, *Diffusion of Innovations* (New York: The Free Press of Glencoe, 1962), pp. 57–75, 208–253.

[14] Herbert Blumer and Philip Hauser, *Movies, Delinquency, and Crime* (New York: Macmillan, 1933).

fenders, accordingly, are grouped by the public into such categories as the thief, the burglar, the robber, the sex offender, and the murderer. Categories such as these furnish the boundaries for the public's view of crime.

On the basis of stereotypes, then, persons construct their conceptual realities of crime. The criminal becomes a *social type.*[15] As a social type, "the criminal" can be understood by the observer as one who possesses attributes that are believed to be characteristic of a class of people. The criminal, as socially typed, is a construct that incorporates a description of what such persons are like, why they act as they do, and how they should act in the future. All that is associated with crime has the possibility of being categorized by the public. Such is the basis of human understanding.

Some systematic evidence exists on the public stereotyping of criminals. In a series of pilot studies the extent and nature of stereotyped images of deviants were investigated.[16] The researcher found, first, public stereotypes for such deviant categories as homosexuals, drug addicts, prostitutes, murderers, and juvenile delinquents. It was then determined that persons also tend to consistently portray each type of deviant in a particular way. Homosexuals were likely to be described as being sexually abnormal, perverted, mentally ill, and maladjusted, whereas marijuana smokers were characterized as persons looking for kicks, escapists, insecure, lacking self-control, and frustrated. It was concluded that "discernible stereotypes of at least several kinds of deviants do exist in our society and that there is a fair amount of agreement on the content of these stereotypes."[17] Hence, imputed deviance, including deviance which may also be criminally defined, is publicly stereotyped. These stereotypes of human behavior are structured and patterned in society.

On a more general level, the category of "criminal" tends to incorporate its own stereotyped set of characteristics. According to public conception, the criminal is a social type. The principal model for the type is the *villain,* one who is feared, hated, and ridiculed. The criminal is generally the "bad guy" in popular conception. Crim-

[15] The concept of social type is from Orrin E. Klapp, *Heroes, Villains, and Fools* (Englewood Cliffs, N.J.: Prentice-Hall, 1962), pp. 1–24.

[16] J. L. Simmons, "Public Stereotypes of Deviants," *Social Problems,* 13 (Fall, 1965), pp. 223–232.

[17] *Ibid.,* p. 229.

inals are the enemies of law and order (desperadoes, rebels, flouters, rogues, troublemakers), villainous strangers (intruders, suspicious isolates, monsters), disloyal and underhanded types (renegades, traitors, deceivers, sneak-attackers, chiselers, shirkers, corrupters), or are among the miscellaneous social undesirables (vagrants, derelicts, convicts, outcasts).[18] Such villains are with us in popular conception, nominally as criminals. The public concept of crime is used to cover a multitude of sins.

But the criminal as a social type incorporates other than the image of villain. He may also be cast in the role of *hero*. Noted outlaws are an example:

> Billy the Kid did not make a good villain because he was blonde, blue-eyed, well built, and rather handsome; women fell for him. He was brave and a square shooter. Such discrepancies in the character of a bad man made him resemble others (Robin Hood, Don Juan, François Villon, Pancho Villa), who perhaps should have been villains but were not.[19]

Paradoxically (perhaps), the villainous criminal can also be a popular favorite of heroic proportions.

A major reason for the ambiguity between villainous and heroic criminal conceptions is that the roles of villain and hero support similar value themes. Both types depend upon aggressiveness, cleverness, and the ability to "outdo" others in some way.

> Not only in fiction but in real life confusion between good guys and bad guys occurs. Since Edwin H. Sutherland's epochal studies, Americans have gotten rather used to the idea that a whitecollar criminal looks very like an honest businessman. Expense account chiseling, kickbacks, payoffs, tax evasion, even a little fraud or larceny, may be all in a day's work. If the old distinction between honesty and dishonesty has become blurred, no less has the quaint notion that "crime does not pay" (if you want to get a laugh from an audience, just smile when you say this). When the Brinks Express robbers were caught a few years back, a housewife remarked, "I was kind of sad. It seemed a shame, when they had only a few days to go before the statute of limitations would have let them keep all that money." A

[18] Klapp, *Heroes, Villains, and Fools*, pp. 50–67.
[19] *Ibid.*, p. 50.

> strange kind of casing is occurring today — good guys do not have to live up to codes, bad guys do not have to be caught and punished (especially if they look enough like good guys); it may be that the distinction is ceasing to be important.[20]

With a bit more humor, Mark Twain observed the same American tendency to respect what is also regarded as criminal:

> And he grew up and married and raised a large family, and brained them all with an ax one night, and got wealthy by all manner of cheating and rascality; and now he is the infernalest wickedest scoundrel in his native village, and is universally respected, and belongs to the legislature.[21]

The ambiguous reaction to crime can be traced in part to the tradition of the *romantic outlaw*. Tales of the maverick who defied the law are legend.

> Even today annual celebrations are devoted to Jesse James at Northfield, Minnesota (because he happened to ride through and rob a bank there), and to Wild Bill Hickock at Deadwood, South Dakota. Were a proposal made to abolish the outlaw tradition, there would probably be a storm of protest from movie-makers, writers, and the public. Crooks like John Dillinger, the "Yellow Kid" Weil, and Al Capone, get wrapped in glamor, even outlaws from other countries, such as Pancho Villa, who, in spite of train robberies and murders, became as much of a celebrity in America as Buffalo Bill; reporters stayed with his staff to tell of the women he kidnapped or how he ordered a thousand-dollar bathtub from a firm in Chicago.[22]

Certainly the romantic outlaw is more than villain. He is also something else — "too good to be a villain, too bad to be a hero, too serious to be a mere clown, too interesting to forget."[23]

Perhaps some criminals capture the modern imagination as *anti-heroes*. As anti-hero, the criminal represents the attempt to make it outside the system. Inevitable failure gives charisma to his noble attempt. And, along the way, such a criminal is likely to assist those

[20] *Ibid.*, pp. 145–146. Also see Nathan Hare, "The Ambivalent Public and Crime," *Crime and Delinquency,* 9 (April, 1963), pp. 145–151.

[21] "Story of the Bad Little Boy," in *The Complete Short Stories of Mark Twain,* ed. by Charles Neider (New York: Bantam Books, 1957), pp. 8–9.

[22] Klapp, *Heroes, Villains, and Fools,* p. 146.

[23] *Ibid.*, p. 147.

who are made to fail in other ways because of the system. Woody Guthrie had Pretty Boy Floyd singing in Shawnee, Oklahoma:

> You say that I'm an outlaw
> You say that I'm a thief
> Here's a Christmas dinner
> For the families on relief

Then adding:

> Now as through this world I ramble
> I see lots of funny men
> Some will rob you with a six gun
> And some with a fountain pen.
> But as through your life you roam
> You won't never see an outlaw
> Drive a family from their home.[24]

Respect for some criminals, in addition, is a product of the American fascination with violence. Violence has become a hallowed tradition in American culture:

> If we could formulate a generalized image of America in the eyes of foreign peoples from the eighteenth century to the present, it would surely include, among other things, a phantasmagoria of violence, from the original Revolution and Indian wars to the sordid history of lynching; from the casual killings of the cowboy and bandit to the machine-gun murders of racketeers. If America has often been considered a country of innocence and promise in contrast to a corrupt and immoral Europe, this sparkling, smiling, domestic land of easygoing friendliness, where it is estimated that a new murder occurs every forty-five minutes, has also glorified personal whim and impulse and has ranked hardened killers with the greatest folk heroes. Founded and preserved by acts of aggression, characterized by a continuing tradition of self-righteous violence against suspected subversion and by a vigorous sense of personal freedom, usually involving the widespread possession of firearms, the United States has evidenced a unique tolerance of homicides.[25]

[24] "Pretty Boy Floyd," *American Folksong, Woody Guthrie,* edited by Moses Asch (New York: Oak Publications, 1961), p. 27.

[25] David Brion Davis, *Homicide in American Fiction, 1798–1860: A Study in Social Values* (Ithaca, N.Y.: Cornell University Press, 1957), pp. vii–viii.

Little wonder, then, that there is public confusion in the evaluation of acts that involve violence. Violence itself has its own legitimacy.

Criminals are not the only social types that fill the public world of crime. Also included are the social types that are associated with criminals. Policemen, lawyers, and detectives have become socially typed through the various forms of communication. The detective, in particular, has been the object of a great deal of characterizing in the mystery novel. Edgar Allan Poe, interested in unraveling puzzles by reasoning, wrote a number of stories in which the detective played the dominant role. In 1852 Charles Dickens introduced readers of *Bleak House* to a Scotland Yard detective, Inspector Bucket. But it was not until Arthur Conan Doyle introduced Sherlock Holmes to the public in "A Study of Scarlet" in the 1880's that the detective story became a public favorite. Sherlock Holmes represented to readers not only a "consulting detective," but a cultured gentleman who transcended the law with his own code of right and wrong. In the world of Holmes the business of upholding the right fell upon the shoulders of private men rather than public officials.[26] Holmes was always, morally and scientifically, beyond the reach of Lestrade of Scotland Yard.

The crime-fighting heroes of today display virtues for another age. These characters are more likely to be found in suspense and science fiction stories than in detective stories.[27] The "private eye," such as Dashiell Hammett's Sam Spade or Raymond Chandler's Philip Marlowe, is a tough guy, cynical, hard-boiled, and hard drinking, who is at war with criminals in his *own* way, often outside the law. Mickey Spillane's Mike Hammer killed numerous innocent people in his pursuits against crime. But perhaps James Bond of Ian Fleming's novels best presents the modern figure in a world of crime. As a secret agent, Bond is licensed to kill — and with great finesse. He is talented also as a lover, sportsman (who cheats), and a connoisseur of fashionable luxuries. Ian Fleming symbolizes something that appeals to every good man.

> What he offers his readers is the beguiling modern dream of life of total self-sufficiency and sophisticated self-indulgence. Soli-

[26] See Martin Maloney, "A Grammar of Assassination," *Etc.*, 11 (Winter, 1954), pp. 83–95.

[27] See Christopher Hibbert, *The Roots of Evil: A Social History of Crime and Punishment* (Harmondsworth, Eng.: Penguin Books, 1966), pp. 302–314.

> tary, composed, self-assured, acting with ritualistic deliberation and meeting his trials single-handedly and resourcefully, Bond is an existential deep-sea diver. In his casual moments (enjoying a good meal or an evening with a lovely woman) he projects the satisfaction of feeling cool and superior; at critical times he demonstrates the capacity of the lone individual to pull through unaided. His only use for society is as a hospital, where he can recoup his strength for the next plunge into the void.[28]

Images such as these have been presented to a wide audience by television and the movies as well as by fictional literature. Detective heroes have been portrayed in leading roles as being "smarter than the cops, craftier than the crooks, too quick to be caught and domesticated by the classiest doll."[29] And we have been presented with the shadowy figure of Perry Mason, a lawyer who behaves like a private detective in preparing his cases. The list need not be extended. It is enough to say that the world of crime is readily before us for the taking.

I am not necessarily being critical of the ways in which the characters of the world of crime are presented. The portrayals by criminologists probably have not been any more convincing. I *do,* however, argue that the world of fiction is also the world of reality. Fiction is fact when it is believed and taken as the object of action. When criminals and their counterparts are characterized in a particular way, they are already becoming social types which find their fulfillment in society. Social reality begins in the imagination.

PUBLIC ATTITUDES TOWARD CRIME

The nature and intensity of the public's concern about crime varies from time to time; it has periodically been acute throughout the twentieth century. Fluctuations in attention to crime are indicated by the perennial appointment of legislative and private committees to

[28] Albert Goldman, "Elegant Narcissist," *The New York Times Book Review,* December 11, 1966, p. 36. (A review of John Pearson, *The Life of Ian Fleming* [New York: McGraw-Hill, 1966].) Also see Lycurgus M. Starkey, Jr., *James Bond's World Values* (Nashville, Tenn.: Abingdon Press, 1966).

[29] Quoted in Hibbert, *The Roots of Evil,* p. 311 (originally from *Time,* October, 1959). Also see Melvin L. De Fleur, "Occupational Roles as Portrayed on Television," *Public Opinion Quarterly,* 28 (Spring, 1964), pp. 57–74.

investigate the crime problem. The public's perception of crime is variable. The construction and diffusion of criminal conceptions are part of a process that is continually changing in substance and intensity.

Public anxiety about crime is now especially critical — in response, the President's Commission on Law Enforcement and Administration of Justice was established in 1965.[30] One part of the Commission's task was to investigate the anxiety itself. Attitudes toward crime were assessed by analyzing national public opinion polls and surveys conducted for the Commission.

The Commission, indeed, found that crime is perceived by the public as one of the most serious of all domestic problems.[31] In a national survey conducted for the Commission by the National Opinion Research Center, citizens were asked to choose from a list of six major domestic problems facing the nation the one to which they had been paying the most attention recently. Crime was the second most frequently selected problem. Only race relations was selected by more people. Furthermore, most persons thought the crime situation in their own community was getting worse. A Gallup survey of April, 1965, showed that this pessimistic perception of the crime problem occurred among many segments of the population — men and women, well educated and less educated, and all age, regional, income, and residential groupings.

Personal *fear* of crime, the Commission found, is especially great about personal safety and to some extent the fear that personal property will be taken. Most intense is the fear of being accosted by a stranger on the street or that a stranger will break into the home and attack them. Although these are the crimes that occur least frequently, fear about them significantly affects personal lives. The Commission reported the following:

> Perhaps the most revealing findings on the impact of fear of crime on people's lives were the changes people reported in their

[30] For the summary report, see President's Commission on Law Enforcement and Administration of Justice, *The Challenge of Crime in a Free Society* (Washington, D.C.: U.S. Government Printing Office, 1967).

[31] See President's Commission on Law Enforcement and Administration of Justice, "Public Attitudes Toward Crime and Law Enforcement," *Task Force Report: Crime and Its Impact — An Assessment* (Washington, D.C.: U.S. Government Printing Office, 1967), pp. 85–95. Or see Jennie McIntyre, "Public Attitudes Toward Crime and Law Enforcement," *Annals of the American Academy of Political and Social Science,* 374 (November, 1967), pp. 34–46.

> regular habits of life. In the high-crime districts surveyed in Boston and Chicago, for example, five out of every eight respondents reported changes in their habits because of fear of crime, some as many as four or five major changes. Forty-three percent reported they stayed off the streets at night altogether. Another 21 percent said they always used cars or taxis at night. Thirty-five percent said they would not talk to strangers any more.[32]

The Commission also found that there are differences in the intensity of concern about crime according to personal characteristics of the population. In a national survey of anxiety about crime, supplemented by a survey in Washington, it was found that Negro women have the highest degree of anxiety, followed in order by Negro men, white women, and white men. Also, anxiety about crime is more pronounced among the lower income levels for both Negroes and whites.[33]

One of the first pieces of research on public attitudes toward crime investigated attitudes of persons to stealing from three kinds of organizations.[34] The main objective of the research was to determine how the size of the victim organization affects public attitudes toward stealing. In general, it was found that if obliged to choose, most persons disapprove less of stealing from large, impersonal business and governmental organizations than from small, personal organizations. The findings were, however, modified by the characteristics of the respondents. It was observed that regardless of organizational size, the lower the socioeconomic status of the respondent the greater the approval of stealing. Similarly, women were more inclined to approve of stealing than men, though they showed the greatest differences in attitudes when the size of the victim or-

[32] President's Commission on Law Enforcement and Administration of Justice, *Task Force Report: Crime and Its Impact — An Assessment,* p. 88.

[33] Phillip H. Ennis, *Criminalization in the United States: A Report of a National Survey,* President's Commission on Law Enforcement and Administration of Justice, Field Survey II (Washington, D.C.: U.S. Government Printing Office, 1967), pp. 72–79; Albert D. Biderman, Louise A. Johnson, Jennie McIntyre, and Adrianne W. Weis, *Report on a Pilot Study in the District of Columbia on Victimization and Attitudes Toward Law Enforcement,* President's Commission on Law Enforcement and Administration of Justice, Field Survey I (Washington, D.C.: U.S. Government Printing Office, 1967), pp. 119–134.

[34] Erwin O. Smigel, "Public Attitudes Toward Stealing as Related to Size of the Victim Organization," *American Sociological Review,* 21 (June, 1956), pp. 320–327.

ganization was considered. The conclusion was that while size of organization affects public attitudes toward stealing, the attitudes are also affected by the characteristics of the respondents.

Similar research was conducted in a study of public attitudes toward the violation of unemployment compensation laws.[35] Three major circumstances were considered: (1) knowledge of the laws, (2) social norms of the respondents, and (3) socioeconomic status. The evidence supported the hypothesis that knowledge of the law plays a part in determining attitudes toward violation of the law. Individuals who approved of the illegal behavior were likely to be ignorant of the law and unaware that violations were involved. It was found that when the social norms are in conflict with the goals of the law, there is a divergence in attitudes toward violation. Respondents who had poor jobs and low socioeconomic status were more inclined to approve of violation of unemployment compensation laws, whereas those who had good jobs and high status were more likely to disapprove of the violations. Finally, the opportunity to violate the law and personal experiences with unemployment increased the tendency to approve or at least be indifferent toward the violation of unemployment compensation laws.

Attitudes toward offenses in which the public itself is the victim may also be considered. Violations of the Federal Food, Drug and Cosmetic Act directly affect the consumer. With such pure food violations as misbranding and adulteration in mind, a sample of consumers was asked to judge selected cases of violation to show how they would react to the violations.[36] The responses of the consumers were then compared with actual decisions in the cases and with possible decisions provided in the federal law. The respondents reacted to the pure food violations without regard for their class position: "That is, even though they vary greatly by income, occupation, and educational level, by degree of awareness and familiarity with these violations, and by amount of organized consumer activity, their choices of penalties do not differ significantly from one such grouping to another."[37] Yet, according to their reactions, the re-

[35] Erwin O. Smigel, "Public Attitudes Toward 'Chiseling' with Reference to Unemployment Compensation," *American Sociological Review,* 18 (February, 1953), pp. 59–67.

[36] Donald J. Newman, "Public Attitudes Toward a Form of White Collar Crime," *Social Problems,* 4 (January, 1957), pp. 228–232.

[37] *Ibid.,* p. 231.

spondents tended to view food adulteration as more comparable to serious traffic violations than to burglary. The respondents, thus, tended to view such violators as "law breakers" rather than "criminals." But pure food offenses against the customer have only recently become a matter of public interest. Greater awareness of this form of violation in the future may be accompanied by a stronger public reaction toward the offenses.

Criminal conceptions also refer to offenses that are without victims. Public knowledge about and reaction to three forms of such offenses (abortion, homosexuality, and drug addiction) were investigated in one study.[38] Respondents in the San Francisco area were asked to indicate the degree to which they approve of changes in social policies toward abortion, homosexuality, and drug addiction. Other questions probed for misconceptions about the facts regarding these activities. The researchers found that the levels of social tolerance for these behaviors varied according to (1) the degree to which the behaviors are interpreted as being dangerous to the participants or to other members of society and (2) the accuracy of their knowledge about the behaviors. Also, it was found that tolerance for abortion, homosexuality, and drug addiction was related to variations in the social background of the respondents. Men were more tolerant than women, younger persons than older persons, educated persons than less educated persons, and Protestants and Jews than Catholics. Finally, regardless of these social correlates of attitudes, it was found that persons were most tolerant of abortion, less tolerant of proposed changes in laws and practices regarding homosexuals, and least accepting of changes in the handling of drug addicts.

Members of a community are likely to develop a pattern of reactions to crime peculiar to their own community. Public reaction to crime within a particular community setting has been studied in research conducted for the President's Commission on Law Enforcement and Administration of Justice in a middle-sized eastern industrial city, given the fictitious name of "Wincanton."[39] A survey of the city's residents indicated a general tolerance of gambling and

[38] Elizabeth A. Rooney and Don C. Gibbons, "Social Reactions to 'Crime Without Victims,'" *Social Problems,* 13 (Spring, 1966), pp. 400–410.

[39] John A. Gardiner, "Public Attitudes Toward Gambling and Corruption," *Annals of the American Academy of Political and Social Science,* 374 (November, 1967), pp. 123–134.

related activities, but hostility toward all forms of official corruption The respondents displayed both a tolerance of illicit services and a demand for honesty on the part of local officials. The residents apparently did not realize the paradox that in order for illicit services to be supplied, dishonesty of local officials was necessary. A major reason for the public ignorance of the connection between gambling and corruption, the study suggests, is that the illegal activities of the officials are hidden from public view, becoming known only during a reform investigation. The following conclusions were offered about the nature and significance of public attitudes toward gambling and corruption:

> First, public attitudes are much more permissive toward gambling than the statutes which are common in the United States; gambling is either positively desired or else not regarded as particularly reprehensible by a substantial proportion of the population. Second, citizens value official honesty and impartial administration of the laws even if they do not expect that all officials will, in fact, live up to these standards. Third, while there was little awareness of the extent of corruption in the city, citizens reacted strongly whenever investigations revealed the relationship between organized crime and local officials. While local residents are inadequately aware of the costs of the support for the services offered by organized crime, they respond positively whenever choices are clearly and dramatically presented to them.[40]

The implication is that the conclusions apply as well to public attitudes toward crime in other communities.

PUBLIC ATTITUDES TOWARD THE CONTROL OF CRIME

Associated with public attitudes toward crime are thoughts on controlling it. Public conceptions develop in regard to law and its enforcement, judicial administration of criminal law, and penal and correctional administration. As with other attitudes, these become patterned within the segments of society. Actions, in turn, find their source in such conceptions.

Attitudes toward the control of crime tend to be moralistic. The

[40] *Ibid.*, p. 134.

surveys regarding beliefs about the causes of crime indicate a concern with the morals of the country and the moral training of youths.[41] A Gallup poll of 1965 showed that few persons blame social conditions or law enforcement for the increase in crime. Rather, most answers reflected poor parental guidance or inadequate home life and supervision of teenagers. In another survey, also asking similar questions about the causes of crime, it was found that 68 per cent of the persons interviewed believed that upbringing or bad environment were the main causes of crime. Few suggested poor or inadequate social conditions.

Although the public attributes an increase in crime to the lowering of moral standards, most would depend on the police and related agencies for controlling crime; connected with this reliance on law enforcement is the generally positive attitude the public has toward the police. According to opinion polls, most of the public has a high opinion of the work of the police. A poll in 1967 showed that 77 per cent of the public had a "great deal" of respect for the police, 17 per cent had "some" respect, and only 4 per cent had "hardly any" respect.[42] Similarly, the national survey in 1965 by the National Opinion Research Center (NORC) showed that 67 per cent of the persons interviewed thought that the police were doing a good to excellent job of enforcing the law.[43] The later finding, however, was qualified by the income, race, and sex of the respondents. It was found in the NORC study that upper income groups are consistently more favorable in their evaluation of the police, that Negroes at all income levels have fairly strong negative attitudes toward the police, and that Negro women are more critical than Negro men of the job the police are doing. Furthermore, although Negroes more than whites feel that the police are not "respectful" to them, persons of both races and sexes tend to feel that the police are not sufficiently respectful.

Nevertheless, in spite of some criticism, there is a general public reliance on the police for the control of crime. Associated with this

[41] See McIntyre, "Public Attitudes Toward Crime and Law Enforcement," pp. 41–44.

[42] George Gallup, "U.S. Public Gives Police Big Vote of Confidence," *The Gallup Report* (Princeton, N.J.: American Institute of Public Opinion, August 30, 1967).

[43] Ennis, *Criminalization in the United States,* pp. 52–72. Also see Phillip H. Ennis, "Crime, Victims, and the Police," *Trans-Action,* 4 (June, 1967), pp. 36–44.

acceptance (and mandate) is the public's willingness to permit the police considerable range in their efforts to control crime. A majority of those (73 per cent) interviewed in Washington, D.C., agreed that the police have the right to act tough when deemed necessary.[44] More than half (56 per cent) thought that there should be more use of police dogs. In the national survey, 52 per cent of the respondents believed that the police should have more power, and 42 per cent believed that police should risk arresting an innocent person rather than risk missing an offender.[45] Yet, the surveys found a concern among the public for protection of the civil rights of the individual in enforcement of the law. Some of this concern is related to a belief that there is discrimination against certain economic and racial groups.

The general positive acceptance of the police in America is a reflection of "the sacredness of the police as a social institution, especially among the less sophisticated lower-middle class — the people with 'Support your local police' bumper stickers who enliven their lives by reading about child molesters in the Sunday supplements."[46] It is not so much that we respect the law, but that we submit to popular sovereignty. Law *enforcement* represents something more and something other than the law. The police are allowed to operate a kind of order that limits any challenge to the social functions of the institution of law enforcement. It is assumed that law enforcement is good in itself. There may be occasional criticisms of incidents of police brutality, but to critically examine law enforcement as an institution is not an especially pressing interest of Americans.

Another indication that the public believes that repressive measures, rather than changes in social conditions, are the most effective means of controlling crime is found in attitudes about court actions. A Gallup survey in 1969 found that 75 per cent of adults believe that the courts do not deal harshly enough with criminals.[47] Only 2 per cent said that the courts in their area deal "too harshly" with criminals, while 13 per cent agreed that the treatment by the courts

[44] Biderman, Johnson, McIntyre, and Weis, *Report on a Pilot Study in the District of Columbia on Victimization and Attitudes Toward Law Enforcement*, pp. 144–149.

[45] Ennis, *Criminalization in the United States*, pp. 58–60.

[46] Edgar Z. Friedenberg, "Hooked on Law Enforcement," *The Nation* (October 16, 1967), pp. 360–361.

[47] *The New York Times*, February 16, 1969, p. 47.

is "about right." Further evidence of the public's desire to crack down on crime was indicated when 58 per cent of the respondents agreed that it was a good idea to give a double sentence to anyone who commits a crime with a gun. Similarly, 71 per cent of the respondents believed that it is a good idea to deny parole to a person convicted of crime a second time.

The public apparently believes that the courts are too lenient in their sentencing practices. Aside from this evaluative matter, the public has a fairly definite idea of the kinds of penalties that the courts should give for specific crimes. This was documented in a study conducted some years ago of the judgments of students in assigning punishments to thirteen selected felonies.[48] On the basis of a questionnaire, the students were asked to respond as if they were judges in criminal cases. A principal finding was a significant discrepancy between the penal law, the application of the law, and the judgments as to how the law should be applied in the assignment of sentences for the crimes. Severe child beating by a father was regarded as much more serious, in the penalty it deserves, than indicated in the law and actual sentences. There was, as well, a consistent and stable hierarchy of crimes and associated penalties in the minds of most of the students. Moreover, there were predictable relationships between an individual's personal characteristics (sex, socioeconomic status, and rural-urban backgrounds) and the punishments he assigned to the offenses. Women were inclined to assign longer prison sentences than men for such offenses as child beating and bigamy and shorter ones for assault with a deadly weapon; persons with an upper class background were inclined to assign longer prison sentences than those with a lower class background for such offenses as bribing a witness and child beating; and persons from rural areas were more inclined than those from urban areas to assign harsher punishments for such crimes as arson, attempted burglary, and grand larceny. To generalize from the findings, the public judgments were assigned according to the crime and its cultural meaning, in relation to the personal characteristics of the evaluators.

More recent research continues to show a pattern of public atti-

[48] Arnold M. Rose and Arthur E. Prell, "Does the Punishment Fit the Crime? A Study in Social Valuation," *American Journal of Sociology,* 61 (November, 1955), pp. 247–259.

tudes toward the punishment of specific offenses. In a national survey conducted in 1967, the public was asked the best way of dealing with an adult convicted of a specific crime.[49] The alternative sentences, from a list of seven crimes ranging from embezzlement to murder, were probation, a short prison sentence with parole, or a long prison sentence. The use of probation found little favor with the public. Considering each of the crimes, only about a quarter of the respondents felt that probation was an appropriate sentence. Only for prostitution, judged more harshly by women than men, did as much as 26 per cent of the public feel probation should be used. A further breakdown by education showed an increasingly severe attitude as the amount of education decreased. That is, those with less than a high school education were the most willing to have someone sent to prison.

Public attitudes toward the control of crime are not always logically consistent. Some ambivalence or even contradiction is to be expected in attitudes toward various means of crime control. Ultimately, opinions are based on valuation. One forced response on an issue may simultaneously call a number of divergent values into play. Consistency in attitudes toward crime and the control of crime is more often an accident than a logical association of underlying values.

Ambivalence in attitudes toward crime control can be found in the public opinion surveys and research studies. A study of adult attitudes toward the control of juvenile delinquency found that respondents in Wisconsin believed delinquents should be punished but, at the same time, that they should be treated.[50] Although differences followed social status, with persons of high social status showing less ambivalence between the espousal of a legalistic-punitive approach and a treatment approach, punishment of the delinquent was generally emphasized whereas at the same time treatment was favored.

A similar pattern of responses can be observed in the national survey which contained questions on prisons and corrections.[51] More than half the adults polled felt that the prison system was doing a

[49] Louis Harris and Associates, *The Public Looks at Crime and Corrections* (Washington, D.C.: Joint Commission on Correctional Manpower and Training, 1968), pp. 11–12.

[50] William P. Lentz, "Social Status and Attitudes Toward Delinquency Control," *Journal of Research in Crime and Delinquency,* 3 (July, 1966), pp. 147–154.

[51] Harris, *The Public Looks at Crime and Corrections,* pp. 7–9.

good job in helping to deal with the problem of crime. (The more education the participant had, the less likely he was to give the prison a positive rating.) But though the majority of the respondents believed in the worth of the prison as a form of punishment, an even larger proportion (72 per cent) felt that rehabilitation should be the main emphasis within the prison. In addition, there was little interest (only 20 per cent) among the respondents in the increased use of parole to release inmates from prison.

A final consideration in public attitudes toward the control of crime is that of attitudes toward the death penalty. Changes in attitudes toward capital punishment are among the most sensitive indicators of shifts in the public's orientation to crime control. There has been a gradual shift in the United States from a punitive reaction to one that is less oriented to punishment. Since 1953 Gallup has been polling the American public on capital punishment, asking: "Are you in favor of the death penalty for persons convicted of murder?"[52] In the 1953 survey, 68 per cent of the national sample favored the death penalty. By 1960 the proportion who favored capital punishment shifted to 51 per cent, and by 1965 the figure had decreased to 45 per cent. In 1966, 42 per cent of the public favored the death penalty.

Other surveys and studies support and amplify the extent to which the public is undergoing changes in attitudes toward capital punishment.[53] The amount of support for the death penalty varies from one segment of the population to another, and shifts in opinion are occurring at varying rates. A greater proportion of men than women favor the death penalty. However, the greatest amount of change in attitude toward capital punishment in the last few years has occurred among men. Also, whereas occupational groups such as law enforcement officers still tend to favor the death penalty, other occupational groups such as psychiatrists, penologists, and social workers are tending to oppose the death penalty.

Attitudinal changes such as these, occurring among the general public and within the segments associated with penal and correc-

[52] George Gallup, "Opposition to the Death Penalty Continues to Mount," *The Gallup Poll* (Princeton, N.J.: American Institute of Public Opinion, July 1, 1966).

[53] See Hugo Adam Bedau (ed.), *The Death Penalty in America* (Garden City, N.Y.: Anchor Books, 1964), pp. 231–236.

tional practices, are likely to affect the control policies of the future. Public attitudes are relevant because basically they are the sources of action. That which is regarded and handled as criminal begins in the minds of persons in some segments of society.

CONSEQUENCES OF CRIMINAL CONCEPTIONS

So it is that conceptions of crime are constructed and diffused throughout the segments of society. And the conceptions are important because of their consequences. But since they vary from one segment to another, they have different effects on the total society. That is, the conceptions most critical in creating a social reality of crime are those held by the power segments of the society. These are the segments that impose their views and actions on others in the name of the whole society. The social reality of crime is basically constructed from the criminal conceptions held by the most powerful segments of society.

Any conception of crime has its own set of consequences. Each conception provides a perspective as to what is regarded as crime, how crime should be controlled, how criminals should be punished and treated, and how the population is to conduct itself in an environment of crime and criminals. All these issues are resolved in actions. As thoughts become deeds, a social reality is constructed.

But the most significant consequence of a criminal conception is the creation of crime. Without the concept of crime, crime would not exist as a phenomenon. It follows that the more concern that surrounds the concept of crime, the greater is the probability that criminal definitions will be formulated and applied. The concept of crime must be reified in order to justify its existence.

CHAPTER TEN

The Politics of Reality

The conceptions of crime within any society are many and varied. The reality of crime is a multifaceted world of an infinite number of realities. But in the social reality that is constructed to cope concretely with crime, some criminal conceptions are more important than others. Particular criminal conceptions, those of the powerful segments of society, ultimately determine the nature of the social reality of crime. These are the criminal conceptions that are responsible for creating crime.

Conceptions of crime — the subjective aspect of the social reality of crime — are constructed with intentions, not merely to satisfy the imagination. We end up with some realities rather than others for good reason — because someone has something to protect. That protection can be achieved by the perpetuation of a certain view of reality. Realities are, then, the most subtle and insidious of our forms of social control. No weapon is stronger than the control of one's world of reality. It is the control of one's mind.

By constructing a reality that we are all to believe in, those in positions of power *legitimize* their authority. That which is believed to be true, to be the "real" nature of things, is good in itself. It is right simply because it *is,* and is not to be questioned or refuted. Believing is accepting. Hence, the reality of crime that is constructed for all of us by those in a position of power is the reality we tend to accept as our own. By doing so, we grant those in power the authority to carry out the actions that best promote their interests.

This is the *politics of reality*. The social reality of crime in politically organized society is constructed as a political act. Both private and governmental groups have a vested interest in constructing particular criminal conceptions that instruct official policy. From beginning to end, then, the construction of the social reality of crime is a political matter.

PERIODIC INVESTIGATIONS OF CRIME

At various times the public is made aware of the crime problem. Public alarm about crime fluctuates from one period to another.[1] And associated with each period is the belief in a new "crime wave." How and why are these waves manufactured? The answer can be found in part in the interests that have something to gain from constructing a reality that includes an aroused fear and anxiety about crime.

Concerted efforts to increase public concern about crime are often achieved by the appointment of committees to investigate what someone regards as the particular crime problem of the time. Crusades on crime have been organized for the explicit purpose of promoting a criminal conception. Realities of crime are shaped by such periodic investigations of crime.

Many of the crime commissions in the last fifty years have been organized in communities to investigate that which some leaders have regarded at the time as the local crime problem. In 1920 a number of civic groups in Cleveland (headed by the Cleveland Bar Association) commissioned a survey of crime. The final report concentrated on the machinery of criminal justice.[2] At about the same time the Chicago Crime Commission was established in response to a sensational case in which a gang of four men killed two armed guards carrying a factory payroll. The Chicago Crime Commission exists to this day, looking into various aspects of crime and criminal justice. Other cities, both in the past and in recent

[1] See Yale Kamisar, "When the Cops Were Not 'Handcuffed.'" *The New York Times Magazine,* November 7, 1965, p. 34.

[2] Roscoe Pound and Felix Frankfurter (eds.), *Criminal Justice in Cleveland* (Cleveland: The Cleveland Foundation, 1922).

times, have established commissions to investigate various aspects of the crime problem.[3]

New York, in particular, has been the setting for numerous criminal investigations. One of the earliest organizations was the Society for the Prevention of Crime, started in 1878. Eventually the Society developed a religious fervor under the leadership of the Reverend Charles Henry Parkhurst. In the 1920's, when a crime wave was the principal topic of conversation, the Society engaged the public by sponsoring an essay contest on how best to reduce crime. Professor Franklin H. Giddings and a panel of prominent citizens awarded the first prize of $2,500 to a former police captain and the second prize of $500 to a police detective. The proposals to curb crime included a criticism of the police commissioner, a recommendation that parole be eliminated, and the suggestion that the heads of prisoners be shaved and that they wear striped uniforms.

Following such efforts, a number of committees and citizen's groups concentrated on specific forms of crime and deviance in New York, especially on prostitution and organized crime. Criminal justice in the city received attention in the 1930's with the Appellate Court's appointment of the Seabury Commission. Considerable graft and corruption in the city government were exposed. Nevertheless, city officials, as could be expected, denounced and then ignored the investigation. Characteristically, Mayor Jimmy Walker responded by condemning those who called for further investigations as "slanderers of the fair name of the City we love."[4]

Crime commissions have been established to investigate the crime problem on the state as well as the local level. In 1925 the Missouri Bar Association called a meeting of civic and business leaders throughout the state to enlist their support for a statewide crime

[3] See Ralph G. Murdy, *Crime Commission Handbook* (Baltimore: Criminal Justice Commission, 1965), pp. 12–35. Also E. Connor, "Crime Commissions and Criminal Procedure in the United States since 1920," *Journal of Criminal Law, Criminology and Police Science,* 21 (May, 1930), pp. 129–144; Allen Eaton, *A Bibliography of Social Surveys* (New York: Russell Sage Foundation, 1930); A. F. Kuhlman (ed.), *A Guide to Material on Crime and Criminal Justice* (New York: H. W. Wilson, 1929); Virgil Peterson, *Crime Commissions in the United States* (Chicago: Chicago Crime Commission, 1945).

[4] William B. Northrop, *The Insolence of Office — the Story of the Seabury Investigations* (New York: G. P. Putnam's Sons, 1932), p. 54.

survey. Research by a staff covered a number of topics, including law enforcement, prosecution, penal sanctions, and corrections.[5] Although recommendations on the criminal justice system were made, few were implemented. The proposals, if they had been instituted, would have destroyed the political machines in the metropolitan areas of the state. Corrupt and inefficient criminal "justice" systems, as well as crime, are not such serious considerations when the interests of those who hold political power are at stake.

Similar commissions, with similar results, completed their tasks in other states during this same period.[6] The conclusion that can be drawn from all these efforts is that crime commissions have been appointed primarily for political reasons. Politicians would like to give the appearance to their constituents that something is being done about crime. But when the recommendations of the commissions go counter to the interests of the politicians, legislation is more likely to be restricted to controlling "the criminal" rather than to be directed toward reforming the criminal justice system. Yet, everyone can be happy with the results of a criminal investigation. Civic, business, and professional groups have been active; the researchers have carried out their study; politicians have fought crime without upsetting the political apparatus; and nothing has changed. All this has been accomplished by appointing a crime commission.

Until recent times, the major experiment with a crime commission on the national level has been the Wickersham Commission. The commission, formally titled the National Commission on Law Observance and Enforcement, and chaired by former United States Attorney General George W. Wickersham, was established by an act of Congress in 1929. From the beginning, the commission was the fulfillment of a campaign promise by Herbert Hoover to conduct a thorough inquiry into the enforcement of the prohibition laws.

Things had been going rather badly for the prohibition laws. Basically they seemed to be unenforceable. Furthermore, the lack of their

[5] Missouri Association for Criminal Justice, *The Missouri Crime Survey* (New York: Macmillan, 1926).

[6] Illinois Association for Criminal Justice, *The Illinois Crime Survey* (Chicago: Illinois Association for Criminal Justice, 1929); Wayne Morris and Ronald H. Beattie, *Survey of the Administration of Justice* (Eugene: University of Oregon Press, 1932).

enforcement was making a mockery of the American legal system. In response, the commission, with a large staff of researchers, assistants, and writers, completed an impressive report that ran to fifteen volumes.[7] Included in the volumes was material that extended beyond the enforcement of prohibition laws to such topics as the causes of crime, crime among the foreign born, child offenders, criminal statistics, the costs of crime, criminal courts, deportation, criminal procedure, and penal institutions.

The recommendations of the Wickersham Commission in regard to its primary focus, the enforcement of prohibition laws, were confusing and contradictory, indicating the desire of the commission to satisfy opposing interests. On the one hand, the federal government could rest with the satisfaction that there were no recommendations for a repeal of the prohibition laws. But on the other hand, the public was told that the laws were unenforceable. Prohibition ended shortly, nevertheless, out of its own exhaustion.

Today it is commonplace to condemn the Wickersham Commission as an ineffectual body and to bemoan the fact that no significant legislation and reform followed as a result of the commission's work. However, the immediate significance of the commission was considerable. For it provided a *forum* for the clash of diverse political, intellectual, and philosophical positions regarding crime and justice in America. That should be worth something, since such conflicts usually remain blurred and disguised from public view.

The lack of any long-term results from the crime commissions of the past is due to a number of factors which are now changing. The more recent crime commissions are closely tied to the power structure of the society. They are composed, moreover, of large technical staffs, representing the most respected institutions in the country. Furthermore, the commissions are organized along bureaucratic lines. Such organization assures some permanence and continuity, and also increases the possibility for the implementation of the proposals by the commissions. Finally, the activities of the commissions are made known today to most of the public. Through mass communication, we are all being presented with the image that crime is a national problem. The whole population is being alerted

[7] See especially National Commission on Law Observance and Enforcement, *Report on the Enforcement of the Prohibition Laws of the United States* (Washington, D.C.: U.S. Government Printing Office, 1931).

to a social reality of crime that is being constructed by government-appointed commissions.

THE PRESIDENT'S CRIME COMMISSION

On March 9, 1966, Lyndon Johnson told the nation:

> *The problems of crime bring us together. Even as we join in common action, we know there can be no instant victory. Ancient evils do not yield to easy conquest. We cannot limit our efforts to enemies we can see. We must, with equal resolve, seek out new knowledge, new techniques, and new understanding.*[8]

Johnson's resolve in a "war on crime" had been confirmed less than a year before (July 23, 1965) in the signing of an Executive Order that established the President's Commission on Law Enforcement and Administration of Justice.

The President's Crime Commission was composed of 19 commissioners, 63 staff members, 175 consultants, and hundreds of advisers. During the investigation, the commission called three national conferences, conducted five national surveys, held hundreds of meetings, and interviewed tens of thousands of persons. A number of publications resulted from the efforts of the commission and its staff. Several Task Force Reports were made on specific subjects and a series of Field Surveys reported the research findings. The investigation is summarized in the volume *The Challenge of Crime in a Free Society*.[9] The general report also contains the commission's recommendations — more than 200 specific proposals.

The appointment of the President's Crime Commission was basically an expedient political move.[10] During the presidential campaign of the previous year, Barry Goldwater had campaigned on the theme of "lawlessness." Although he lost the election, the

[8] President Lyndon B. Johnson, Message to the Congress, March 9, 1966.

[9] President's Commission on Law Enforcement and Administration of Justice, *The Challenge of Crime in a Free Society* (Washington, D.C.: U.S. Government Printing Office, 1967).

[10] See Isidor Silver, "Crime and Punishment," *Commentary,* 45 (March, 1968), pp. 68–73; Isidor Silver, "Introduction," *The Challenge of Crime in a Free Society* (New York: Avon, 1968), pp. 17–36.

theme became ingrained in the public's reality of crime. Johnson, recognizing the fears upon which the theme of "lawlessness" played, reacted by organizing something very American: a commission that would identify a broad evil, a thorough study of that problem, and proposals that would offend no one. Moreover, a "war on crime" would divert the public's attention from a nasty and unpopular war abroad to a common evil at home.

The commission was composed of "men and women of distinction," most of the members being ignorant of the problem they were supposed to analyze. All the commissioners, however, had a vested interest in the analysis of the crime problem. In typical Johnson consensus style, the commission's composition was a careful balance of recognized constituencies: members from the law enforcement establishment, lawyers, judges, the mayor of New York, a publisher, a university president, a couple of law professors, a civil rights leader, and two women. Although the group covered a range of opinion about crime, the report was noncontroversial and clearly within the bounds of the established political and legal order.

The recommendations of the commission reflect the "liberal" thinking of the Johnson consensus. The specific recommendations are related to the commission's conclusion that crime reduction is possible by the "vigorous" pursuit of the following objectives:

> First, society must seek to prevent crime before it happens by assuring all Americans a stake in the benefits and responsibilities of American life, by strengthening law enforcement, and by reducing criminal opportunities.
>
> Second, society's aim of reducing crime would be better served if the system of criminal justice developed a far broader range of techniques with which to deal with individual offenders.
>
> Third, the system of criminal justice must eliminate existing injustices if it is to achieve its ideals and win the respect and cooperation of all citizens.
>
> Fourth, the system of criminal justice must attract more people and better people — police, prosecutors, judges, defense attorneys, probation and parole officers, and corrections officials with more knowledge, expertise, initiative, and integrity.
>
> Fifth, there must be much more operational and basic re-

> search into the problems of crime and criminal administration, by those within and without the system of criminal justice.
>
> Sixth, the police, courts, and correctional agencies must be given substantially greater amounts of money if they are to improve their ability to control crime.
>
> Seventh, individual citizens, civic and business organizations, religious institutions, and all levels of government must take responsibility for planning and implementing the changes that must be made in the criminal justice system if crime is to be reduced.[11]

With the expenditure of enough energy and money, the reasoning goes, crime can be abolished without any significant alteration of American institutions.

Certainly the President's Crime Commission did not suggest any major alteration in the American legal system. For the commission, the causes of crime were to be found in the nature of individuals ("criminals") and in social conditions. That criminal law is in itself the "cause" of crime was not considered. No assessment was offered of the use of the criminal law as a sanction for human behavior.[12] The criminal law as a force in defining and perpetuating crime was not conceived of as being part of the reality of the crime problem. For the commission, crime is not that which the law defines as criminal, but is an evil that exists in spite of the law. Such evil, according to the President's Commission, can be eradicated in an ultimate victory over crime.

The President's Crime Commission has thus provided us with a particular conception of the reality of crime. The war on crime has become a political weapon to accomplish the objectives of those in positions of power. Moreover, the criminal reality that is being constructed for us is resulting in a reality of events. Our state of mind is leading to a particular kind of social order.

THE LAW AND ORDER CHALLENGE

The war on crime at the end of the 1960's culminated in legislation that has consequences for the future reality of crime. The legisla-

[11] President's Commission on Law Enforcement and Administration of Justice, *The Challenge of Crime in a Free Society*, p. vi.

[12] Herbert L. Packer, "Copping Out," *New York Review of Books*, 9 (October 12, 1967), pp. 17–20.

tion gave those who use crime as a political weapon the criminal reality they desired. The war on crime was thus escalated to the lofty issue of "law and order" in society.

On June 19, 1968, Lyndon Johnson signed the Omnibus Crime Control and Safe Streets Act. As originally conceived, the bill was to assist state and local governments in reducing the incidence of crime by increasing the effectiveness of law enforcement and criminal administration.[13] By the time the bill was passed, however, several controversial amendments were added embodying the increasing concern with law and order. One amendment (Title II) was a deliberate attempt to overturn previous Supreme Court decisions that supposedly were responsible for "coddling criminals" and "handcuffing the police." In the bill that was enacted, all voluntary confessions and eyewitness identifications — regardless of whether a defendant has been informed of his rights of counsel — could be admitted in federal trials. In another provision (Title III) state and local law enforcement agencies were given broad license to tap telephones and engage in other forms of eavesdropping. Law enforcement officials were permitted to engage in these practices for brief periods without even a court order. A final provision of the bill provided that any persons convicted of "inciting a riot or civil disorder," "organizing, promoting, encouraging, or participating in a riot or civil disorder," or "aiding and abetting any person in committing" such offenses shall be disqualified for employment by the federal government for five years. In the background of the law was the attempt to control by means of the criminal law any behavior that would threaten the established social and political order.

In signing the Crime Bill, President Johnson sounded a cautious note.[14] Though stating that the bill contained "more good than bad," he said that Congress "has taken a potentially dangerous step by sanctioning eavesdropping and wiretapping by federal, state, and local officials in an almost unlimited variety of situations." If the nation is not careful, he observed, some provisions of the bill "could result in producing a nation of snoopers bending

[13] Richard Harris, "Annals of Legislation: The Turning Point," *The New Yorker* (December 14, 1968), pp. 68–179.

[14] "Transcript of Johnson's Statement on Signing Crime and Safety Bill," *The New York Times,* June 20, 1968, p. 23.

through the keyholes of the homes and offices in America, spying on our neighbors." Despite such shortcomings, however, the president concluded that the new law "will help lift the stain of crime and the shadow of fear from the streets of our communities."

The law and order issue continues to be a politically potent device. In the presidential campaign of 1968, each of the candidates developed his own version of law and order as a battle cry for the campaign. Richard Nixon, then the Republican candidate, touched it off in his acceptance speech at Miami, charging that "some of our courts in their decisions have gone too far in weakening the peace forces as against the criminal," and adding that "if we are to restore order and respect for law in this country, there's one place we're going to begin: we're going to have a new Attorney General of the United States of America."[15] In even greater detail, Nixon presented his position on law and order in a paper "Toward Freedom from Fear." His position was made clear:

> Just as justice dictates that innocent men go free, it also means that guilty men must pay the penalty for their crimes. It is this second part of justice to which the nation must begin to address itself in earnest. . . . By now Americans, I believe, have learned the hard way that a society that is lenient and permissive for criminals is a society that is neither safe nor secure for innocent men and women.[16]

Hubert Humphrey, the Democratic candidate, responded by promising to halt "rioting, burning, sniping, mugging, traffic in narcotics and disregard for law." But he added that "the answer lies in reasoned effective action by our authorities, not in attacks on our courts, our laws or our Attorney General."

The former governor of Alabama, George Wallace, running as an independent candidate, took the most extreme position on the law and order issue. His solution was simple: free the police of all restraint. Wallace repeated his position every place he went, usually bringing the house down with the passage: "If you walk out of this hotel tonight and someone knocks you on the head,

[15] Quoted in Fred J. Cook, "There's Always A Crime Wave — How Bad's This One?" *The New York Times Magazine,* October 6, 1968, p. 38. The quotations from the other presidental candidates are also in Cook's article.

[16] Quoted in Albert J. Reiss, "Crime, Law and Order as Election Issues," *Trans-Action,* 5 (October, 1968), p. 3.

he'll be out of jail before *you're* out of the hospital, and on Monday morning they'll try the policeman instead of the criminal. That's right, we're going to have a *police* state for folks who burn the cities down. They aren't going to burn any more cities." The law and order issue was also becoming a racist euphemism for suppressing the demands of blacks in the urban ghettoes.

The law and order issue became part of the public domain by the end of the campaign. Even the candidates for lesser offices assisted by jumping on the law and order bandwagon. Other political men, such as J. Edgar Hoover, whose job as director of the FBI was assured by Nixon's election, contributed as well. Hoover's statement perhaps best captures the implication of the demand for law and order. By the time of election, Hoover could proclaim with all seriousness: "Justice is incidental to law and order." A distinct conceptual reality of crime and justice had been established.

CRIME AND LEGITIMACY OF AUTHORITY IN A FREE SOCIETY

The drive for law and order brings into sharp focus questions about the nature of the state and the relation of the individual to the state. In particular, the conflict between two fundamental rights is made clear in the law and order issue. That conflict involves, on the one hand, the state's right to protect its citizens and property and, on the other, the citizen's right to individual freedom. Moreover, the question arises of the extent to which the state can claim and exercise authority over the citizenry.

According to the democratic principle, the state's power is legitimate only when it is so regarded by the citizens. Furthermore, the state's authority to govern is legitimate only as long as certain constitutional guarantees are not violated in the course of governing. When the state's use of power to control others does not rest on consent and legal guarantees, the authority of the state is illegitimate and need not be obeyed. In fact, obeying illegitimate authority would be an unprincipled act. A society can only be "a free society," to use the phraseology of the President's Crime Commission, when the authority of the state is legitimate.

In the fervor of the war on crime and in the issue of law and order, basic individual rights have been jeopardized. Parts of the

Omnibus Crime Control and Safe Streets Act are undoubtedly unconstitutional (making suspect the legitimacy of the government). By statute, Congress has violated several provisions of the Constitution and decisions of the Supreme Court that guarantee individual rights. The Bill of Rights is in danger of being tacitly repealed in the name of law and order. For the moment at least, the forces that would restrict individual freedom are dominating the forces that would protect the individual from the aggression of the state.

The civil liberties of the citizen are further being attacked by prominent legal authorities. By the end of 1968, such persons as Judge Henry J. Friendly of the United States Court of Appeals in New York were proposing constitutional amendments that would substantially limit the self-incrimination clause of the Fifth Amendment.[17] Former governor Thomas E. Dewey, in his endorsement of the Friendly proposal, even went beyond the proposal by suggesting that "we could get along just as well if we repealed the Fifth Amendment." Proposals such as these have the possibility of establishing a government tyranny through the cause of law and order. In trying to promote a free society, these forces could easily negate the very principle of a free society.

More recently President Nixon has affirmed the tendency toward the restriction of civil liberties. Soon after his election, Nixon advanced an anti-crime program for the District of Columbia that would deprive the citizen of a basic civil liberty.[18] Nixon asked for authority "whereby dangerous hard-core recidivists could be held in temporary pretrial detention when they have been charged with crimes and when their continued pretrial release presents a clear danger to the community." This "preventive detention" proposal is a breach of the legal doctrine that presumes innocence until guilt is proved in court. We have reached a point in the war on crime in which serious consideration can be given to the reversal of the presumption of a citizen's innocence in favor of the presumption of the citizen's guilt.

The state has attempted to obtain support for its anti-civil libertarian challenge by claiming that such actions must be taken

[17] See Sidney E. Zion, "How It Would Be Without the Fifth," *The New York Times*, December 8, 1968, p. E 9.

[18] Fred P. Graham, "When Bail Is a License for Crime," *The New York Times,* February 2, 1969, p. E 11.

in order to control "violence." Increased use of police power has been justified as necessary to combat civil disorder. But the paradox is that the violence that the police attempt to control is inspired in many instances by the police themselves. And more important, much of the violence in these situations is actually committed by the police.

The state, quite understandably, does not regard its own actions as violence, or if such actions are considered, they are defined at best as "legitimate violence." So it is that looting of property during race "riots" is defined as violence by the state, but killing of looters is legitimate.[19] And those who would peaceably demonstrate against injustices of various kinds are subject to similar displays of police rioting and violence.[20] Many people tend to be led to a belief in the justified use of force by the state.

> American society has always endorsed legitimate violence. In fact, most of us do not consider it violence at all. Respect for law has become one of the nastiest features of the American character. Anything we can get legitimated passes without question. We feel free to destroy Vietnam as long as we enjoy the complicity of its officially recognized government — even though we know that government to be a fictional piece of apparatus we ourselves helped to install. And any disruptive social group to which lawlessness can be imputed is a fair target for violent suppression.[21]

Law enforcement can in itself be a form of instant violence. Those who call for law and order are supporters of this "legitimate violence," since it is being used to defend the established social order.

Violence, then, is the most direct form of state power. And since law is a monopoly of the state, violence when carried out by the state is usually legal.[22] But when the citizens no longer grant

[19] See *Report of the National Advisory Commission on Civil Disorders* (New York: Bantam Books, 1968), pp. 299–336.

[20] *Rights in Conflict, A Report Submitted by Daniel Walker to the National Commission on the Causes and Prevention of Violence* (New York: Bantam Books, 1968).

[21] Edgar Z. Friedenberg, "Legitimate Violence," *The Nation* (June 24, 1968), p. 822. Also see Paul Goodman, "Reflections on Civil Disobedience," *Liberation* (July–August, 1968), pp. 11–15.

[22] H. L. Nieburg, "Violence, Law and the Social Process," *American Behavioral Scientist,* 11 (March–April, 1968), pp. 17–19.

the state the authority to conduct violence, such violence is no longer legitimate, no matter how legal it may be. The time may be coming when state power exercised through the threat or use of violence will no longer be regarded as legitimate. No government can rule — practically or morally — without legitimacy. Power is legitimate only when it is granted by the citizenry. The law and order challenge has brought into the open the conflict between those who grant legitimacy to state violence and those who do not. A conceptual reality of crime is being constructed which recognizes this conflict. The result is not yet clear. Only the future holds the resolution. Let us hope that the war on crime will not be won if it means the further legitimation of state violence and the denial of individual freedom.

CONCLUSION

Crime begins in the mind. In this sense a conceptual reality of crime is constructed. But the consequence of such construction is a world of actions and events; that is, a phenomenal reality. The whole developmental complex of conception and phenomenon, in reference to crime, is the construction of the social reality of crime.

As I have argued throughout this book, crime is a definition of human conduct that becomes part of the social world. Furthermore, the most important conceptions of crime are those held by the powerful segments of society. Criminal definitions in their official formulations, consequently, are the most powerful means of social control, used to control actions which conflict with the interest of those who create these criminal definitions. Such is the dynamic process of the construction of the social reality of crime.

In recent times the theme of law and order has shaped the official conception of crime. That conception of reality has already influenced the phenomenal reality of crime. The state has used its power through the law to define as criminal what it regards as a threat to the social and political order. Crime has become a political weapon that is used to the advantage of those who control the processes of government.

In many ways, the war on crime has become a substitute for the older war on internal communism. Crime today is similarly being billed as "a threat to the American way of life."[23] We are all being told to join the struggle. "What can the individual citizen do?" The campaign calls us:

> Officials have stated that the police, the courts and the correctional agencies, acting alone, cannot control the problem. Crime and delinquency *can* be reduced when each citizen recognizes that it is his problem, too, and when he becomes personally involved in the struggle. In fact, it is maintained that the *only* answer to reducing crime significantly is *vigorous citizen action.*[24]

There is no end. The conceptions, with their inflammatory rhetoric, and the consequential events go on. It can only be hoped that in constructing the social reality of crime the protection of individual rights will also be included. The social reality of crime is indeed very much a part of the modern world. In constructing this reality, some of the most important problems of modern times are being played out.

[23] *Crime Control Projects for Citizens and Their Organizations* (New York: National Council on Crime and Delinquency, 1968), p. 4.

[24] *Crime, Delinquency and You,* pamphlet printed by Kemper Insurance for the National Council on Crime and Delinquency, Chicago, 1967, p. 1. Various anti-crime groups for citizens are discussed in Murdy, *Crime Commission Handbook,* pp. 36–43.

Index to Names

Abramowitz, E., 188*n*
Adler, M. J., 32*n*
Akers, R. L., 16*n*, 21*n*, 81*n*, 217*n*, 242*n*
Albert, R. S., 163*n*
Allen, F. A., 170*n*
Allott, A. W., 53*n*
Allport, G. W., 13*n*-14*n*
Amir, M., 249*n*, 251*n*
Anderson, C. D., 152*n*
Anderson, R. T., 269*n*
Ares, C. E., 144*n*
Arnold, T. W., 31*n*
Attenborough, R. L., 48*n*
Auerbach, C. A., 33*n*
Babst, D. V., 194*n*
Bachmuth, R., 282*n*
Bachrach, P., 13*n*
Ball, J. C., 216*n*, 264*n*
Ballard, K. B., Jr., 193*n*, 194*n*
Baltzell, D., 231*n*
Banfield, L., 152*n*
Banton, M., 19*n*, 114*n*, 115*n*, 129*n*
Baratz, M. S., 13*n*
Barrett, E. L., Jr., 104*n*
Barron, M. L., 229*n*
Beattie, R. H., 252*n*, 306*n*
Becker, H., 8*n*, 14
Becker, H. S., 16*n*, 93*n*, 243*n*
Bedua, H. A., 185*n*, 301*n*
Bell, D., 60*n*, 231*n*
Bellamy, E., 75
Bendix, R., 8*n*
Bensing, R. C., 232*n*
Bentler, R. A., 217*n*
Berger, B., 8*n*
Berger, P., 13*n*, 15*n*, 22*n*
Berk, B. B., 180*n*
Beutel, F., 279*n*
Bevan, W., 163*n*
Bianchi, H., 5*n*
Biderman, A. D., 293*n*, 298*n*
Bierstedt, R., 6*n*, 11*n*
Bittner, E., 19*n*, 114*n*
Black, D. J., 124-125, 125-126, 128*n*, 130*n*
Blackstone, W., 51
Blaisdell, D. C., 12*n*, 31*n*
Blaustein, A. P., 152*n*
Bloch, H. A., 215*n*
Blumberg, A. S., 19*n*, 149, 150*n*, 157
Blumer, H., 235*n*, 285*n*
Boggs, S. L., 228*n*
Bordua, D. J., 16*n*, 19*n*, 118*n*, 121*n*, 135*n*, 219*n*, 226*n*
Brannon, W. T., 272*n*
Briar, S., 20*n*, 128, 130*n*, 243
Bridgman, P. W., 5*n*
Broom, L., 285*n*
Brown, E. C., 51*n*
Brown, R., 7*n*
Brown, R. S., 257*n*
Bruce, P. A., 87*n*
Bryan, J. H., 259-260
Buckley, W., 9*n*
Bullock, H. A., 142*n*, 232*n*
Bunge, M., 5*n*
Burgess, R. L., 21*n*, 242*n*
Burnham, D., 124*n*
Cadwallader, M. L., 265
Calhoun, G. M., 44, 45-46
Cameron, M. O., 252*n*, 273*n*
Cantor, N., 5*n*
Cantrel, H., 239
Carlin, J. E., 152*n*, 153, 154, 156*n*
Carter, R. M., 165*n*, 166*n*
Chambliss, W. J., 17*n*, 95-96, 118*n*, 189*n*
Chandler, R., 290
Chapin, B., 58*n*
Chell, E. P., 67
Chilton, R. J., 226*n*
Christiansen, K. O., 257*n*
Christopher, T. W., 81
Cicourel, A. V., 19*n*, 150*n*
Clark, A. L., 22*n*, 245*n*, 278*n*
Clark, J. P., 19*n*, 113*n*, 225*n*, 236*n*
Clark, R. E., 194*n*
Claster, D. S., 266*n*

Clemmer, D., 176*n*
Cleveland, G., 75
Clinard, M. B., 86*n*, 135*n*, 181, 200*n*, 225*n*, 230*n*, 236*n*, 238*n*, 248*n*, 249*n*, 250, 253*n*, 254*n*, 255*n*, 257, 266, 269-270, 273
Cloward, R. A., 173*n*, 174*n*, 175*n*, 201*n*, 202*n*, 212, 227*n*
Cohen, A. K., 219*n*, 236*n*
Cohen, J., 181*n*
Cohen, M. R., 7*n*
Cohn, B. S., 52*n*, 53
Coke, E., 51
Commager, H. S., 74*n*, 76*n*
Connor, E., 305*n*
Cook, F. J., 312*n*
Cook, T. I., 13*n*
Cooley, R. W., 112*n*
Cooper, P., 75
Corsini, R. J., 246*n*
Coser, L. A., 10*n*
Cottrell, L. S., Jr., 285*n*
Crawford, P. L., 197*n*
Cressey, D. R., 173, 174*n*, 177-178, 178*n*, 179*n*, 181, 183, 189*n*, 190*n*, 200, 211*n*, 221*n*, 222*n*, 254*n*
Cumming, E., 114*n*
Cumming, I., 114*n*
Dahrendorf, R., 9, 10, 11, 38*n*, 39*n*
Davis, D. B., 289
Davis, E. E., 36*n*
Davis, F. J., 36*n*, 263*n*, 281*n*
DeFleur, L. B., 227*n*
DeFleur, M. L., 20*n*, 211*n*, 239*n*, 240*n*, 291*n*
Dean, C. W., 194*n*
Depew, F. M., 81*n*
Derrett, M., 52*n*
Deutscher, I., 90*n*
Dewey, T. E., 314
Dickens, C., 290
Dickson, D. T., 93*n*
Dietrick, D. C., 219*n*
Dimants, R., 171*n*
Dinitz, S., 237, 238
Donnelly, R. C., 107*n*
Douglas, J. D., 3*n*
Dow, T. E., Jr., 22*n*
Doyle, A. C., 290
Drivers, E. D., 251*n*
Dudden, A. P., 74*n*
Duggan, T. J., 194*n*
Dumpson, J. R., 197*n*
Duncan, J., 52*n*
Dunn, C. W., 81
Easton, D., 11*n*
Eaton, A., 305*n*
Edell, L., 114*n*
Edward I, King of England, 110
Edward II, King of England, 110
Ehrlich, H. J., 112*n*
Ehrmann, H. B., 190*n*
Ehrmann, H. W., 12*n*, 31*n*
Elliott, D. S., 236*n*
Elliott, M. A., 229*n*, 258*n*
Elman, R. M., 202*n*
Empey, L. T., 181*n*
England, R. W., Jr., 219*n*-220*n*
Engler, R., 12*n*, 31*n*
Enniss, P. H., 126*n*, 293*n*, 297*n*, 298*n*
Erikson, E. H., 215*n*
Erikson, K. T., 16*n*, 17*n*, 62*n*, 280, 281
Esselstyn, T. C., 117*n*
Evan, W. M., 37*n*
Fanin, L. F., 238*n*
Feldman, H. W., 262-263
Ferdinand, T. N., 225*n*
Ferracuti, F., 232*n*, 252*n*
Fiddle, S., 264*n*
Fielding, H., 110
Finestone, H., 262*n*, 264*n*
Finkel, R. H., 185*n*
Fleming, I., 290-291
Foote, C., 94*n*, 132*n*, 144*n*
Foster, A., 257*n*
Foster, H. H., Jr., 36*n*, 88*n*
Frank, J., 31*n*, 159*n*
Frankel, E., 251*n*
Frankfurter, F., 304*n*
Friedenberg, E. Z., 215*n*, 298, 315*n*
Friedmann, W., 32, 41, 76*n*
Friedrich, C. J., 51*n*
Friendly, A., 284*n*
Friendly, H. J., 314
Frum, H. S., 265*n*-266*n*
Fuller, R. C., 16*n*
Gable, R. W., 12*n*, 31*n*
Galanter, M., 52*n*
Galbraith, J. K., 41*n*
Gallup, G., 297*n*, 301
Galtung, J., 178*n*
Garabedian, P. G., 176*n*
Garceau, O., 12*n*, 31*n*
Gardiner, J. A., 295
Garfinkel, H., 142*n*
Gaudet, F. J., 166*n*
Geis, G., 30*n*, 31, 230*n*, 232*n*, 254, 255, 260*n*
Gellhorn, W., 59
George, H., 75
Gershenovitz, A., 226*n*
Gerth, H. H., 11*n*, 38*n*

Gerver, I., 160*n*
Gibbons, D. C., 23*n*, 182*n*, 265, 295*n*
Gibbs, J. P., 16*n*, 22*n*, 245*n*, 278*n*
Giddings, F. H., 305
Gillin, J. L., 249*n*, 251*n*
Gipson, L. H., 57*n*
Glaser, D., 176*n*, 179*n*, 182*n*, 184*n*, 194*n*, 195*n*, 241
Glueck, E. T., 246*n*
Glueck, S., 246*n*
Goebel, J., Jr., 51*n*, 111*n*
Goffman, E., 13*n*, 173*n*
Goldfarb, R., 144*n*, 284*n*
Goldman, A., 290-291
Goldman, N., 19*n*, 116*n*, 117*n*
Goldstein, A. S., 160*n*
Goldstein, J., 104*n*
Goldwater, B., 308
Goodman, P., 215*n*
Gordon, C. W., 90*n*
Gottfredson, D. M., 193*n*, 194*n*
Graham, F. P., 314*n*
Green, E., 168*n*
Grimshaw, A. D., 135*n*, 232*n*
Grodzins, M., 258*n*
Gross, L., 6*n*, 8*n*
Gross, S. Z., 171*n*
Gruen, E. S., 47*n*
Gusfield, J. R., 92*n*
Guthrie, W., 289
Hall, J., 17*n*, 70, 71-72, 73-74, 106
Halleck, S. L., 160*n*
Hammett, D., 290
Hammond, P. Y., 12*n*, 31*n*
Handy, W., 232*n*, 249*n*, 250*n*
Hannigan, A. St. J., 53*n*-54*n*
Hanson, N. R., 6*n*
Hardin, C. M., 12*n*, 31*n*
Hare, N., 288*n*
Harris, G. E., 65*n*
Harris, G. S., 166*n*
Harris, L., 300*n*
Harris, R., 311*n*
Hart, H. M., Jr., 37*n*
Hartung, F. E., 189*n*, 208, 254*n*
Harvey, W. B., 53*n*
Haskins, G. L., 34*n*, 61*n*, 62*n*, 63*n*, 64*n*
Hauser, P., 285*n*
Hawkins, C., 163*n*
Hyner, N. S., 169*n*
Heisenberg, W., 5*n*
Henderson, A. M., 14*n*
Hibbert, C., 290*n*, 291*n*
Hirshi, T., 5*n*
Hoebel, E. A., 31*n*, 37*n*
Hollingshed, A. B., 217*n*
Holmes, O. W., 31*n*
Homans, G. C., 7
Honingmann, J. J., 16*n*
Hook, S., 5*n*
Hooton, E. A., 246*n*
Hoover, H., 306
Hoover, J. E., 313
Horowitz, I. L., 11*n*, 18*n*, 236*n*
Horton, P. B., 56-57
Howard, J., 153
Humphrey, H., 312
Hurst, J. W., 31*n*, 58*n*
Huxley, J., 14*n*
Hyman, H. H., 60*n*
Hyneman, C. S., 13*n*
Jackman, N. R., 260*n*
Jacob, H., 139
Jacobs, J. A., 199-200
James, R. M., 163*n*, 164*n*
Jeffery, C. R., 16*n*, 17*n*, 21*n*, 36*n*, 47*n*, 242
Jeudwine, J. W., 49*n*
Johns, W. L., 66*n*
Johnson, A. W., 66*n*
Johnson, E. H., 188*n*, 195*n*
Johnson, G. B., 129*n*, 222*n*
Johnson, L. A., 293*n*, 298*n*
Johnson, L. B., 308, 309, 311-312
Johnson, R. C., 274*n*
Kadish, S. H., 104*n*
Kallet, A., 79
Kalven, H., Jr., 161*n*, 162, 164*n*
Kamisar, Y., 304*n*
Kaplan, A., 7*n*, 11*n*
Karreker, C. H., 111*n*
Kassebaum, G. G., 178*n*
Katz, E., 284*n*
Kay, B., 237*n*
Kefauver, E., 81
Kelley, A., 189
Kempton, M., 202
Kennedy, W. C., 178*n*
Kenney, J. P., 252*n*
Kephart, W. M., 130*n*
Key, V. O., Jr., 12*n*, 31*n*
Kinch, J. W., 238*n*
King, C. E., 172*n*
Kirchheimer, O., 16*n*-17*n*, 56, 95*n*, 140*n*
Kitsuse, J. I., 16*n*, 219*n*, 279*n*
Klapp, O. E., 286*n*, 287-288
Klapper, J. T., 284*n*
Klein, J., 262*n*
Knowlton, R. E., 157*n*
Kobrin, S., 199*n*, 200*n*, 227*n*, 268*n*
Korn, R., 181*n*
Kuhlman, A. F., 305*n*

Kunkel, W., 47
LaFave, W. R., 101*n*, 105, 130, 131, 132*n*
Lacey, F. W., 94
Ladinsky, J., 153*n*
Lamb, R. D., 79
Lander, B., 226*n*
Landis, J. R., 236*n*
Lane, R., 111*n*, 255*n*
Lasswell, H. D., 11*n*
Latham, E., 12*n*, 31*n*
Lejins, P., 5*n*
Lehman, W., 152*n*
Lemert, E. M., 22*n*, 152*n*, 245*n*, 247, 252*n*, 258*n*, 266*n*, 271-272, 273*n*
Lentz, W. P., 22*n*-23*n*, 225*n*, 300*n*
Leslie, G. R., 56-57
Levy, L. W., 58*n*
Lewis, A. H., 65*n*
Leznoff, M., 262*n*
Liebowitz, M., 18*n*, 236*n*
Liell, J. T., 118*n*
Lindesmith, A. R., 17*n*, 92*n*, 93-94, 231, 264*n*
Llewellyn, K. N., 31*n*
Lloyd, H. D., 75
Logan, N., 216*n*
Loiseaux, P. R., 163*n*
Lombroso, C., 246
Lorber, J., 21*n*
Lottier, S., 223*n*
Lowi, T., 41*n*
Luckmann, T., 15*n*, 22*n*
Lunt, P. S., 217*n*
Lymon, J. L., 110*n*
Lynd, H. M., 235
McCleary, R., 174*n*
McClintock, F. H., 249, 251*n*
McConnell, G., 12*n*, 31*n*
McCord, J., 196*n*
McCord, W., 196*n*
McCorkle, L. W., 181*n*
McDonald, J. F., 266*n*
McIntyre, J., 23*n*, 292*n*, 293*n*, 297*n*, 298*n*
MacIver, R., 9*n*, 14, 198*n*
Mack, R. W., 11*n*
McKay, H. D., 225*n*, 266*n*
McNamara, J. H., 121*n*
Malamud, D. I., 197*n*
Malinowski, B., 37*n*
Maloney, M., 290*n*
Mann, R. D., 164*n*
Matza, D., 5*n*, 219*n*, 220*n*, 243, 244*n*
Mark, M., 13*n*
Marx, K., 38*n*
Maurer, D. W., 260*n*, 273*n*
Maxwell, G., 236*n*
Mayfield, P. N., 163*n*
Mead, G. H., 235*n*
Mercer, J. R., 16*n*
Merton, R. K., 221*n*, 229*n*, 285*n*
Messinger, S. L., 153, 175*n*
Michael, J., 32*n*
Miller, D., 7*n*
Miller, F. W., 143*n*
Miller, P., 51*n*, 61*n*
Miller, S. M., 282*n*
Miller, W. B., 197*n*, 198*n*, 218*n*
Millis, H. A., 12*n*, 31*n*
Mills, C. W., 11*n*, 38*n*
Mintz, M., 79*n*, 80*n*
Mitchell, R. E., 119*n*
Mitchell, W. C., 13*n*
Monroe, L. J., 217*n*
Montgomery, R. E., 12*n*, 31*n*
Morison, S. E., 74*n*, 76*n*, 77*n*
Morris, R., 216*n*
Morris, R. B., 62*n*
Morris, R. E., 160*n*
Morris, T., 222*n*, 279-280
Morris, W., 306*n*
Morris, W. A., 110*n*
Moses, E. R., 222*n*
Mouledoux, J. C., 135*n*, 178*n*-179*n*, 257*n*
Mueller, G. O. W., 86*n*
Muller, H. J., 14*n*
Munoz, L., 263*n*
Murdy, R. G., 305*n*, 317*n*
Murray, E., 237, 238*n*
Murray, R. K., 135*n*, 257*n*
Myerhoff, B. G., 220*n*
Myerhoff, H. L., 220*n*
Mylonas, A. D., 23*n*
Nadel, S. F., 13*n*, 14
Nagel, E., 7*n*
Nagel, S. S., 166*n*
Nathanson, M., 6*n*
Naughton, T. R., 111*n*
Nedrud, D. R., 151*n*
Nelson, H. L., 58*n*
Newman, D. J., 78*n*, 145*n*, 146, 147-148, 149, 294-295
Nicholas, B., 46*n*
Nieburg, H. L., 315*n*
Niederhoffer, A., 19*n*, 121, 123, 215*n*
Nisbet, R. A., 8*n*, 221*n*
Nixon, R. M., 312, 314
Nolde, H. C., 189
Northrop, W. B., 305*n*
Nye, F. I., 215*n*, 217*n*
Oaks, D. H., 152*n*

O'Donnell, J., 264*n*
Ohlin, L. E., 170-171, 171*n*, 172, 174*n*, 194*n*, 201*n*, 212, 227*n*
Olson, V. J., 217*n*
O'Neal, P., 249*n*
O'Toole, R., 260*n*
Packer, H. L., 58*n*, 106*n*, 257n-258*n*, 310*n*
Paget, D., 188*n*
Pappenfort, D. M., 171*n*
Parker, I. C., 54-55
Parkhurst, C. H., 305
Parsons, T., 13*n*, 14
Pearl, A., 181*n*
Pearson, J., 291*n*
Peel, R., 110
Peltason, J., 140*n*
Perrow, C., 13*n*, 180*n*
Peterson, R. A., 249*n*
Peterson, V. W., 268*n*, 305*n*
Pettigrew, T. F., 232*n*
Pfantz, H. W., 227*n*, 236*n*
Phillips, D. L., 262*n*
Phillips, W., 75
Piliavin, I., 20*n*, 128, 130*n*, 179*n*, 243
Pittman, D. J., 90*n*, 232*n*, 249*n*, 250*n*
Piven, F. F., 202*n*
Piven, H., 171*n*
Ploscowe, M., 86*n*, 87*n*
Poe, E. A., 290
Polk, K., 226*n*
Polsky, N., 273*n*
Porter, C. O., 152*n*
Porterfield, A. L., 232*n*
Pound, R., 17*n*, 30, 31, 32-35, 36, 50*n*, 51*n*, 137*n*, 304*n*
Powers, E., 62*n*, 196*n*
Preiss, J. J., 112*n*
Prell, A. E., 299*n*
Preston, W., Jr., 135*n*-136*n*, 258*n*
Quinney, R., 3*n*, 4*n*, 15*n*, 20*n*, 29*n*, 86*n*, 135*n*, 211*n*, 225*n*, 226*n*, 230*n*, 236*n*, 239*n*, 240*n*, 248*n*, 249*n*, 250, 254*n*, 255*n*, 257, 266, 269-270, 273
Rabow, J., 181*n*
Rankin, A., 144*n*
Reckless, W. C., 5*n*, 23*n*, 214*n*, 224*n*, 237, 238, 267, 268*n*
Reed, J. P., 172*n*
Reich, C. A., 42
Reisman, F., 181*n*
Reiss, A. J., Jr., 19*n*, 118*n*, 124*n*, 124-125, 125-126, 128*n*, 130*n*, 216*n*, 227*n*, 240*n*
Remington, F. J., 143*n*
Rhodes, A. L., 227*n*, 240*n*
Riley, J. W., Jr., 284*n*-285*n*
Riley, M. W., 284*n*-285*n*
Ringold, S. M., 188*n*
Robinson, D., Jr., 107*n*
Robinson, W. S., 54, 163*n*
Rodzinowicz, L., 109*n*-110*n*
Roebuck, J. B., 265, 273*n*-274*n*
Rogers, E. M., 22*n*, 285*n*
Rooney, E. A., 23*n*, 295*n*
Roosevelt, F. D., 80
Roosevelt, T., 76
Rose, A. M., 299*n*
Rosen, L., 282*n*
Ross, E. A., 29-30
Rubington, E., 90*n*
Rusche, G., 16*n*-17*n*, 95*n*
St. John, C. W., 166*n*
Savitz, L. D., 185*n*, 189*n*
Sayles, G. O., 49*n*
Scarpitti, F. R., 180*n*, 236*n*, 238*n*
Schermerhorn, R. A., 13*n*
Schilling, W., 12*n*, 31*n*
Schlink, F. J., 79
Schmid, C. F., 226*n*
Schofield, M., 260-261, 262
Schrage, C., 8*n*, 179*n*
Schroeder, O., 232*n*
Schubert, G., 139*n*
Schuessler, K. F., 189*n*
Schur, E. M., 30*n*, 89*n*, 93*n*, 158, 248*n*, 264*n*, 274*n*
Schutz, A., 6*n*, 14
Schwartz, M., 239*n*
Schwartz, R. D., 278*n*
Segerstedt, T. T., 279*n*
Sellin, T., 16*n*, 142*n*, 185*n*, 189*n*, 190
Selvin, H. C., 5*n*
Selznick, P., 37*n*
Shallo, J. P., 112*n*
Shannon, L. W., 223*n*
Shaw, C. R., 199-200, 225*n*, 266*n*
Sheldon, W. H., 246*n*
Sherman, J., 75
Sherry, A. H., 96
Shibutani, T., 13*n*, 235*n*, 239*n*
Shinn, C. H., 55*n*
Shirley, G., 55
Short, J. F., Jr., 197*n*, 215*n*, 217*n*, 238*n*, 240*n*
Sibley, M. Q., 258*n*
Siebert, F. S., 58*n*
Silver, A., 135*n*
Silver, I., 308*n*
Silverstein, L., 152*n*
Simmel, G., 10*n*-11*n*
Simmons, J. L., 286

Simon, R. J., 164*n*
Sinclair, A., 91-92
Sklar, R. B., 172*n*
Skolnick, J. H., 19*n*, 108, 122, 123, 133*n*, 136*n*, 150*n*, 194*n*, 278*n*
Small, A. W., 30
Smigel, E. O., 294*n*
Smith, B., 111*n*
Smith, D. R., 127*n*
Smith, J. M., 58*n*
Snyder, G. H., 12*n*, 31*n*
Solmes, A., 110*n*
Spengel, I., 227*n*
Spier, R. B., 232*n*
Spillane, M., 290
Starkey, L. M., Jr., 291*n*
Stedman, M. S., 12*n*, 31*n*
Stephenson, R. M., 180*n*
Sternberg, D., 170*n*
Stinchcombe, A. L., 19*n*, 119*n*
Stoddard, E. R., 124*n*
Stone, J., 33*n*
Stratton, J. R., 179*n*
Street, D., 176*n*, 180*n*
Strodtbeck, F. L., 163*n*, 164*n*, 197*n*, 238*n*
Sturz, H., 144*n*
Suchman, E. A., 263*n*, 263-264
Sudnow, D., 19*n*, 148*n*
Suffet, F., 144*n*
Surrency, E. C., 51*n*
Sutherland, E. H., 17*n*-18*n*, 20*n*, 83, 84, 181, 189*n*, 190*n*, 200, 210, 211, 222*n*, 230*n*, 240*n*, 255*n*, 271*n*, 272*n*
Svalastoga, K., 251*n*
Swanson, A. H., 82*n*
Sykes, G. M., 172*n*, 173, 173*n*, 175, 176*n*, 177, 219*n*, 220*n*, 244*n*
Szasz, T. S., 160*n*, 161
Taber, M., 171*n*
Taft, D. R., 229*n*
Taft, P., 232*n*
Tangri, S. S., 239*n*
Tannenbaum, F., 22*n*, 245
Tappan, P. W., 82*n*, 84, 85, 165*n*
Thorelli, H. B., 73*n*, 74*n*
Thrasher, F. M., 226
Tittle, C. R., 179*n*
Tittle, D. P., 179*n*
Trebach, A. S., 159*n*, 166*n*
Truman, D., 12*n*, 31*n*, 139*n*
Tufts, E., 200*n*
Turk, A. T., 16*n*, 17*n*, 20*n*
Turner, H. A., 12*n*, 31*n*
Turner, R. H., 239*n*
Twain, M., 288
Tyler, G., 268*n*
Van Lanengham, D. E., 171*n*
Van Tyne, C. H., 59*n*
Van Vechten, C. C., 221*n*
Vernon, D. H., 81*n*
Vines, K., 139
Vinter, R. D., 180*n*
Vold, G. B., 17*n*, 18*n*, 182*n*, 231*n*
Von Hentig, H., 246*n*
Voss, H. L., 240*n*
Wade, A. L., 253*n*
Walker, D., 315
Walker, J., 305
Wallace, G., 312-313
Wallerstein, J. S., 215*n*
Ward, D. A., 178*n*
Ward, L. F., 30
Wardlow, A., 258*n*
Warner, W. L., 217*n*
Washburne, G. A., 57*n*
Weber, G. H., 179*n*
Weber, M., 11*n*, 14
Weis, A. W., 293*n*, 298*n*
Weisberg, B., 107*n*
Wellford, C., 176*n*
Wenninger, E. P., 225*n*, 236*n*
Westley, W. A., 19*n*, 120, 232*n*, 262*n*
Westwood, G., 262*n*
Wheeler, S., 119*n*, 176, 179*n*
Whyte, W. F., 226*n*
Wickersham, G. W., 306
Wiley, H. W., 78
Wilkins, L. T., 165*n*-166*n*
Wilks, J. A., 222*n*, 224*n*
Williams, R. M., Jr., 10, 258*n*
Willie, C. V., 226*n*
Willoughby, W. R., 12*n*, 31*n*
Wilner, D. M., 178*n*
Wilson, J. Q., 19*n*, 114*n*, 119
Winick, C., 264*n*
Winthrop, J., 61-62
Witmer, H. L., 196*n*, 200*n*
Woetzel, R. K., 230
Wolff, H. J., 46*n*
Wolff, K. H., 11*n*
Wolfgang, M. E., 129*n*, 189, 220*n*, 232*n*, 249*n*, 250*n*, 251*n*, 252*n*
Wood, A. L., 19*n*, 155, 156*n*
Wright, G., 163*n*
Wrong, D., 13*n*
Wyle, C. J., 215*n*
Yablonsky, L., 227*n*
Zald, M., 179*n*, 180*n*
Zeigler, H., 139*n*
Zeisel, H., 161*n*, 162, 164*n*
Zion, S. E., 214*n*

Index to Subjects

Abortion:
public attitudes on, 295
regulation of, 89-90
Abortion Law Reform Association, 89
Accused (*see* Defendant)
Acquittal, 149
Action (*see* Social action)
Active interests, defined, 39
Adjudication (*see also* Trial):
nontrial, in pretrial procedings, 143-145
use of, 145
Administration:
of capital punishment, 184-190
of criminal justice, 40, 137-168
of prisons, 173, 177-184
of probation and parole, 170-171
special interest groups and, 18-20
Adolescents (*see* Juvenile)
Adultery laws, 87
Adversary principle of justice, 150
Advertising regulation, 80, 81
Africa, British law in, 52, 53-54
Age distribution of offenses, 213-217
Alcoholism (*see* Drunkenness)
Ambivalence in stereotyping criminals, 287-291
American Colonies:
Justice and government in, 137
law enforcement in, 110-111
laws: criminal law development, 60-65; English common law and, 50-52, 57-59; political order and, 58-69; Sunday laws, 66; on vagrancy, 96
settlement and development diversities, 51
American Indians, regulation of, 54
American Law Institute, 99
Amnesty for offenders, 184
Ancient Greece, criminal law in, 45-46
Ancient Rome, criminal law in, 46-47
Anglo-Saxons, legal system of, 48
Antihero, criminals as, 288-289
Antiloyalist laws, 58-59
Antimiscegenation statutes, 87
Anti-Saloon League, 91
Antitrust laws:
attitudes on breaches of, 254-255
historic development of, 73-77
Appeal of sentencing, 158
Acquittal, 164-165
Armed robbery, 265
Arraignment, 144, 157
Arrest, 101
bases of initial charge, 144
community attitudes on, 115
complexity of relationships in, 124
decision-making after, 141
discretion and, 114, 127-129, 129-136
juvenile, 116-117, 127-128
objectives of, 130-132
pretrial proceedings after, 143-145
for prevention, 132
for protection, 131
rate: police organization and, 119; race and, 129-130
record (*see* Criminal record)
Association, differential, 20-21
behavior learning and, 211-212
criminal behavior and, 240-241, 242
Attitudes on crime (*see* Public conceptions of crime)
Authority (*see also* Social control):
legitimization of, 303-304; crime and, 313-316
police command system, 118
of prison staff, 177
relations in social collectives, 36

Bail:
alternatives to, 144
injustices in procedures, 143-144
Bastardy laws, 87
Behavior (*see also* Criminal behavior; Personal action patterns; Social action):
crime as definition of, 15-16, 43
crime definitions and, 16-18

criminal vs. noncriminal, 207
law and regulation of, 40
morality protection, 86-97
normative systems and, 20-21, 210
patterns (*see* Personal action patterns)
professional, of lawyers, 156-157
reference group and, 239-240
regulation of private, 132-133
sexual conduct regulation, 86-90
social meaning and, 22-23
social organization and understanding, 207
systems of regulating, 36
Biblical authority, law and, 61-65
Bill of Rights, 51, 314
Black market practices, 254, 255
Blood-feud, British, 48
"Blue laws" (*see* Sunday laws)
Body of Liberties, Massachusetts Bay Colony, 62
Boston Delinquency Project, 197, 198
Bow Street Runners, England, 110
Burglary, 70-73
attitudes on, 293-294
charge reduction, 148
Business ethics:
lawful behavior and, 230-231
nature of violations of, 253-256
organized crime and, 231

Call girls, 259-260
Cambridge-Somerville Youth Study, 196, 198
Capital laws, 62-64
Capital punishment, 184-190
arguments favoring, 189-190
characteristics of executed, 186, 188-189
decline in use, 185-186, 190
discretion and, 184-186
functions of, 190
public attitudes on, 301-302
regional variations in, 186, 187
Capitalism, ethics of, 230-231
Career patterns:
in criminal law practice, 153-156
of offenders, 248
Carrier's Case of 1473, England, 70-73
Casework approach:
of prevention, 196
of probation officers, 171
Caveat emptor attitude, 77, 78
Causation:
as criminology theory, 5-7
social, 6
Chicago Area Project, 199-200
Chicago Crime Commission, 304
Christianity, criminal law and, 48
Churches (*see* Religion)
Cities (*see* Urban areas)
Citizens (*see* Community; Public conceptions of crime)
Civil liberties:
due process: police concepts, 123; right of, 107
law and order challenge and, 313-314
of offenders, 203
personal protection against state action, 106, 107-108
preventive detention concept and, 314
public concern with, 298
Clemency, 184, 186, 188
Colonies, criminal law development in, 49-56 (*see also* American colonies)
Command system, police, 118
Common law:
antitrust legislation tradition in, 73-74
English, American colonies and, 50-52, 57-59
Commissions on crime, 291-292, 304-312 (*see also* President's Commission on Law Enforcement and Administration of Justice)
Commitment:
action decision and, 243-244
of political offenders, 257
Communication:
behavior learning and, 210
crime conception diffusion and, 22-23
order in prisons, 174
police communications center, 118
Communism scare, 135
Communist Control Act (1954), 60
Community (*see also* Public conceptions of crime):
anxiety over sex crimes, 84-85
community development programs, 198-201
crime prevention programs, 195-202; conflict and, 197-198; whole community and, 201
criminal behavior and, 222, 224-228
implications of action programs, 201-202
juvenile aid programs, 201-202
law enforcement and: expectations on, 115-116, 117; homogeneity and, 115-117
personal action patterns and reactions of, 244-248
police and, 113-118; attitudes on police, 115-116, 232, 290-291, 297-298; expectations and police action, 115-116,

117; homogeneity and, 115-117; police discretion and, 114-118, 130-132; police encounters with, 120, 124-129; police mobilization, 124-125; role of police, 113-118, 125-127; violence and, 232
public order offenses and, 259-264
setting and reaction to crime, 295-296
treatment centers for prisoners, 181
Commutation of sentences, 184, 186, 188
Competency determination, 160
Comstock Act (1873), 87, 88
Conceptions of crime (*see* Public conceptions of crime)
Conduct (*see* Behavior; Criminal behavior; Personal action patterns; Social action)
Confessions, admissibility of, 106, 107, 311
Confidence men, 271-272
Conflict:
community prevention programs and, 197-198
criminal definitions and, 17
functions of social, 10-11
interest structure and, 39
juvenile crime and neighborhood, 226-227
juvenile subcultures and, 227
power struggle and, 11
in social structure, 9-11
Conformity:
to law, 229
of prisoners, 176-177
Conscientious objectors, 258
Consensus:
model of criminal law, 32
in social structure, 9-10, 208
Consequences:
behavior and anticipated, 21
criminal behavior maintenance by, 242-243
Constitution, U.S.:
Bill of Rights, 51, 314
Eighteenth Amendment, 90-92
Fifth Amendment, 107, 314
Fourteenth Amendment, 74, 107
Fourth Amendment, 107
on interstate commerce, 74
law and order concept and, 314
on law enforcement, 187
on right of counsel, 151
on right of jury trial, 161
on self-incrimination, 107, 314
Sixth Amendment, 151, 161
Consumers, offenses against, 294-295
Conviction (*See also* Sentencing; Verdict):
agreement, plea bargaining and, 146-148
effects of criminal, 202-204, 247-248
guilty pleas and, 144, 145
judge vs. jury on, 164-165
minority group membership and, 142
type of counsel and, 152-153
Covenant, Puritan, 61-65
Conventional offense behavior, 264-267
Correction system, 169-204 (*see also* Prison)
emphasis on correction, 169-170
custody objectives of, 173, 174, 175
organization of, 103
power segment and, 17-18
public attitudes on, 301
punishment vs. treatment-oriented, 169
variations in, 170
Corruption, attitudes on, 296
Counsel (*see* Lawyer)
Counseling in prisons, 181
Courts (*see also* Judge; Sentencing; Supreme Court, U.S.; Trial):
arraignment, 144, 157
decision-making by, 140-143; extra-legal factors and, 141-142; variations in, 141-143
discretion use by, 140-143
interest groups and, 139-140
juvenile, 170
law and order concept and, 314
as law-givers, 106
organization of, 150
pleas, 144-150
politics and, 138-140
probation revocation hearings, 172
prosecution and nontrial adjudication, 143-150
public attitudes on, 298-300
on right of counsel, 151
role in legal system, 101, 102-103
variations in systems, 142-143
Crime, 15-24 (*see also* Criminal behavior; Criminal definitions; Offense; and specific topic)
communication and diffusion of concepts, 22-23, 24
criminal conceptions and creation of, 15, 20-22, 24, 302
heterogeneous vs. homogeneous concept of society and, 208-210
as human conduct definition, 43
man and society in theory of, 8-15

police organization and recording, 119-120
relation to legal system, 3-4
theories: 4-8, 24-25; causation, 5-7; construction, 7-8; epistemology, 4-5; ontology, 4

Crime prevention:
arrest for, 132
capital punishment and, 189-190
casework approach to, 196
community programs, 195-202
imprisonment and, 181-184
nature of, 316-317
preventive detention concept, 314
public attitudes on, 296-302

Criminal behavior, 248-273 (*see also* Offense; and specific topic)
age-sex structure, 213-217
community variations in, 222, 224-228
conventional offenses, 264-267
crime study and, 4
development and criminal definitions, 20-22, 24, 210-213
ecology of patterns, 222-228
ethnic-racial structure, 220-222
learning, 210-213; opportunity and, 211-212; situation and, 211-212
objectivity definition, 212
occasional property offenses, 252-253
occupational offenses, 253-256
operant nature of, 21
political offenses, 236, 256-259
probability terminology, 212-213
professional offenses, 267, 270-273
public morals and, 132-133
public order offenses, 90, 259-264
rates, 211
rationalization of, 254-255
regional variations in, 222, 223-224
social class and, 217-220
structural sources, 213-222
violent personal offenses, 249-252

Criminal definitions:
application of, 18-20, 24
behavior patterns and probability of, 20-22, 24, 210-213
communication of, 22-23, 24
as crime creation, 15-16, 20-22, 24, 302
formulation of, 16-18, 24
objectivity and, 212
removal of, 202-204

Criminal law, 4, 29-42 (*see also* specific law and/or topic)
American cultural hypocrisy and, 229-230
consensus model, 32
historic emergence, 40, 44-56; American frontier law, 54-56; ancient Greece, 45-46; ancient Rome, 46-47; in colonies and territories, 49-56, 57-59; in England, 47-49; interests and, 43-97; Massachusetts Bay Colony, 62-64; political order and, 56-60; religion and, 60-70; social context, 44; standards and, 40, 50
interests and, 17-18, 18-20, 43-97
justice concept and, 137-168
philosophies of, 29-30
political order protection and, 56-60
power segments and, 17-18
public welfare and, 77
sociology of, 32-35

Criminal record:
of committers of violent crimes, 249
sentencing and previous, 168

Criminals (*see* Defendant; Offender)

Culture (see also Society):
assimilation of prison, 176
behavior and, 20-21
general themes, 228-233
reaction to crime and, 277-281
violence in American, 231-232, 289

Custody objectives of prisons, 173, 174, 175

Custom, as rule system, 36*n*

Death penalty (*see* Capital punishment)

Decision-making (*see also* Discretion):
in capital punishment administration, 184-186
in identity creation, 235
interest groups and, 12, 140
judicial, 140-143; hidden factors in, 137-138; interest groups and, 140
in law enforcement, 105
in parole granting, 191, 192-194
in prisons, 174
by probation officers, 172
in sentencing, 165-166
stages in legal system, 101

Declaration of Independence, 51

Defendant (*see also* Offender):
decision-making on, 141
judicial discretion and, 138-139
jury trial as choice of, 161-162
legal representation of, 151-153
legal rights of, 151
manipulation by lawyers, 157
presentence investigation, 165
right of counsel, 106, 107-108
as witness for himself, 159

Defense attorney, 150

in jury selection, 162-163
as mediator, 156
in plea bargaining, 148-149
presentence investigation and, 165
provision of, 151-153
public defender systems, 152
trial role of, 157
witness use by, 159-160
Delinquency subculture, 219, 227
Demeanor, arrest and, 127-128
Democracy:
in ancient Greece, 45-46
criminal law and American, 51
paradoxical ideology in political, 56-57
police organization and governmental, 109
state power over individual in, 313-314
Detached worker prevention programs, 196-197
Detention (*see* Prison)
Deterrence (*see* Crime prevention)
Deviance:
law violation as social, 236
manipulation of deviancy definition, 212-222
perspectives in study of, 16
primary vs. secondary, 247
stereotypes of deviants, 286
Differential association, 20-21
behavior learning and, 211-212
criminal behavior and, 240-241, 242
Diffusion of criminal concepts, 281-285
Discretion (*see also* Decision-making):
in capital punishment administration, 184-186
in commutation of execution, 186, 188
in judicial process, 140-143
in judicial system, 138-139
in law administration, 40
in pardon granting, 188
in parole granting, 191, 192-194
police (*see* Police, discretion)
Disorderly conduct arrest, 132
Domesday Survey, England, 48
Dormant laws, enforcement of, 133-134
Drug addiction:
criminal laws on, 85, 92-94
patterns in, 262-264
personal meaning of, 263-264
public attitudes on, 295
reasons for, 262-263
stereotypes of addicts, 286
Drug industry:
federal inquiry into, 81-82
pure food and drug laws, 77-82, 294-295
Drunkenness, 90-92
arrests for, 131
conviction of alcoholics for, 90
Due process:
police concepts of, 123
right of, 107
Durham-Humphrey Amendment (1951) of Federal Food, Drug and Cosmetic Act, 80
Durham insanity determination, 160

Eavesdropping, 106, 311
Economy (*see also* Business ethics):
increasing complexities, 77-78
interests and economic order, 35, 38
legislation in control of, 73-77, 254-255
Educational order, interests and, 38
Eighteenth Amendment, 90-92
Elementary tort, criminal law vs., 44
Enforcement (*see* Law enforcement)
England (*see* Great Britain)
Epistemology, 4-5
Escobedo v. Illinois (1964), 108
Espionage Acts (1917-1918), 59
Ethnic group, criminal behavior and, 220-222
Execution (*see* Capital punishment)
Experience:
action and, 235
theories and meaning of, 4
Expert witnesses, 160-161

Family, sexual conduct regulation and protection of, 86-87
Fear of crime, 292-293
Federal Bureau of Investigation (FBI), 109
on average sentences, 167
on crime and sex and race, 213*n*-214*n*
on ethnic distribution of crime, 221
on regional distribution of crime, 223
on urban crime, 224
Federal Bureau of Narcotics, 93
Federal Food and Drug Act (1906), 79
Federal Food, Drug and Cosmetic Act (1935), 80, 294-295
Federal government (*see also* Constitution, U.S.; Supreme Court, U.S.):
antinarcotic laws, 93
civil liberties and, 313-316
crime studies, 306-313 (*see also* President's Commission on Law Enforcement and Administration of Justice)
drug industry inquiry, 81-82
judicial system diversity, 142
law enforcement agencies, 111-112

police in protection of interests, 135-136
subversion statutes, 59-60
violence as form of power of, 315-316
Felonies:
jury trial for, 161
plea bargaining in, 146-148
plea attitudes on punishment for, 299
Feudalism, criminal law and, 48
"Firm" lawyers, 153-156
Fifth Amendment, 107, 314
Forgery:
action patterns in, 252-253
prosecution manner, 162
Formal interests, defined, 38-39
Fornication laws, 86
Fourteenth Amendment, 74, 107
Fourth Amendment, 107
Free enterprise ethic, behavior and, 230-231
Frontier:
behavior and ethic of, 229
criminal law development in, 54-56

Gambling, attitudes on, 296
Gang activity:
development, in juveniles, 226-227
progression to adult offenses, 264-266, 268
rural areas, 225
work with gangs, 196-198
Gault case, 151
Geographic variaton:
criminal behavior, 223-224
executions, 186, 187
parole granting, 191, 192-193, 194
sentencing practices, 167, 168
Ghana, British law in, 53
Gideon v. Wainwright (1963), 107
God, word of, 61-65
Government (*see also* Federal government; States):
British, criminal law emergence and, 47-49
justice and interests of, 140
interests and nature of, 40-42
police organization and nature of, 109, 135
political protest and law enforcement, 56-60, 134-136
Great Britain:
abortion regulation, 89
common law: in American colonies, 50-52, 57-59; antitrust legislation tradition in, 73-74; in India and Africa, 52-54
community attitudes on police, 115
drug addiction approach, 93-94
homosexuality laws, 89
law enforcement history, 109-110
legal concept of theft, 70-73
political unfication and criminal law, 47-49
Sunday laws, 65, 66, 69
vagrancy law development, 94-96
Wolfenden Report on prostitution, 88-89
Group experiences, behavior and, 239-241
Group support, 238
occupational violations and, 255
of political offenders, 258-259
of professional offenders, 272-273
Group theory for offenders, 182
Groups, social differentiation and, 10
Guilty pleas, 101
convictions under, 144, 145
judicial necessity of, 146
jury trial and, 161, 162
negotiation of, 145-150

Halfway houses for prisoners, 181
Harlem (New York City) detached worker program, 197
Harrison Act (1914), 92-93
Hero, criminal as, 287-289
Hierarchies:
in organized crime, 267-268, 269
prison, 173-174
Homicide (*see* Murder)
Homosexuality, 260-262
criminal penalties for, 89
life style in, 261-262
objectives in arrests for, 132
public attitudes on, 295
social role learning in, 260-261
stereotypes of homosexuals, 286
Humanism, 13
Hypocrisy, behavior and, 229-230

Identification of offenders, 311
Identity:
achievement of sense of, 234-239;
criminal behavior and, 236-239, 241-242
aspiration achievement and, 235, 236
concepts, delinquency and, 237-239
crises, 235-236; sex differences in, 215-216
importance of, 235-236
maintenance of non-criminal self-concept, 253-254
nonconformity and search for, 13
reference group and, 239-240

self-definition and definitions of others, 245-246
shared reality worlds and, 239
sources of personal, 234
Ideology:
conflict and diversity of, 9
criminally defined behavior and, 208-210, 236
drug abuse and, 262-263
full enforcement and, 104
justice as abstract, 137
occupational, of legal agents, 19-20
paradoxical, in political democracy, 56-57
police (*see* Police, ideology)
of political offenders, 258-259
in politics, 257
prison inmate code, 175-177
Illegal evidence, regulation of, 106, 107
Immigration and Nationality Act (1952), 60
Imprisonment (*see* Prison)
Incest laws, 86
India, British law in, 52-53
Indictment:
as basis for charge, 144
minority group membership and, 142
Individual lawyers, 153-156
Intention, in crime conception, 303-304
Interactions, personal action patterns and, 210, 244-245
Interests:
analyzing in law, 35
antitrust legislation and, 74-76
categorization, 34-35, 38
courts and, 139-140
criminal definition application and, 16-18, 18-20
criminal law formulation and, 43-97
defined, 38, 39
differential structure of, 37-38
food and drug laws and, 80
institutional orders of, 38
law as representation of, 40
operating in prisons, 174
organization of, 12, 38-39
political order and, 30-32, 38, 41-42
political parties as, 74, 75
Pound's classification, 32-35
power structure and, 12, 39
prohibition and, 91-92
public policy and, 11-13, 39
public vs. private, 41-42
structure, 37-39; conflict-power concept, 39; in contemporary society, 40-42
Sunday laws and, 67-70
theories of, 30-31, 32-35
vagrancy laws and, 95-96
Internal Security Act (1950), 59-60
Interpersonal contacts:
interpretation of mass media and, 285
violence as result of, 249-252
Interpretation of statutes, enforcement and, 104
Investigations of crime, 304-313 (*see also* President's Commission on Law Enforcement and Administration of Justice)
Isolation of police, 113-114

Jail (*see* Prison)
Job training for juveniles, 201
Judge (*see also* Sentencing; Verdict):
discretion of, 139
early itinerant British, 49
instructions in trial, 157
judgment, plea and, 144-145
plea negotiation and, 149-150
role of, 150
sentencing, 165-168; background and attitudes and, 166-168
trial by, 158
verdict, jury's verdict vs., 164-165
Jury:
background, influence of, 162-163, 163-164
choice of, 157, 162-163
foreman selection, 163
influence of jurors, 164
participation of jurors, 163-164
verdict, judges' verdicts vs., 164-165; rendition of, 157
waiver of, 162
Jury trial, 161-165
criminal justice and, 162
social factors and, 162-164
use of, 161-162
Justice:
administration of, 137-168
adversary system and, 150
politics and, 138-140
as symbol, 137
Justices of the peace, England, 110
Juvenile:
behavior, 215-216; characteristics of area and, 226-227; community reactions and, 245-246; self-concept and, 237-239; social class and, 215, 217, 218-220
community aid for, 201-202

crime prevention programs with, 196-198
drug experimentation patterns, 262-264
offenders: age distribution, 213, 214-215; factors in case disposition, 127-128; progression to adult offenses, 264-266, 268; public conceptions on delinquency causes, 297; rural, 253
patterns of handling, 116-117
rights of legal representation, 151
self-reporting of delinquency, 214-215
sexual deviance, 87
social class: behavior and, 215, 217, 218-220; learning traditions and, 218-220
subculture development by, 227
Juvenile courts, 170

Kefauver-Hart Drug Act (1962), 81
Kinship order, 38, 48

Labeling regulations, 80, 81
Law (*see also* Capital laws; Criminal law; and specific topic):
American legal system, 102-103
conformity to, 229
as dynamic process, 37
interests and, 32-35
interpretation and enforcement, 104
New Deal, 76-77
in politically organized society, 36-37
as social force, 32, 33-34, 36-37
Law and order challenge, 308-309, 310-313, 316
civil liberties and, 313-314
Law enforcement, 101-136 (*see also* Discretion; and specific topic)
American colonies, 110-11
community and, 113-118, 296-302
development of British, 109-110
idea of full, 104
legal regulation of, 105-108
offense situation and, 129-136
organizational demands and, 104
orientation and, 104
police ideology and, 120-124
police organization and, 118-120
political protest and, 56-60, 134-136
power segments and, 17
procedural restrictions and, 104
public attitudes on, 296-302
of sexual psychopath laws, 84-85
special interests and, 18-20
Sunday laws, 67, 133-134
systems, described, 108-113
types of, 111

"Laws and Liberties," Massachusetts Bay Colony, 62-64
Lawyer (*see also* Defense attorney; Prosecutor):
criminal: behavior and ethics of, 156-157; career patterns of, 153-156; competition for cases, 154-155
criminal and civil compared, 155
individual and "firm" compared, 153-156
in manipulation of defendants, 157
reference plans, 152
rights of accused for representation, 151-153
stereotypes of, 290, 291
types of legal representation, 152-153
Learning criminal behavior patterns, 210-213, 240-244
Legal aid system, 152
Liberties (*see* Civil liberties)
Lord's Day Alliance, 133-134

McCarran Act (1950), 59-60
McCarran-Walter Act (1952), 60
McGowan v. Maryland, 68-69
McNabb v. United States (1943), 107
Mallory v. United States (1957), 107
Mapp v. Ohio (1961), 107
Marriage, legal protection as institution, 86-87
Marshal, Office of U.S., 112
Maryland, Sunday Law of, 68-69
Mass media, criminal conceptions and, 281-285
Massachusetts:
colonial: adultery laws, 87; Bill of Rights, 137; Puritan ethic and reaction to crime, 280-281; Scriptures and Law in, 60-65
Sunday Law, 67-68
Massiah v. United States (1964), 108
Metropolitan Police Act (1829), England, 110
Mining camp regulation, 55-56
Minority groups, punishment and, 142
Miranda v. Arizona (1966), 108
Missouri, crime survey in, 305-306
M'Naghten test, 160
Mobilization for Youth, New York City, 201-202
Mobilization of police, 124-125
Morality (*see* Public morals)
Murder:
action patterns in, 250, 251
indictment for, 142

prosecution for, 162
public attitudes on execution for, 301

National Commission on Law Observance and Enforcement, 306-307
National Organization for Decent Literature, 88
Natural law concepts, 51
Negotiation of pleas, 145-150
Neutralization of legal norms, 243-244
New Deal legislation, 76-77
New Jersey, Sunday Law of, 69
New Weight Act (1919), 79
New York City:
crime investigations, 305
Youth Board, 197
New York State:
drug addiction law, 85
Sunday laws, 66-67, 68, 133-134
Nolo contendere plea, 144
Nontrial adjudication, 143-145
Norman conquest, British law and, 48-49
Nonconformity, self-identity search and, 13
Norms (*see also* Ideology):
attitudes and, 278-279
behavior and, 20-21, 210
conflict and, 9
criminal definitions and, 207
neutralization of legal, 243-244
occupational violations and, 255-256
physical, in definition of offenders, 246-247
political offenses and, 257-258
professional, for criminal lawyers, 156-157
of reaction, 278-279
as rule system, 36*n*
in sexual psychopath definition, 84-85
violent behavior and, 252
Not guilty pleas, 145

Objective reality, 4-5
Obscenity regulation, 87-88
Occupation:
attitude on capital punishment and, 301-302
occupational offenses, 253-256; attitudes on, 294-295
organization and ideology of legal agents, 19-20
police: occupational ideology, 120-124; variations in, 118-119
Offender, 4 (*see also* Defendant; Juvenile, offenders)
career of, defined, 248
civil rights of, 203
decision-making on, 141
group support of, 18; defined, 248; political, 258-259; professional, 272-273
indictment, 142, 144
presentence investigation, 165
provision for release, 143-144
removal of criminal definition from, 202-204
role in crime creation, 127-129
treatment as patient, 84
Offense, 248-273 (*see also* specific offense)
age-sex distribution, 213-217
case disposition and nature of, 143
community distribution of, 222, 224-228
concurrent, 147
conventional offense behavior, 264-267
decision-making on, 129-136, 141
dropped charges, 147-148
ethnic-racial distribution, 220-222
jury trial and, 161, 162
occupational offense behavior, 253-256
organized offense behavior, 231, 267-270
plea bargaining and, 147; concurrent, 147; dropped charges, 147-148; reduced charges, 148-149
police organization and recording, 119-120
political (*see* Political protest)
professional, 270-273
property offense behavior, 252-253, 265-267, 293-294
public order offenses, 259-264
reduction of charges, 148-149
regional distribution, 222, 223-224
rehabilitative therapy and, 182-183
sentencing and, 166; capital punishment, 185, 186, 187; public attitudes on, 299, 300
situation of, law enforcement and, 129-136
social class distribution, 217-220
violent personal offenses, 249-252
Omnibus Crime Control and Safe Streets Act (1968), 311, 313-314
On-the-spot citation, 143
Ontology, 4
Operant nature of criminal behavior, 242-243
Opportunity, criminal behavior learning and, 211-212
Order (*see* Peace keeping; Public order)
Organized crime, 23, 267-270

business patterns and, 231
career of persons in, 268-269
group support of, 272-273
hierarchic structure of, 267-268, 269
legal system and, 269-270
socioeconomic factors and, 268

Pardon, criminal, 184, 188
Parole, 190-195 (*see also* Probation)
administration of, 170-171
average period of, 194
conditions of, 194-195
discretion in, 191, 192-194
extent of use, 170, 190-191
possibilities for, 149
pretrial, 144
regulation and supervision, 194-195
role of parole officer, 195
violation of, 194, 195
Peace keeping:
law enforcement and, 114
political protest and, 135
Personal action patterns, 234-274 (*see also* Behavior; Criminal behavior; social action)
achievement of sense of self, 234-239
association, identification, and commitment, 239-244
community development and, 198-199
criminal definitions and, 210-213; as responses to, 244-248; structuring and, 20-22
criminal trials and, 158-159
defined, 234
development of, 21-22; interactions and, 210, 244-245
personal meaning of, 274
possibilities for, 13-14
social reactions and, 244-248
structuring, 20-22, 213-222
Personal offenses, violent, 249-252
Petty theft, 148
Physical stereotypes of criminals, 246-247
Pinkerton's National Detective Agency, 112
Planned Parenthood Federation, 90
Plea, 144-150 (*see also* Guilty pleas)
decision-making on, 141
negotiation of, 101, 145-150; advantages, 149-150; conviction and, 146-148; interactions of prosecution and defense in, 148
offenses following, 157
options in, 144-145
trial and, 145
Pluralism:
political process and, 12-13
social force and legal, 333
Police (*see also* Law enforcement): anti-Negro attitudes, 130
community and: attitudes on, 115-116, 232, 290-291, 297-298; community expectations on enforcement, 115-116, 117; community homogeneity and, 115-117; discretion use and, 114-118, 130-132; encounters with citizens, 120, 124-129; mobilization and, 124-125; public order offense behavior, 259-264; role in community, 113-118; social roles, 125-127; violence and, 232
cynicism of, 122-123
discretion, 104-105; arrest decision, 114, 127-129; community and, 114-118, 130-132; dormant law enforcement, 133-134; political protest and, 134-136; public morals and, 132-133; race and, 129-130; rural areas, 117
dual function, 114
ideology, 120-124; due process and, 123; image of "troublemaker," 128-129; on police work, 121-122; precinct vs. academy, 121-122; training and, 120-122; violence use and, 123-124; working personality and, 122
isolation of, 113-114
legal regulation of, 105-108
mobilization, 124-125
occupational roles, 118-119
organization, 118-120; bureaucratization, 118; command system, 118; communications center, 118; in democratic vs. authoritarian states, 109; effectiveness and, 119; functional divisions, 118-119; isolation and, 113-114; professionalization, 108; reported crimes and, 119-120
private police agencies, 112
problems, 106, 120; of rookies, 121-122
professionalization of, 108
role: in American legal system, 101, 102; in community, 113-118, 125-127; control-freedom dilemma, 106; in crime creation, 126-127; in dormant law enforcement, 133-134; dual, 114; social, 125-127; supportive, 114-115, 131
socioeconomic distribution, 120-121
state and federal systems, 111-112
stereotypes of, 104, 290-291
support by, 114-115, 131

training, effects of, 120-122
violence: attitudes on, 232, 298; ideology and, 123-124; political protest and, 135
violence control and, 315
Police calls, nature of, 114-115
Political parties:
criminal justice and, 139
political leadership and, 139
as pressure groups, 74, 75
Political protest, 236, 256-259
government interests and, 140
law enforcement and, 134-136
police discretion and, 134-136
restrictions on, 57-60
treason concept in American colonies, 57-58, 58-59
violence and, 232
Politics (*see also* Government; Political parties; Political protest):
ancient Greece, 45-46
crime commissions and, 306
criminal definitions and, 15-16
criminal law formulations and, 43, 47-49, 56-60
interests and, 30-32, 38, 41-42
of judges, sentencing and, 168
justice and, 138-140
law and order and, 308-309, 310-313
law organization and, 36-37
pluralist concept of process, 12-13
political parties and, 139
Populist party, 74
Positivism, 5
Power (*see also* Interests):
conflict and struggle for, 11
crime commissions and, 307
criminal definition formulation and, 17-18
interest structure and, 12, 39
social organization and, 11-13
treatment policies and, 17-18
Prescription drug violations, 255-256
Presentence investigations, 165
President's Commission on Law Enforcement and Administration of Justice, 308-312
composition, 308, 309
on crime and delinquency, 222*n*
on institutional treatment of criminals, 181*n*
on nature of crime, 310
on organized crime, 268-269
on parole, 191, 193, 194
on public conceptions of crime, 292-293, 295-296
on responsibilities of prosecutor, 151*n*
on sanctions on criminals, 203
Pressure groups (*see* Interests)
Pretrial parole, 144
Pretrial proceedings, 143-145
Prevention (*see* Crime prevention)
Preventive detention concept, 314
Primary deviation, secondary deviation vs., 247
Primitive law, criminal law vs., 44
Prison:
administration, 173, 177-184; decision-making in, 174
assimilation of prison culture, 176
balance of punitive and treatment goals, 180-181
communication in, 174
correctional interest groups, 174
custody objectives of, 173, 174, 175
follow-up study of inmates, 183
goal achievement by prisoners, 174-175
group relations principle used in, 181
hierarchies in, 173-174
internal order maintenance, 173
pains of imprisonment, 175
population type, rehabilitation and, 182
prisoner conformity, 176-177
prisoner participation in therapy, 170*n*, 179-180
public attitudes on, 301
reimprisonment, 182-184
social organization, 172-177
staff: attitudes on prisoners, 180; authority of, 177, 178-179; relations with prisoners, 177
treatment-oriented, 177-184; administration, 180-181; authority problems in, 177, 178-179; effectiveness of therapy, 181-183; interpersonal relations in, 178-180; interprisoner relations in, 179-180; objectives of therapeutic vs. custodial staff, 178-179; paradox in, 177-178; positive reactions of inmates, 180; prisoner participation in treatment, 170*n*, 179-180; program implementation, 182-183; treatment techniques, 181
Private police agencies, 112
Private vengeance, 44
"Probable cause," establishment of, 141
Probation, 170-172 (*see also* Parole)
administration of, 170-171
increasing use of, 170
officers: context of decisions, 170-171; orientation of, 171; sentencing and, 165-166; variations in decisions, 172

organizational problems, 171-172
probationer handling problems, 171-172
revocation of, 172
successful completion of, 170, 172
Professional offenders, 266-267, 270-273 (*see also* Organized crime)
careers of, 271-273
described, 270-271
reasons for leaving crime, 267
recruitment of, 272-273
Professionalization of police, 108
Prohibition, 91-92, 306-307
Prohibition party, 91
Property offenses:
arrests in clearing, 266-267
conventional, 265-266
occasional, 252-253
public attitudes on, 293-294
rural, 253
Prosecutor:
decision-making by, 141
discretion of, 130
importance of skill of, 151
interactions with defense in plea bargaining, 148-149
jury selection by, 162-163
role of, 101, 102, 150-151, 157
witness use by, 159-160
Prostitution:
action and culture patterns in, 259-260
laws on, 88-89
objectives in arrests for, 132-133
Protection, arrests for, 131
Psychiatrists:
power of, in criminal trials, 160-161
sexual psychopath laws and, 83-85
Psychotherapy for offenders, 181, 182
Public (*see* Community)
Public conceptions of crime, 277-302
attention to crime, 291-296
consequences of, 302
control of crime, 296-302
crime investigations and, 304-305
diffusion of, 281-285
intention and, 303-304
knowledge and, 279-280
Puritan ethic and, 280-281
social reaction and, 277-281
on social types of criminals, 285-291
Public defender systems, 152
Public morals:
concern with, 297
protective legislation on, 86-97; enforcement of, 132-133
Public order:
drunkenness and, 90
interests and, 38
legislation in protecting, 86-87
offenses against, 90, 259-264
Public policy:
criminal law administration and, 138-139
establishment of, 43
interests and, 11-13, 16, 37-38, 39
law as form of, 40
power and value allocation and, 11-12
Public welfare, protection of, 77
Publicity:
crime commissions and, 307-308
criminal conception diffusion and, 281-285
sexual psychopath laws and, 83
violence emphasis in, 232
Pure food and drug laws, 77-82, 294-295
Puritans:
adultery laws, 87
criminal law development and, 60-65
ethic of: lawful behavior and, 230; reaction to crime and, 280-281

Race:
attitudes on police and, 297-298
behavior as reaction to, 222
conviction and punishment and, 142
criminal behavior and, 220-222
execution patterns and, 186, 188-189
police discretion and, 129-130
violent behavior and, 135, 252
Race riots, 135
Rape:
action patterns in, 250-251
laws on, 86
Rationalizations of criminal conduct, 254-255
Rationing violations, 254
Reality:
causation statement and, 5-6
conceptual and phenomenal, 15
constructs based on social, 6-7
formation of conceptions of, 277
objective, 4-5
social action and, 14-15
as social construction, 22
Regional distribution (*see* Geographic distribution)
Rehabilitation (*see also* Prison, treatment-oriented):
effectiveness of prison, 181-184
rise of ideal of, 170
Reimprisonment, 182-184

Reinforcement of criminal conduct, 242-243
Religion:
abortion reform and, 90
attitude on crime and, 295
criminal law foundation and, 60-70
of judges, sentencing and, 168
Sunday laws and, 65-70, 133-134, 267-270
Repeated offenders, 182-183
Research methodology, 7
Responsibility, legal, 160
Right of counsel, 106, 107-108, 151
Riot policing, 232
Risk taking by offenders, 266-267
Robbery:
attitudes on, 293-294
shoplifting, 252
Romantic outlaw concept, 288
Rural areas:
attitudes on sentencing, 299-300
criminal behavior in, 222, 224-225; property offenses, 253
juvenile gangs in, 225
law enforcement: agencies, 111; development, 111; discretion in, 117
prohibition and, 91, 92

Sanctions:
administration of criminals, 278-279
on criminal offenders, 203-204
Seabury Commission on Crime, 305
Search and seizure, 107
Secondary deviation, primary deviation vs., 247
Security (*see also* Political protest):
legislation and national, 135-136
social interests and, 34, 35
Sedition Act (1798), 58, 59
Self-help community programs, 198-201
Self-image (*see* Identity)
Self-incrimination, 106, 107, 314
Semiprofessional criminals, 265
Sentencing, 101, 102, 157, 165-168, 169 (*see also* Conviction; Verdict)
appeal of, 158
decision-making in, 141, 165-166
legal representation and, 153
minority group membership and, 142
modification of, 184
necessity for mandatory, 149
penal law limits and, 166, 168
plea bargaining and, 146-148
postponing, 144
presentence investigation, 165
previous criminal record and, 168
public attitudes on, 299-300
responsibility for, 165
variations in, 166
Sex factor:
attitudes and: on capital punishment, 301; on crime, 295; on police, 297, 298; on sentencing, 299
criminal offenses distributed by, 213-217
identity problems and, 215-216
role as juror and, 163-164
Sex offenses (*see also* Homosexuality; Prostitution):
problem of, 82-86
public response to, 84-85
Sexual conduct regulation, 86-90
Sexual psychopath laws, 82-86
definition of sexual psychopath, 82, 84-85
enforcement of, 84-85
Sherley Amendment, Federal Food and Drug Act, 79
Sherman Act (1890), 75, 76
Sheriffs, 111, 117
"Shire-reeve" office, England, 110
Shoplifting, 252
Situation:
criminal behavior and, 211-212, 242
identity concepts and, 235-238
Sixth Amendment, 151, 161
"Slavery" laws, 87
Smith Act (1940), 59
Social action:
activity and, 278-279
alternatives and, 274
concepts of, 13-15
criminal definitions and, 267-270
drift and commitment standards, 243-244
factors in, 16-18, 20-21
political protest and, 134-136
social reality and, 14-15
Social class (*see also* Socioeconomic factors):
ancient Greece, 45-46
criminal behavior and, 217-220
juvenile: behavior and, 215, 217, 218-220; motivation and, 218-220
youth learning patterns and, 218-220
Social control (*see also* Authority):
law as formal, 36-37
variations in systems, 36
Social force, law as, 33-34
Social meaning, behavior and, 22-23
Social organization, 37-38
behavior and, 207

coercion and, 11
commitment of political offenders to, 257
Conflict and, 9-11
consensus and, 9-10, 208
constraint and, 11
crime and, 208
as differentiated interest structure, 37-38
disruption, roots of, 10-11
enforcement and, 104-105
law and, 36-37
of penal custody, 172-177
power and, 11-13
rule systems and, 36*n*-37*n*
segmental, 208-210
in social collectives, 36
Social process, 8-9
Social reactions:
to crime, 277-281
definitional conferral and, 245
norms of, 278-279
personal action patterns and, 244-248
Social reform, 30
Social role:
learning by homosexuals, 260-261
in police-citizen encounters, 125-127
of prisoners, 175-177
Social types, conceptions of criminal, 285-291
Social workers:
detached worker programs, 196-197
probation and parole and, 171
Socialization:
differential association and, 240
political, 257
Society (*see also* Culture; Social Organization; and specific topic):
behavior and, 16-18, 20-21
characterization of, 35
conflict vs. consensus in, 9-11
crime conceptions and, 8-15, 22-23, 24
homogeneous vs. heterogeneous, 208-209
interests in contemporary, 40-42
general cultural themes in, 228-233
law and, 32, 33-34
power and, 11-13
social process, 8-9
Society for the Prevention of Crime, 305
Socioeconomic factors (*see also* Social class):
attitude and: on capital punishment, 301-302; on crime, 294-295, 295-296; on police, 297-298; on sentencing, 299-300
in city areas, crime and, 226-228
in clemency granting, 188
in concern about crime, 293
criminal justice and, 152-153, 188
in juror influence, 164
in jury participation, 163-164
jury choice and, 163
organized crime and, 268
police candidates distributed by, 120-121
in violence, 252
"Solo" lawyers, 153-156
Special interests (*see* Interests)
Standing mute, 144-145
States (*see also* specific state):
antinarcotic laws, 93
on civil rights of offenders, 203
courts, variations in, 142
crime commissions, 305-306
law enforcement agencies, 111, 112
sexual psychopath laws, 82
Stereotypes:
of criminals, 285-291; physical, 246-247
of detectives, 290-291
of homosexuals, 286
of lawyers, 290, 291
of police, 104, 290-291
Stigma of criminal conviction, 203-204, 247-248
Street-corner groups, 196-197
Subversion statutes, 59-60 (*see also* Political protest)
Summons serving, 143
Sunday laws, 65-70
American colonies, 66
British, 65, 66, 69
changes in substance, 66-67
enforcement, 67, 133-134
pressure groups and, 67-70, 133-134
Supportive role of police, 114-115, 131
Supreme Court, U.S.:
on protection of person, 106, 107-108
on right of counsel, 151
on Sunday laws, 68-69
on Virginia antimiscegenation law, 87
Suspects (*see* Defendant; Offender)

Territories, criminal law development in, 49-56
Testimony in criminal trials, 159-161
Theft, laws on, 70-73
Tradition, as rule system, 36*n*
Treason, 57-59 (*see also* Political protest)
Trial:
adjudication vs., 145

capital crimes, 190
decision-making in, 141
evidence and, 143
extralegal considerations in, 158-159
by judges, 158
jury, 161-165 (*see also* Jury trial)
reasons for, 157
steps in, 157-158
testimony and witnesses, 159-161
variations in, 158
Twelve Tables, Law of the, 46-47

Unemployment compensation laws, violation of, 294
Urban areas:
attitudes on sentencing, 299-300
crime commissions, 304-305
criminal behavior in, 222, 224-228; variations within cities, 225-228
law enforcement in, 111

Vagrancy laws, 94-97
evaluation of, 96-97
objectives of vagrancy arrests, 132
origin of, 94-96
use of, 94
Value judgments (*see also* Ideology):
allocation of, 11-12
on prostitution, 260
Vandalism, 253
Verdict (*see also* Sentencing):
jury compared with judges', 164-165
jury rendition of, 157
Victim role:
in crime creation, 126-127
in violent behavior, 250-251
Villain, criminal as, 286-288
Violence, 249-252
as American cultural trait, 231-232, 289
control of, 315
as form of state power, 315-316
perceptions of, 251-252
police: attitudes on, 232, 298; community and, 232; ideology and, 123-124; political protest and, 135
Virginia, early criminal law, in, 87
Voir dire examination, 162-163
Volstead Act, 91-92
Voorhis Act (1940), 59

"Watch and Ward" officers, England, 110
Weeks v. United States (1914), 107
Westward migration, criminal law and, 54-56
Wickersham Commission on Crime, 306-307
Wiretapping, 106, 311
Witnesses:
in criminal trials, 159-161; defendant as witness for himself, 159; defense use of, 159-160
expert, 160-161
Wolfenden Report on Prostitution, England, 88-89
Woman's Christian Temperance Union, 91
Work projects:
for juveniles, 201
of prisons, 181